# PIRATE CLUB

## BRAINWASH ESCAPE VICTIMS

### VOL: 2

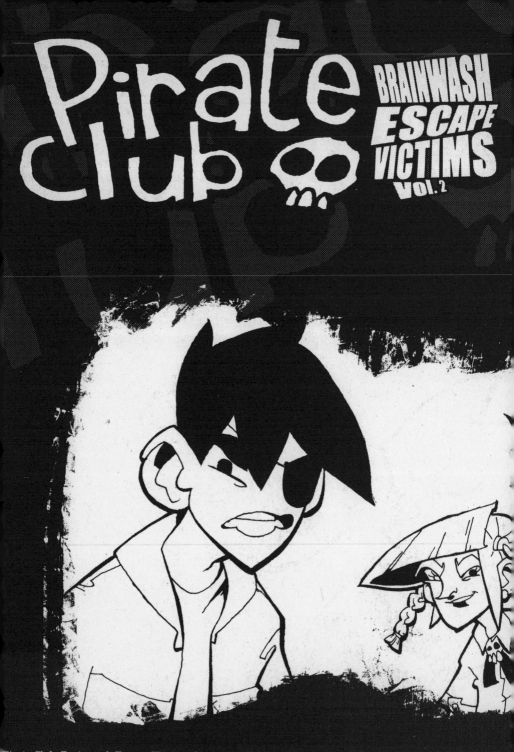

Pirate Club: Brainwash Escape Victims, [Sept. 2006]. Published by SLG Publishing, P.O. Box 26427, San Jose, CA 85159-6427. Pirate Club is tm and c 2005 Derek Hunter, all rights reserved. no part of this publication may be reproduced without the permission of Derek Hunter and SLG Publishing, except for purposes of review. For a free catalog, call 1-800-866-8929 or visit our website at www.slavelabor.com. Printed in Canada.

art & story by:
# derek hunter.
### script assists:
## elias pate & bryan young.

## PIRATE CLUB: BRAINWASH ESCAPE VICTIMS. VOLUME TWO

CREATED BY: DEREK HUNTER
WRITTEN AND DRAWN BY: DEREK HUNTER
SCRIPT ASSISTANCE: ELIAS PATE AND BRYAN YOUNG
BOOK DESIGN AND LAYOUT: DEREK HUNTER, RACHEL HUNTER

## SLAVE LABOR GRAPHICS

DAN VADO: PRESIDENT
JENNIFER DE GUZMAN: EDITOR-IN-CHIEF
DEB MOSKYOK: DIRECTOR OF SALES

## A VERY SPECIAL THANKS GOES OUT TO:

RACHEL KAY HUNTER
MY MOM AND DAD FOR MOVING BACK TO SWEDEN AND LETTING RACHEL AND I LIVE IN THEIR HOME FOR FREE, MY CHILDHOOD
FRIENDS AND THE ADVENTURES WE HAD TOGETHER (THUD, THE YAKS, NICK GRUNDY, CHRIS RICHARDS, TACHIERA BOYS,
STEPHENS BOYS, BRYAN WHITNEY, TROOP 228, MATT WILEY, NINJA NINI'S, ETC.), DAN VADO AND THE SLG CREW, ELIAS AND
MICHELLE PATE, BRYAN YOUNG AND HIS PATIENCE, SHANE HILLMAN, JEFFREY CRUZ, KERRY JACKSON AND THE X96 GEEK
SHOW, RYAN, ERIN, AND QUENTIN OTTLEY, CHAD HURD, MIMI AND NIGHT FLIGHT COMICS, DR. VOLTS, BRYAN DOBROW, JAKE
BELL, DRESSED TO KILL SKATE CREW, THE BOYS AND GIRLS AT SATURDAY SHORTS.COM, ALAN TEW, MANFRED NEBER, MEL
MILTON, PERRY STEWART, ALL OF THE MEMBERS OF THE PIRATE CLUB, THE GREAT RETAILERS THAT SUPPORT INDY BOOKS,
EVERYONE ELSE WHO GAVE THIS BOOK A CHANCE, AND YOU.

WWW.PIRATECLUB.COM     WWW.SLAVELABOR.COM

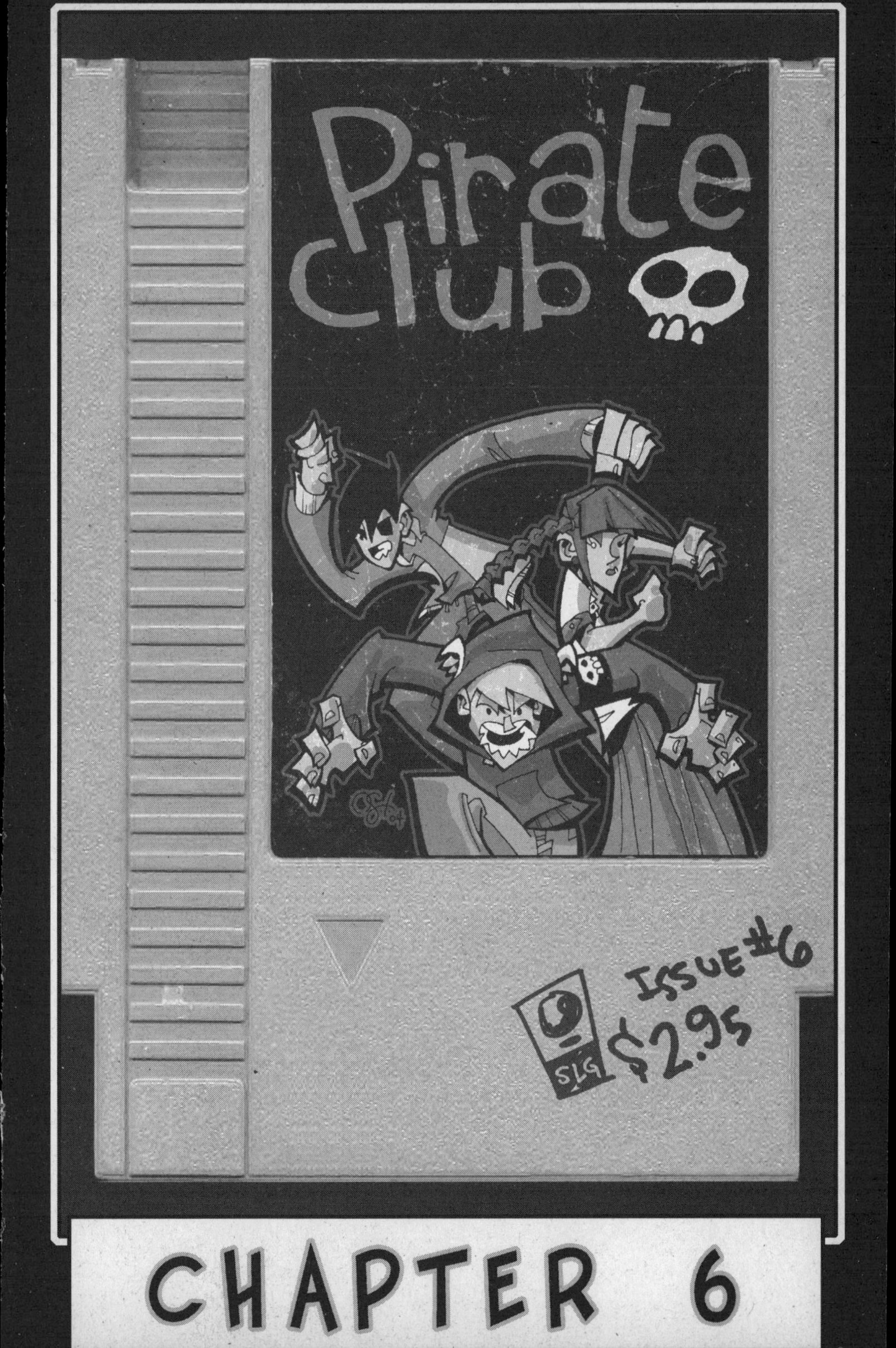
Pirate Club
ISSUE #6
SLG
$2.95

# CHAPTER 6

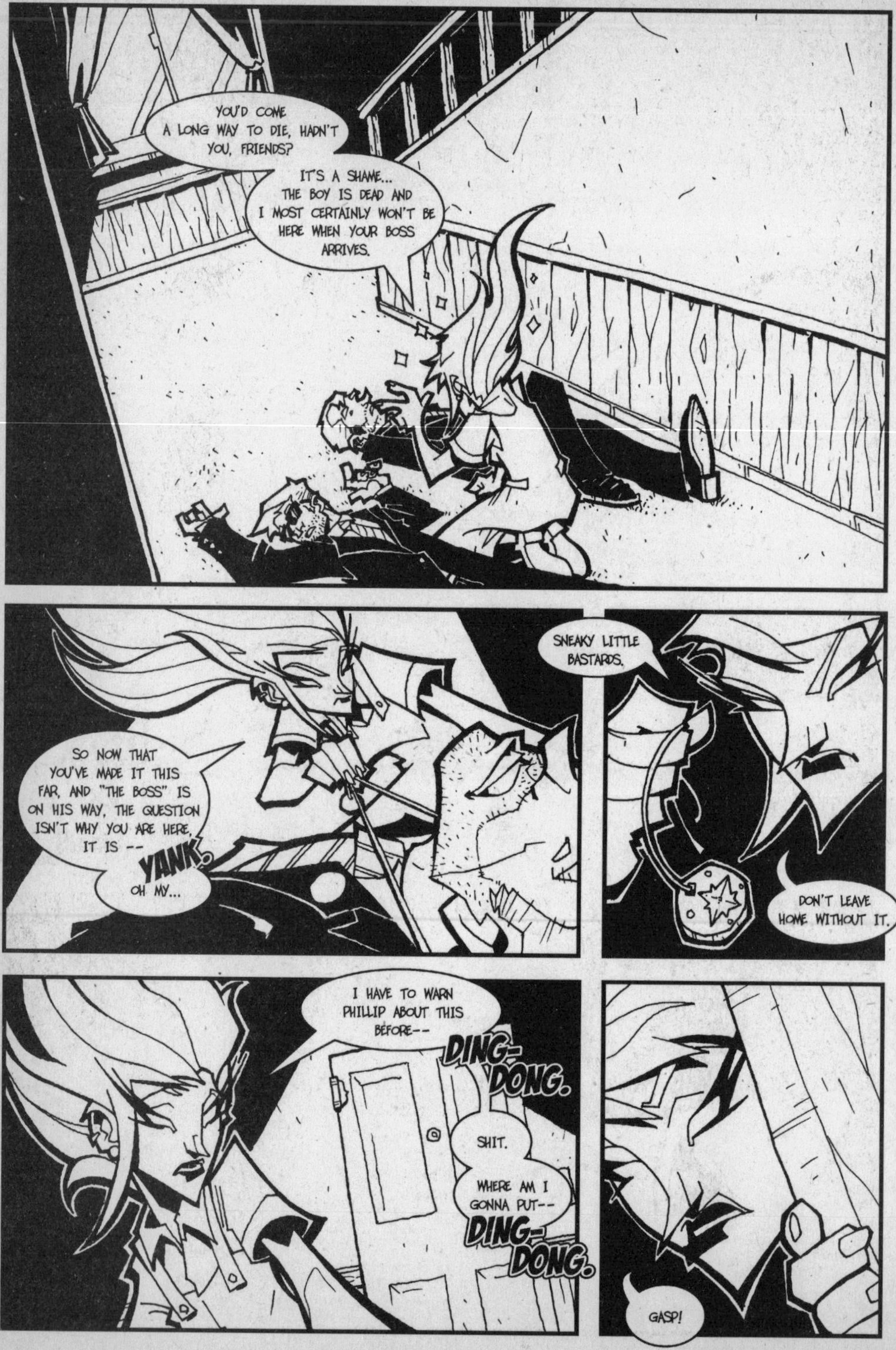
YOU'D COME A LONG WAY TO DIE, HADN'T YOU, FRIENDS?
IT'S A SHAME... THE BOY IS DEAD AND I MOST CERTAINLY WON'T BE HERE WHEN YOUR BOSS ARRIVES.
SO NOW THAT YOU'VE MADE IT THIS FAR, AND "THE BOSS" IS ON HIS WAY, THE QUESTION ISN'T WHY YOU ARE HERE, IT IS --
YANK.
OH MY...
SNEAKY LITTLE BASTARDS.
DON'T LEAVE HOME WITHOUT IT.
I HAVE TO WARN PHILLIP ABOUT THIS BEFORE--
DING-DONG.
SHIT.
WHERE AM I GONNA PUT--
DING-DONG.
GASP!

RUN! RUN! RUN!
FOOOOM!
JOHN?! A VIDEO GAME?! HOW DO WE GET OUTTA HERE?!
I DUNNO, BEARCLAW!
LOOKS LIKE WE HAVE TO MAKE IT BACK THE WAY WE CAME, THAT FAT-ASS HAS THE EXIT BLOCKED!
ONCE WE GET BACK THE WAY WE CAME, WE CAN--OOF!

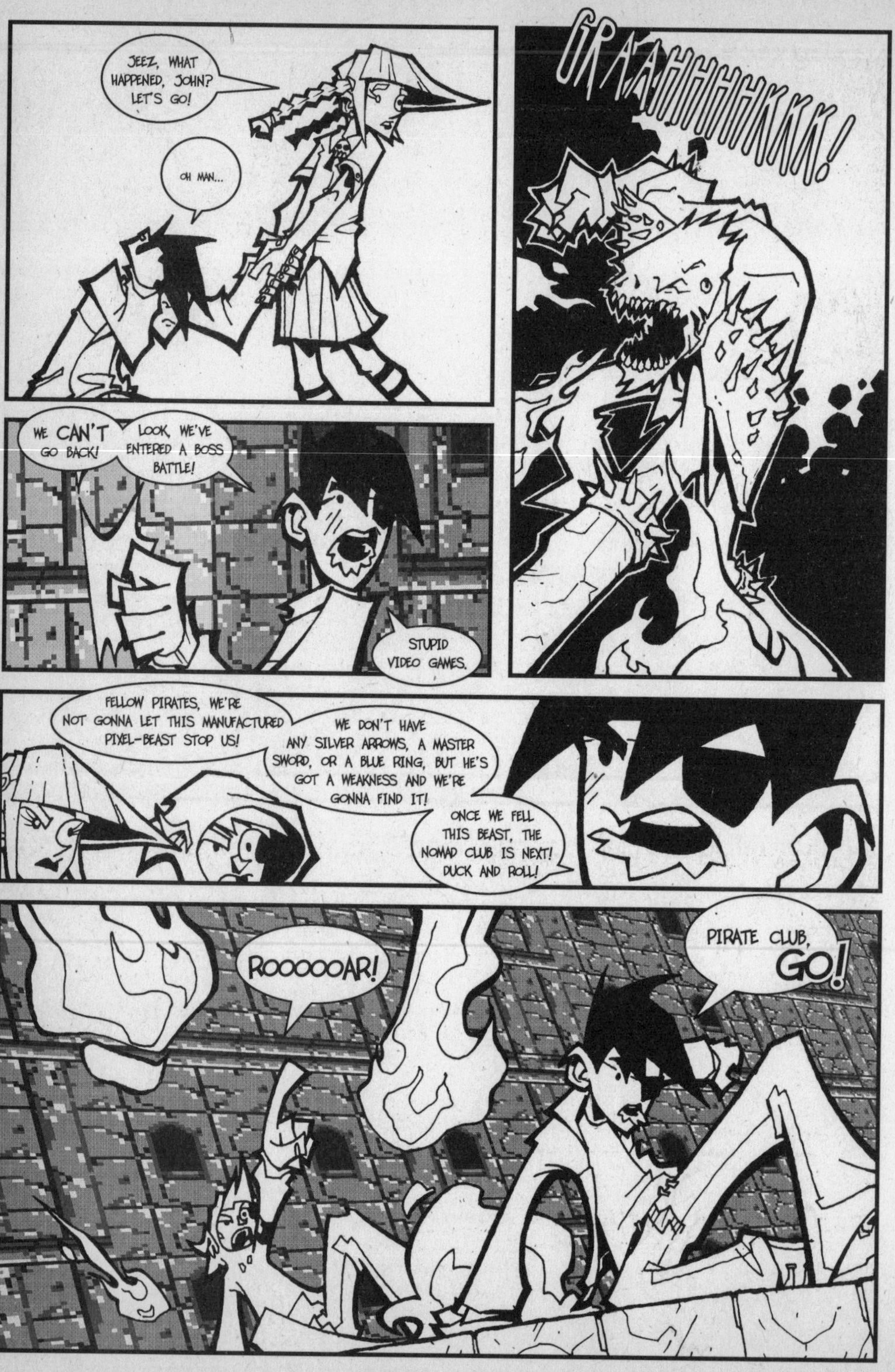
JEEZ, WHAT HAPPENED, JOHN? LET'S GO!
OH MAN...
GRAAAHHHHKKKK!
WE CAN'T GO BACK!
LOOK, WE'VE ENTERED A BOSS BATTLE!
STUPID VIDEO GAMES.
FELLOW PIRATES, WE'RE NOT GONNA LET THIS MANUFACTURED PIXEL-BEAST STOP US!
WE DON'T HAVE ANY SILVER ARROWS, A MASTER SWORD, OR A BLUE RING, BUT HE'S GOT A WEAKNESS AND WE'RE GONNA FIND IT!
ONCE WE FELL THIS BEAST, THE NOMAD CLUB IS NEXT! DUCK AND ROLL!
ROOOOOAR!
PIRATE CLUB, GO!

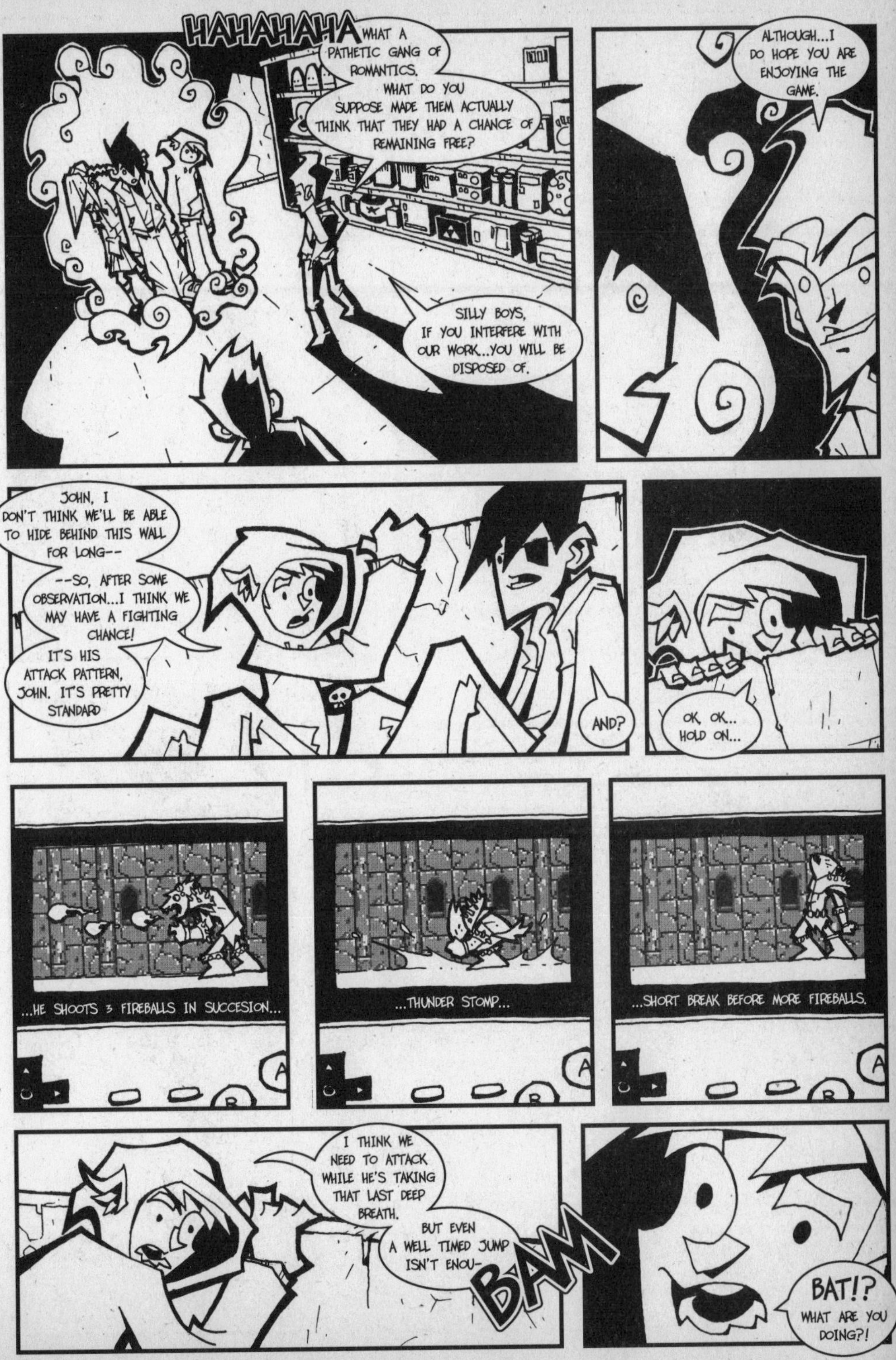
HAHAHAHA
WHAT A PATHETIC GANG OF ROMANTICS.
WHAT DO YOU SUPPOSE MADE THEM ACTUALLY THINK THAT THEY HAD A CHANCE OF REMAINING FREE?
SILLY BOYS, IF YOU INTERFERE WITH OUR WORK...YOU WILL BE DISPOSED OF.
ALTHOUGH...I DO HOPE YOU ARE ENJOYING THE GAME.
JOHN, I DON'T THINK WE'LL BE ABLE TO HIDE BEHIND THIS WALL FOR LONG--
--SO, AFTER SOME OBSERVATION...I THINK WE MAY HAVE A FIGHTING CHANCE!
IT'S HIS ATTACK PATTERN, JOHN. IT'S PRETTY STANDARD
AND?
OK, OK.. HOLD ON...
...HE SHOOTS 3 FIREBALLS IN SUCCESION...
A
B
...THUNDER STOMP...
A
B
...SHORT BREAK BEFORE MORE FIREBALLS.
A
B
I THINK WE NEED TO ATTACK WHILE HE'S TAKING THAT LAST DEEP BREATH.
BUT EVEN A WELL TIMED JUMP ISN'T ENOU-
BAM
BAT!? WHAT ARE YOU DOING?!

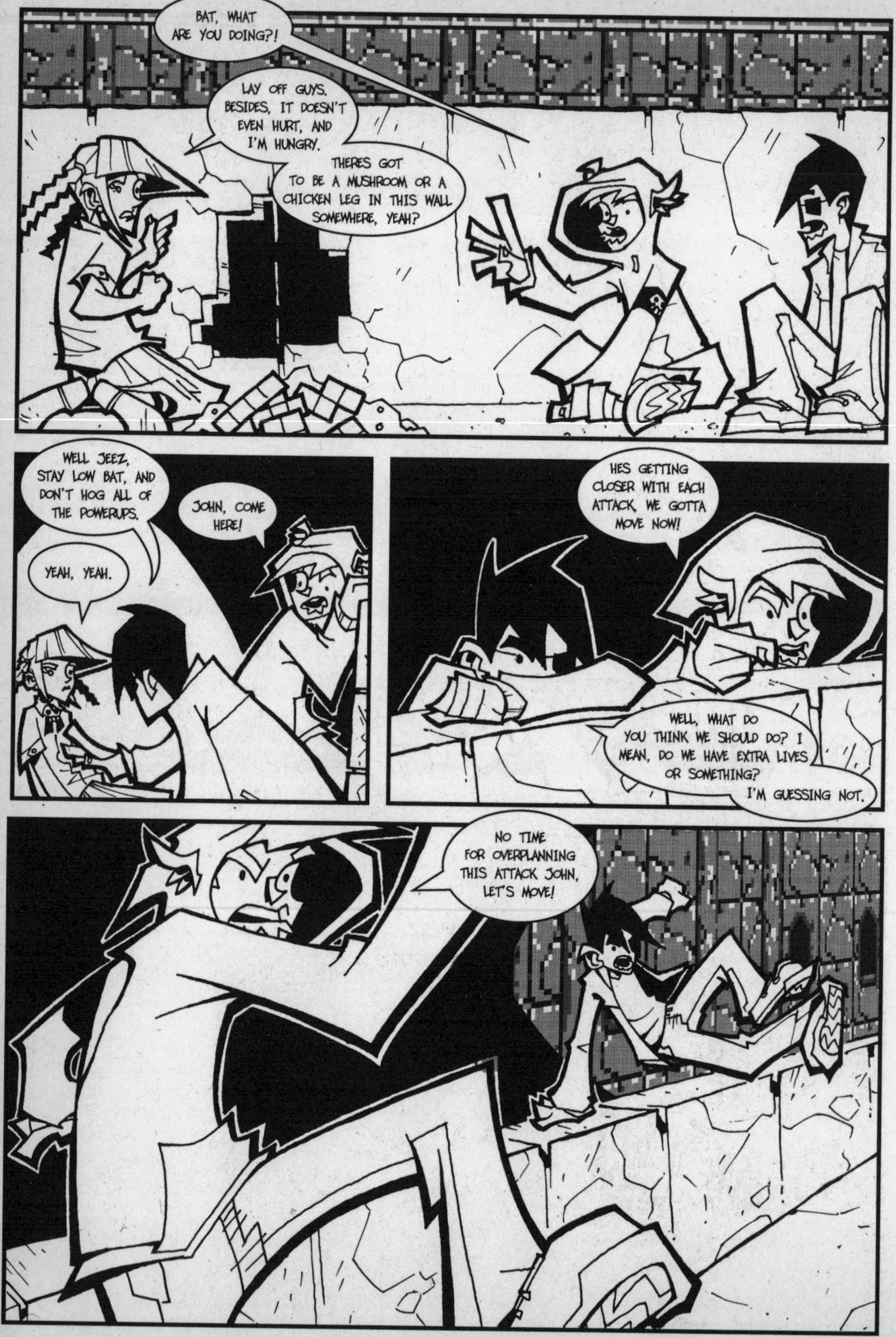
BAT, WHAT ARE YOU DOING?!
LAY OFF GUYS. BESIDES, IT DOESN'T EVEN HURT, AND I'M HUNGRY.
THERES GOT TO BE A MUSHROOM OR A CHICKEN LEG IN THIS WALL SOMEWHERE, YEAH?
WELL JEEZ, STAY LOW BAT, AND DON'T HOG ALL OF THE POWERUPS.
JOHN, COME HERE!
YEAH, YEAH.
HES GETTING CLOSER WITH EACH ATTACK, WE GOTTA MOVE NOW!
WELL, WHAT DO YOU THINK WE SHOULD DO? I MEAN, DO WE HAVE EXTRA LIVES OR SOMETHING?
I'M GUESSING NOT.
NO TIME FOR OVERPLANNING THIS ATTACK JOHN, LET'S MOVE!

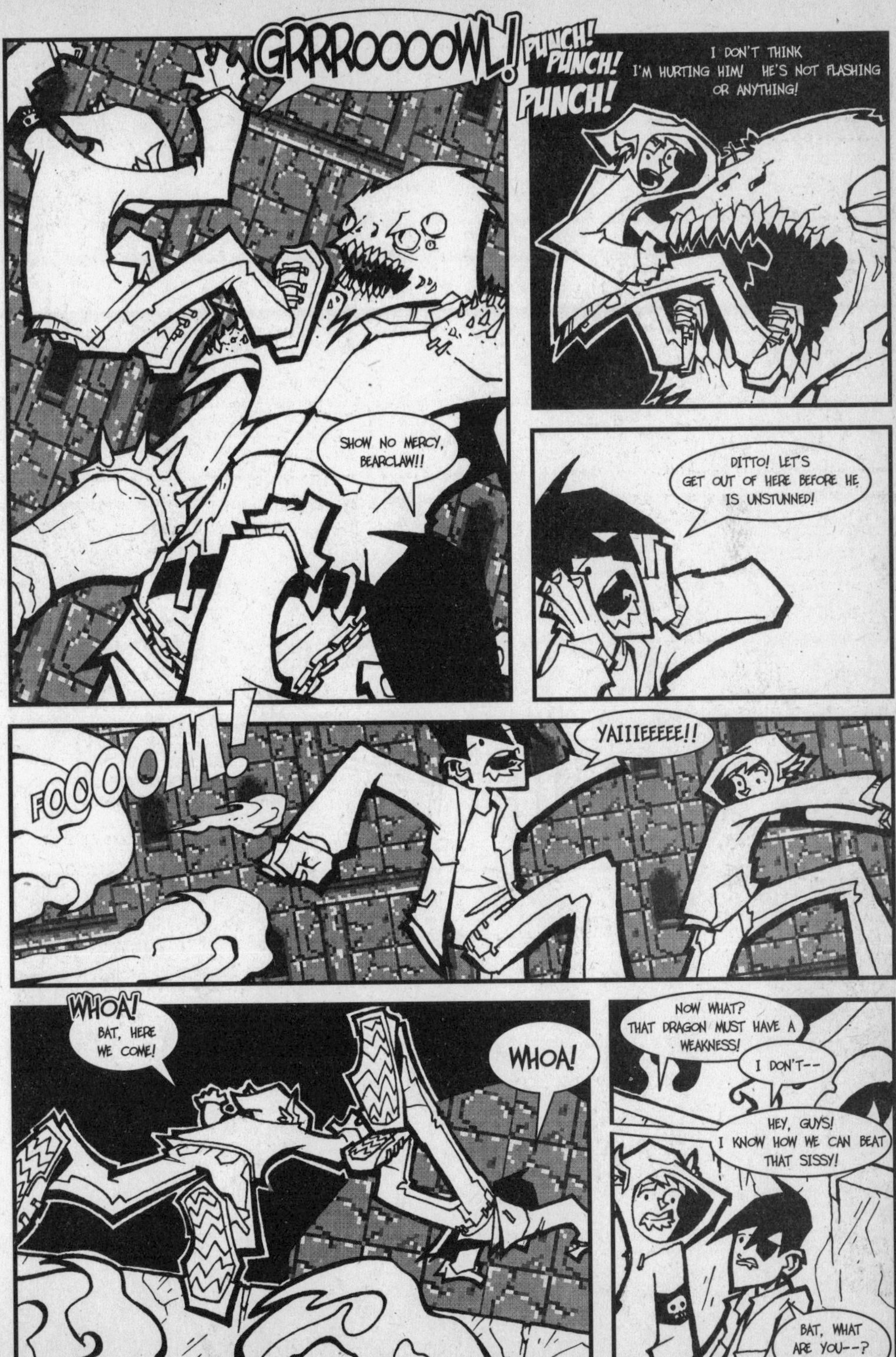
GRRROOOOWL!
PUNCH! PUNCH! PUNCH!
I DON'T THINK I'M HURTING HIM! HE'S NOT FLASHING OR ANYTHING!
SHOW NO MERCY, BEARCLAW!!
DITTO! LET'S GET OUT OF HERE BEFORE HE IS UNSTUNNED!
FOOOOM!
YAIIIEEEEE!!
WHOA!
BAT, HERE WE COME!
WHOA!
NOW WHAT? THAT DRAGON MUST HAVE A WEAKNESS!
I DON'T--
HEY, GUYS! I KNOW HOW WE CAN BEAT THAT SISSY!
BAT, WHAT ARE YOU--? WHOA..

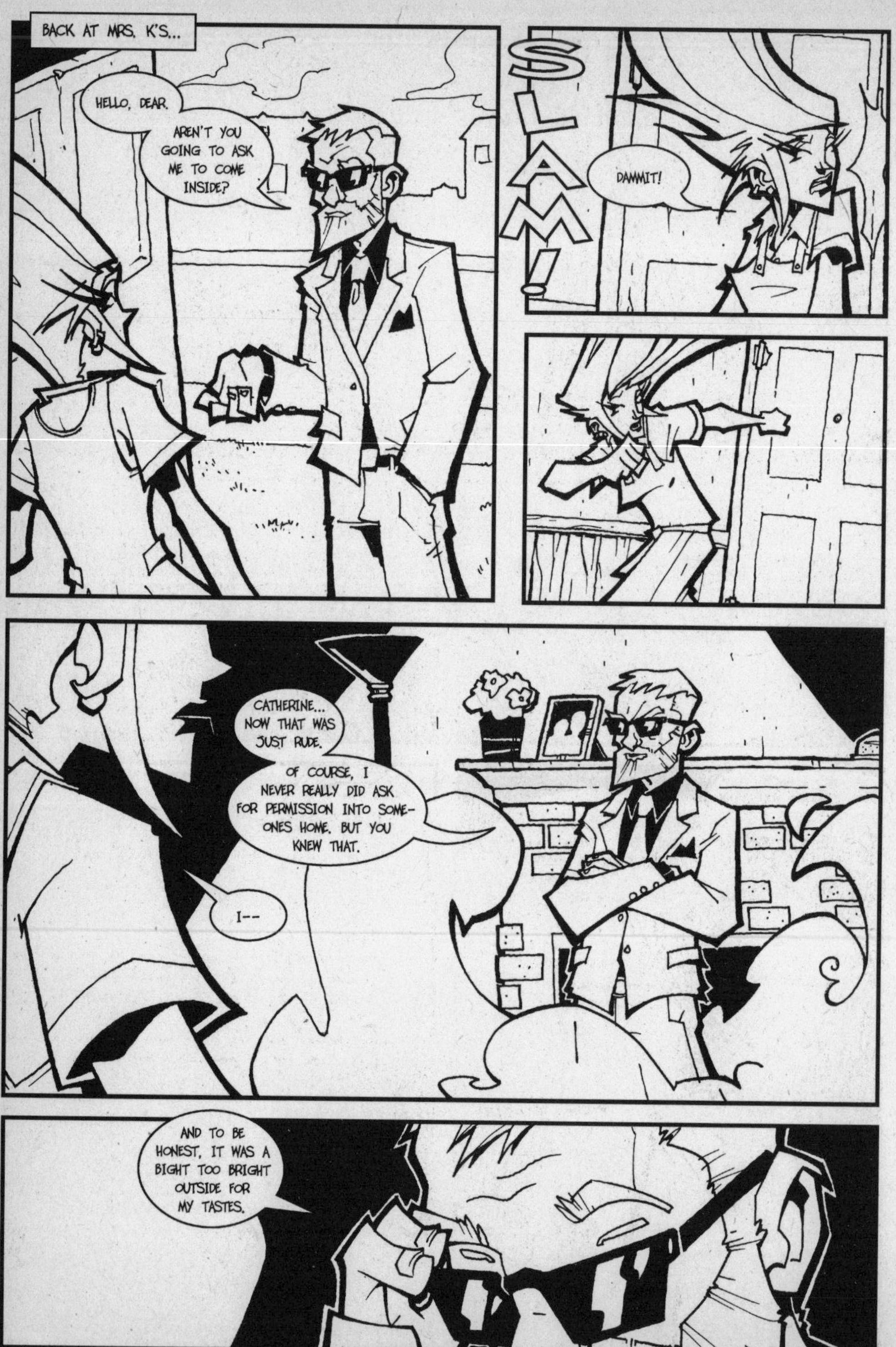
BACK AT MRS. K'S...
HELLO, DEAR.
AREN'T YOU GOING TO ASK ME TO COME INSIDE?
SLAM!
DAMMIT!
CATHERINE... NOW THAT WAS JUST RUDE.
OF COURSE, I NEVER REALLY DID ASK FOR PERMISSION INTO SOME-ONES HOME. BUT YOU KNEW THAT.
I--
AND TO BE HONEST, IT WAS A BIGHT TOO BRIGHT OUTSIDE FOR MY TASTES.

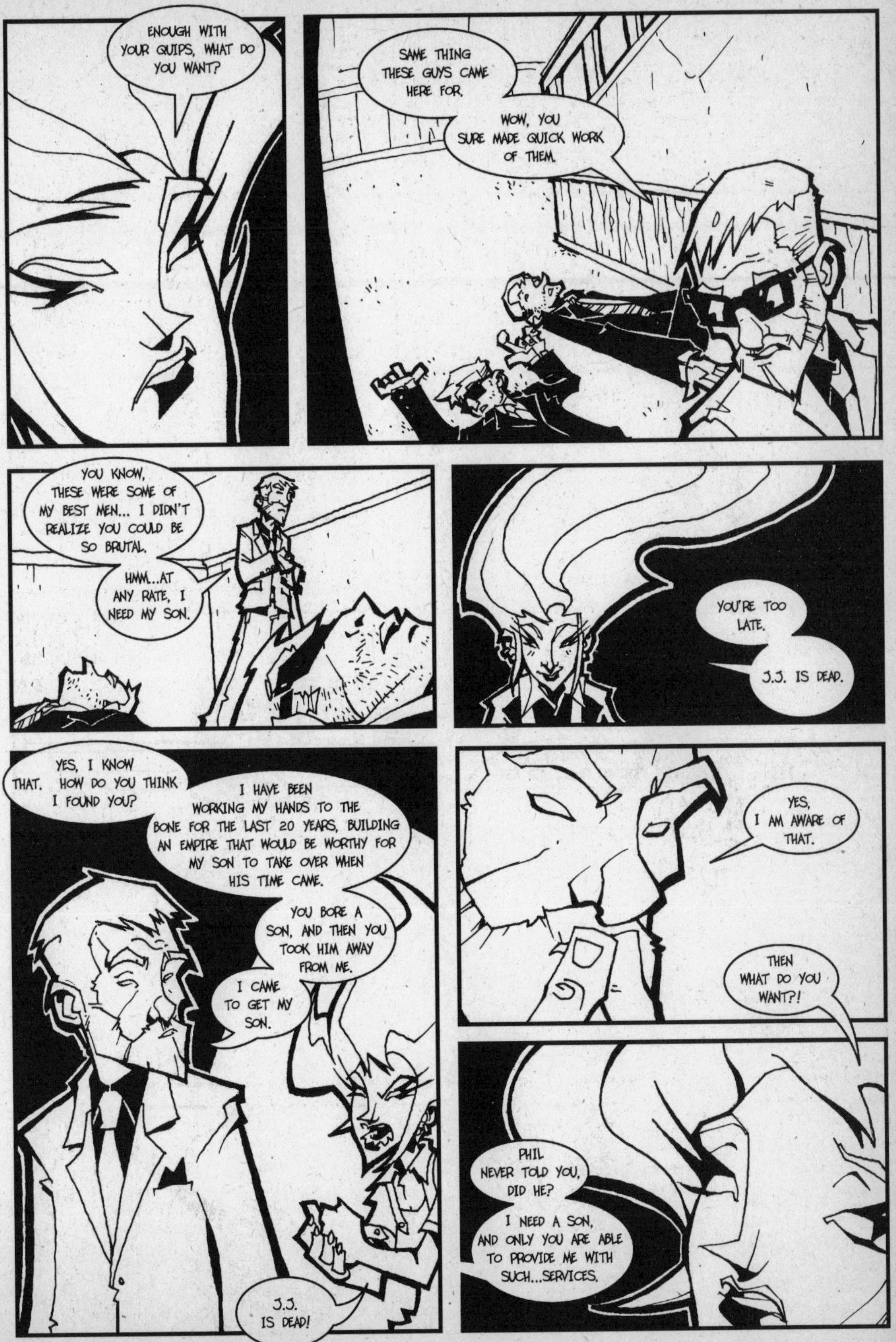
ENOUGH WITH YOUR QUIPS, WHAT DO YOU WANT?
SAME THING THESE GUYS CAME HERE FOR.
WOW, YOU SURE MADE QUICK WORK OF THEM.
YOU KNOW, THESE WERE SOME OF MY BEST MEN... I DIDN'T REALIZE YOU COULD BE SO BRUTAL.
HMM...AT ANY RATE, I NEED MY SON.
YOU'RE TOO LATE.
J.J. IS DEAD.
YES, I KNOW THAT. HOW DO YOU THINK I FOUND YOU?
I HAVE BEEN WORKING MY HANDS TO THE BONE FOR THE LAST 20 YEARS, BUILDING AN EMPIRE THAT WOULD BE WORTHY FOR MY SON TO TAKE OVER WHEN HIS TIME CAME.
YOU BORE A SON, AND THEN YOU TOOK HIM AWAY FROM ME.
I CAME TO GET MY SON.
J.J. IS DEAD!
YES, I AM AWARE OF THAT.
THEN WHAT DO YOU WANT?!
PHIL NEVER TOLD YOU, DID HE?
I NEED A SON, AND ONLY YOU ARE ABLE TO PROVIDE ME WITH SUCH...SERVICES.

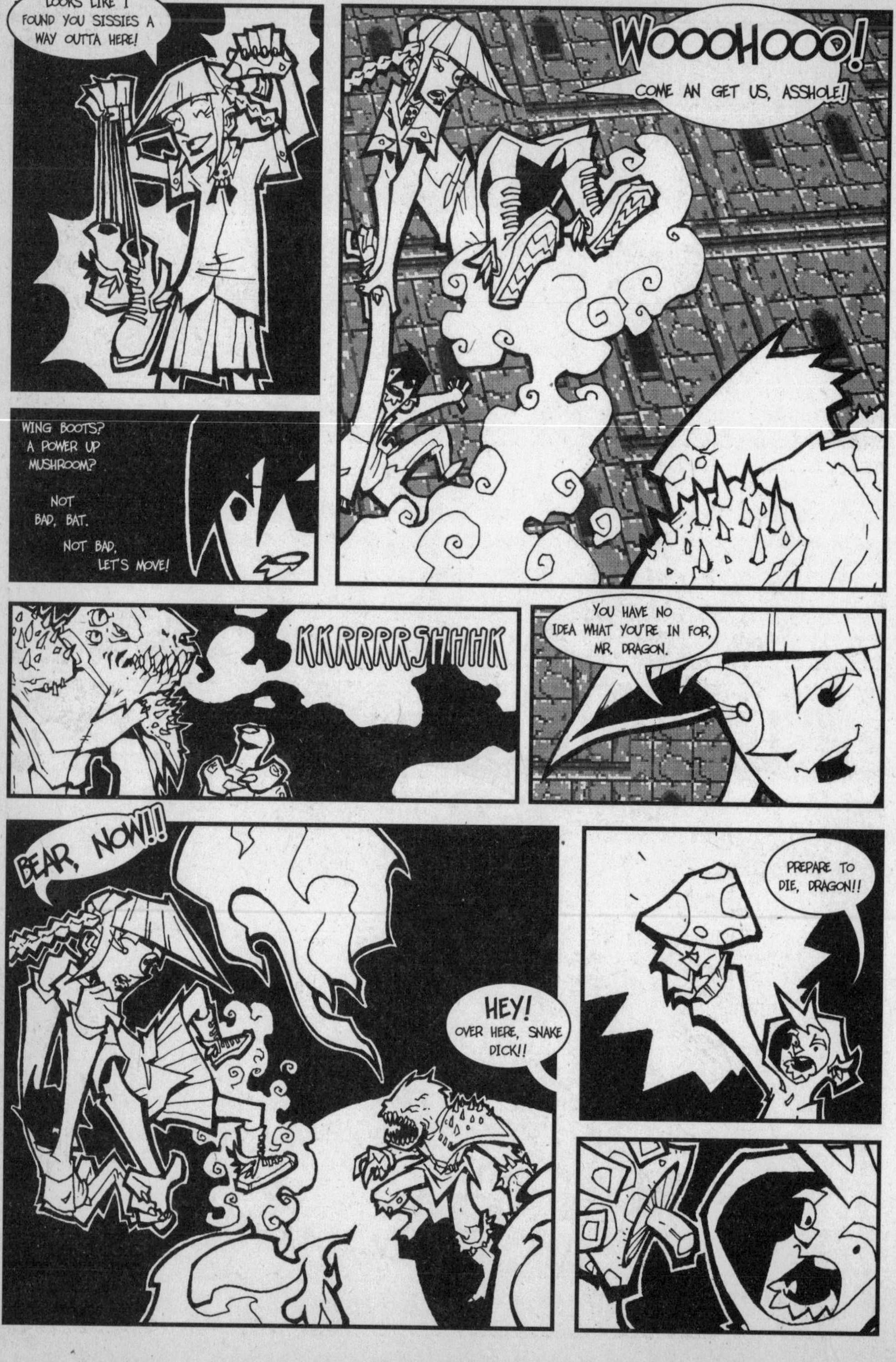

LOOKS LIKE I FOUND YOU SISSIES A WAY OUTTA HERE!
WOOOHOOO!
COME AN GET US, ASSHOLE!
WING BOOTS? A POWER UP MUSHROOM?
NOT BAD, BAT.
NOT BAD, LET'S MOVE!
KKRRRRRSHHHK
YOU HAVE NO IDEA WHAT YOU'RE IN FOR, MR. DRAGON.
BEAR, NOW!!
HEY! OVER HERE, SNAKE DICK!!
PREPARE TO DIE, DRAGON!!

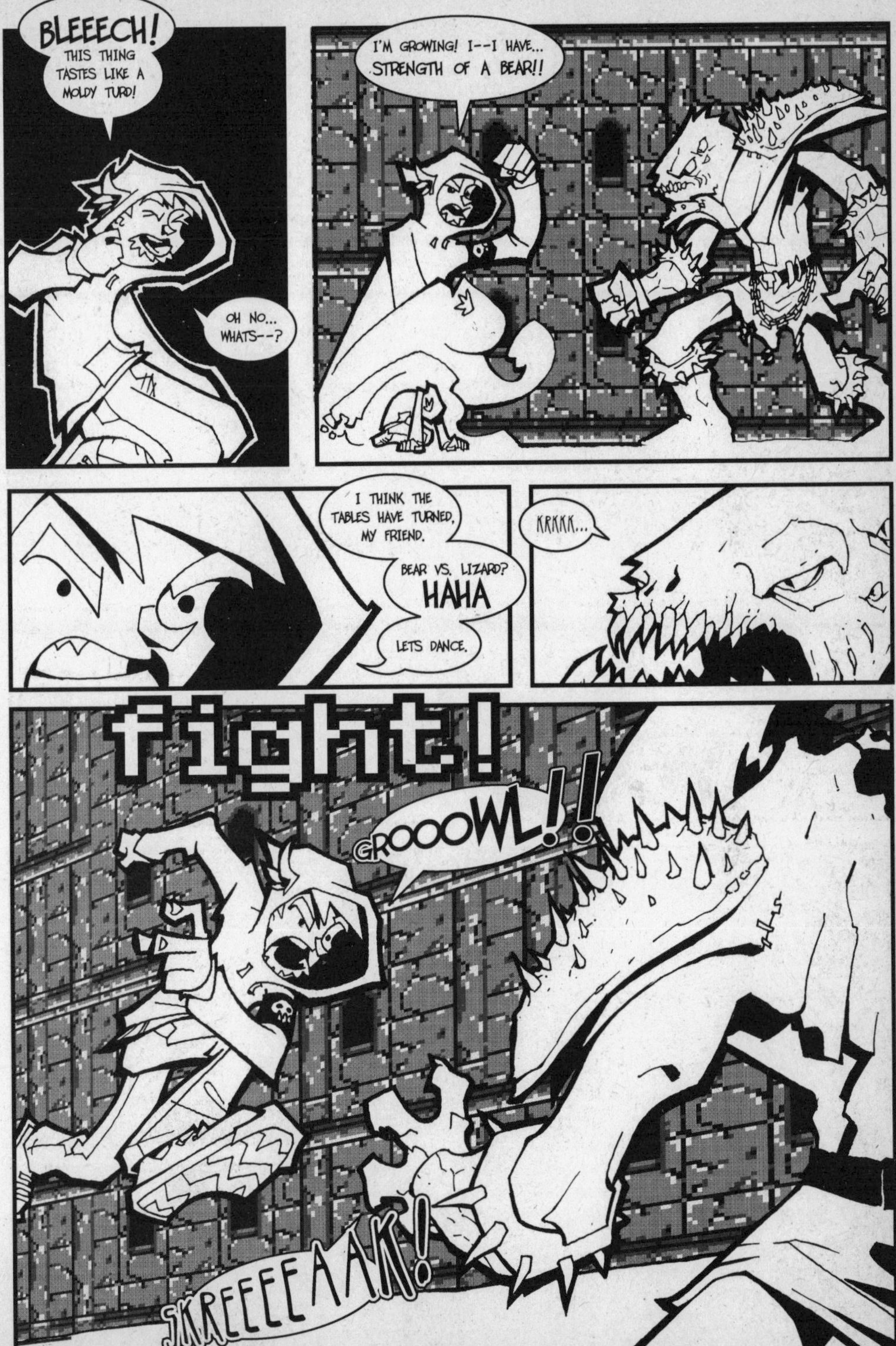
BLEEECH! THIS THING TASTES LIKE A MOLDY TURD!
OH NO... WHATS--?
I'M GROWING! I--I HAVE... STRENGTH OF A BEAR!!
I THINK THE TABLES HAVE TURNED, MY FRIEND.
BEAR VS. LIZARD? HAHA
LETS DANCE.
KRKKK...
fight!
GROOOWL!!!
SKREEEEAAK!

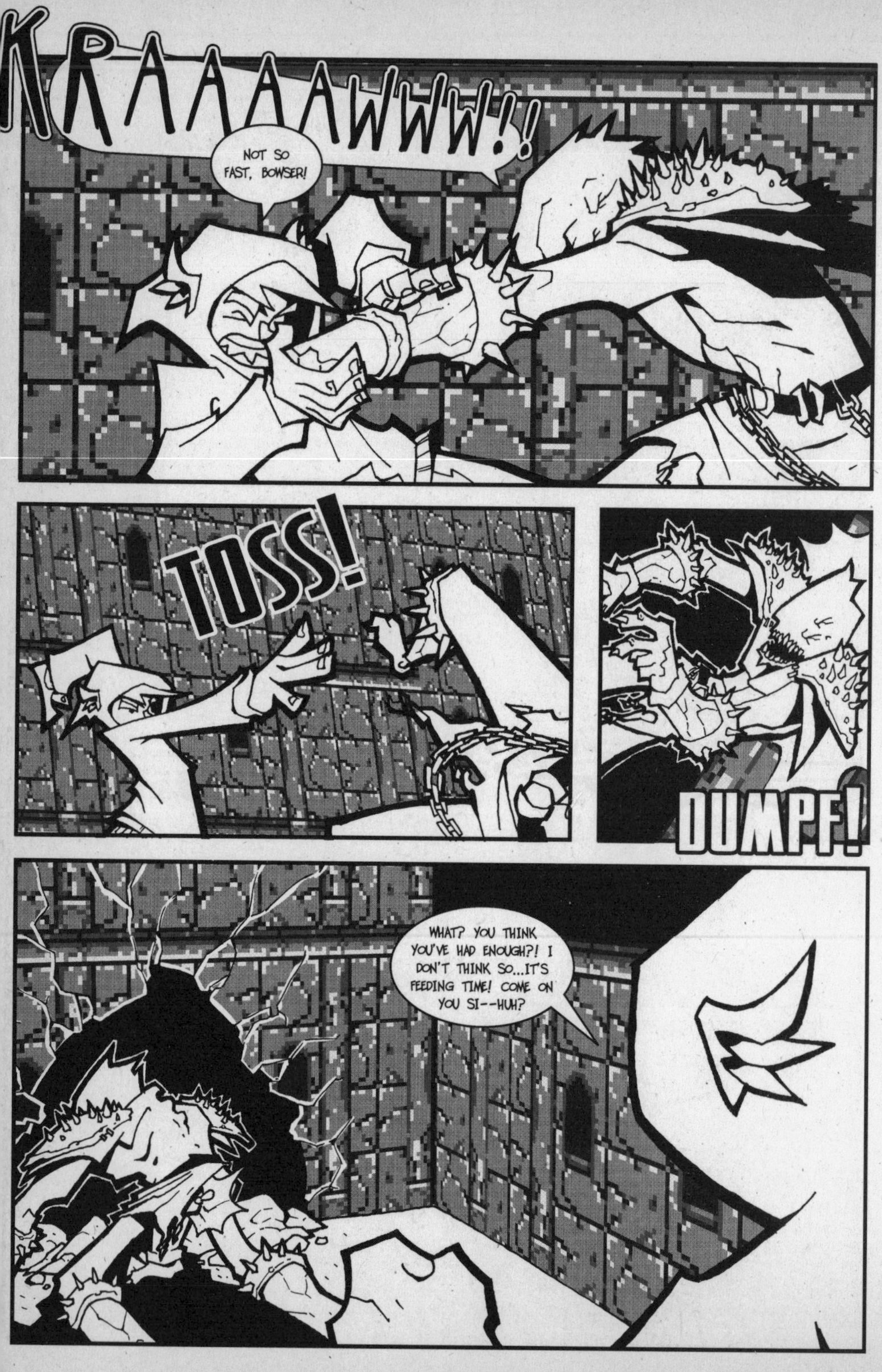
KRAAAAWWW!!
NOT SO FAST, BOWSER!
TOSS!
DUMPF!
WHAT? YOU THINK YOU'VE HAD ENOUGH?! I DON'T THINK SO...IT'S FEEDING TIME! COME ON YOU SI--HUH?

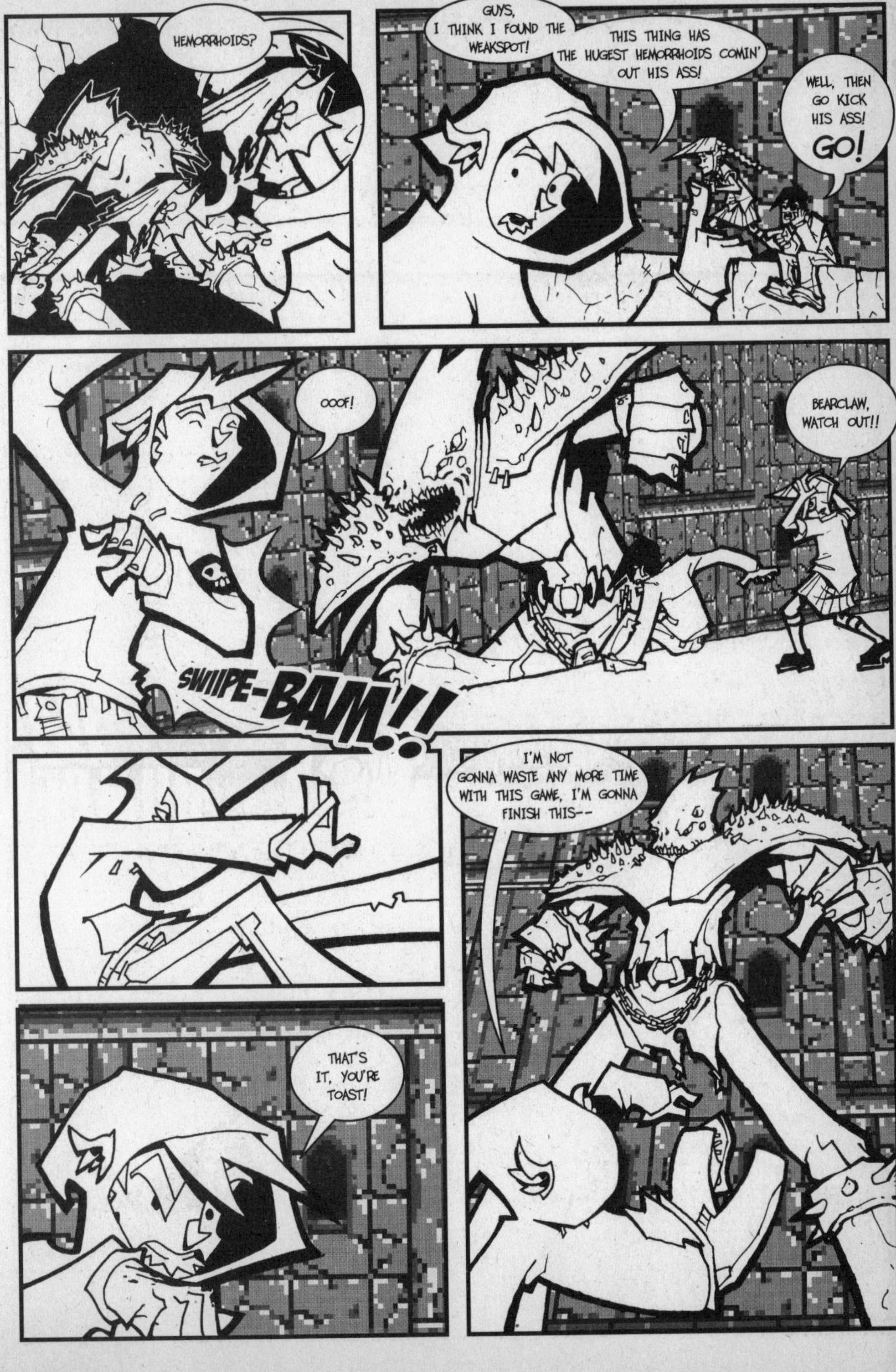
HEMORRHOIDS?
GUYS, I THINK I FOUND THE WEAKSPOT!
THIS THING HAS THE HUGEST HEMORRHOIDS COMIN' OUT HIS ASS!
WELL, THEN GO KICK HIS ASS! GO!
OOOF!
BEARCLAW, WATCH OUT!!
SWIIPE-BAM!!
I'M NOT GONNA WASTE ANY MORE TIME WITH THIS GAME, I'M GONNA FINISH THIS--
THAT'S IT, YOU'RE TOAST!

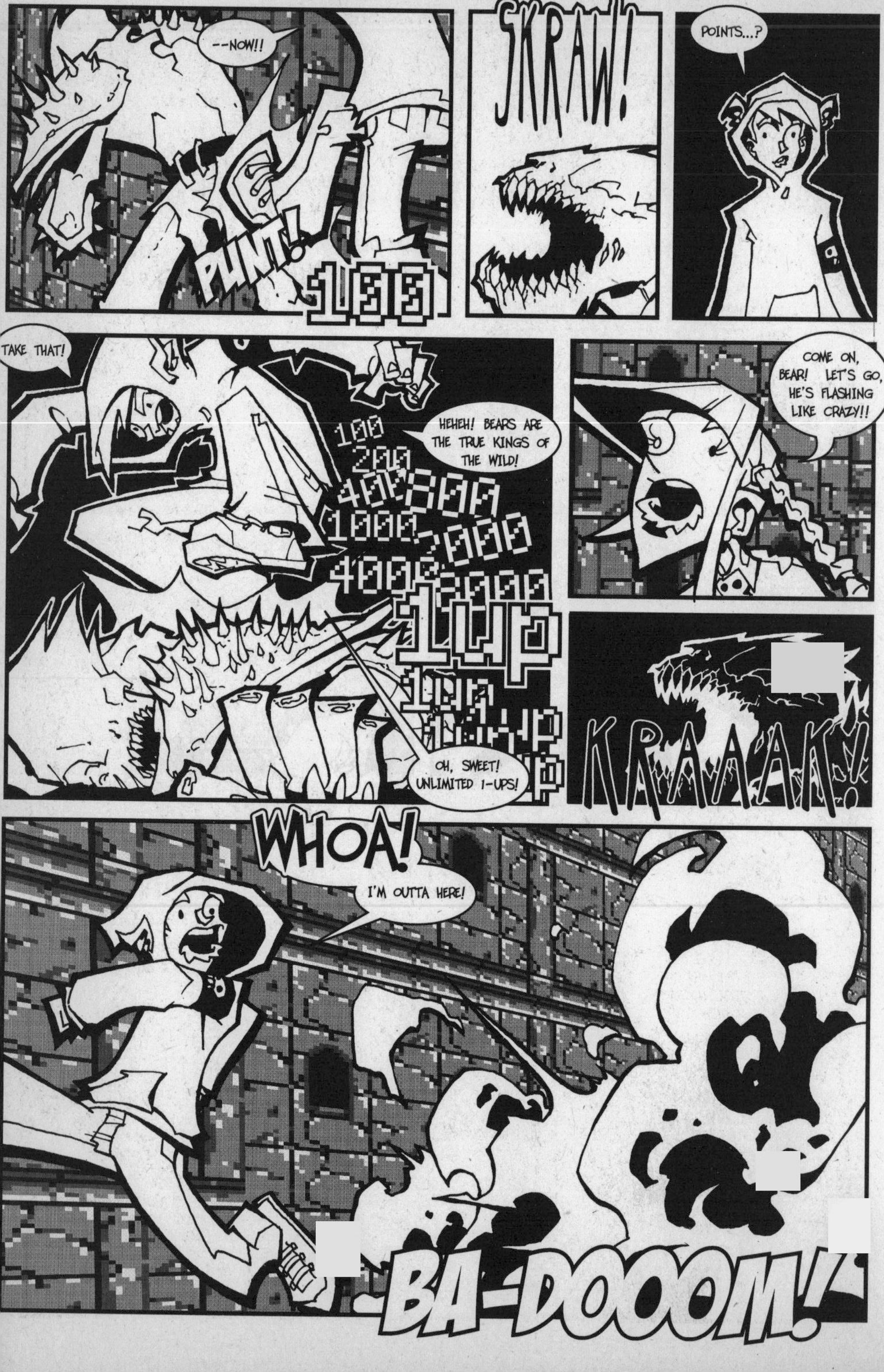

--NOW!!
PUNT!
100
SKRAW!
POINTS...?
TAKE THAT!
HEHEH! BEARS ARE THE TRUE KINGS OF THE WILD!
100
200
400
800
1000
2000
4000
8000
1UP
OH, SWEET! UNLIMITED 1-UPS!
COME ON, BEAR! LET'S GO, HE'S FLASHING LIKE CRAZY!!
KRAAAK!
WHOA!
I'M OUTTA HERE!
BA-DOOOM!

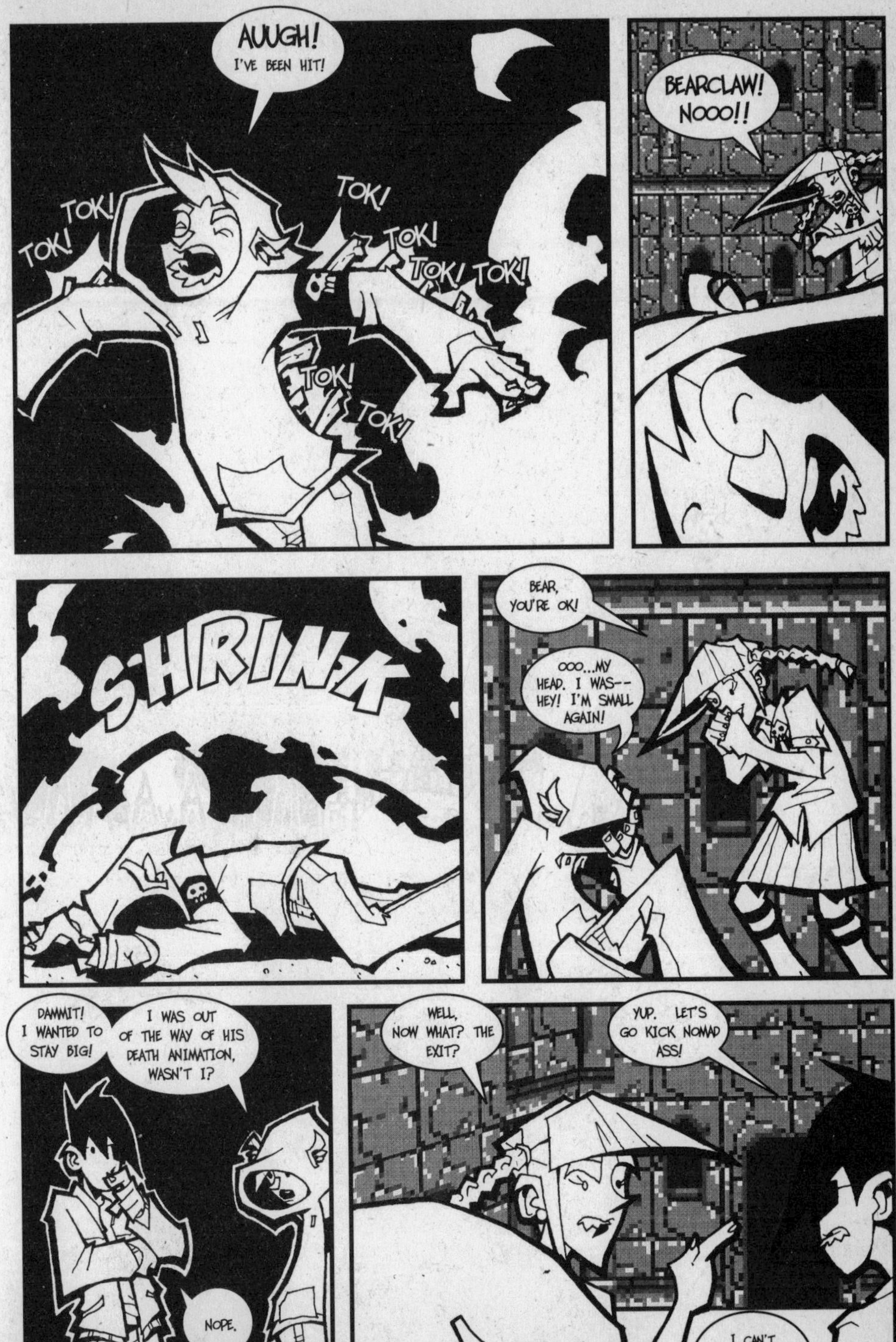
AUUGH!
I'VE BEEN HIT!
TOK! TOK!
TOK!
TOK! TOK! TOK!
TOK! TOK!
BEARCLAW! NOOO!!
S-H-R-I-N-K
BEAR, YOU'RE OK!
OOO...MY HEAD. I WAS--HEY! I'M SMALL AGAIN!
DAMMIT! I WANTED TO STAY BIG!
I WAS OUT OF THE WAY OF HIS DEATH ANIMATION, WASN'T I?
NOPE.
WELL, NOW WHAT? THE EXIT?
YUP. LET'S GO KICK NOMAD ASS!
I CAN'T BELIEVE I LOST MY POWER UP.

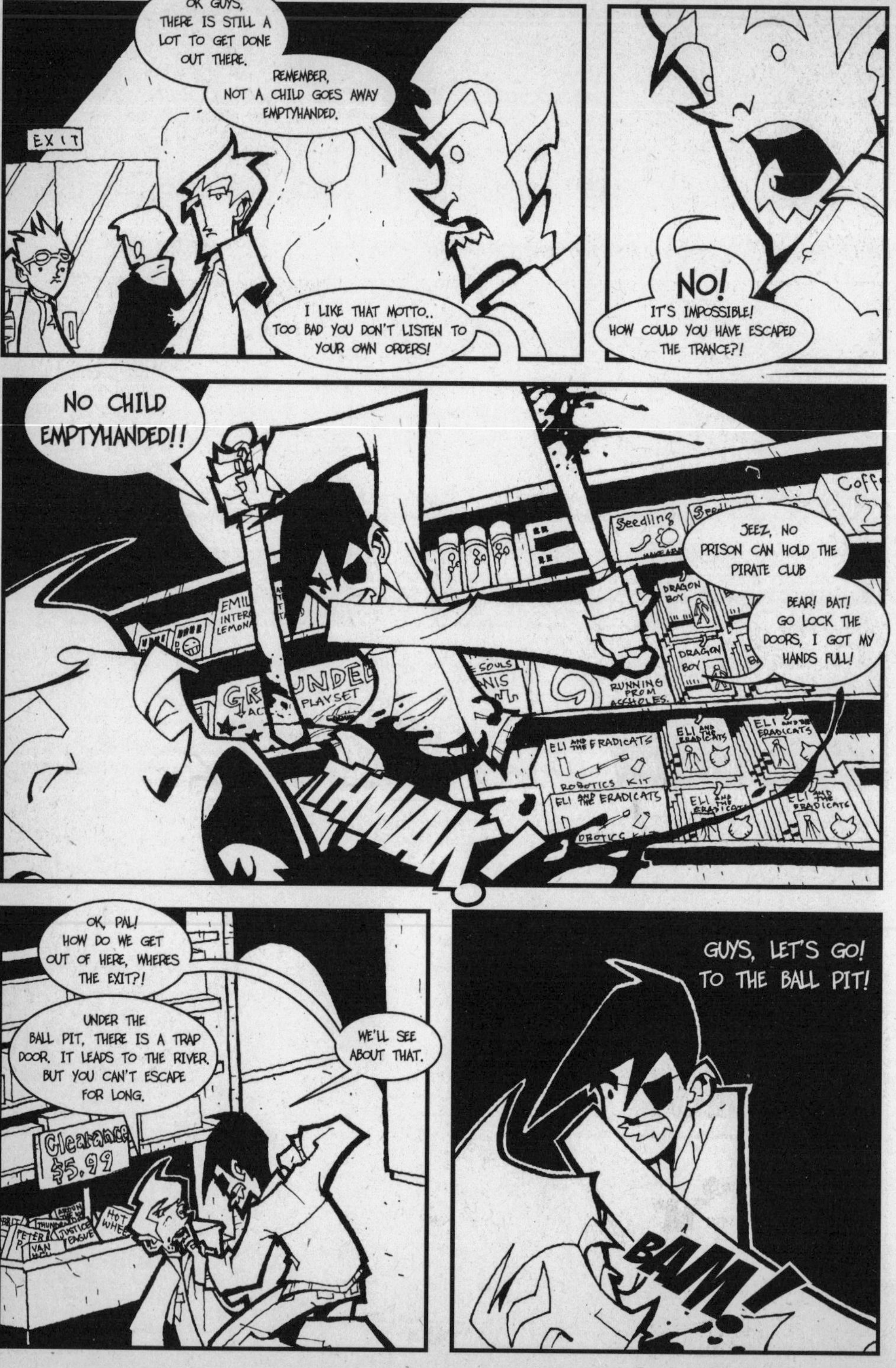
OK GUYS, THERE IS STILL A LOT TO GET DONE OUT THERE.
REMEMBER, NOT A CHILD GOES AWAY EMPTYHANDED.
EXIT
I LIKE THAT MOTTO.. TOO BAD YOU DON'T LISTEN TO YOUR OWN ORDERS!
NO!
IT'S IMPOSSIBLE! HOW COULD YOU HAVE ESCAPED THE TRANCE?!
NO CHILD EMPTYHANDED!!
JEEZ, NO PRISON CAN HOLD THE PIRATE CLUB
BEAR! BAT! GO LOCK THE DOORS, I GOT MY HANDS FULL!
THWAK!
OK, PAL! HOW DO WE GET OUT OF HERE, WHERES THE EXIT?!
UNDER THE BALL PIT, THERE IS A TRAP DOOR. IT LEADS TO THE RIVER, BUT YOU CAN'T ESCAPE FOR LONG.
WE'LL SEE ABOUT THAT.
Clearance $5.99
GUYS, LET'S GO! TO THE BALL PIT!
BAM!

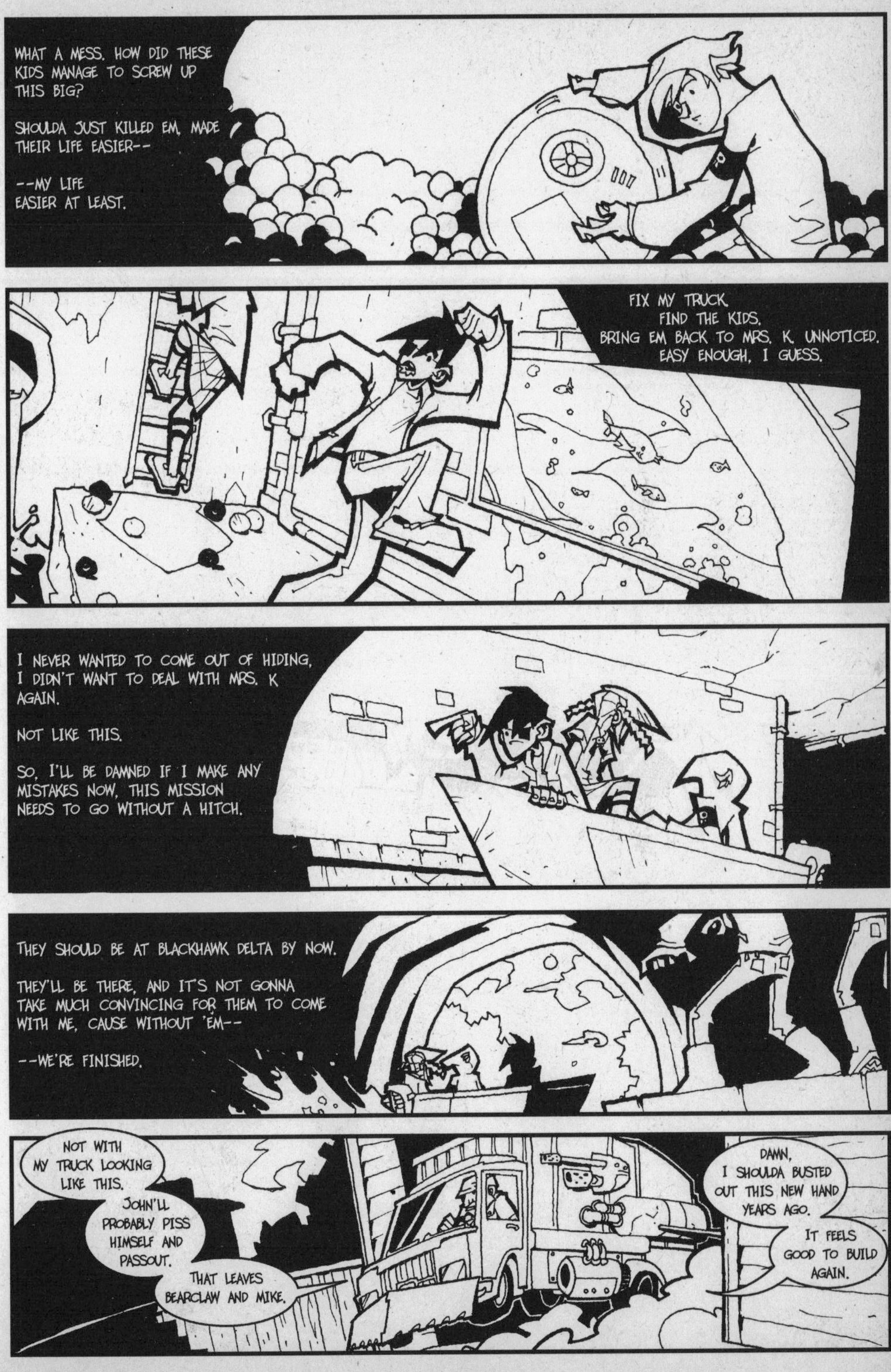
WHAT A MESS. HOW DID THESE KIDS MANAGE TO SCREW UP THIS BIG?
SHOULDA JUST KILLED EM, MADE THEIR LIFE EASIER--
--MY LIFE EASIER AT LEAST.
FIX MY TRUCK. FIND THE KIDS. BRING EM BACK TO MRS. K. UNNOTICED. EASY ENOUGH, I GUESS.
I NEVER WANTED TO COME OUT OF HIDING, I DIDN'T WANT TO DEAL WITH MRS. K AGAIN.
NOT LIKE THIS.
SO, I'LL BE DAMNED IF I MAKE ANY MISTAKES NOW, THIS MISSION NEEDS TO GO WITHOUT A HITCH.
THEY SHOULD BE AT BLACKHAWK DELTA BY NOW.
THEY'LL BE THERE, AND IT'S NOT GONNA TAKE MUCH CONVINCING FOR THEM TO COME WITH ME, CAUSE WITHOUT 'EM--
--WE'RE FINISHED.
NOT WITH MY TRUCK LOOKING LIKE THIS.
JOHN'LL PROBABLY PISS HIMSELF AND PASSOUT.
THAT LEAVES BEARCLAW AND MIKE.
DAMN, I SHOULDA BUSTED OUT THIS NEW HAND YEARS AGO.
IT FEELS GOOD TO BUILD AGAIN.

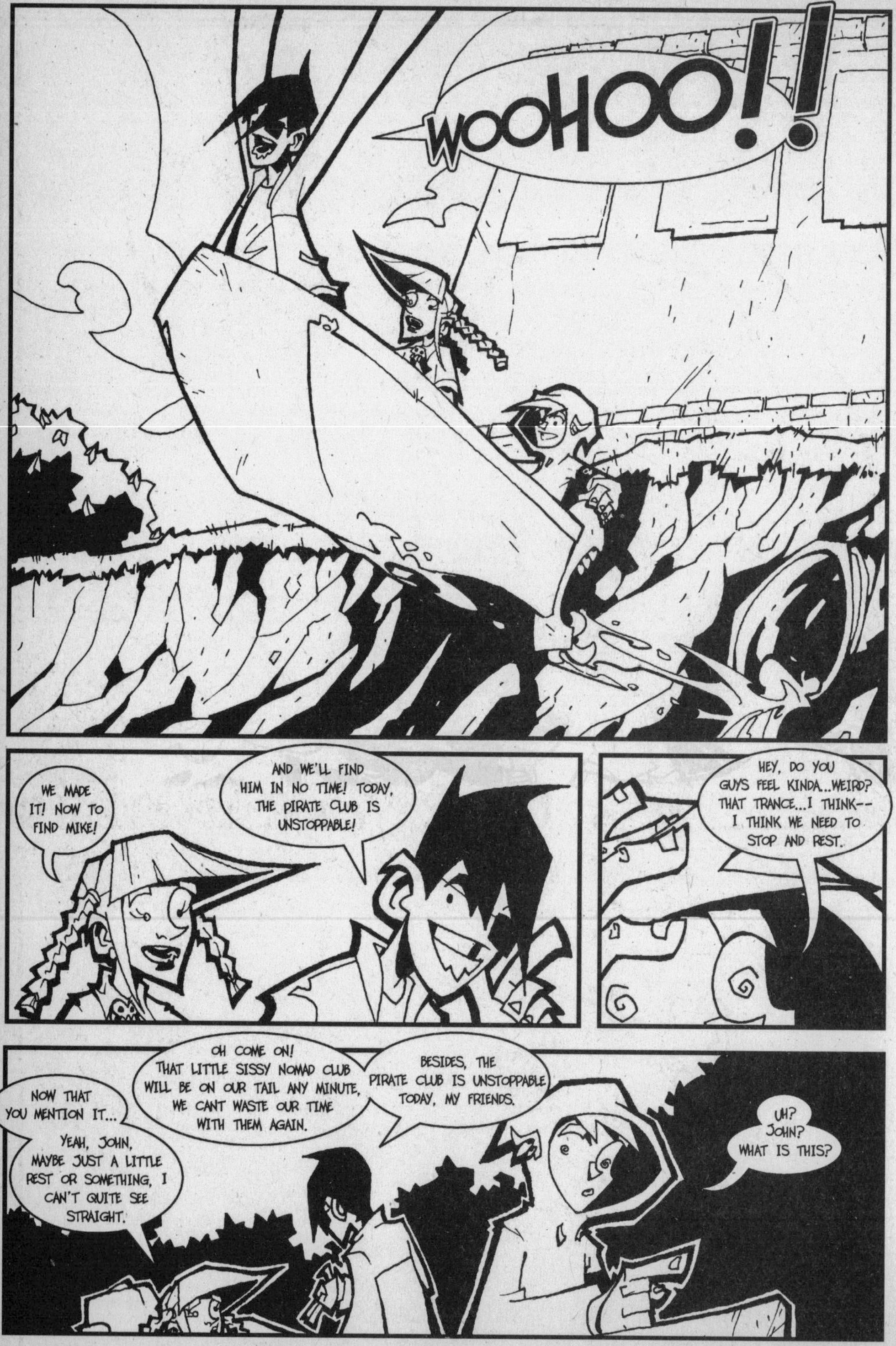
WOOHOO!!
WE MADE IT! NOW TO FIND MIKE!
AND WE'LL FIND HIM IN NO TIME! TODAY, THE PIRATE CLUB IS UNSTOPPABLE!
HEY, DO YOU GUYS FEEL KINDA...WEIRD? THAT TRANCE...I THINK--I THINK WE NEED TO STOP AND REST.
NOW THAT YOU MENTION IT...
YEAH, JOHN, MAYBE JUST A LITTLE REST OR SOMETHING, I CAN'T QUITE SEE STRAIGHT.
OH COME ON! THAT LITTLE SISSY NOMAD CLUB WILL BE ON OUR TAIL ANY MINUTE, WE CANT WASTE OUR TIME WITH THEM AGAIN.
BESIDES, THE PIRATE CLUB IS UNSTOPPABLE TODAY, MY FRIENDS.
UH? JOHN? WHAT IS THIS?

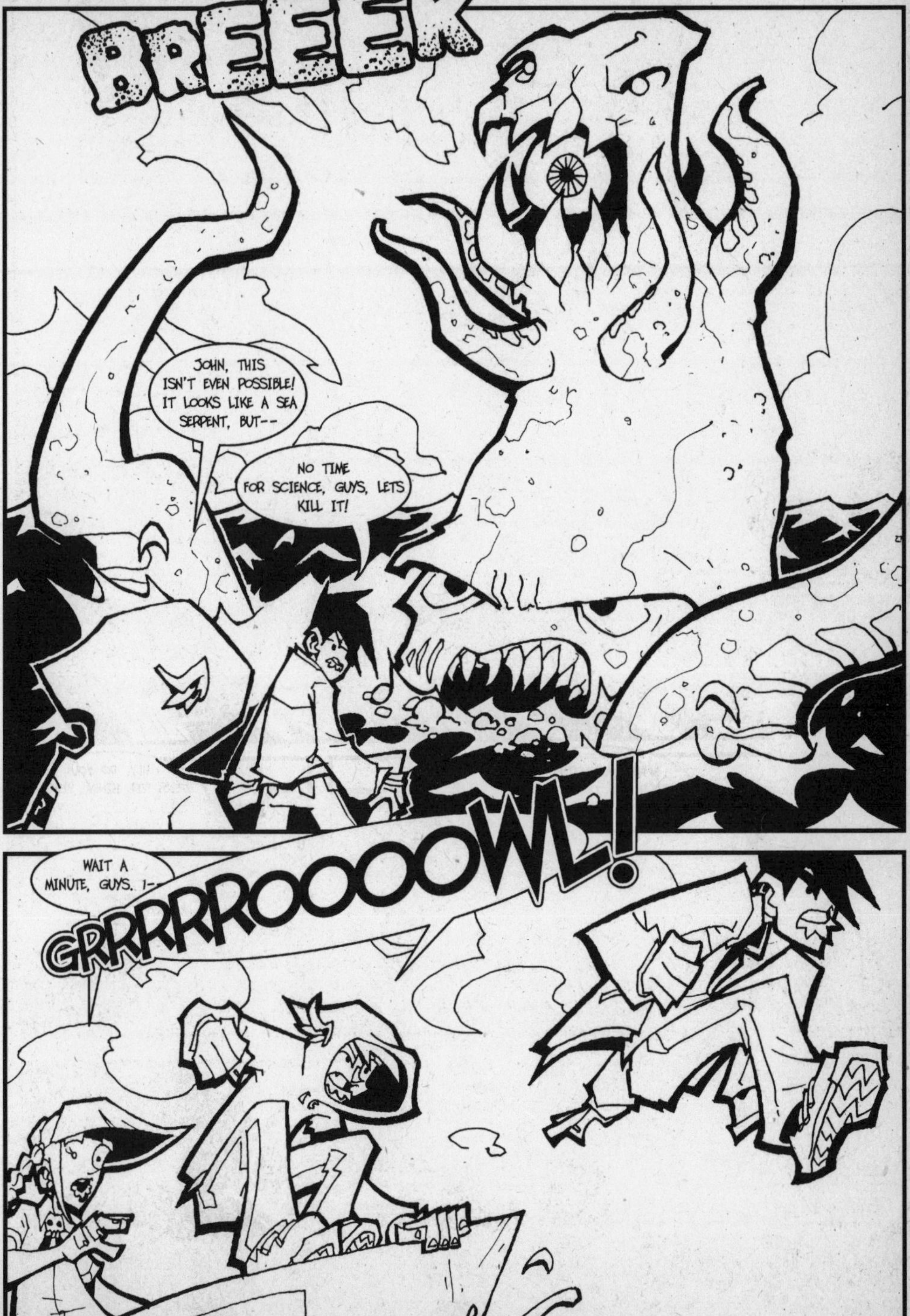
BREEEK
JOHN, THIS ISN'T EVEN POSSIBLE! IT LOOKS LIKE A SEA SERPENT, BUT--
NO TIME FOR SCIENCE, GUYS, LETS KILL IT!
WAIT A MINUTE, GUYS. I--
GRRRRROOOOOWL!

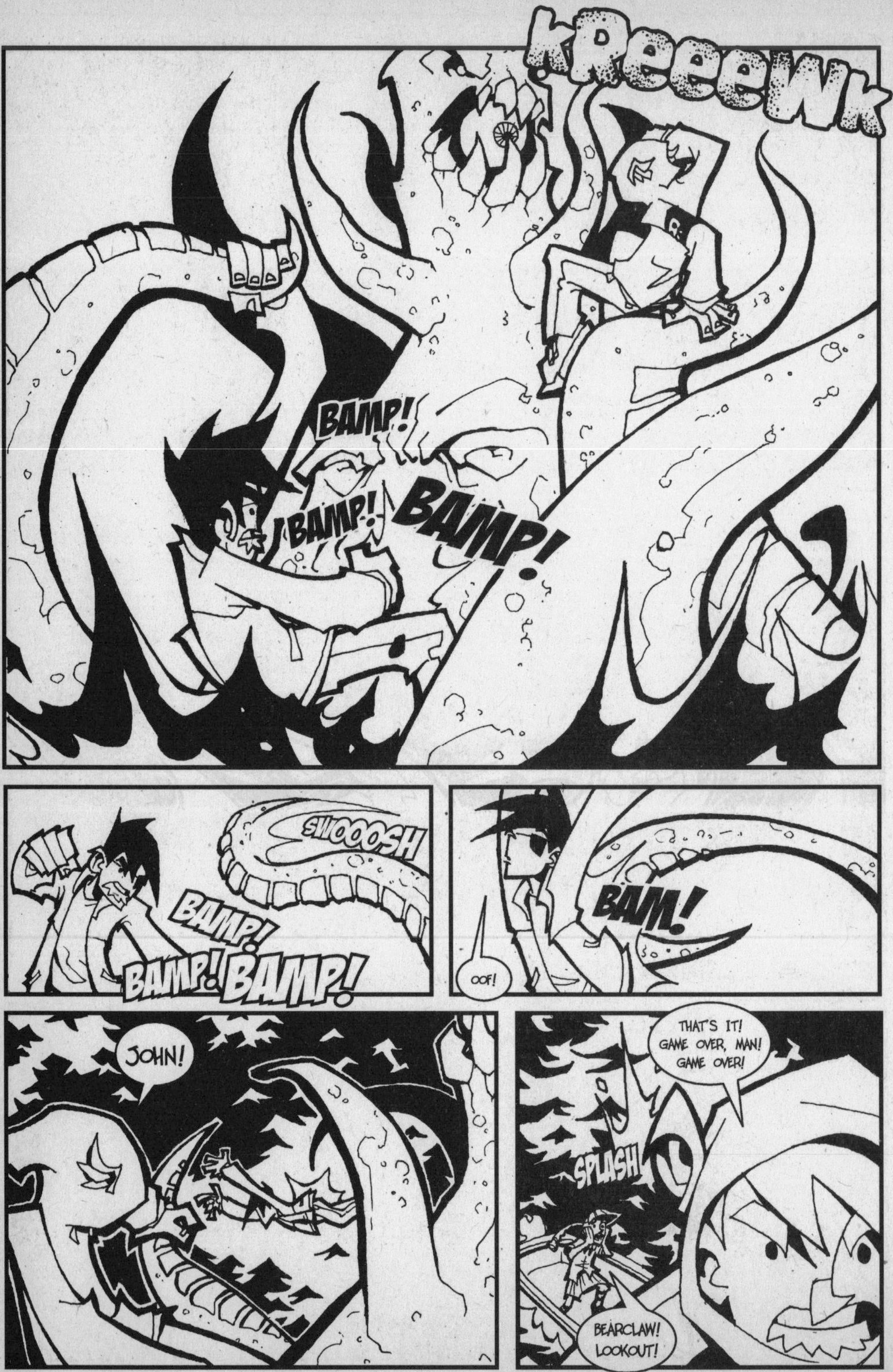
kReeeWk
BAMP!
BAMP!
BAMP!
SWOOOSH
BAMP!
BAMP!
BAMP!
BAM!
OOF!
JOHN!
THAT'S IT! GAME OVER, MAN! GAME OVER!
SPLASH!
BEARCLAW! LOOKOUT!

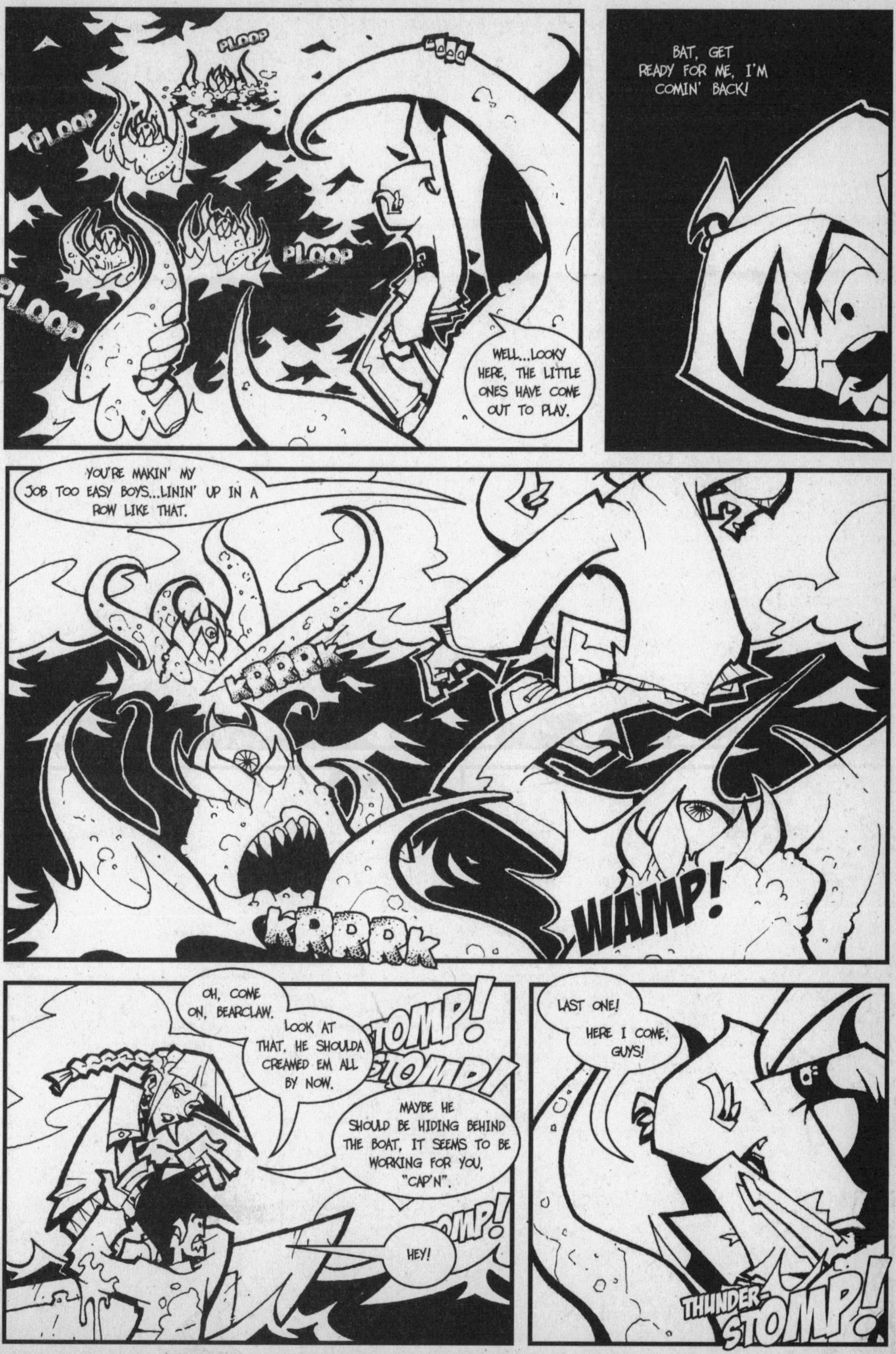

PLOOP
PLOOP
PLOOP
PLOOP
PLOOP
WELL...LOOKY HERE, THE LITTLE ONES HAVE COME OUT TO PLAY.
BAT, GET READY FOR ME, I'M COMIN' BACK!
YOU'RE MAKIN' MY JOB TOO EASY BOYS...LININ' UP IN A ROW LIKE THAT.
KRRRK
KRRRK
WAMP!
OH, COME ON, BEARCLAW.
LOOK AT THAT. HE SHOULDA CREAMED EM ALL BY NOW.
STOMP!
STOMP!
MAYBE HE SHOULD BE HIDING BEHIND THE BOAT, IT SEEMS TO BE WORKING FOR YOU, "CAP'N".
HEY!
LAST ONE!
HERE I COME, GUYS!
THUNDER-STOMP!

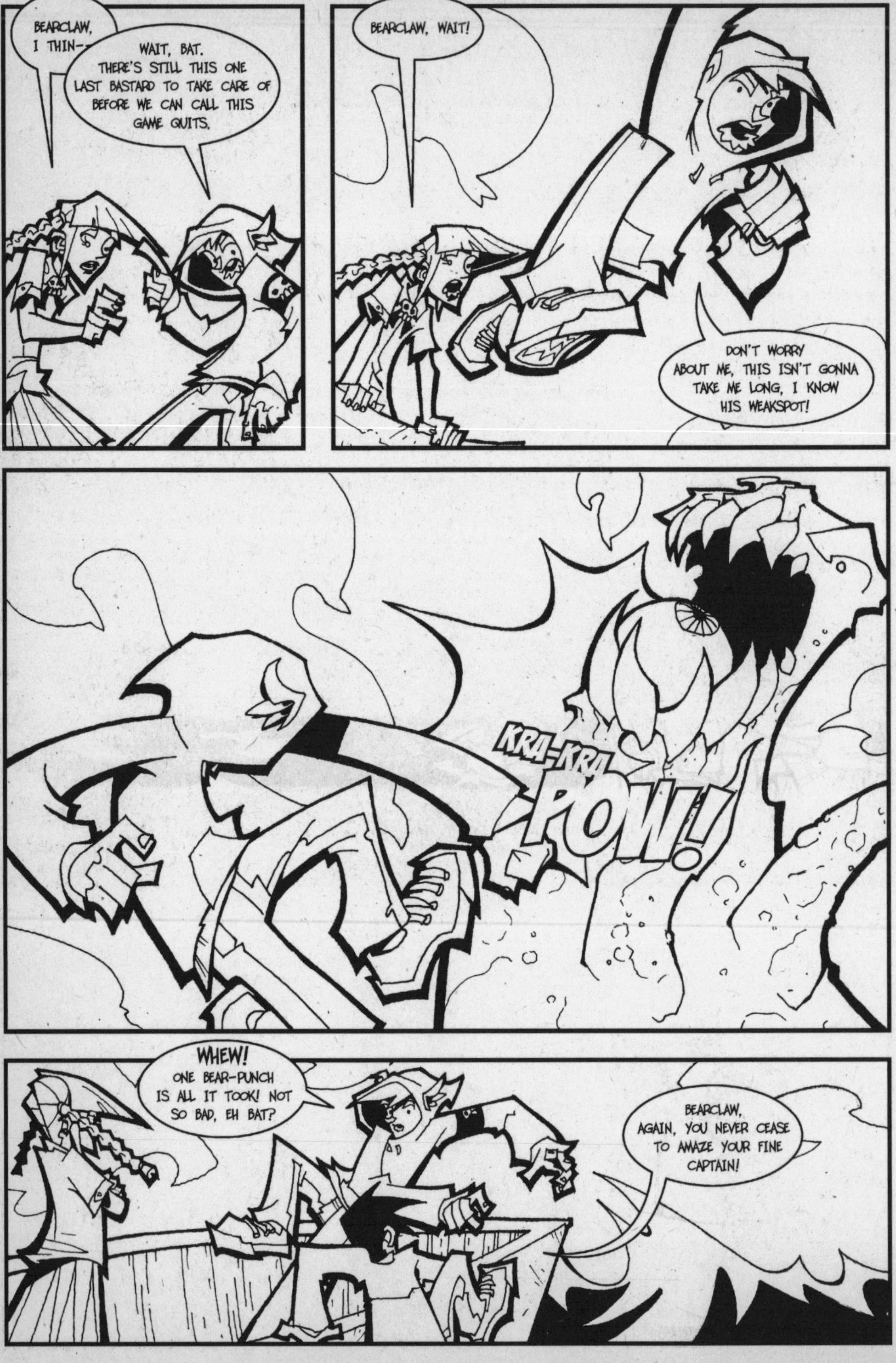
BEARCLAW, I THIN--
WAIT, BAT. THERE'S STILL THIS ONE LAST BASTARD TO TAKE CARE OF BEFORE WE CAN CALL THIS GAME QUITS.
BEARCLAW, WAIT!
DON'T WORRY ABOUT ME, THIS ISN'T GONNA TAKE ME LONG, I KNOW HIS WEAKSPOT!
KRA-KRA POW!
WHEW! ONE BEAR-PUNCH IS ALL IT TOOK! NOT SO BAD, EH BAT?
BEARCLAW, AGAIN, YOU NEVER CEASE TO AMAZE YOUR FINE CAPTAIN!

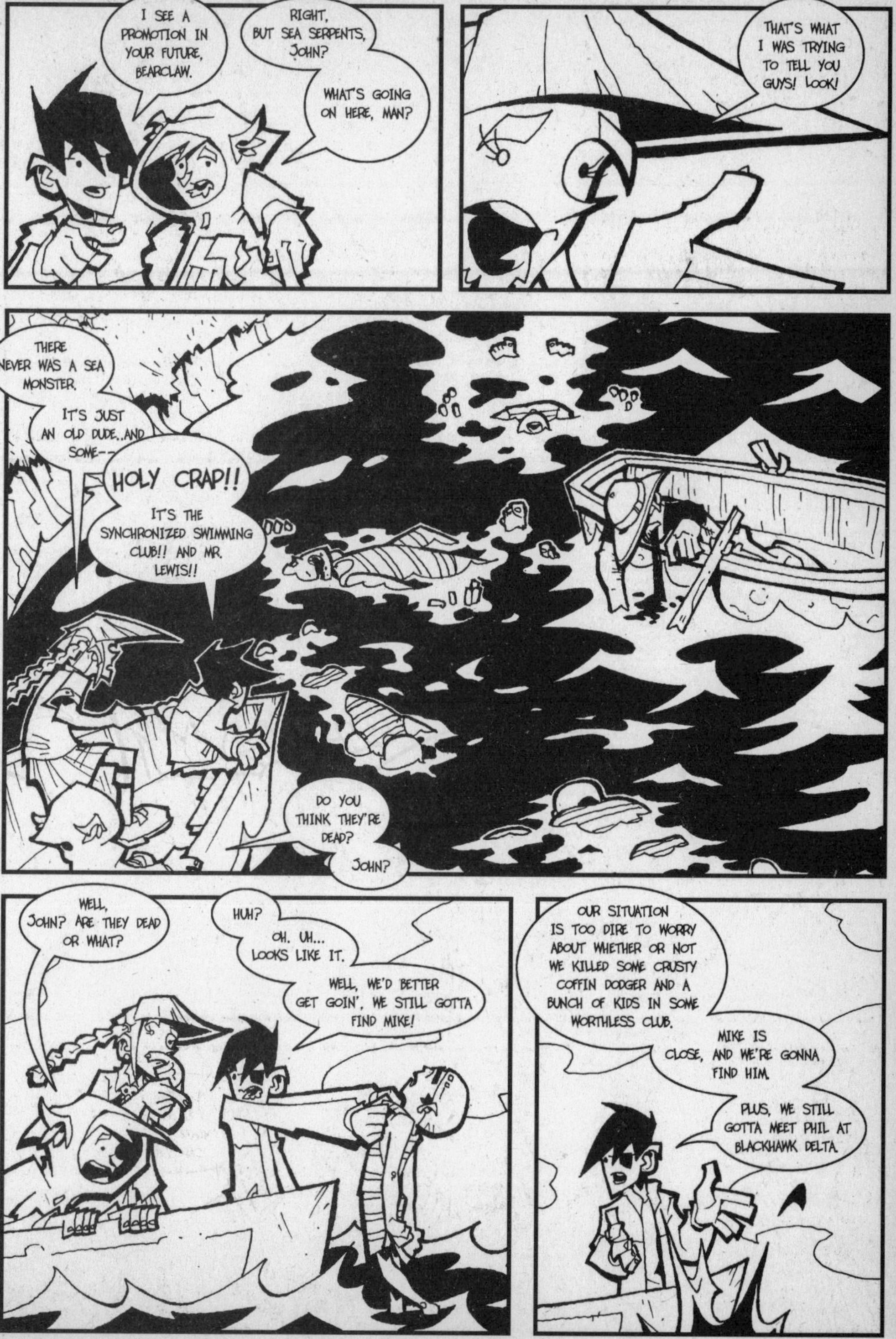
I SEE A PROMOTION IN YOUR FUTURE, BEARCLAW.
RIGHT, BUT SEA SERPENTS, JOHN?
WHAT'S GOING ON HERE, MAN?
THAT'S WHAT I WAS TRYING TO TELL YOU GUYS! LOOK!
THERE NEVER WAS A SEA MONSTER.
IT'S JUST AN OLD DUDE..AND SOME--
HOLY CRAP!!
IT'S THE SYNCHRONIZED SWIMMING CLUB!! AND MR. LEWIS!!
DO YOU THINK THEY'RE DEAD?
JOHN?
WELL, JOHN? ARE THEY DEAD OR WHAT?
HUH?
OH. UH... LOOKS LIKE IT.
WELL, WE'D BETTER GET GOIN', WE STILL GOTTA FIND MIKE!
OUR SITUATION IS TOO DIRE TO WORRY ABOUT WHETHER OR NOT WE KILLED SOME CRUSTY COFFIN DODGER AND A BUNCH OF KIDS IN SOME WORTHLESS CLUB.
MIKE IS CLOSE, AND WE'RE GONNA FIND HIM.
PLUS, WE STILL GOTTA MEET PHIL AT BLACKHAWK DELTA.

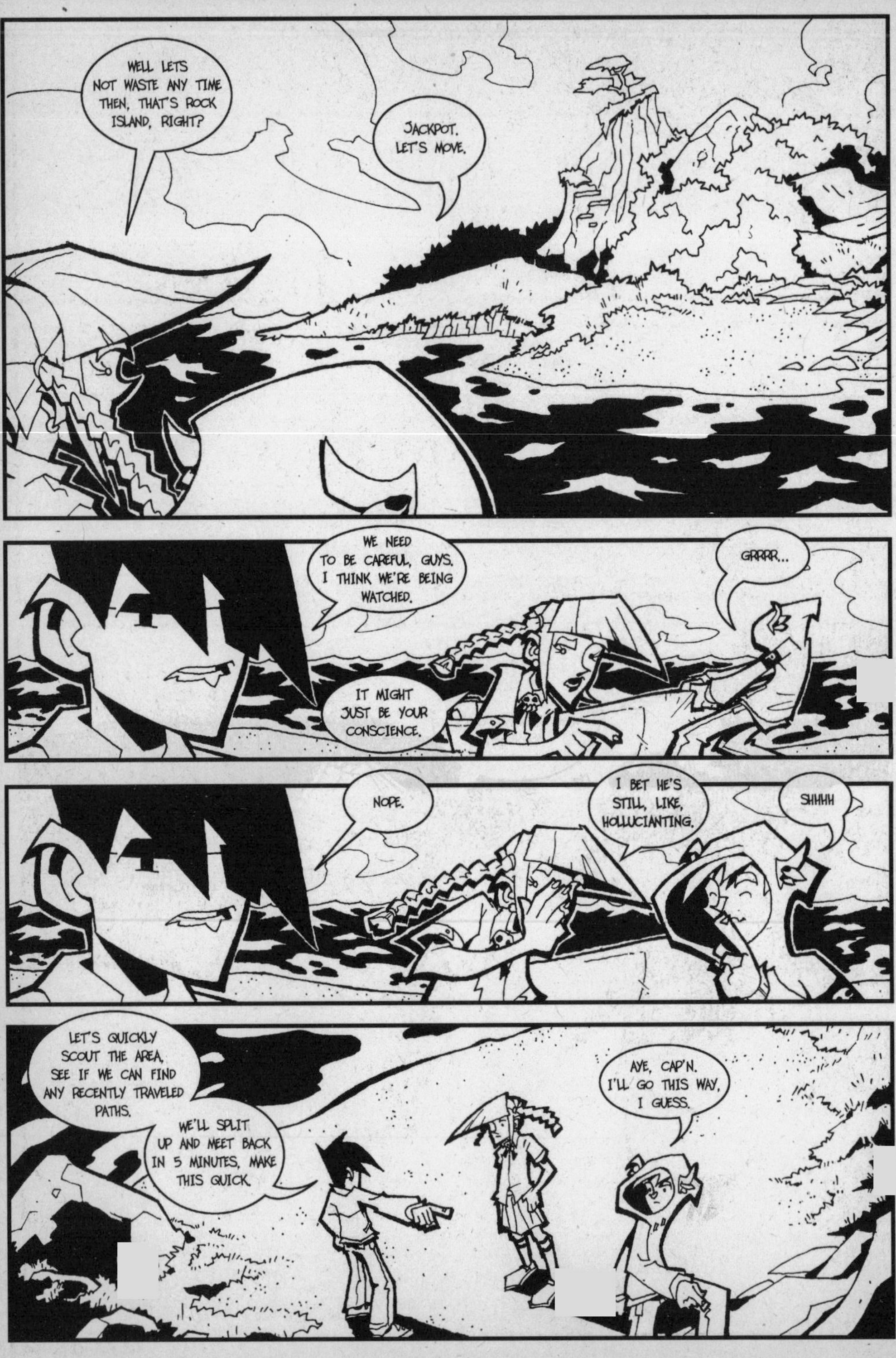
WELL LETS NOT WASTE ANY TIME THEN, THAT'S ROCK ISLAND, RIGHT?
JACKPOT. LET'S MOVE.
WE NEED TO BE CAREFUL, GUYS. I THINK WE'RE BEING WATCHED.
GRRRR...
IT MIGHT JUST BE YOUR CONSCIENCE.
NOPE.
I BET HE'S STILL, LIKE, HOLLUCIANTING.
SHHHH
LET'S QUICKLY SCOUT THE AREA, SEE IF WE CAN FIND ANY RECENTLY TRAVELED PATHS.
WE'LL SPLIT UP AND MEET BACK IN 5 MINUTES, MAKE THIS QUICK.
AYE, CAP'N. I'LL GO THIS WAY, I GUESS.

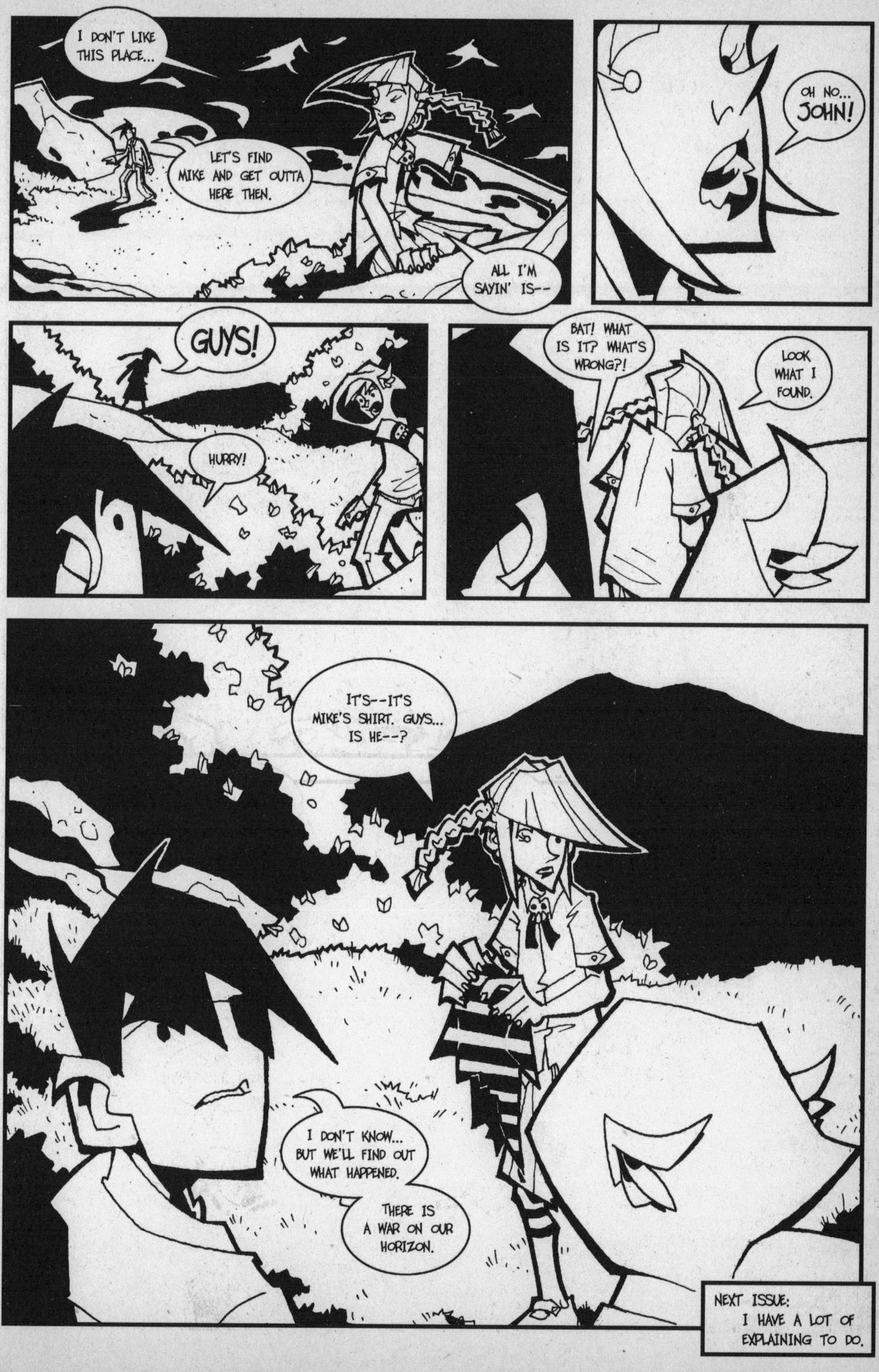

I DON'T LIKE THIS PLACE...
LET'S FIND MIKE AND GET OUTTA HERE THEN.
ALL I'M SAYIN' IS--
OH NO... JOHN!
GUYS!
HURRY!
BAT! WHAT IS IT? WHAT'S WRONG?!
LOOK WHAT I FOUND.
IT'S--IT'S MIKE'S SHIRT. GUYS... IS HE--?
I DON'T KNOW... BUT WE'LL FIND OUT WHAT HAPPENED.
THERE IS A WAR ON OUR HORIZON.
NEXT ISSUE: I HAVE A LOT OF EXPLAINING TO DO.

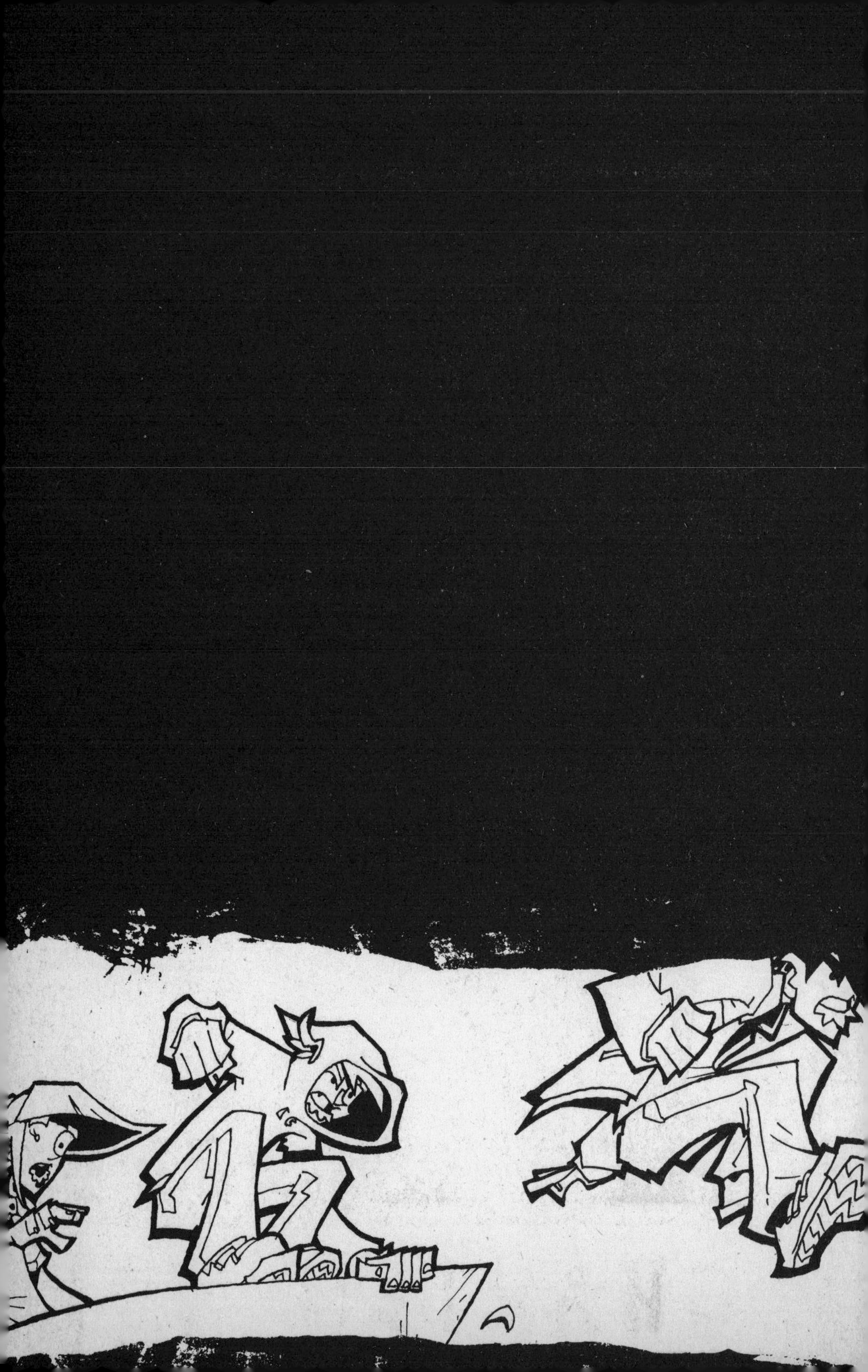

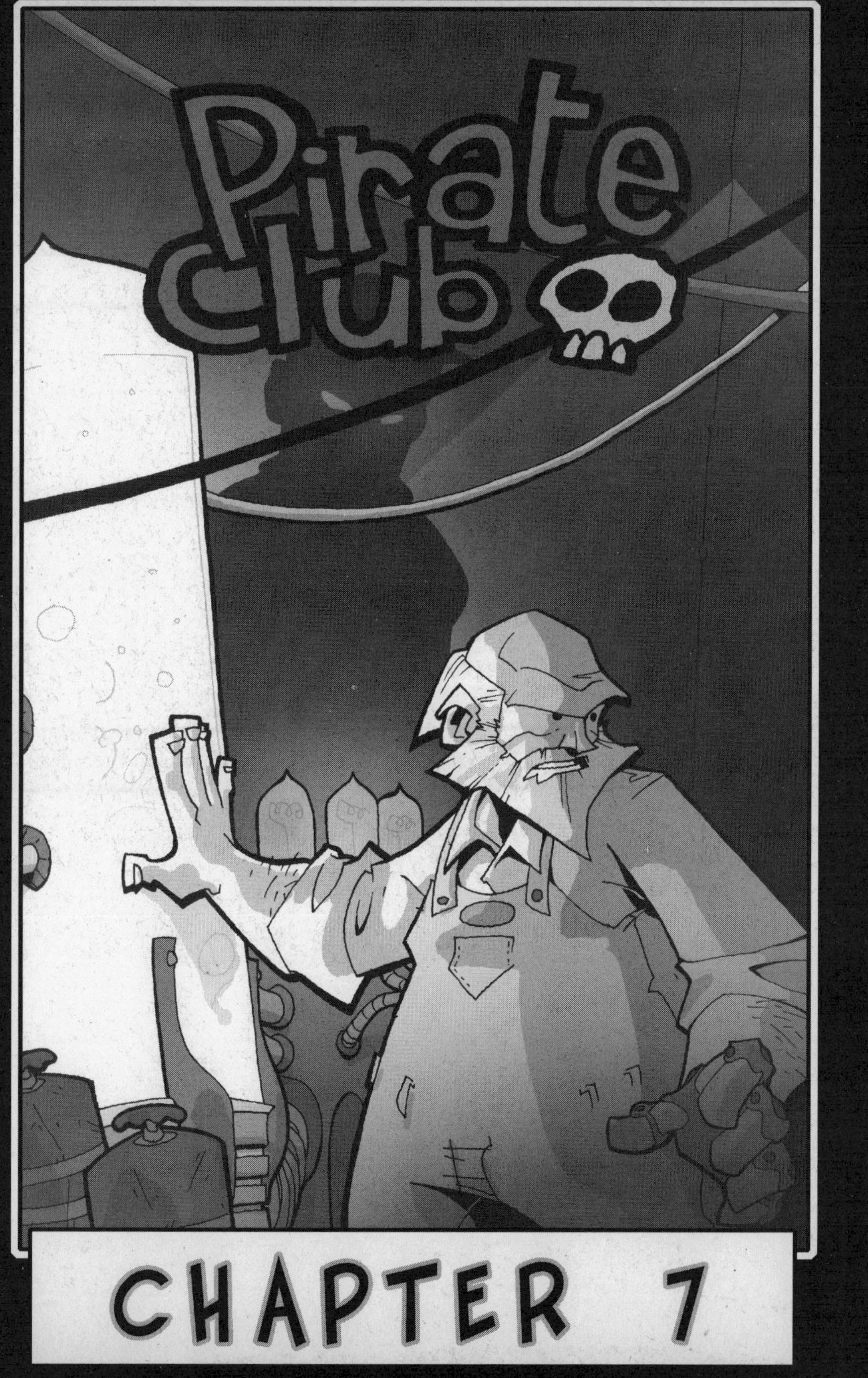
Pirate club

# CHAPTER 7

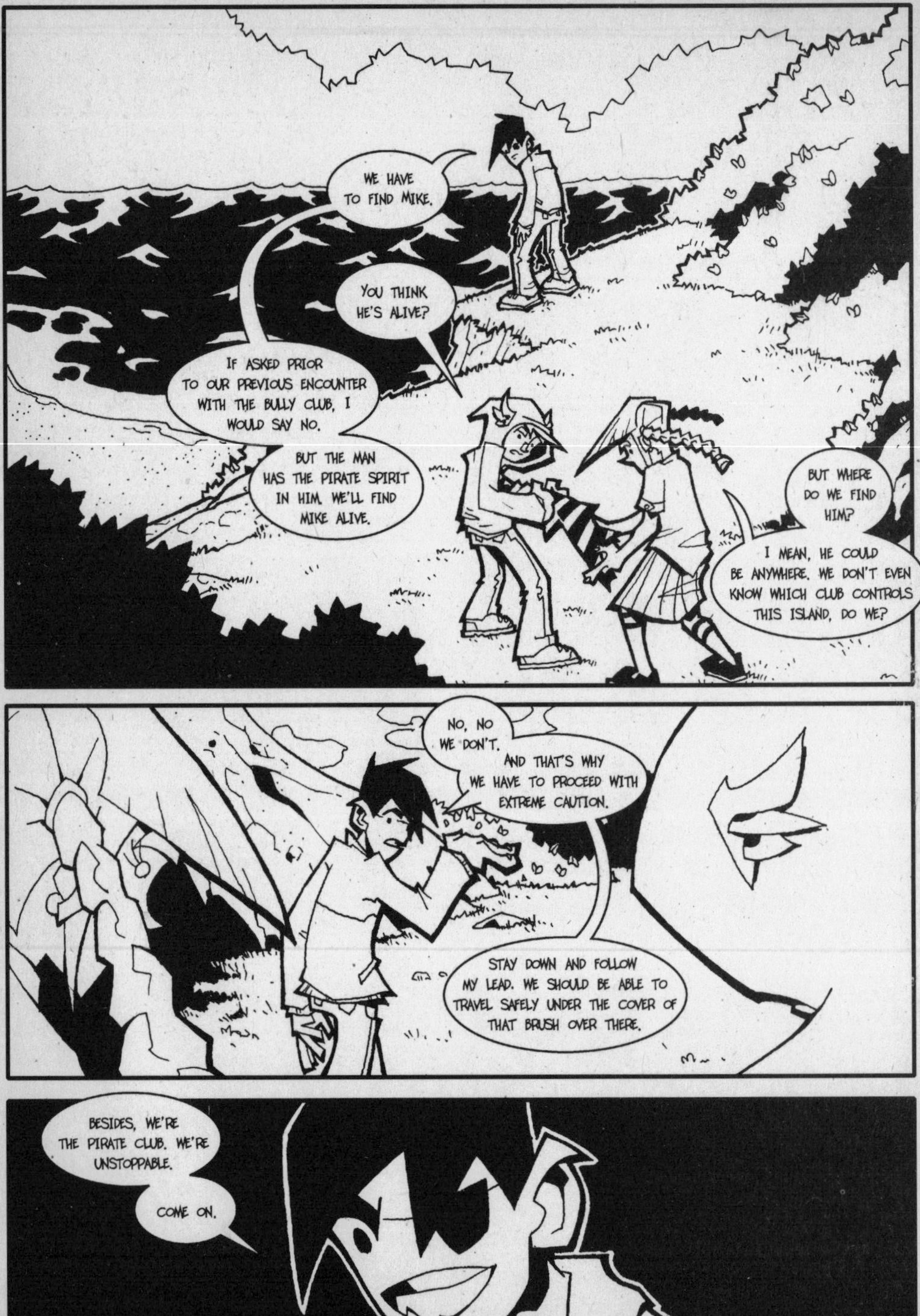
WE HAVE TO FIND MIKE.
YOU THINK HE'S ALIVE?
IF ASKED PRIOR TO OUR PREVIOUS ENCOUNTER WITH THE BULLY CLUB, I WOULD SAY NO.
BUT THE MAN HAS THE PIRATE SPIRIT IN HIM. WE'LL FIND MIKE ALIVE.
BUT WHERE DO WE FIND HIM?
I MEAN, HE COULD BE ANYWHERE. WE DON'T EVEN KNOW WHICH CLUB CONTROLS THIS ISLAND, DO WE?
NO, NO WE DON'T.
AND THAT'S WHY WE HAVE TO PROCEED WITH EXTREME CAUTION.
STAY DOWN AND FOLLOW MY LEAD. WE SHOULD BE ABLE TO TRAVEL SAFELY UNDER THE COVER OF THAT BRUSH OVER THERE.
BESIDES, WE'RE THE PIRATE CLUB. WE'RE UNSTOPPABLE.
COME ON.

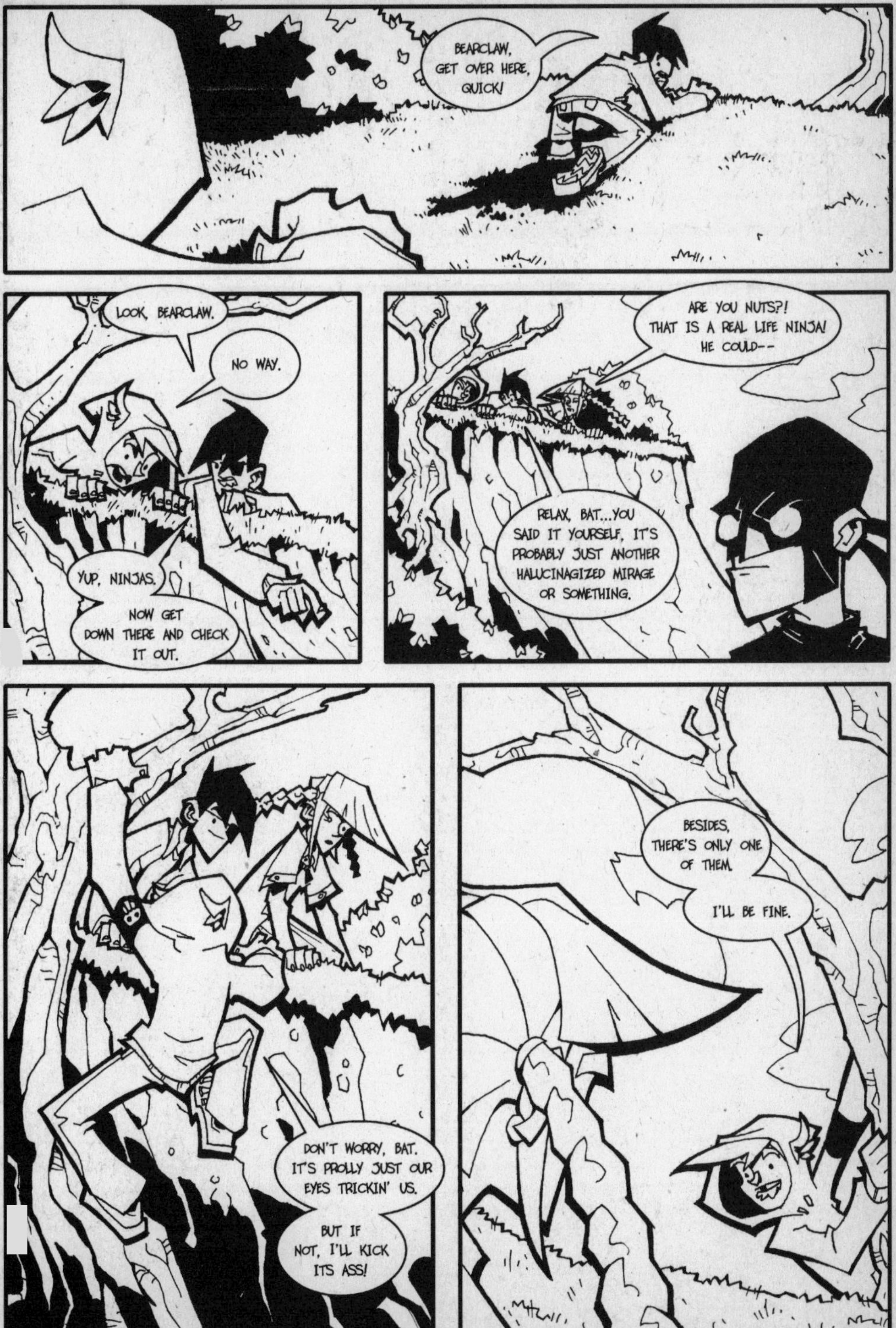
BEARCLAW, GET OVER HERE, QUICK!
LOOK, BEARCLAW.
NO WAY.
YUP, NINJAS.
NOW GET DOWN THERE AND CHECK IT OUT.
ARE YOU NUTS?! THAT IS A REAL LIFE NINJA! HE COULD--
RELAX, BAT...YOU SAID IT YOURSELF, IT'S PROBABLY JUST ANOTHER HALUCINAGIZED MIRAGE OR SOMETHING.
DON'T WORRY, BAT. IT'S PROLLY JUST OUR EYES TRICKIN' US.
BUT IF NOT, I'LL KICK ITS ASS!
BESIDES, THERE'S ONLY ONE OF THEM.
I'LL BE FINE.

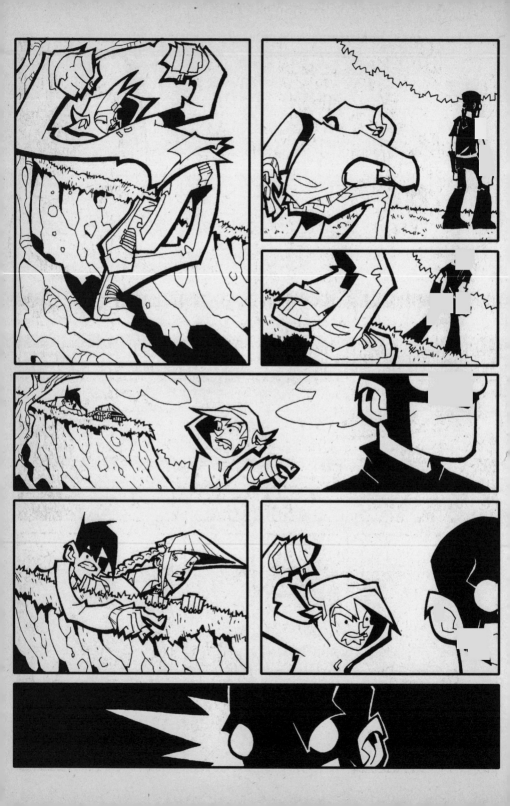

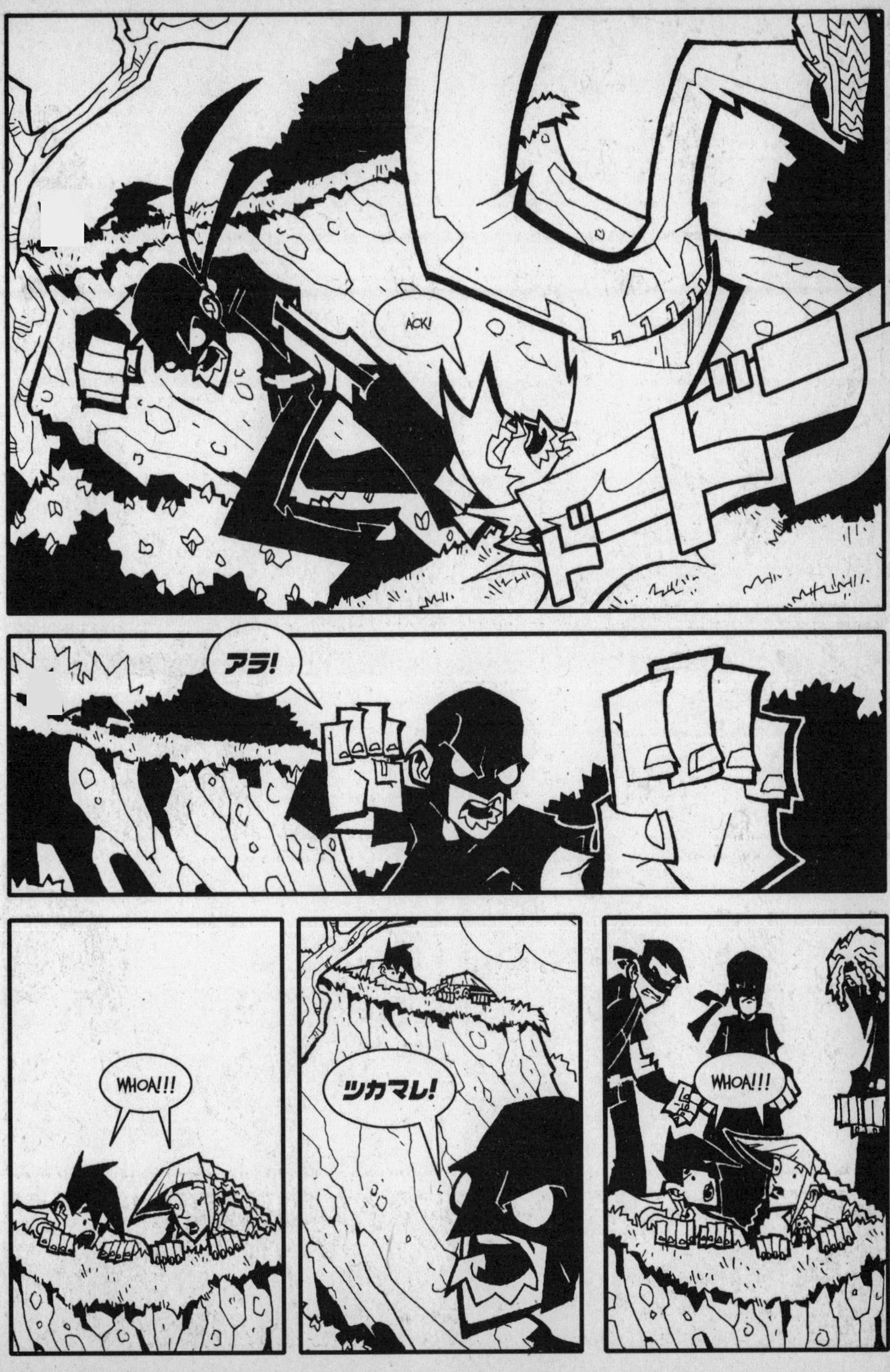
ACK!
アラ!
WHOA!!!
ツカマレ!
WHOA!!!

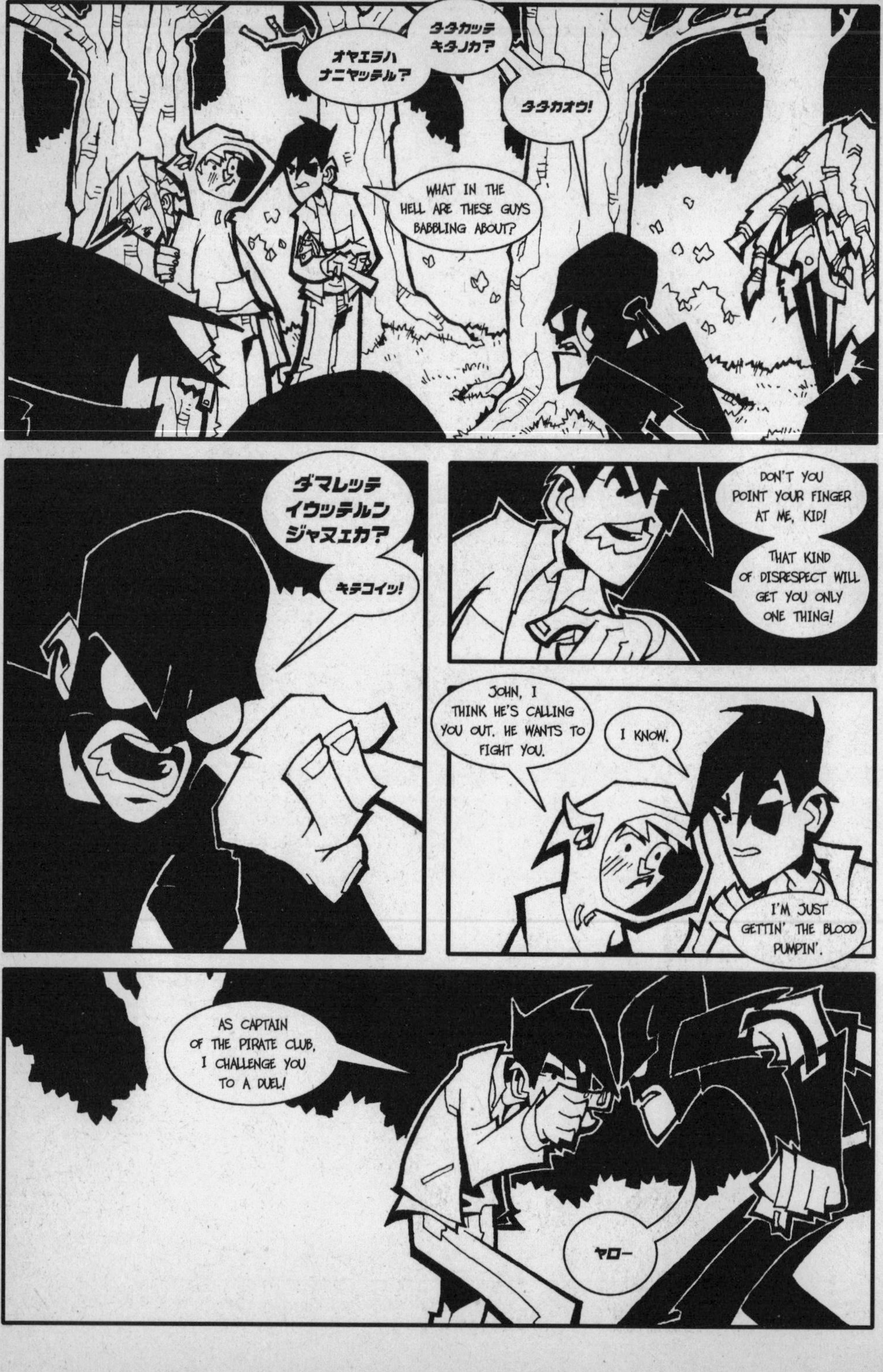

オヤエラハ ナニヤッテル?
タタカッテ キタノカ?
タタカオウ!
WHAT IN THE HELL ARE THESE GUYS BABBLING ABOUT?
ダマレッテ イウッテルン ジャヌェカ?
キテコイッ!
DON'T YOU POINT YOUR FINGER AT ME, KID!
THAT KIND OF DISRESPECT WILL GET YOU ONLY ONE THING!
JOHN, I THINK HE'S CALLING YOU OUT. HE WANTS TO FIGHT YOU.
I KNOW.
I'M JUST GETTIN' THE BLOOD PUMPIN'.
AS CAPTAIN OF THE PIRATE CLUB, I CHALLENGE YOU TO A DUEL!
ヤロー

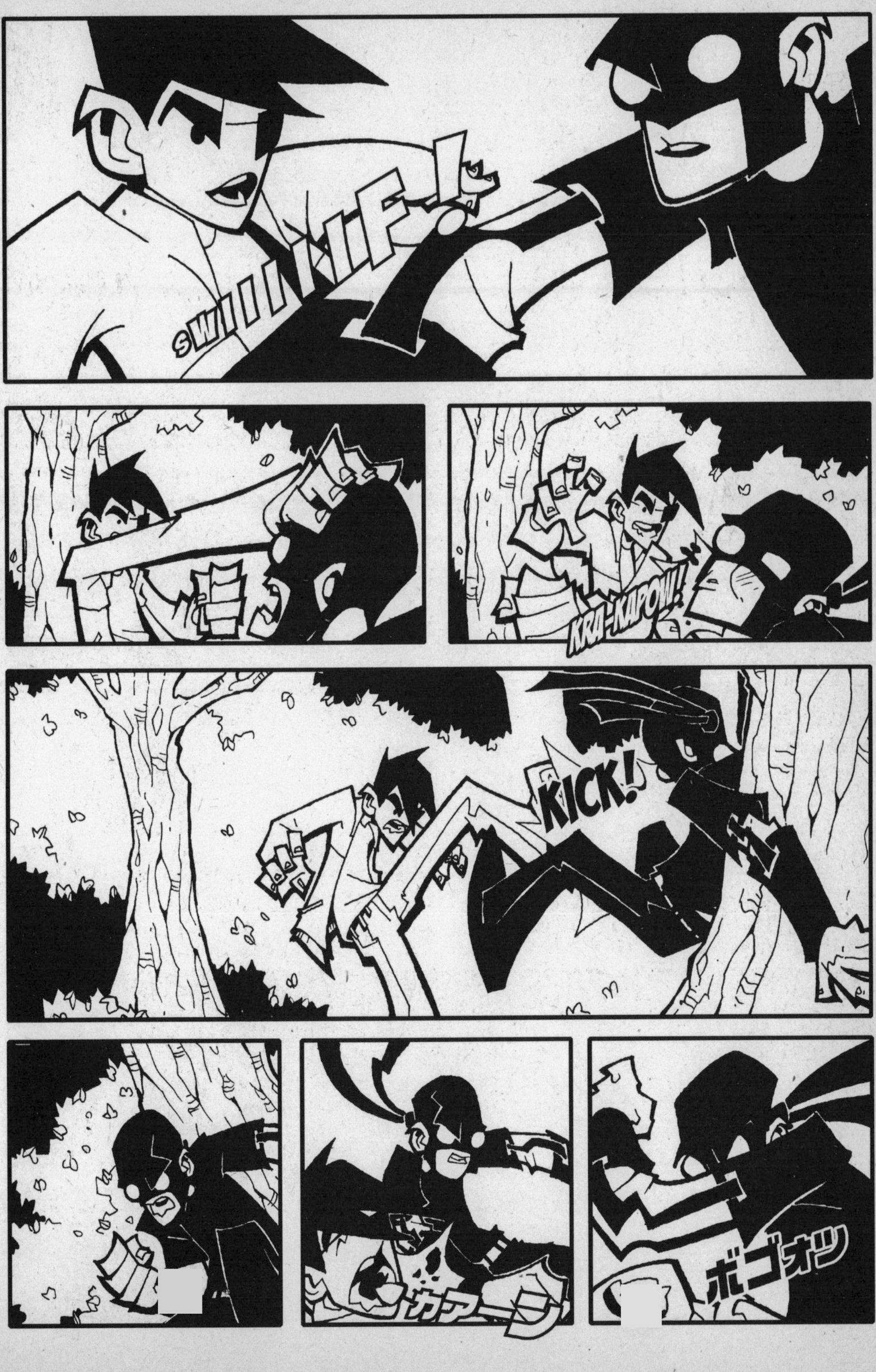
SWIIIIIIIF!
KRA-KAPOW!
KICK!
カアーン
ボゴオッ

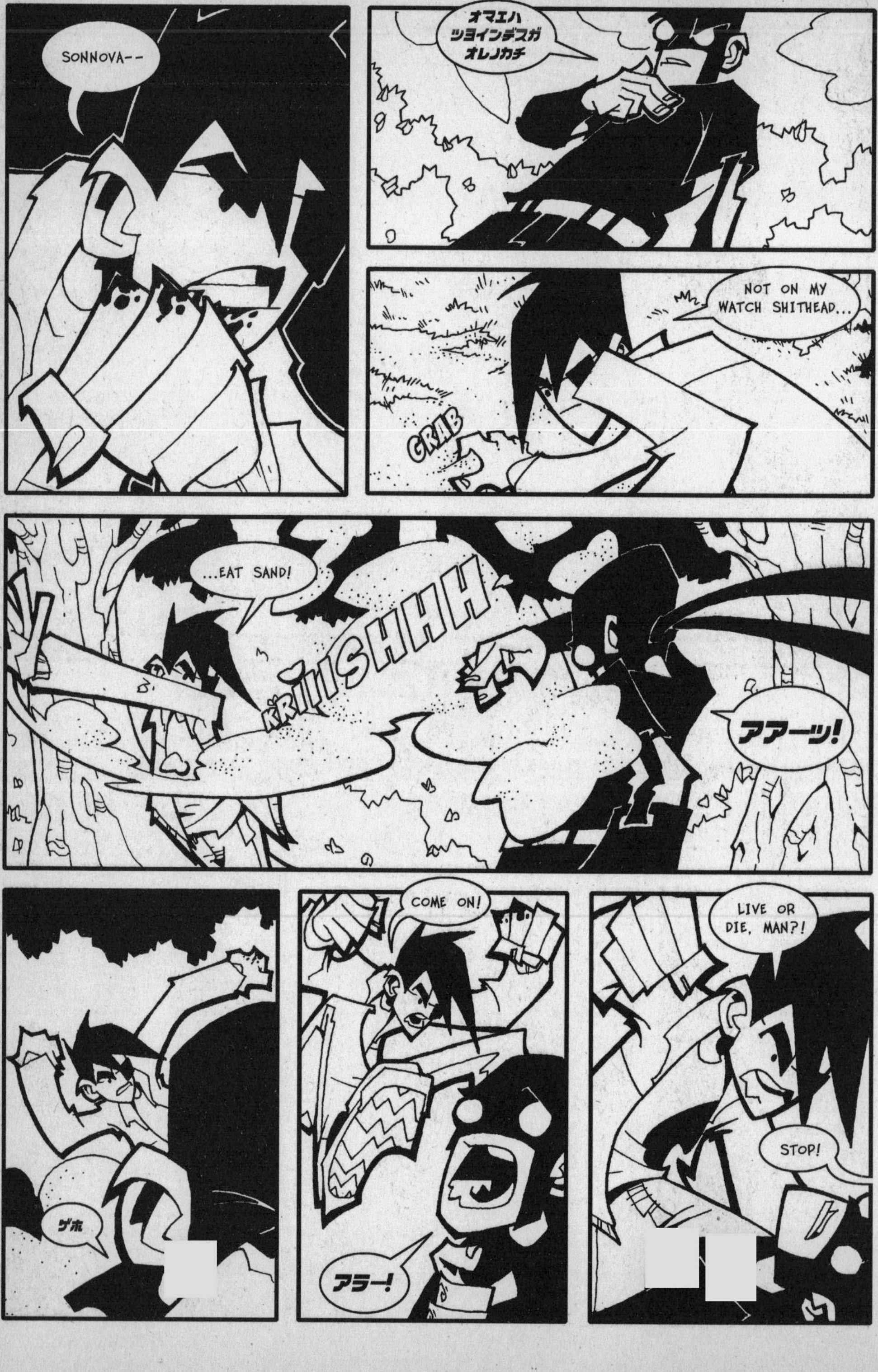
SONNOVA--
オマエハ
ツヨインデスガ
オレノカチ
NOT ON MY WATCH SHITHEAD...
GRAB
...EAT SAND!
KRIIIISHHH
アアーッ!
ゲホ
COME ON!
アラー!
LIVE OR DIE, MAN?!
STOP!

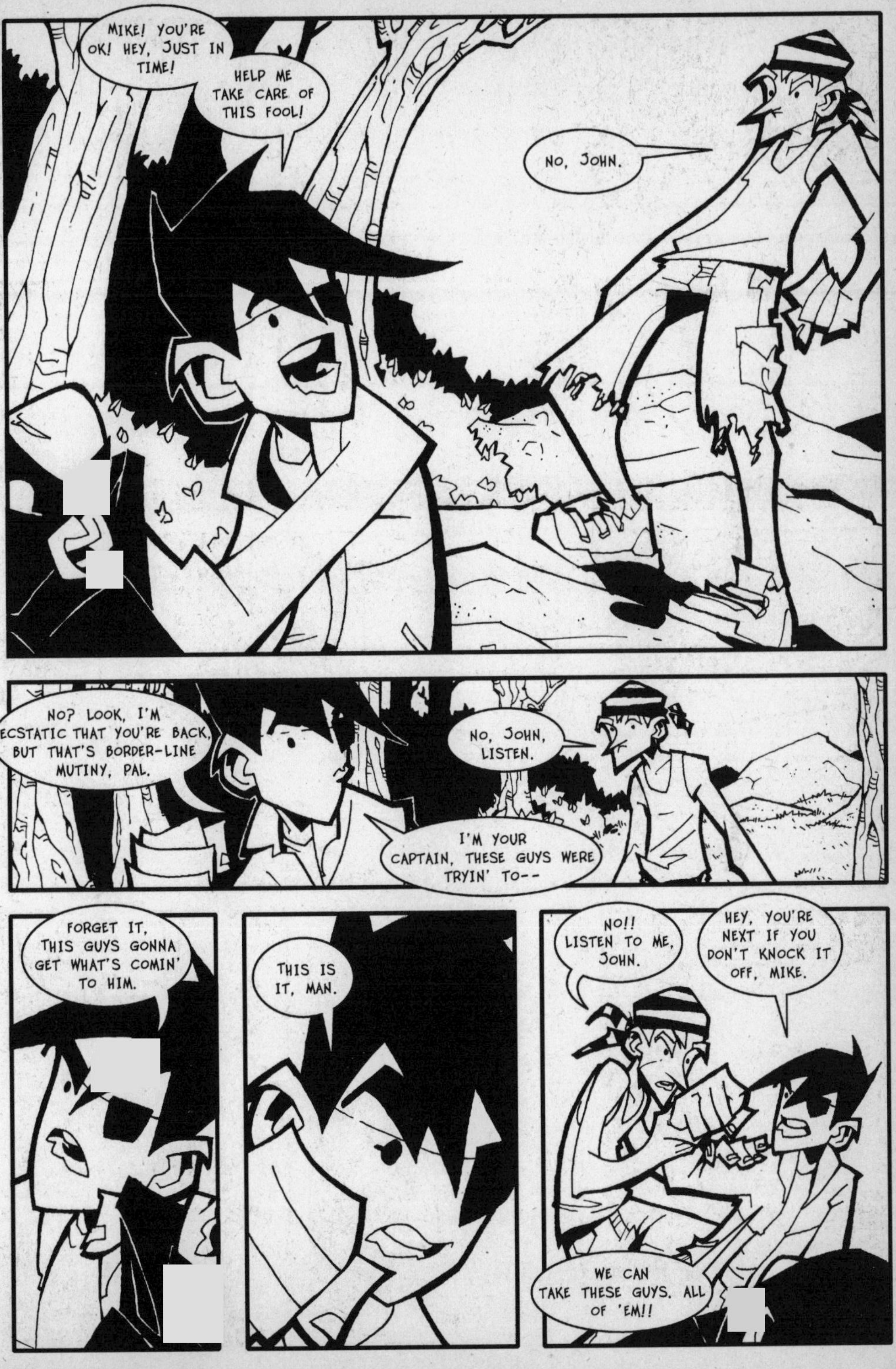
MIKE! YOU'RE OK! HEY, JUST IN TIME!
HELP ME TAKE CARE OF THIS FOOL!
NO, JOHN.
NO? LOOK, I'M ECSTATIC THAT YOU'RE BACK, BUT THAT'S BORDER-LINE MUTINY, PAL.
NO, JOHN, LISTEN.
I'M YOUR CAPTAIN, THESE GUYS WERE TRYIN' TO--
FORGET IT, THIS GUYS GONNA GET WHAT'S COMIN' TO HIM.
THIS IS IT, MAN.
NO!! LISTEN TO ME, JOHN.
HEY, YOU'RE NEXT IF YOU DON'T KNOCK IT OFF, MIKE.
WE CAN TAKE THESE GUYS. ALL OF 'EM!!

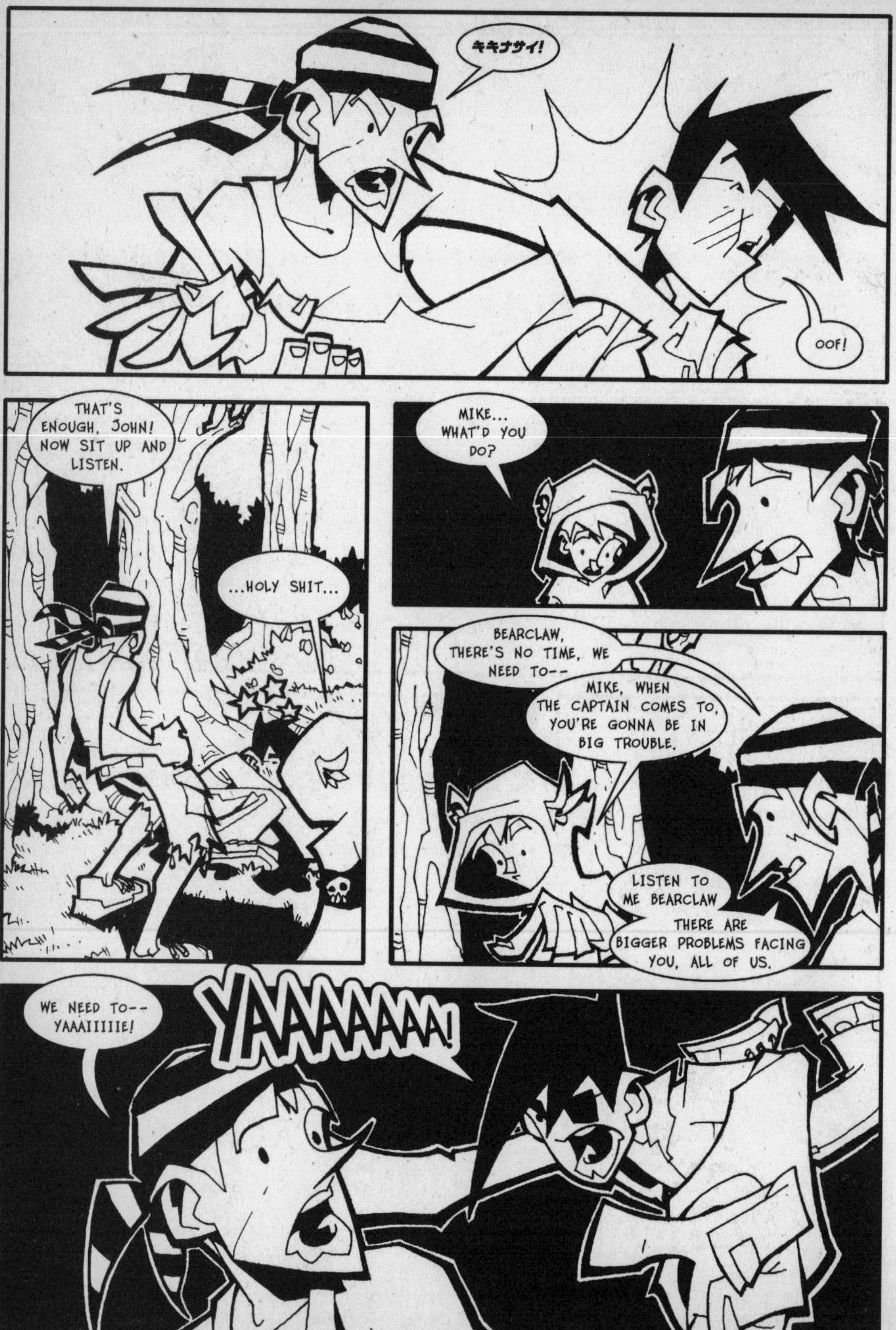
キキナサイ!
OOF!
THAT'S ENOUGH, JOHN! NOW SIT UP AND LISTEN.
...HOLY SHIT...
MIKE... WHAT'D YOU DO?
BEARCLAW, THERE'S NO TIME, WE NEED TO--
MIKE, WHEN THE CAPTAIN COMES TO, YOU'RE GONNA BE IN BIG TROUBLE.
LISTEN TO ME BEARCLAW
THERE ARE BIGGER PROBLEMS FACING YOU, ALL OF US.
WE NEED TO-- YAAAIIIIIE!
YAAAAAAA!

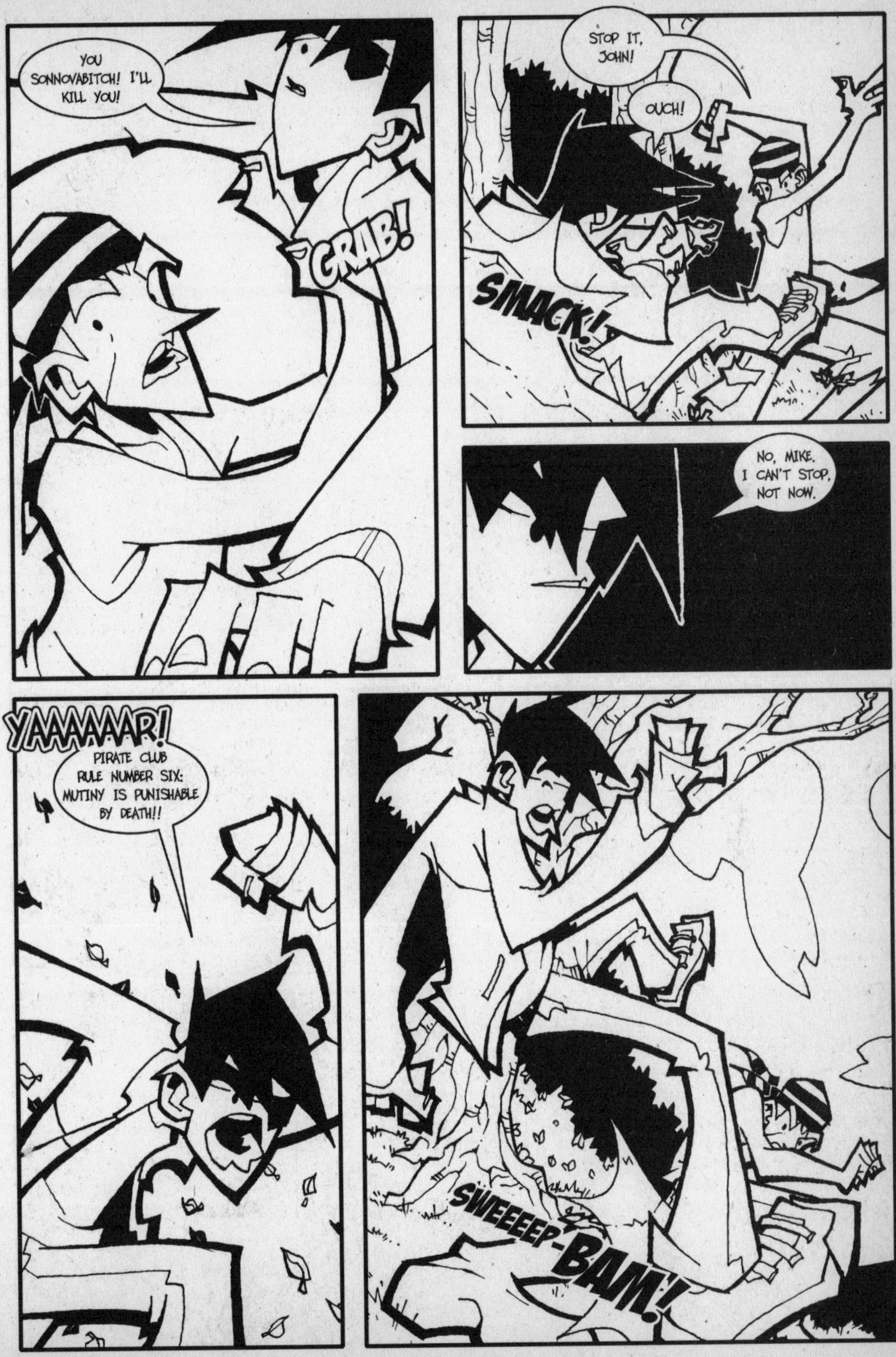

YOU SONNOVABITCH! I'LL KILL YOU!
GRAB!
STOP IT, JOHN!
OUCH!
SMACK!
NO, MIKE. I CAN'T STOP, NOT NOW.
YAAAAAAR!
PIRATE CLUB RULE NUMBER SIX: MUTINY IS PUNISHABLE BY DEATH!!
SWEEEEP-BAM!

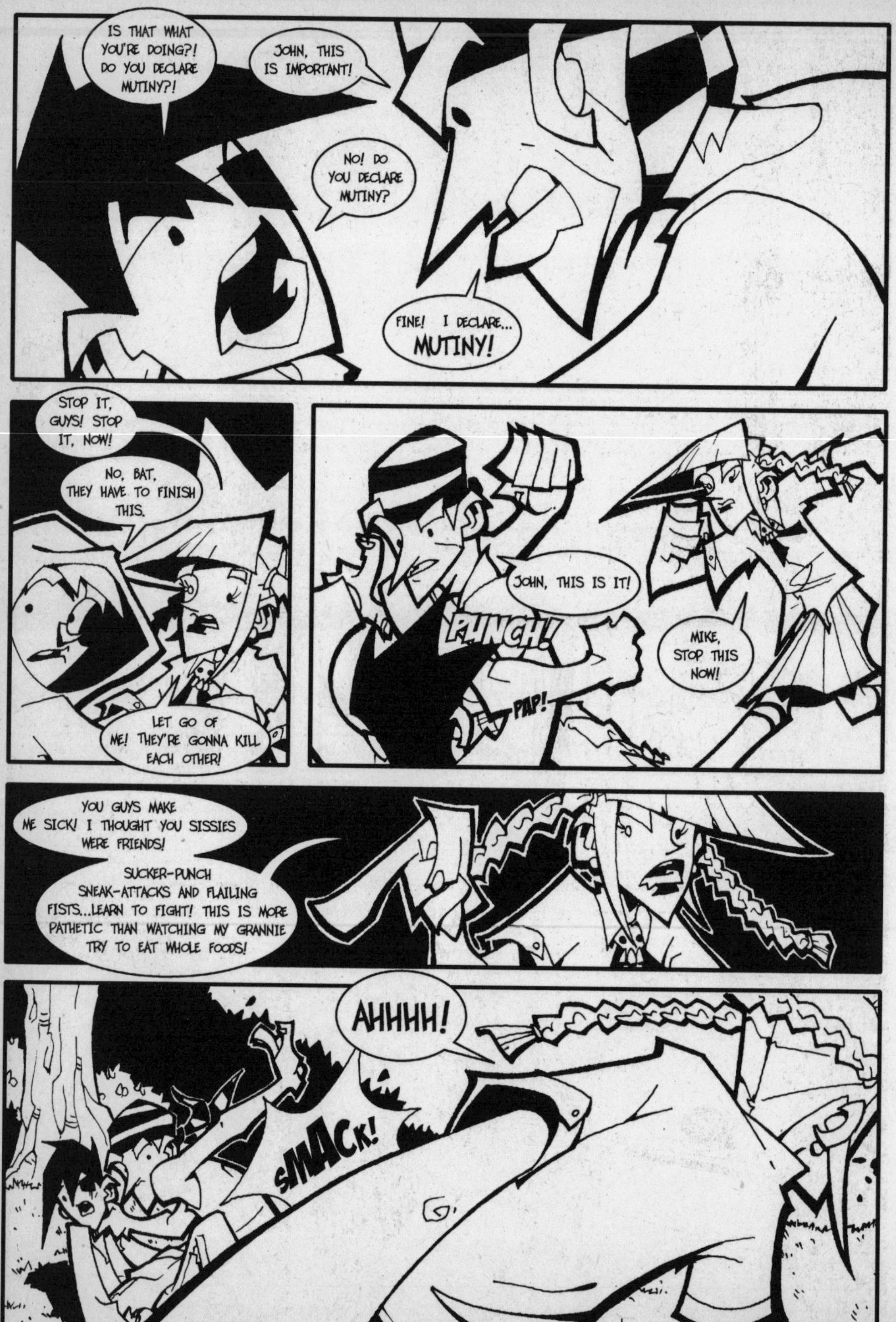
IS THAT WHAT YOU'RE DOING?! DO YOU DECLARE MUTINY?!
JOHN, THIS IS IMPORTANT!
NO! DO YOU DECLARE MUTINY?
FINE! I DECLARE... MUTINY!
STOP IT, GUYS! STOP IT, NOW!
NO, BAT, THEY HAVE TO FINISH THIS.
LET GO OF ME! THEY'RE GONNA KILL EACH OTHER!
JOHN, THIS IS IT!
PUNCH!
PAP!
MIKE, STOP THIS NOW!
YOU GUYS MAKE ME SICK! I THOUGHT YOU SISSIES WERE FRIENDS!
SUCKER-PUNCH SNEAK-ATTACKS AND FLAILING FISTS...LEARN TO FIGHT! THIS IS MORE PATHETIC THAN WATCHING MY GRANNIE TRY TO EAT WHOLE FOODS!
AHHHH!
SMACK!

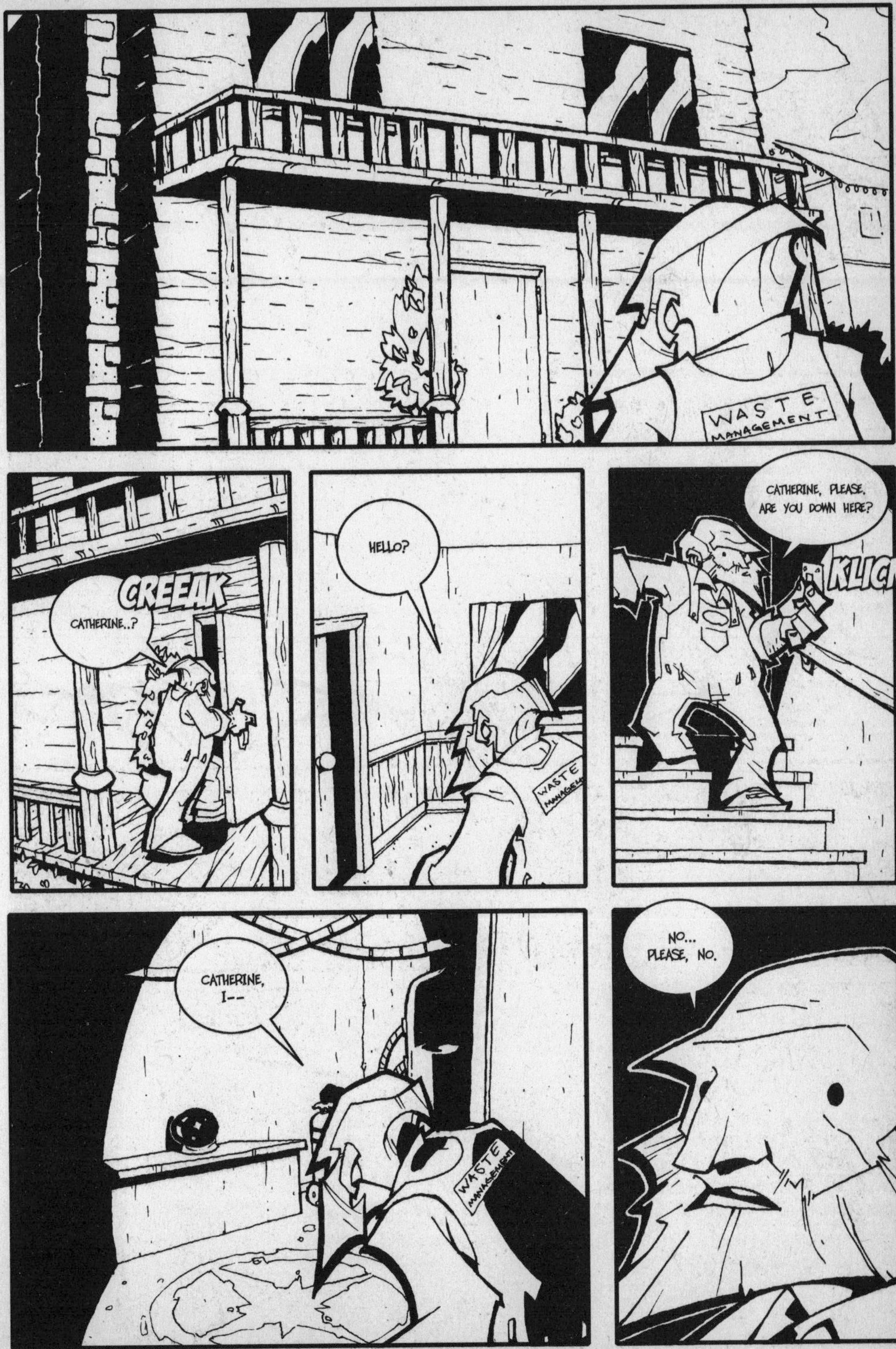
WASTE MANAGEMENT
CREEAK
CATHERINE..?
HELLO?
CATHERINE, PLEASE. ARE YOU DOWN HERE?
KLICK
CATHERINE, I--
NO... PLEASE, NO.

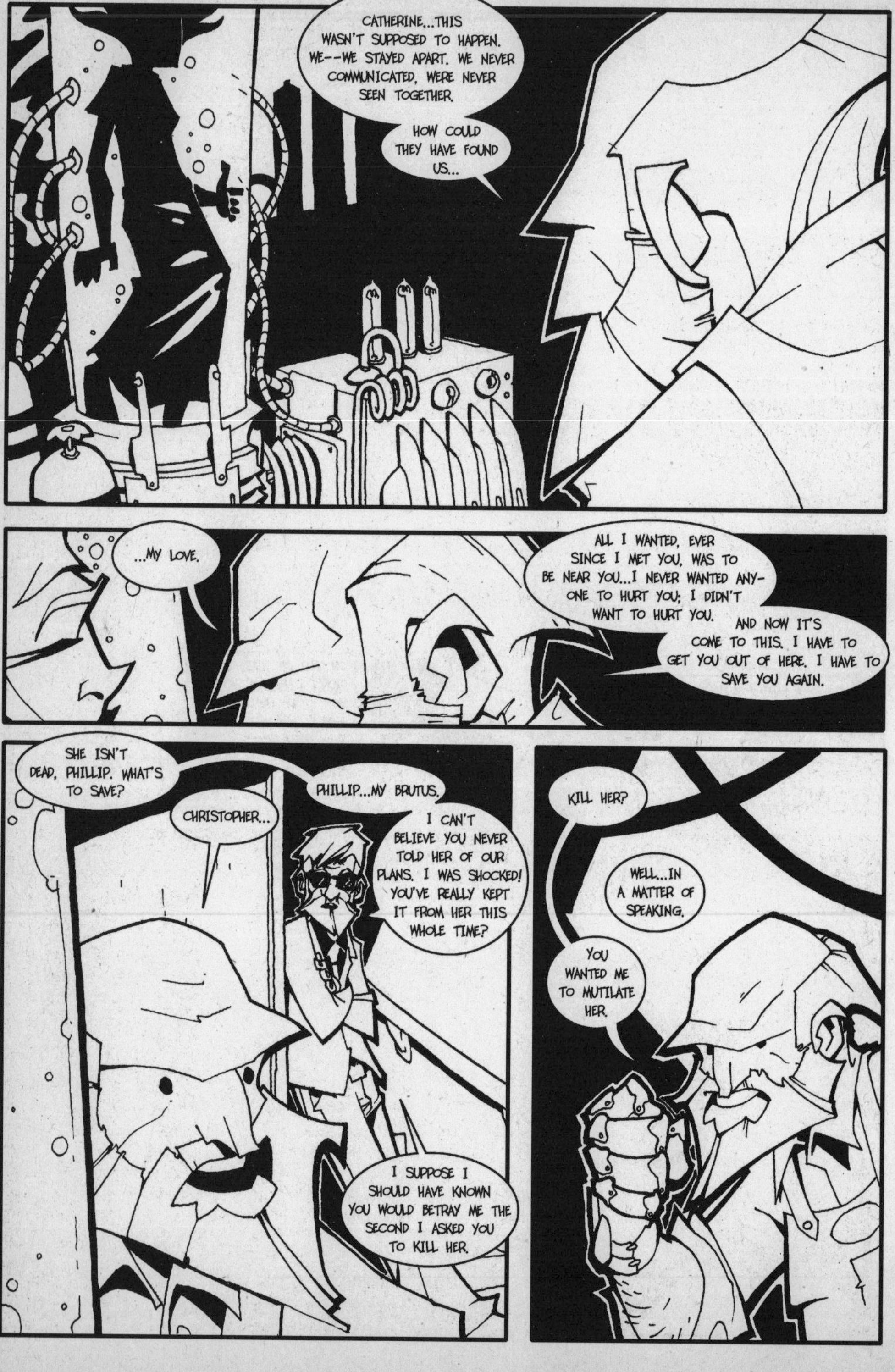
CATHERINE...THIS WASN'T SUPPOSED TO HAPPEN. WE--WE STAYED APART. WE NEVER COMMUNICATED, WERE NEVER SEEN TOGETHER.
HOW COULD THEY HAVE FOUND US...
...MY LOVE.
ALL I WANTED, EVER SINCE I MET YOU, WAS TO BE NEAR YOU...I NEVER WANTED ANYONE TO HURT YOU; I DIDN'T WANT TO HURT YOU.
AND NOW IT'S COME TO THIS. I HAVE TO GET YOU OUT OF HERE. I HAVE TO SAVE YOU AGAIN.
SHE ISN'T DEAD, PHILLIP. WHAT'S TO SAVE?
CHRISTOPHER...
PHILLIP...MY BRUTUS.
I CAN'T BELIEVE YOU NEVER TOLD HER OF OUR PLANS. I WAS SHOCKED! YOU'VE REALLY KEPT IT FROM HER THIS WHOLE TIME?
I SUPPOSE I SHOULD HAVE KNOWN YOU WOULD BETRAY ME THE SECOND I ASKED YOU TO KILL HER.
KILL HER?
WELL...IN A MATTER OF SPEAKING.
YOU WANTED ME TO MUTILATE HER.

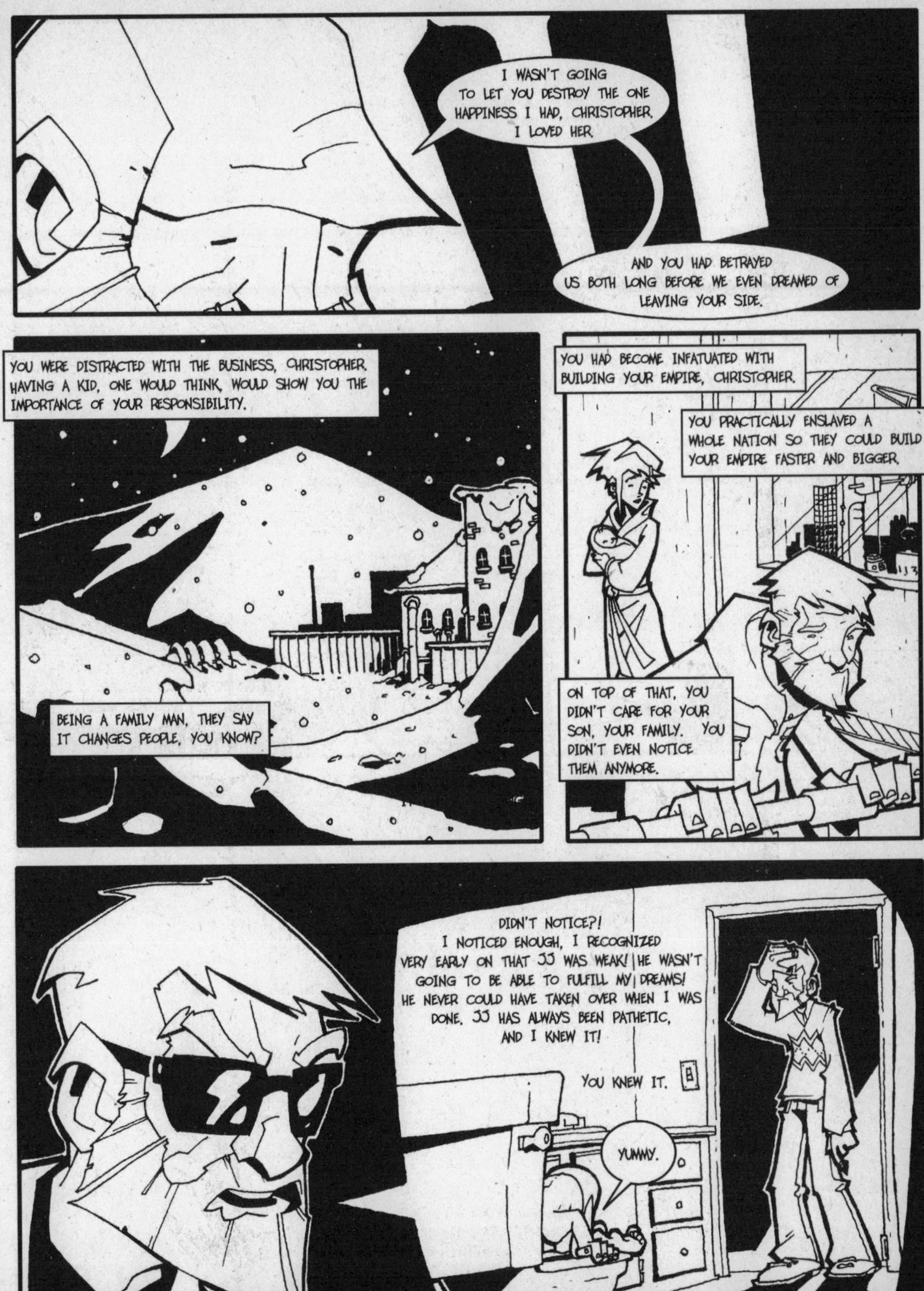
I WASN'T GOING TO LET YOU DESTROY THE ONE HAPPINESS I HAD, CHRISTOPHER. I LOVED HER.
AND YOU HAD BETRAYED US BOTH LONG BEFORE WE EVEN DREAMED OF LEAVING YOUR SIDE.
YOU WERE DISTRACTED WITH THE BUSINESS, CHRISTOPHER. HAVING A KID, ONE WOULD THINK, WOULD SHOW YOU THE IMPORTANCE OF YOUR RESPONSIBILITY.
BEING A FAMILY MAN, THEY SAY IT CHANGES PEOPLE, YOU KNOW?
YOU HAD BECOME INFATUATED WITH BUILDING YOUR EMPIRE, CHRISTOPHER.
YOU PRACTICALLY ENSLAVED A WHOLE NATION SO THEY COULD BUILD YOUR EMPIRE FASTER AND BIGGER.
ON TOP OF THAT, YOU DIDN'T CARE FOR YOUR SON, YOUR FAMILY. YOU DIDN'T EVEN NOTICE THEM ANYMORE.
DIDN'T NOTICE?! I NOTICED ENOUGH, I RECOGNIZED VERY EARLY ON THAT JJ WAS WEAK! HE WASN'T GOING TO BE ABLE TO FULFILL MY DREAMS! HE NEVER COULD HAVE TAKEN OVER WHEN I WAS DONE. JJ HAS ALWAYS BEEN PATHETIC, AND I KNEW IT!
YOU KNEW IT.
YUMMY.
YOU WERE A MASTER BUILDER AND I NEEDED YOU TO BUILD ME SOMETHING GREATER THAN MY OWN SON.

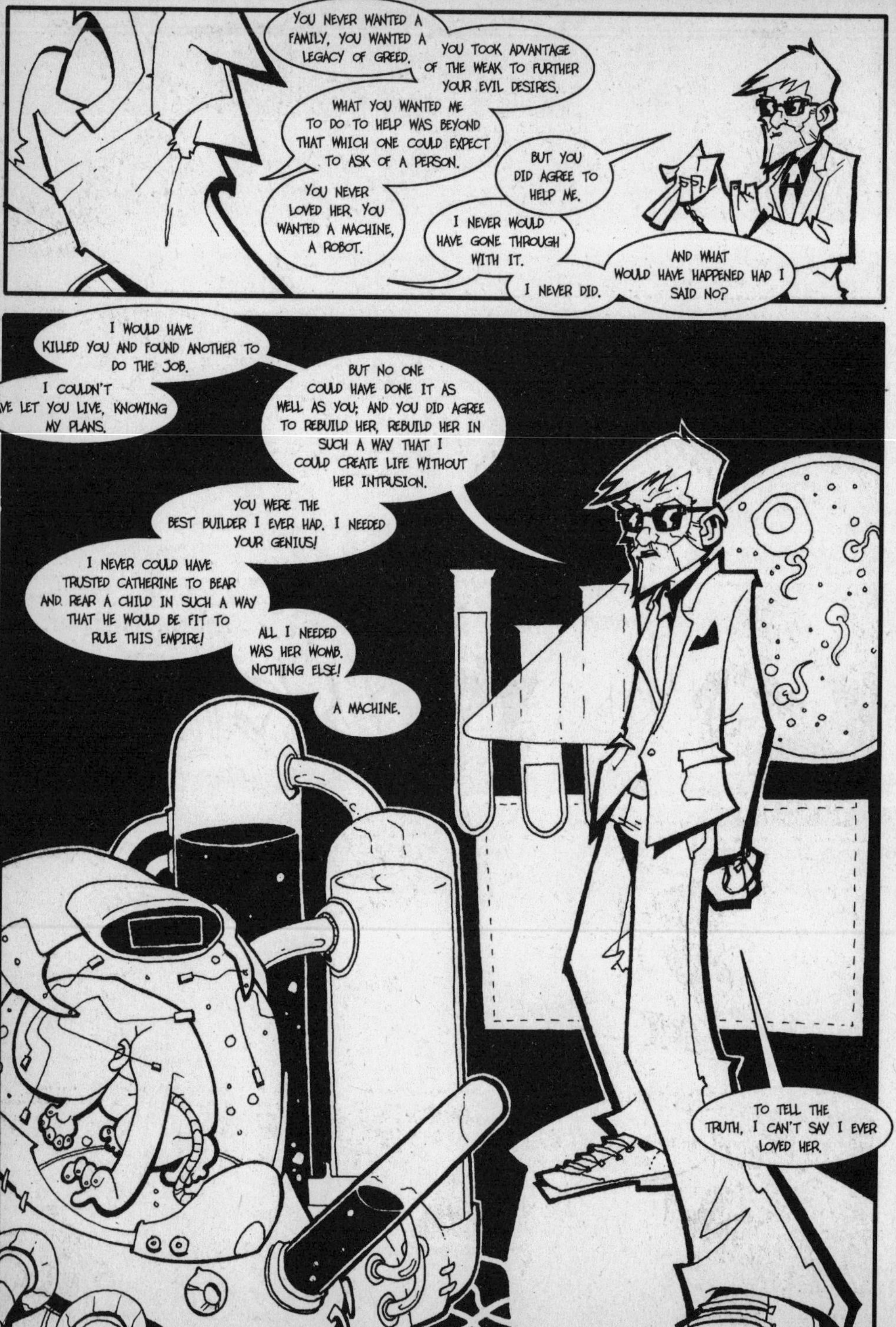
YOU NEVER WANTED A FAMILY, YOU WANTED A LEGACY OF GREED.
YOU TOOK ADVANTAGE OF THE WEAK TO FURTHER YOUR EVIL DESIRES.
WHAT YOU WANTED ME TO DO TO HELP WAS BEYOND THAT WHICH ONE COULD EXPECT TO ASK OF A PERSON.
YOU NEVER LOVED HER. YOU WANTED A MACHINE, A ROBOT.
BUT YOU DID AGREE TO HELP ME.
I NEVER WOULD HAVE GONE THROUGH WITH IT.
I NEVER DID.
AND WHAT WOULD HAVE HAPPENED HAD I SAID NO?
I WOULD HAVE KILLED YOU AND FOUND ANOTHER TO DO THE JOB.
I COULDN'T HAVE LET YOU LIVE, KNOWING MY PLANS.
BUT NO ONE COULD HAVE DONE IT AS WELL AS YOU; AND YOU DID AGREE TO REBUILD HER, REBUILD HER IN SUCH A WAY THAT I COULD CREATE LIFE WITHOUT HER INTRUSION.
YOU WERE THE BEST BUILDER I EVER HAD. I NEEDED YOUR GENIUS!
I NEVER COULD HAVE TRUSTED CATHERINE TO BEAR AND REAR A CHILD IN SUCH A WAY THAT HE WOULD BE FIT TO RULE THIS EMPIRE!
ALL I NEEDED WAS HER WOMB. NOTHING ELSE!
A MACHINE.
TO TELL THE TRUTH, I CAN'T SAY I EVER LOVED HER.

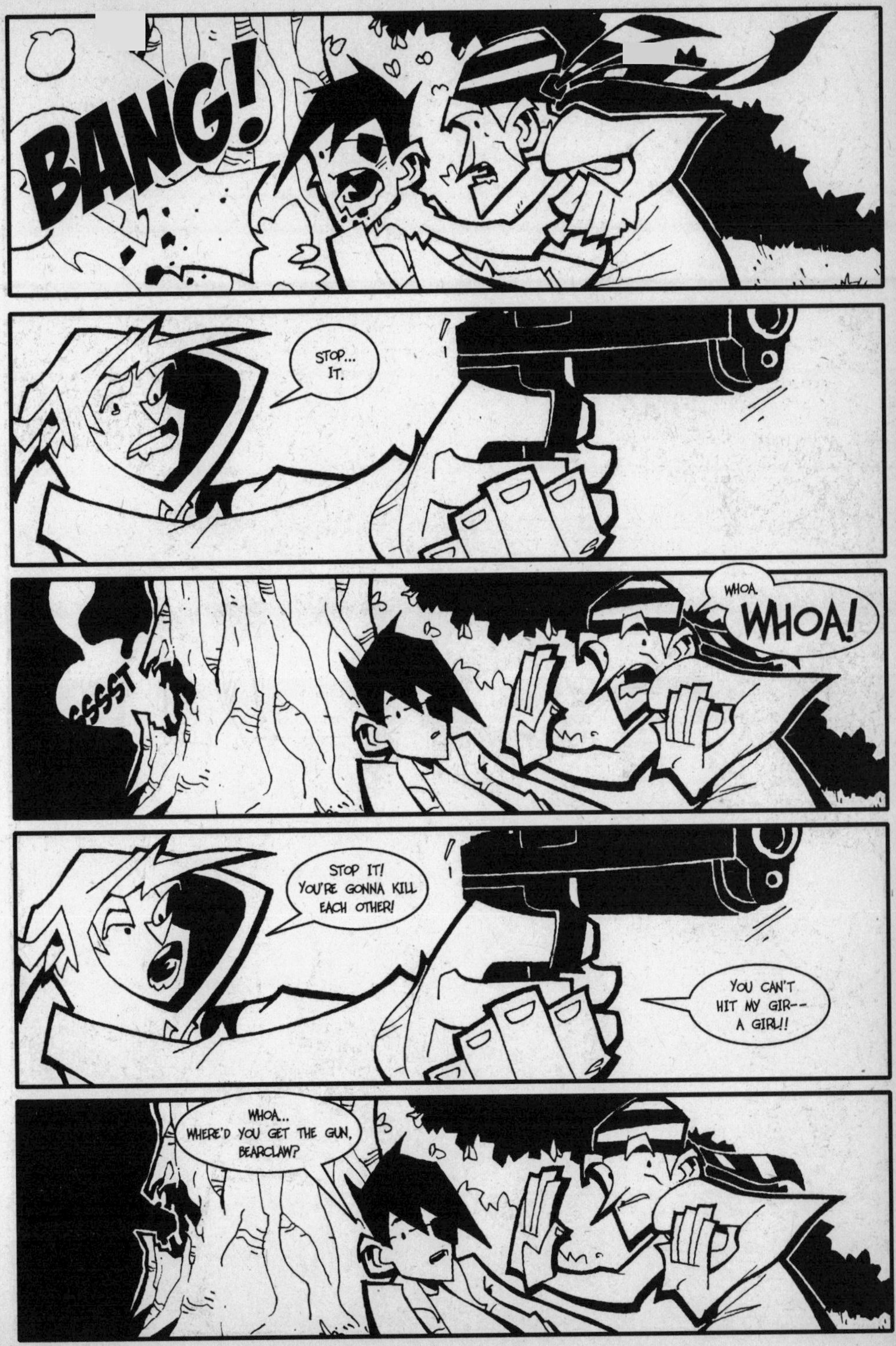
BANG!
STOP... IT.
SSSST
WHOA. WHOA!
STOP IT! YOU'RE GONNA KILL EACH OTHER!
YOU CAN'T HIT MY GIR-- A GIRL!!
WHOA... WHERE'D YOU GET THE GUN, BEARCLAW?

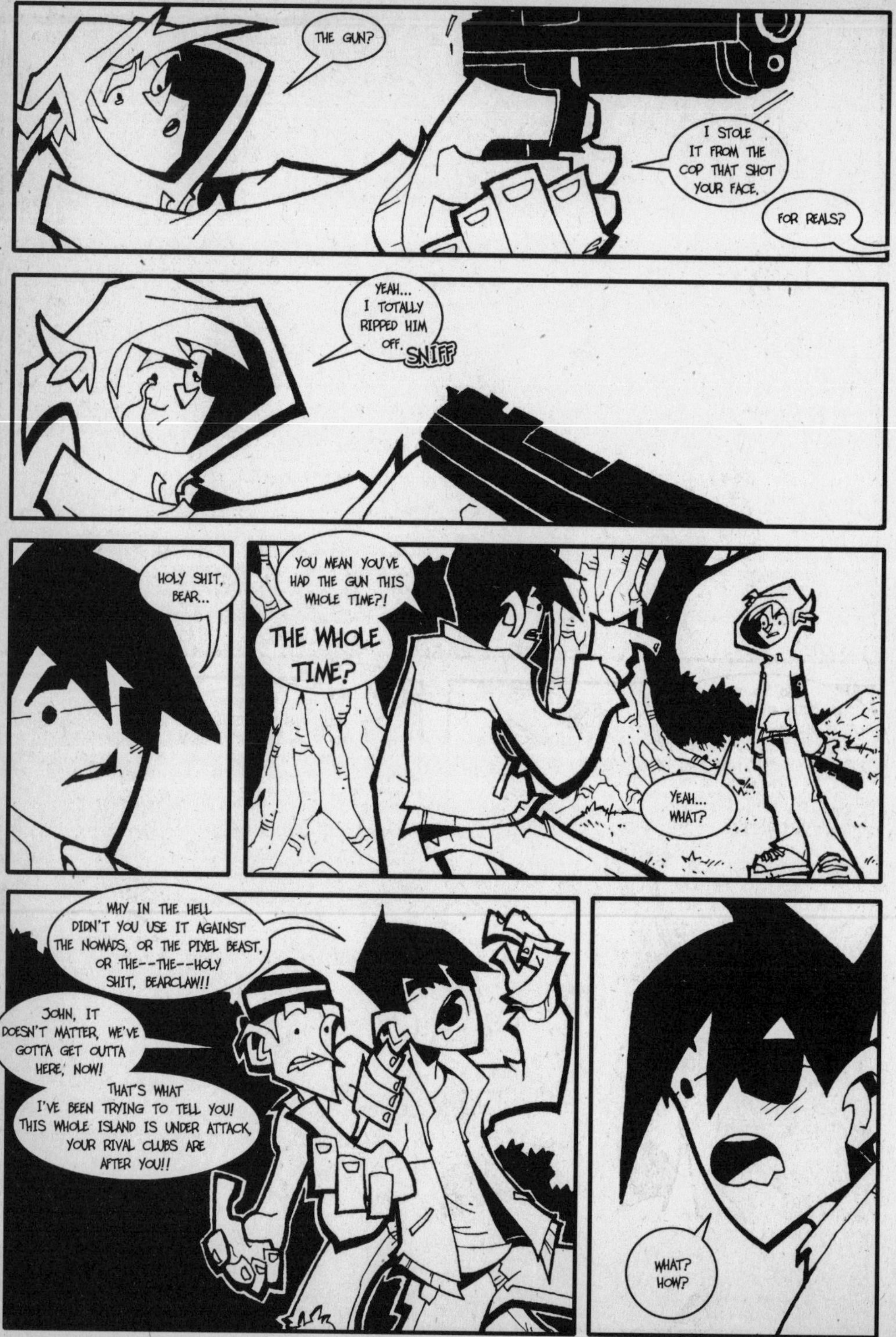
THE GUN?
I STOLE IT FROM THE COP THAT SHOT YOUR FACE.
FOR REALS?
YEAH... I TOTALLY RIPPED HIM OFF.
SNIFF
HOLY SHIT, BEAR...
YOU MEAN YOU'VE HAD THE GUN THIS WHOLE TIME?!
THE WHOLE TIME?
YEAH... WHAT?
WHY IN THE HELL DIDN'T YOU USE IT AGAINST THE NOMADS, OR THE PIXEL BEAST, OR THE--THE--HOLY SHIT, BEARCLAW!!
JOHN, IT DOESN'T MATTER, WE'VE GOTTA GET OUTTA HERE, NOW!
THAT'S WHAT I'VE BEEN TRYING TO TELL YOU! THIS WHOLE ISLAND IS UNDER ATTACK, YOUR RIVAL CLUBS ARE AFTER YOU!!
WHAT? HOW?

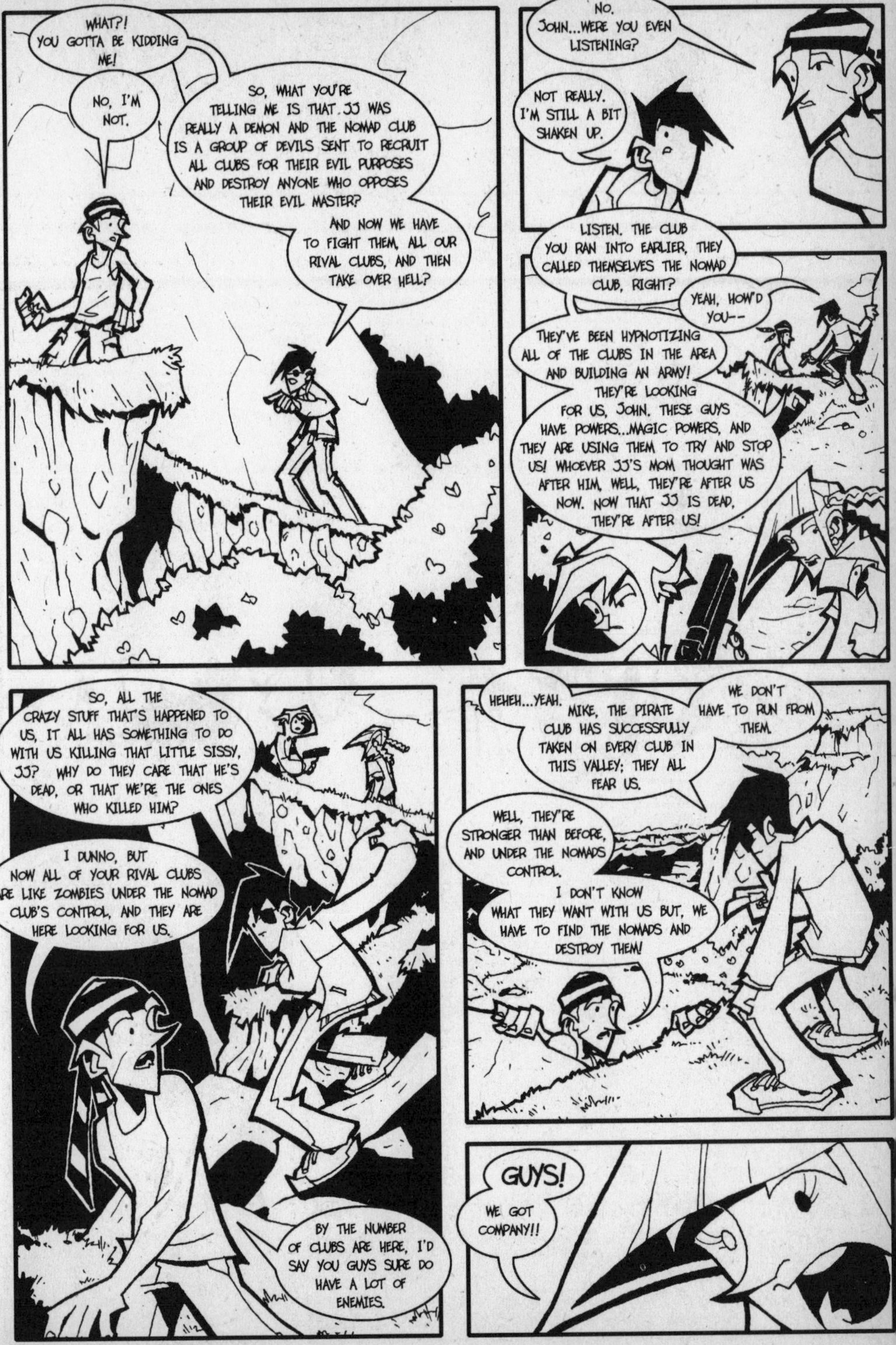
WHAT?! YOU GOTTA BE KIDDING ME!
NO, I'M NOT.
SO, WHAT YOU'RE TELLING ME IS THAT JJ WAS REALLY A DEMON AND THE NOMAD CLUB IS A GROUP OF DEVILS SENT TO RECRUIT ALL CLUBS FOR THEIR EVIL PURPOSES AND DESTROY ANYONE WHO OPPOSES THEIR EVIL MASTER?
AND NOW WE HAVE TO FIGHT THEM, ALL OUR RIVAL CLUBS, AND THEN TAKE OVER HELL?
NO. JOHN...WERE YOU EVEN LISTENING?
NOT REALLY. I'M STILL A BIT SHAKEN UP.
LISTEN. THE CLUB YOU RAN INTO EARLIER, THEY CALLED THEMSELVES THE NOMAD CLUB, RIGHT?
YEAH, HOW'D YOU--
THEY'VE BEEN HYPNOTIZING ALL OF THE CLUBS IN THE AREA AND BUILDING AN ARMY! THEY'RE LOOKING FOR US, JOHN. THESE GUYS HAVE POWERS...MAGIC POWERS, AND THEY ARE USING THEM TO TRY AND STOP US! WHOEVER JJ'S MOM THOUGHT WAS AFTER HIM, WELL, THEY'RE AFTER US NOW. NOW THAT JJ IS DEAD, THEY'RE AFTER US!
SO, ALL THE CRAZY STUFF THAT'S HAPPENED TO US, IT ALL HAS SOMETHING TO DO WITH US KILLING THAT LITTLE SISSY, JJ? WHY DO THEY CARE THAT HE'S DEAD, OR THAT WE'RE THE ONES WHO KILLED HIM?
I DUNNO, BUT NOW ALL OF YOUR RIVAL CLUBS ARE LIKE ZOMBIES UNDER THE NOMAD CLUB'S CONTROL, AND THEY ARE HERE LOOKING FOR US.
BY THE NUMBER OF CLUBS ARE HERE, I'D SAY YOU GUYS SURE DO HAVE A LOT OF ENEMIES.
HEHEH...YEAH.
WE DON'T HAVE TO RUN FROM THEM.
MIKE, THE PIRATE CLUB HAS SUCCESSFULLY TAKEN ON EVERY CLUB IN THIS VALLEY; THEY ALL FEAR US.
WELL, THEY'RE STRONGER THAN BEFORE, AND UNDER THE NOMADS CONTROL.
I DON'T KNOW WHAT THEY WANT WITH US BUT, WE HAVE TO FIND THE NOMADS AND DESTROY THEM!
GUYS!
WE GOT COMPANY!!

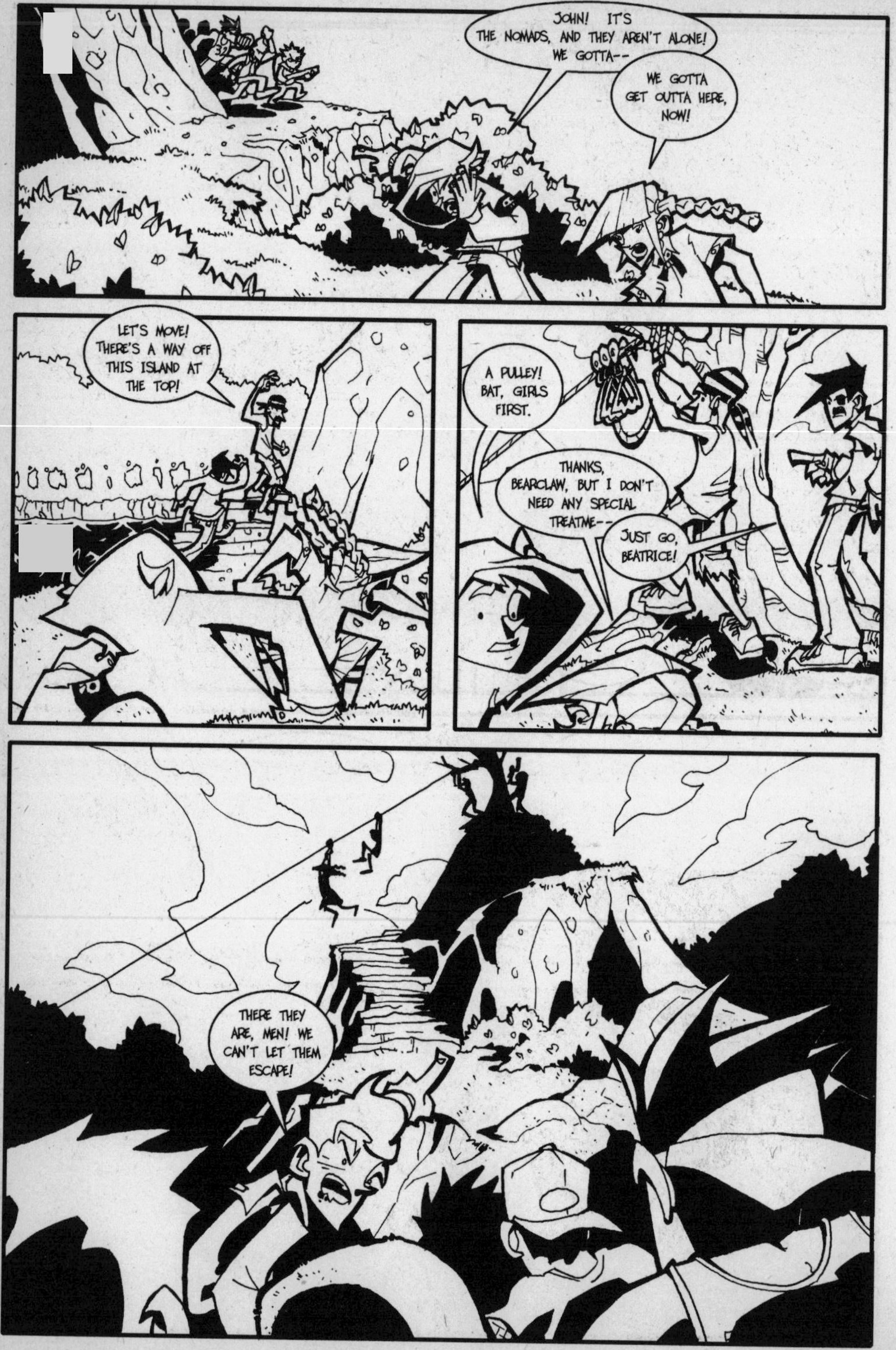
JOHN! IT'S THE NOMADS, AND THEY AREN'T ALONE! WE GOTTA--
WE GOTTA GET OUTTA HERE, NOW!
LET'S MOVE! THERE'S A WAY OFF THIS ISLAND AT THE TOP!
A PULLEY! BAT, GIRLS FIRST.
THANKS, BEARCLAW, BUT I DON'T NEED ANY SPECIAL TREATME--
JUST GO, BEATRICE!
THERE THEY ARE, MEN! WE CAN'T LET THEM ESCAPE!

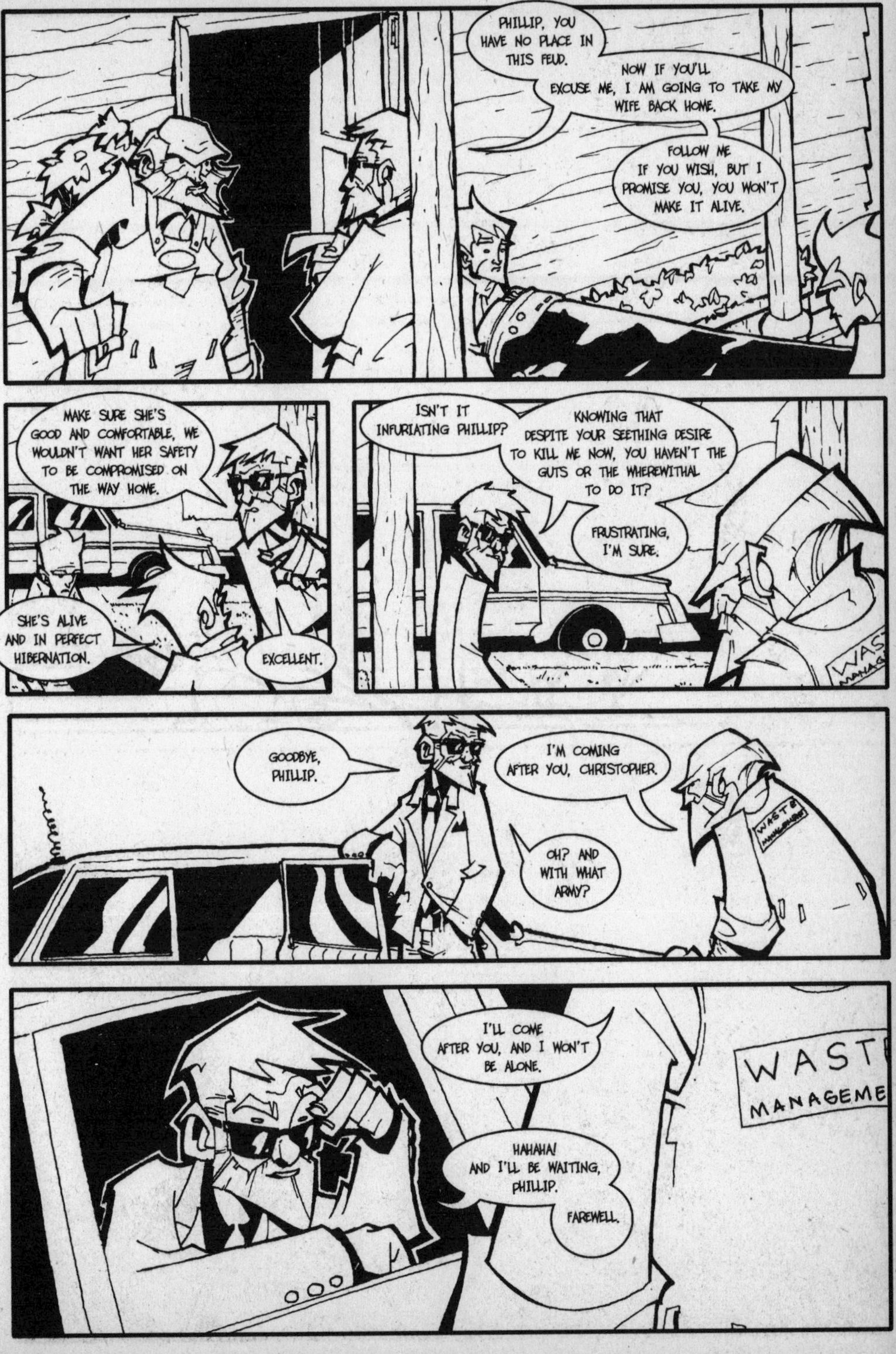
PHILLIP, YOU HAVE NO PLACE IN THIS FEUD.
NOW IF YOU'LL EXCUSE ME, I AM GOING TO TAKE MY WIFE BACK HOME.
FOLLOW ME IF YOU WISH, BUT I PROMISE YOU, YOU WON'T MAKE IT ALIVE.
MAKE SURE SHE'S GOOD AND COMFORTABLE, WE WOULDN'T WANT HER SAFETY TO BE COMPROMISED ON THE WAY HOME.
SHE'S ALIVE AND IN PERFECT HIBERNATION.
EXCELLENT.
ISN'T IT INFURIATING PHILLIP?
KNOWING THAT DESPITE YOUR SEETHING DESIRE TO KILL ME NOW, YOU HAVEN'T THE GUTS OR THE WHEREWITHAL TO DO IT?
FRUSTRATING, I'M SURE.
GOODBYE, PHILLIP.
I'M COMING AFTER YOU, CHRISTOPHER.
OH? AND WITH WHAT ARMY?
I'LL COME AFTER YOU, AND I WON'T BE ALONE.
WASTE MANAGEME
HAHAHA! AND I'LL BE WAITING, PHILLIP.
FAREWELL.

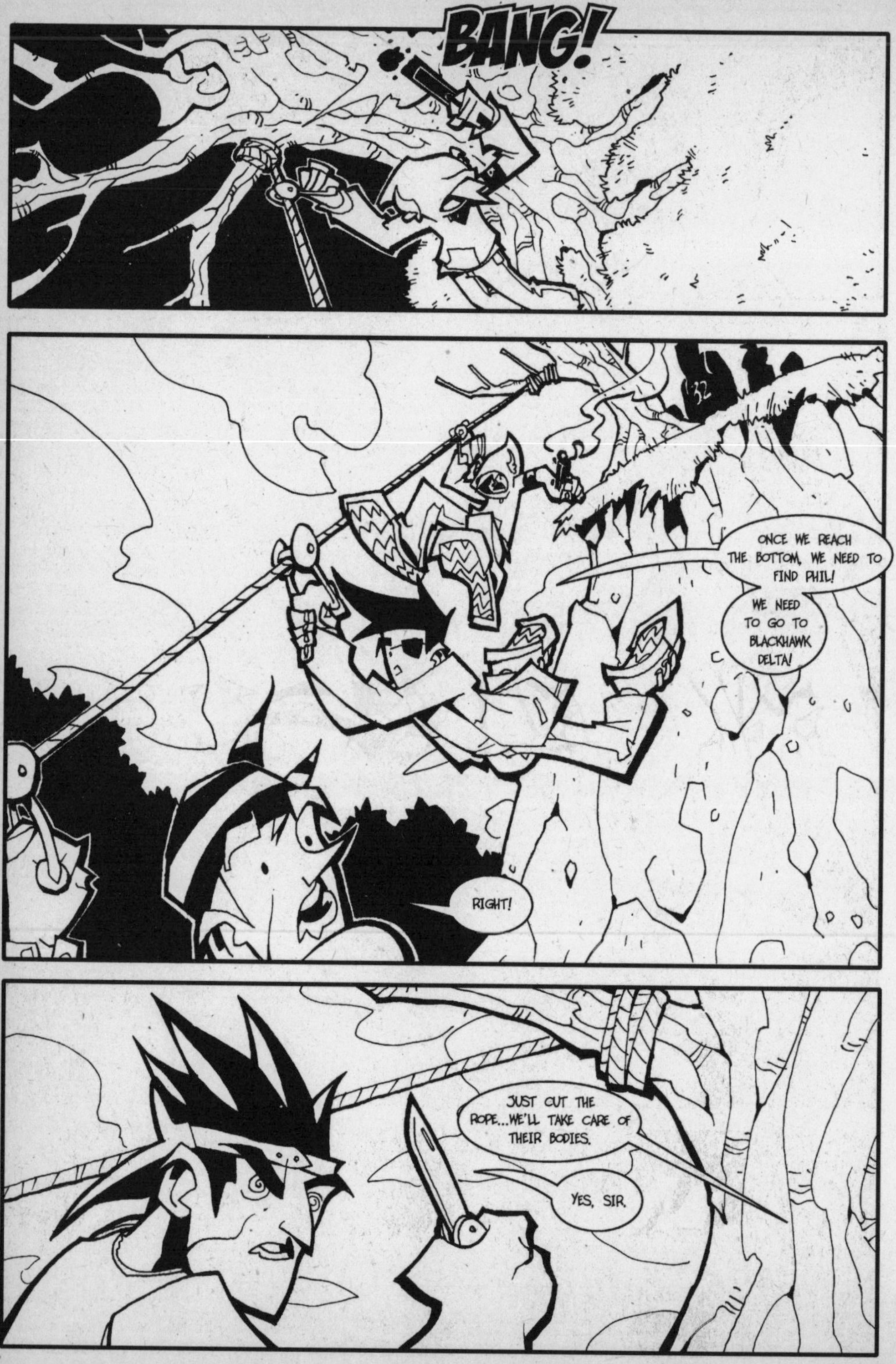
BANG!
ONCE WE REACH THE BOTTOM, WE NEED TO FIND PHIL!
WE NEED TO GO TO BLACKHAWK DELTA!
RIGHT!
JUST CUT THE ROPE...WE'LL TAKE CARE OF THEIR BODIES.
YES, SIR.

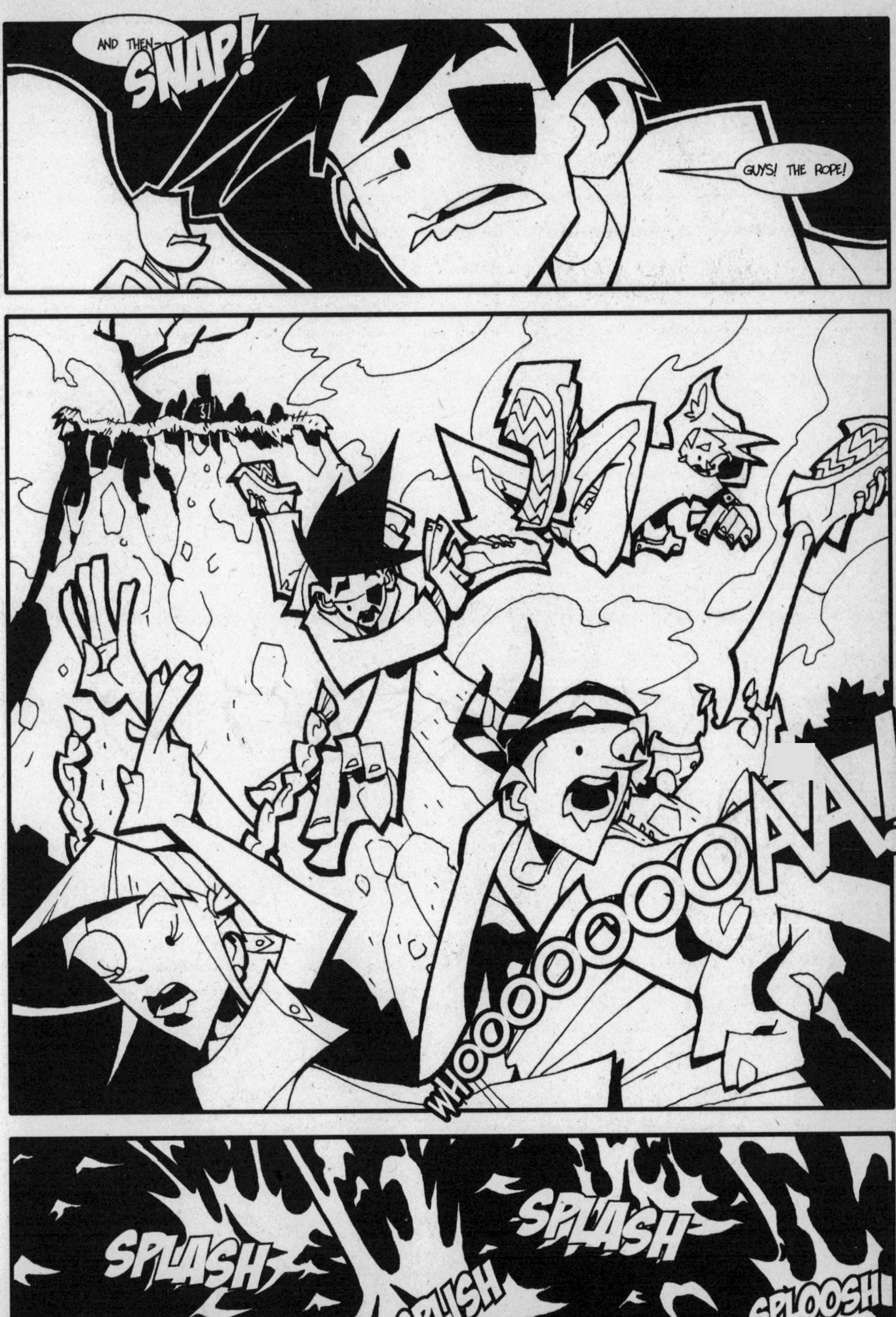
AND THEN—
SNAP!
GUYS! THE ROPE!
WHOOOOOOOOAA!
SPLASH
SPLASH
SPLISH
SPLOOSH!

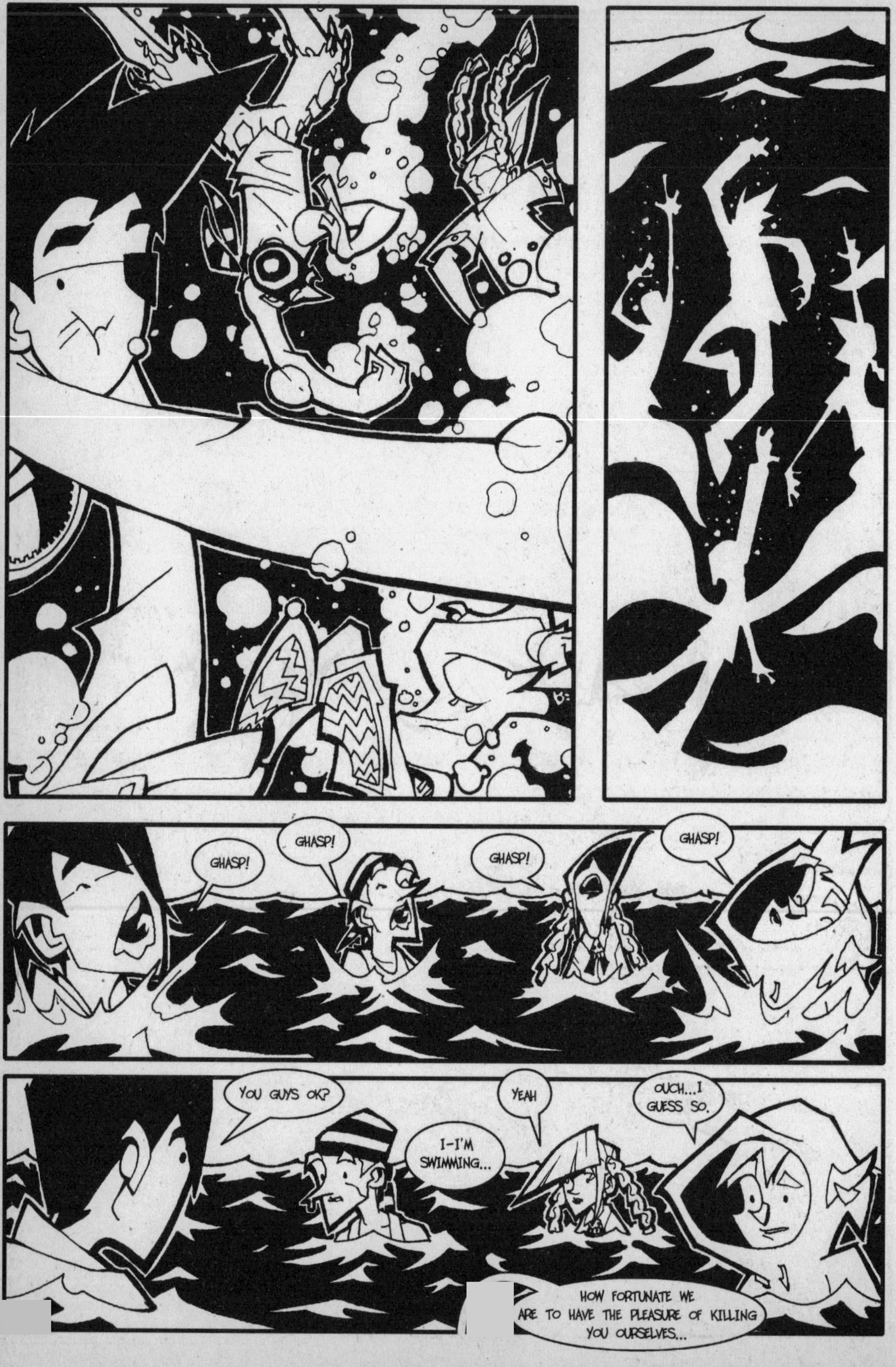
GHASP!
GHASP!
GHASP!
GHASP!
YOU GUYS OK?
I-I'M SWIMMING...
YEAH
OUCH...I GUESS SO.
HOW FORTUNATE WE ARE TO HAVE THE PLEASURE OF KILLING YOU OURSELVES...

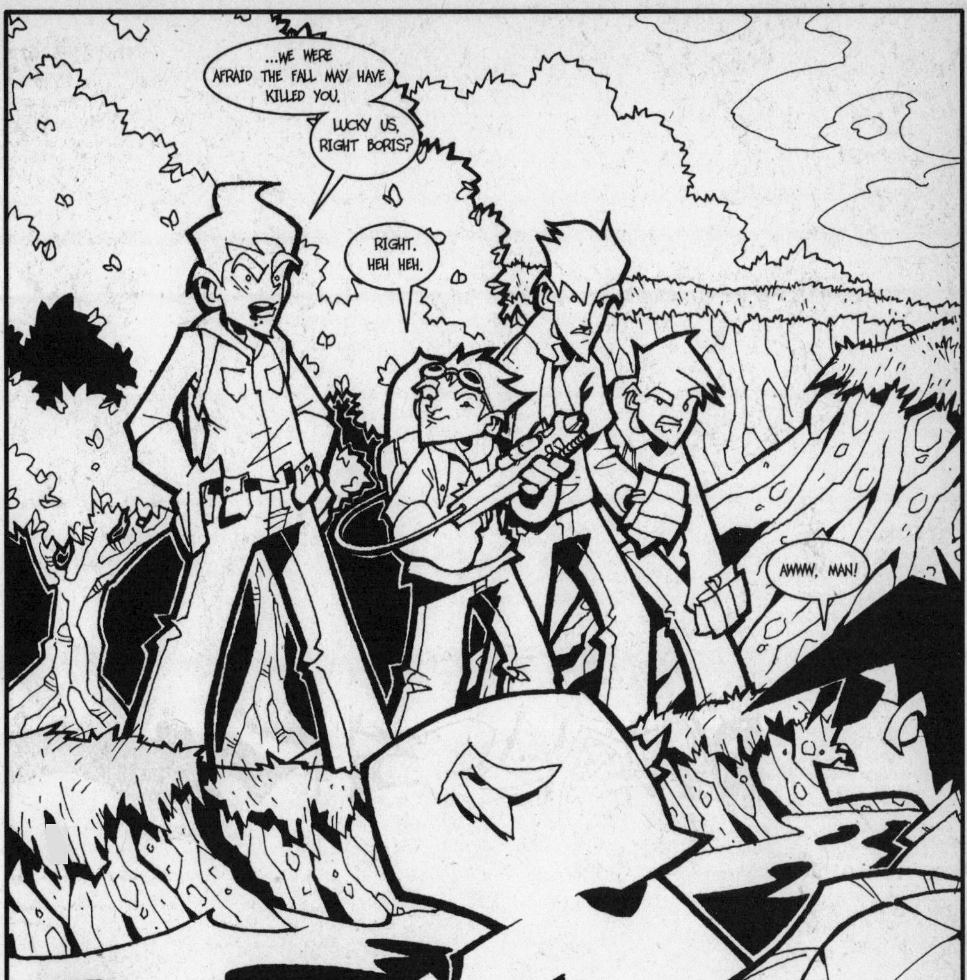
...WE WERE AFRAID THE FALL MAY HAVE KILLED YOU.
LUCKY US, RIGHT BORIS?
RIGHT. HEH HEH.
AWWW, MAN!

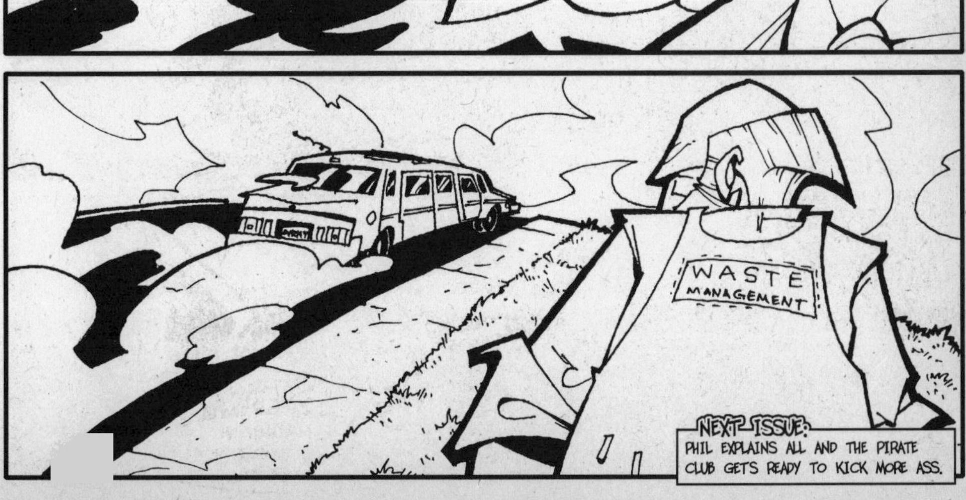
WASTE MANAGEMENT
NEXT ISSUE:
PHIL EXPLAINS ALL AND THE PIRATE CLUB GETS READY TO KICK MORE ASS.

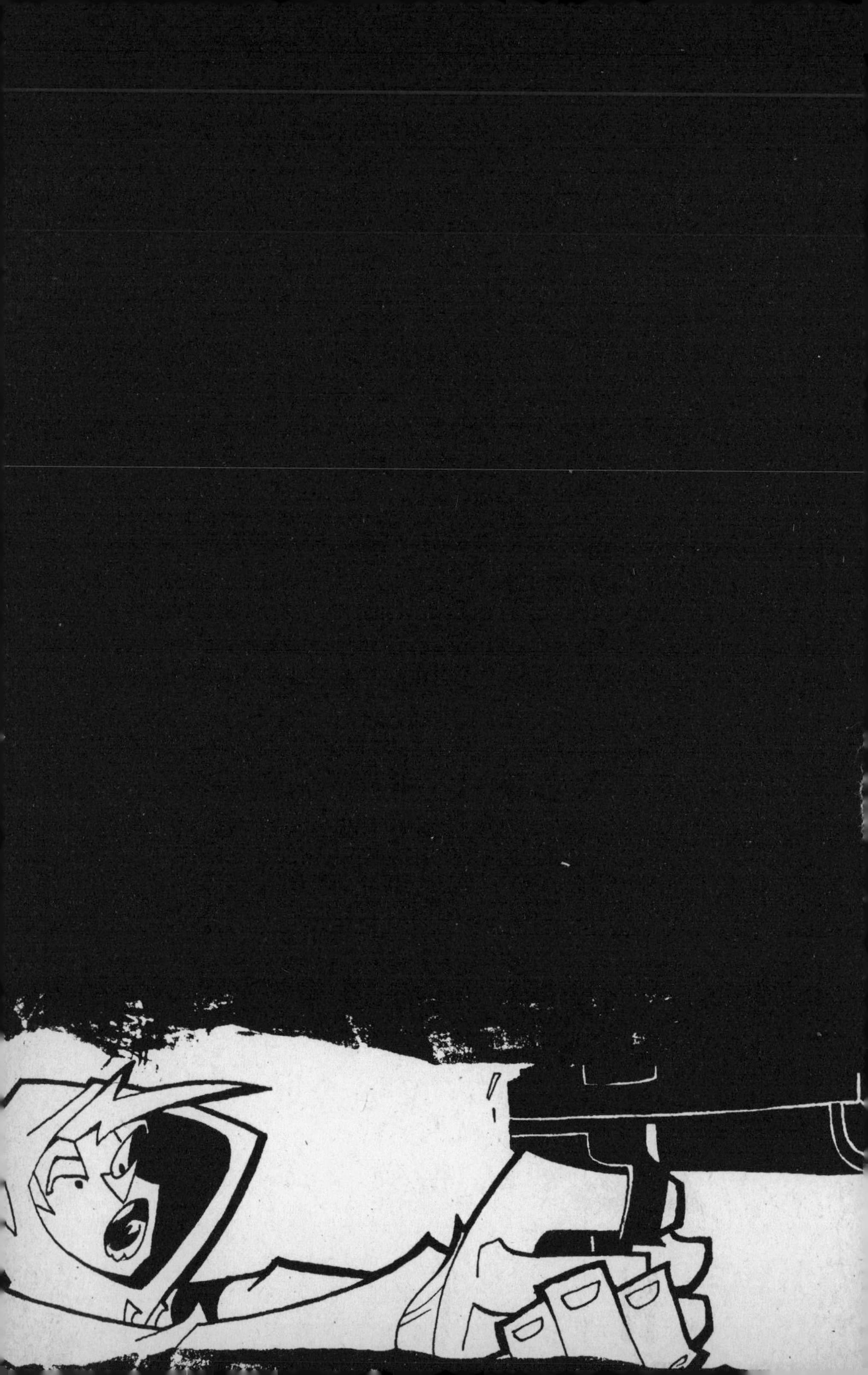

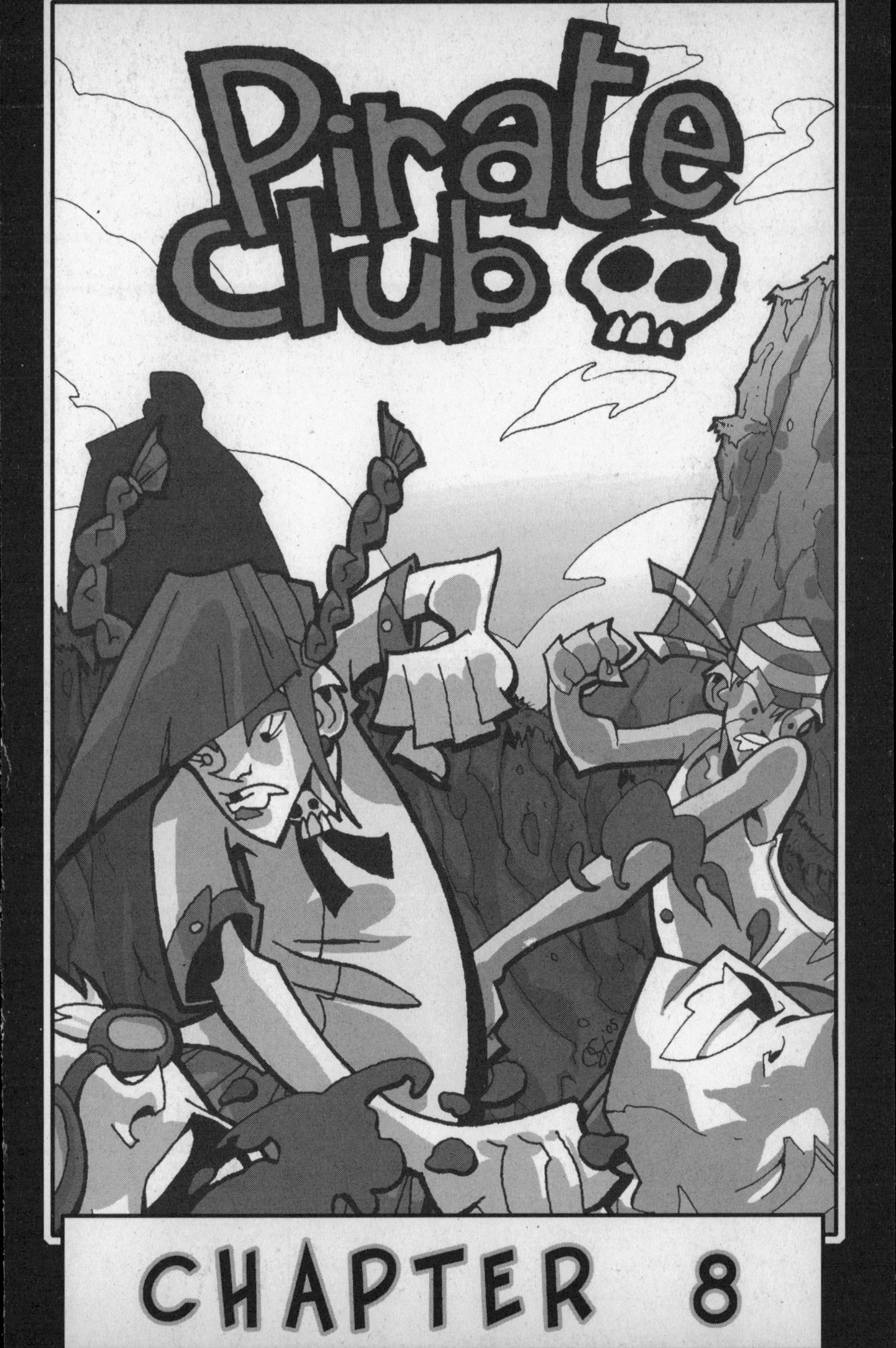
Pirate Club

# CHAPTER 8

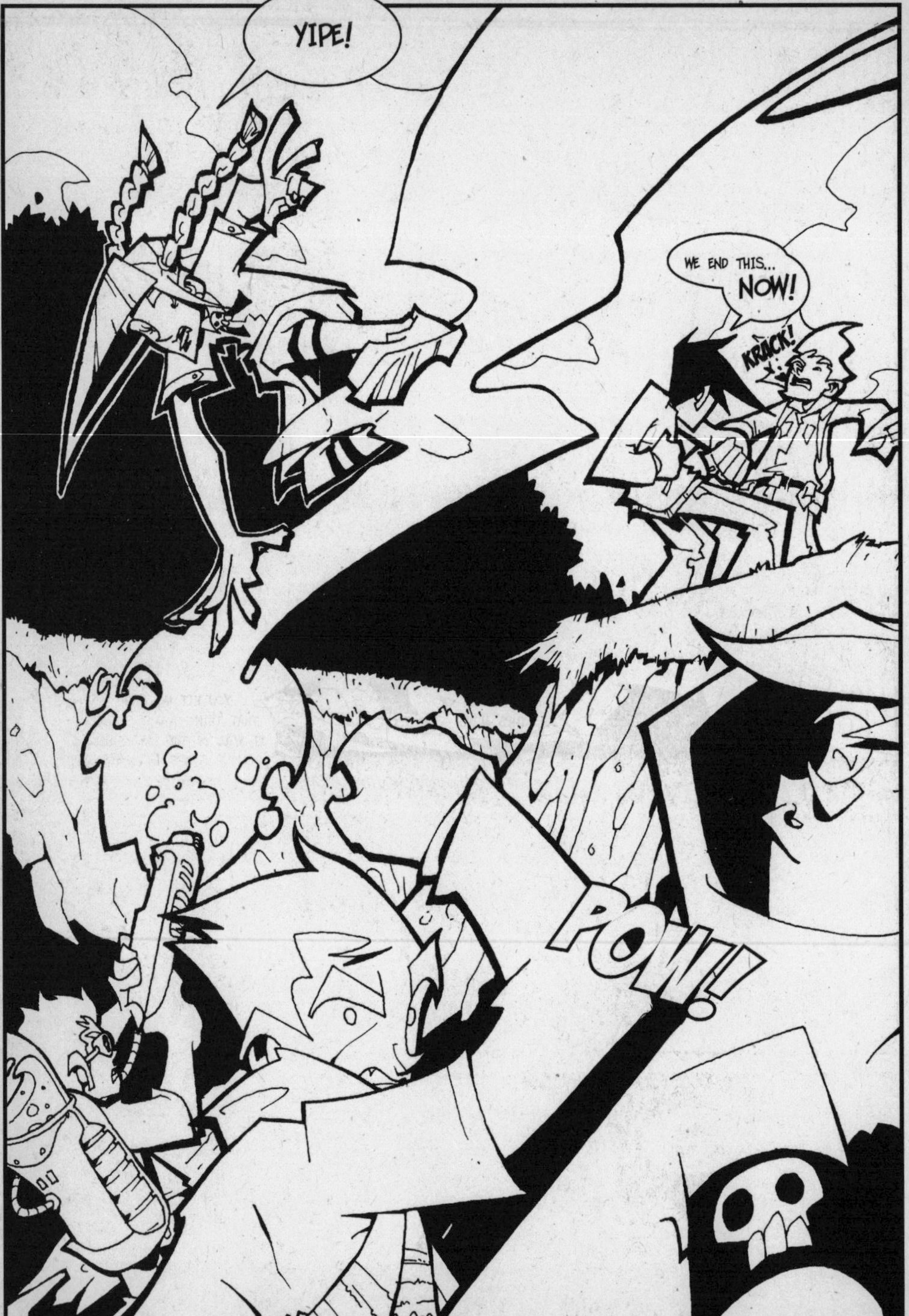
YIPE!
WE END THIS... NOW!
KRACK!
POW!

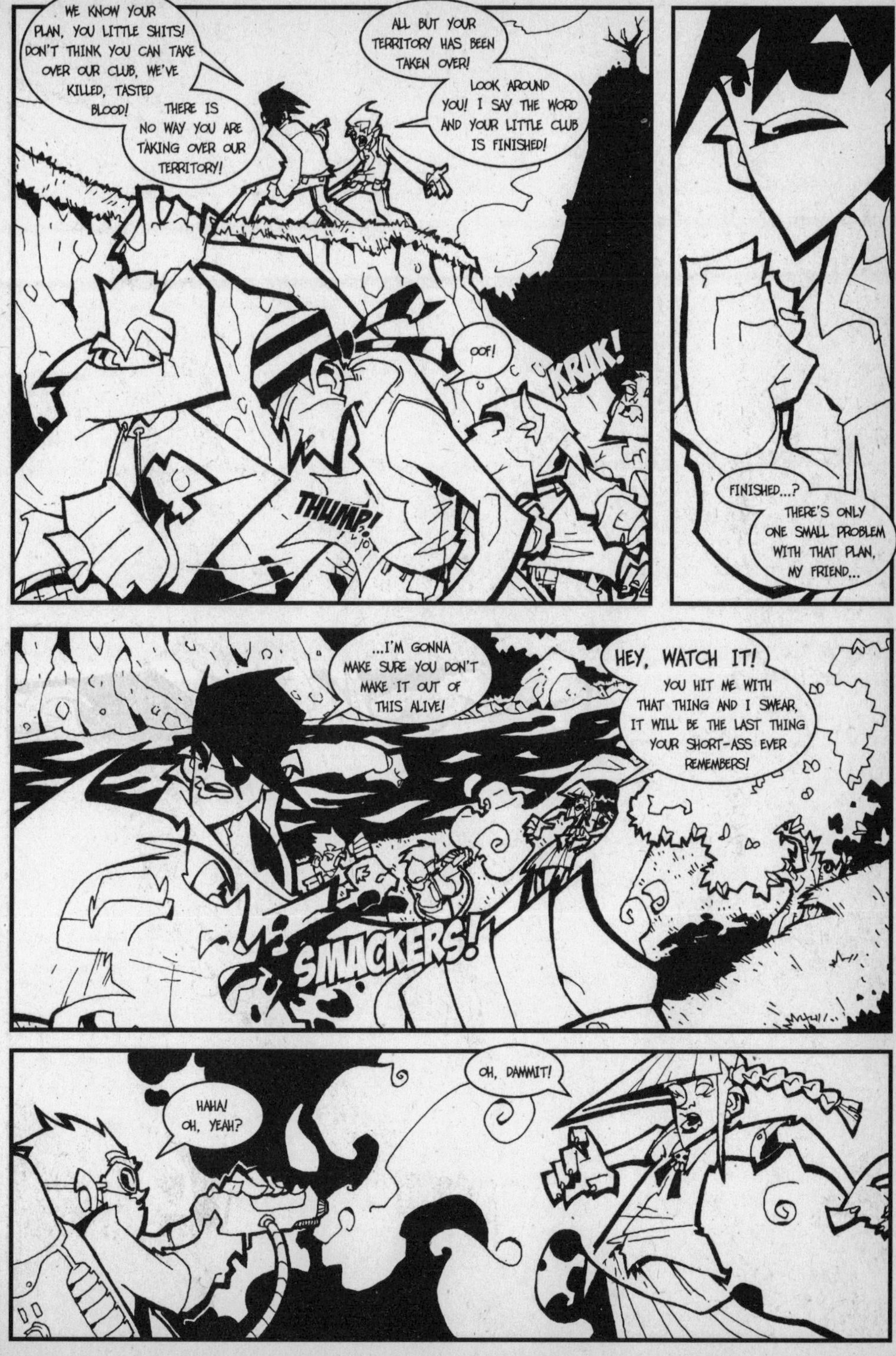
WE KNOW YOUR PLAN, YOU LITTLE SHITS! DON'T THINK YOU CAN TAKE OVER OUR CLUB, WE'VE KILLED, TASTED BLOOD!
THERE IS NO WAY YOU ARE TAKING OVER OUR TERRITORY!
ALL BUT YOUR TERRITORY HAS BEEN TAKEN OVER!
LOOK AROUND YOU! I SAY THE WORD AND YOUR LITTLE CLUB IS FINISHED!
OOF!
KRAK!
THUMP!
FINISHED...?
THERE'S ONLY ONE SMALL PROBLEM WITH THAT PLAN, MY FRIEND...
...I'M GONNA MAKE SURE YOU DON'T MAKE IT OUT OF THIS ALIVE!
HEY, WATCH IT!
YOU HIT ME WITH THAT THING AND I SWEAR, IT WILL BE THE LAST THING YOUR SHORT-ASS EVER REMEMBERS!
SMACKERS!
HAHA! OH, YEAH?
OH, DAMMIT!

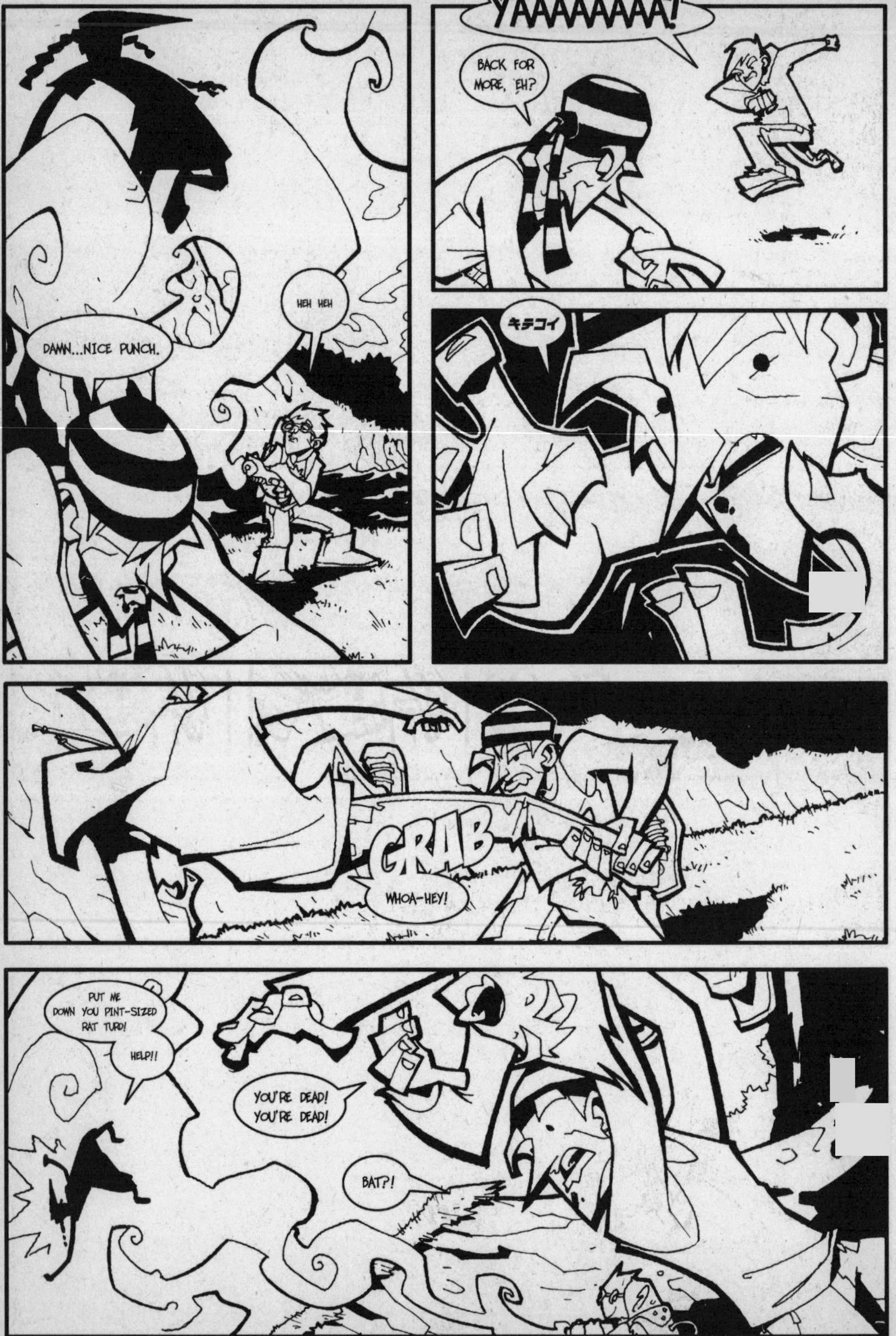
DAMN...NICE PUNCH.
HEH HEH
YAAAAAAAA!
BACK FOR MORE, EH?
キテコイ
CRAB
WHOA-HEY!
PUT ME DOWN YOU PINT-SIZED RAT TURD!
HELP!!
YOU'RE DEAD! YOU'RE DEAD!
BAT?!

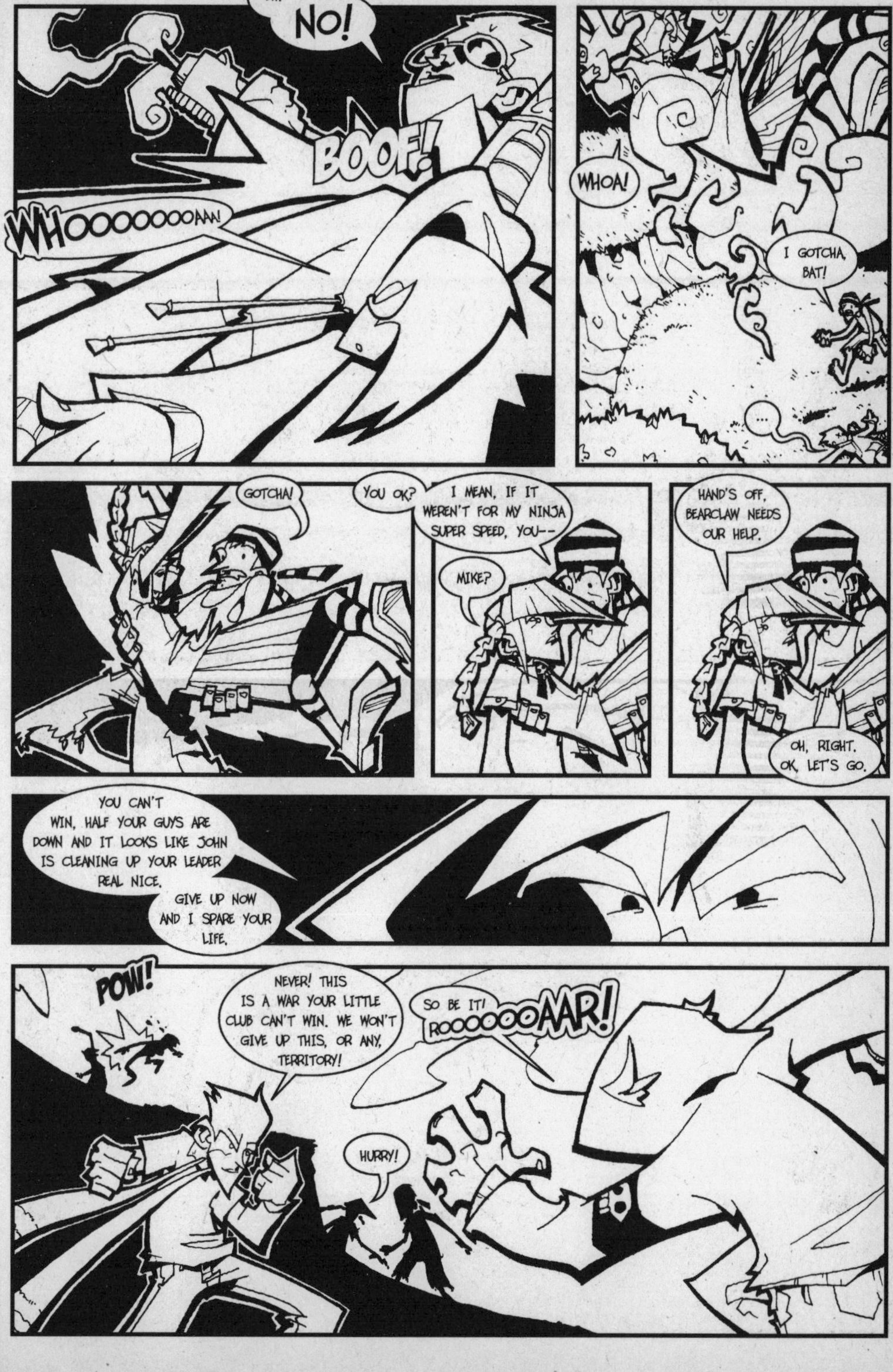
EH?
NO!
BOOF!
WHOOOOOOOOAAA!
WHOA!
I GOTCHA, BAT!
...
GOTCHA!
YOU OK?
I MEAN, IF IT WEREN'T FOR MY NINJA SUPER SPEED, YOU--
MIKE?
HAND'S OFF, BEARCLAW NEEDS OUR HELP.
OH, RIGHT. OK, LET'S GO.
YOU CAN'T WIN, HALF YOUR GUYS ARE DOWN AND IT LOOKS LIKE JOHN IS CLEANING UP YOUR LEADER REAL NICE.
GIVE UP NOW AND I SPARE YOUR LIFE.
POW!
NEVER! THIS IS A WAR YOUR LITTLE CLUB CAN'T WIN. WE WON'T GIVE UP THIS, OR ANY, TERRITORY!
SO BE IT!
ROOOOOOAAR!
HURRY!

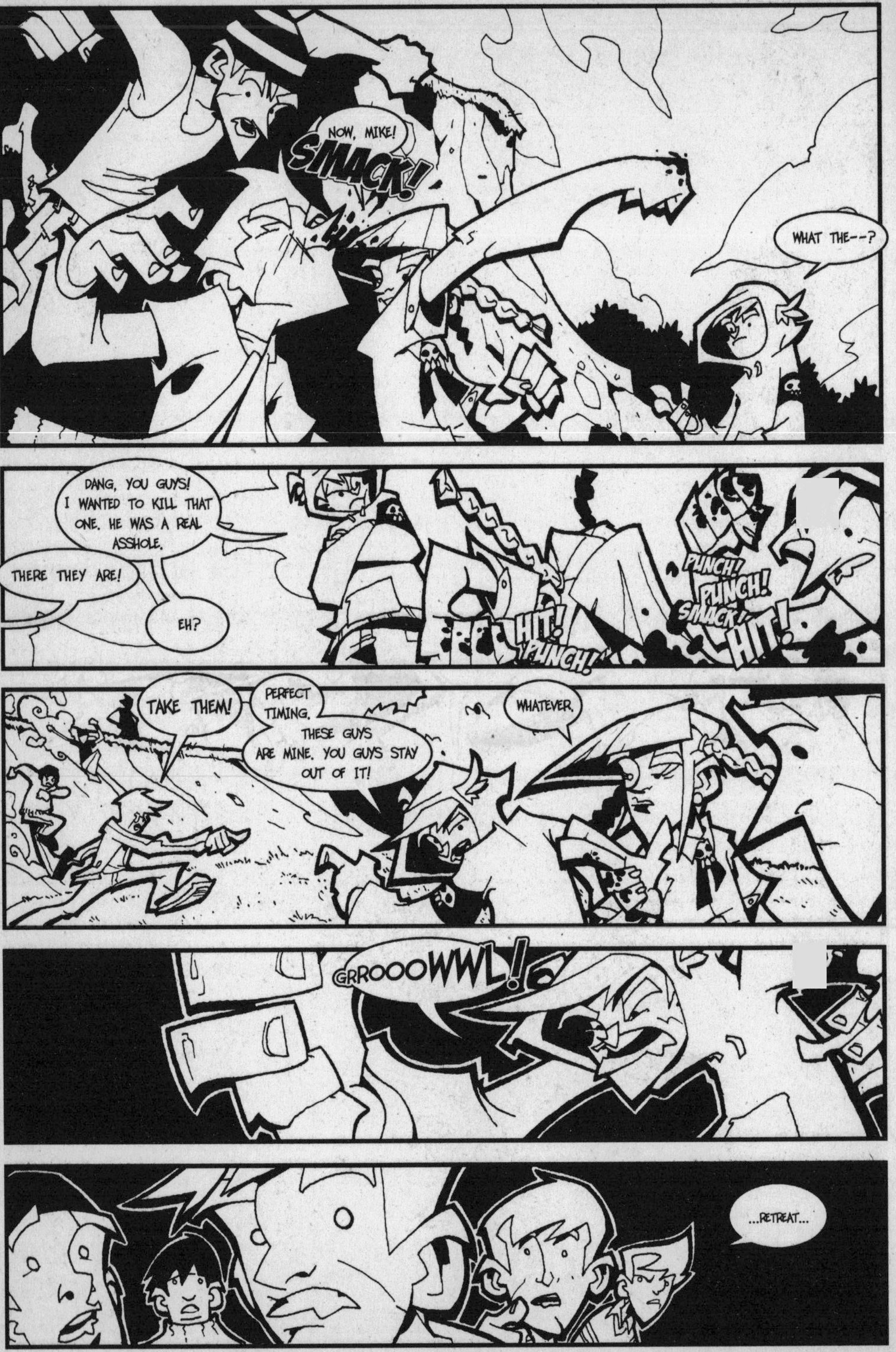
NOW, MIKE!
SMACK!
WHAT THE--?
DANG, YOU GUYS! I WANTED TO KILL THAT ONE. HE WAS A REAL ASSHOLE.
THERE THEY ARE!
EH?
HIT!
PUNCH!
PUNCH!
PUNCH!
SMACK!
HIT!
TAKE THEM!
PERFECT TIMING.
THESE GUYS ARE MINE. YOU GUYS STAY OUT OF IT!
WHATEVER.
GRROOOWWL!
...RETREAT...

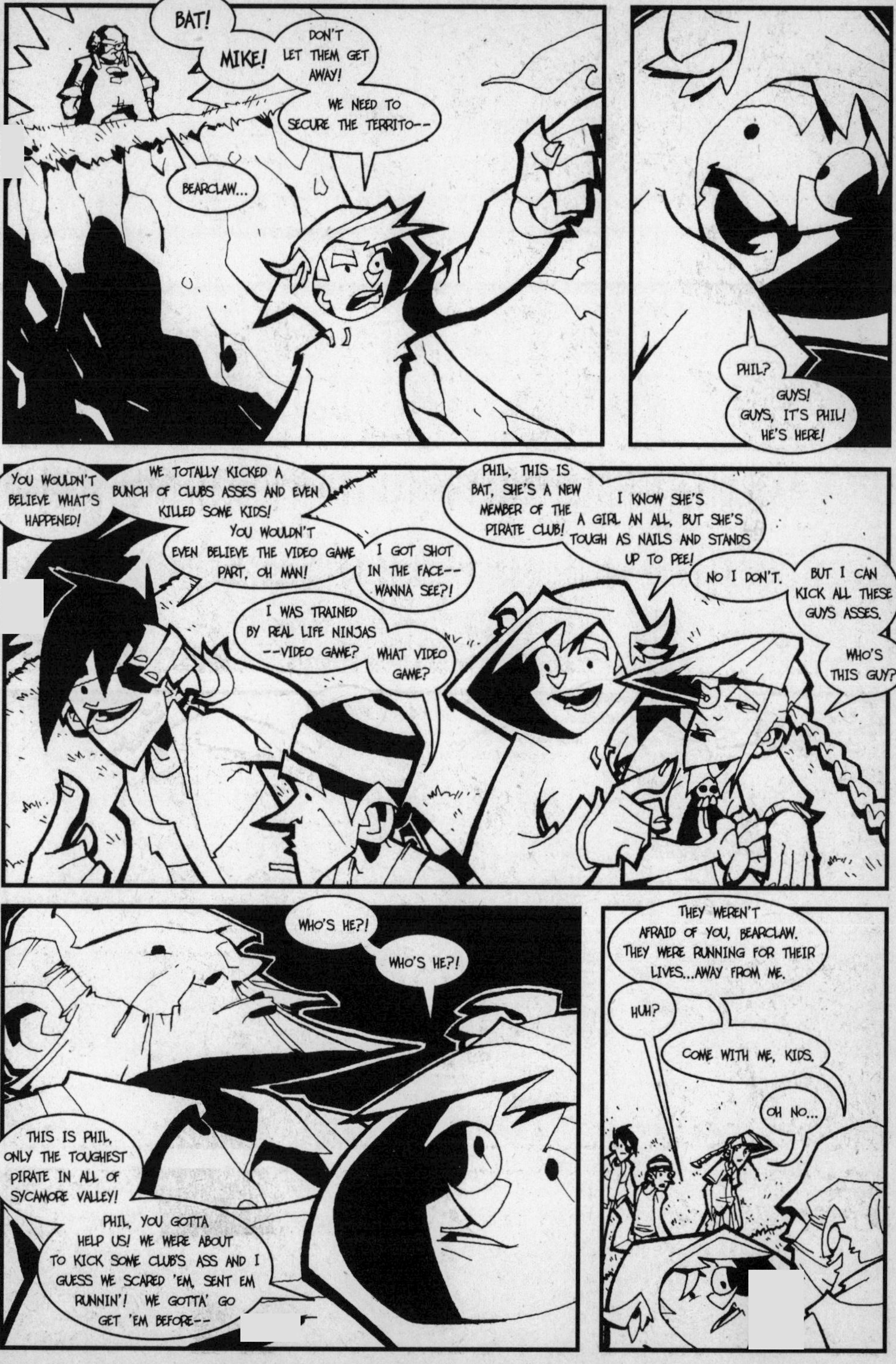
BAT!
MIKE!
DON'T LET THEM GET AWAY!
WE NEED TO SECURE THE TERRITO--
BEARCLAW...
PHIL?
GUYS! GUYS, IT'S PHIL! HE'S HERE!
YOU WOULDN'T BELIEVE WHAT'S HAPPENED!
WE TOTALLY KICKED A BUNCH OF CLUBS ASSES AND EVEN KILLED SOME KIDS!
YOU WOULDN'T EVEN BELIEVE THE VIDEO GAME PART, OH MAN!
I GOT SHOT IN THE FACE--WANNA SEE?!
I WAS TRAINED BY REAL LIFE NINJAS --VIDEO GAME?
WHAT VIDEO GAME?
PHIL, THIS IS BAT, SHE'S A NEW MEMBER OF THE PIRATE CLUB!
I KNOW SHE'S A GIRL AN ALL, BUT SHE'S TOUGH AS NAILS AND STANDS UP TO PEE!
NO I DON'T.
BUT I CAN KICK ALL THESE GUYS ASSES.
WHO'S THIS GUY?
WHO'S HE?!
WHO'S HE?!
THIS IS PHIL, ONLY THE TOUGHEST PIRATE IN ALL OF SYCAMORE VALLEY!
PHIL, YOU GOTTA HELP US! WE WERE ABOUT TO KICK SOME CLUB'S ASS AND I GUESS WE SCARED 'EM, SENT EM RUNNIN'! WE GOTTA' GO GET 'EM BEFORE--
THEY WEREN'T AFRAID OF YOU, BEARCLAW. THEY WERE RUNNING FOR THEIR LIVES...AWAY FROM ME.
HUH?
COME WITH ME, KIDS.
OH NO...

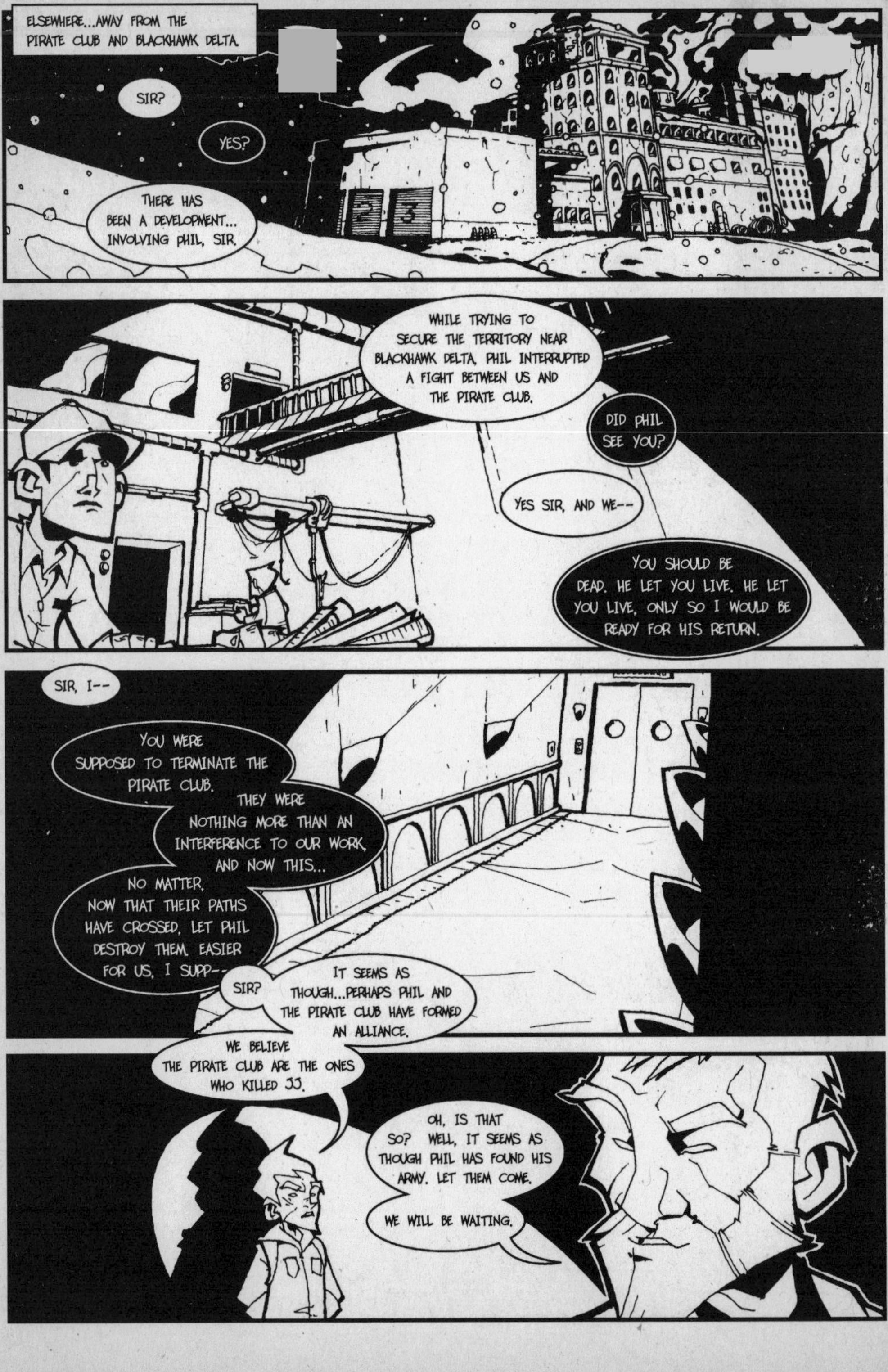
ELSEWHERE...AWAY FROM THE PIRATE CLUB AND BLACKHAWK DELTA.
SIR?
YES?
THERE HAS BEEN A DEVELOPMENT... INVOLVING PHIL, SIR.
WHILE TRYING TO SECURE THE TERRITORY NEAR BLACKHAWK DELTA, PHIL INTERRUPTED A FIGHT BETWEEN US AND THE PIRATE CLUB.
DID PHIL SEE YOU?
YES SIR, AND WE--
YOU SHOULD BE DEAD. HE LET YOU LIVE. HE LET YOU LIVE, ONLY SO I WOULD BE READY FOR HIS RETURN.
SIR, I--
YOU WERE SUPPOSED TO TERMINATE THE PIRATE CLUB.
THEY WERE NOTHING MORE THAN AN INTERFERENCE TO OUR WORK, AND NOW THIS...
NO MATTER. NOW THAT THEIR PATHS HAVE CROSSED, LET PHIL DESTROY THEM. EASIER FOR US, I SUPP--
SIR?
IT SEEMS AS THOUGH...PERHAPS PHIL AND THE PIRATE CLUB HAVE FORMED AN ALLIANCE.
WE BELIEVE THE PIRATE CLUB ARE THE ONES WHO KILLED JJ.
OH, IS THAT SO? WELL, IT SEEMS AS THOUGH PHIL HAS FOUND HIS ARMY. LET THEM COME.
WE WILL BE WAITING.

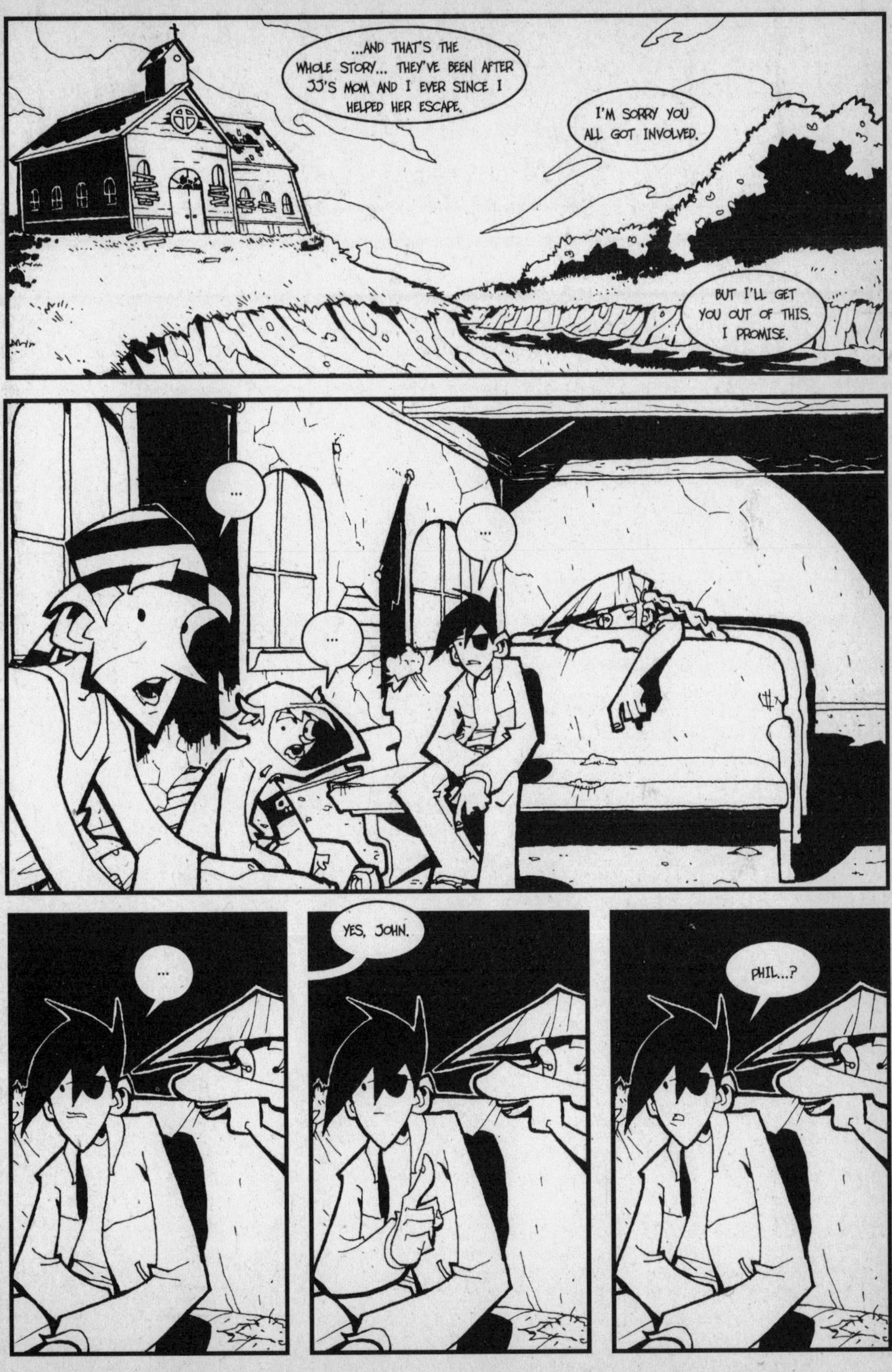
...AND THAT'S THE WHOLE STORY... THEY'VE BEEN AFTER JJ'S MOM AND I EVER SINCE I HELPED HER ESCAPE.
I'M SORRY YOU ALL GOT INVOLVED.
BUT I'LL GET YOU OUT OF THIS. I PROMISE.
...
...
...
...
YES, JOHN.
PHIL...?

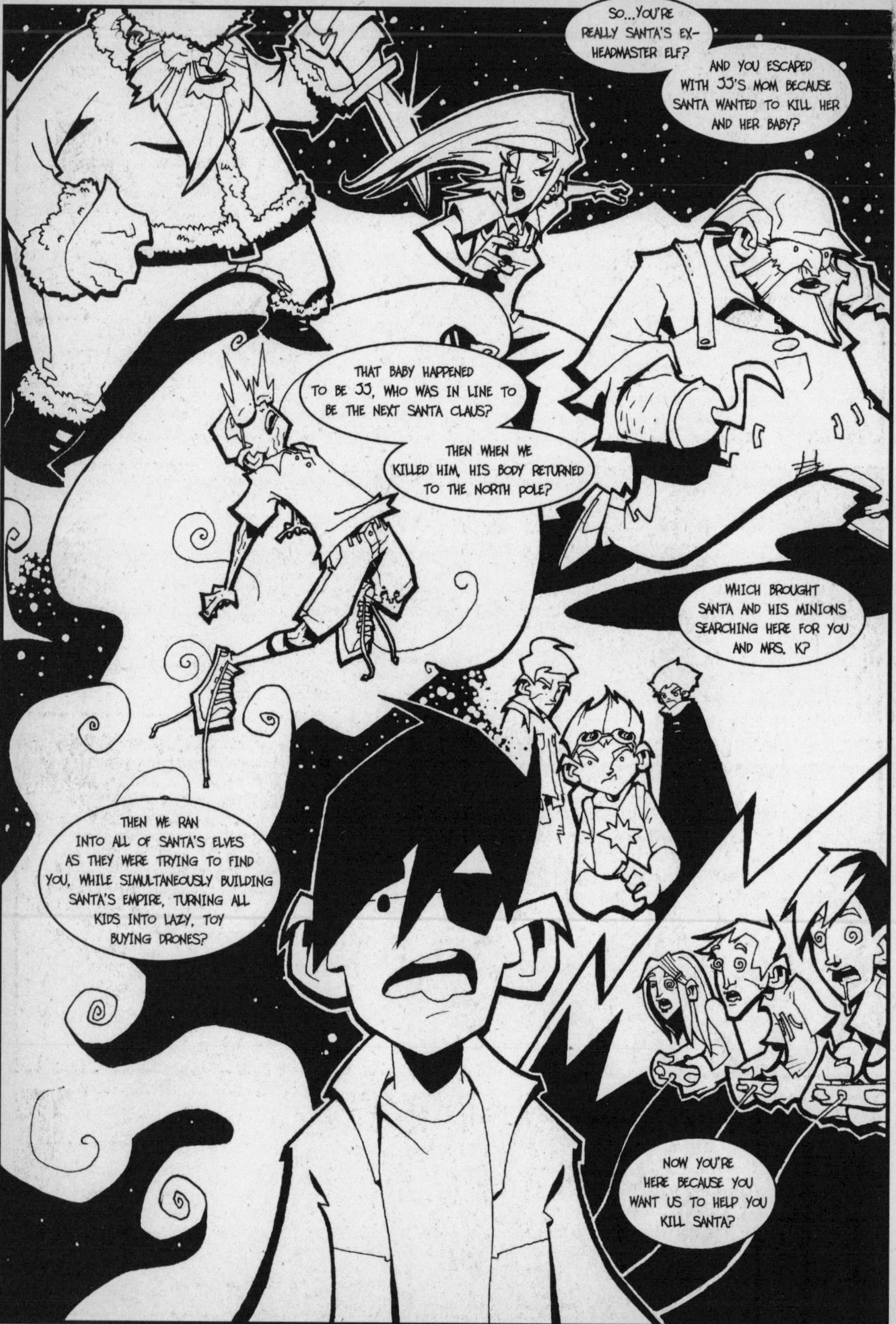
SO...YOU'RE REALLY SANTA'S EX-HEADMASTER ELF?
AND YOU ESCAPED WITH JJ'S MOM BECAUSE SANTA WANTED TO KILL HER AND HER BABY?
THAT BABY HAPPENED TO BE JJ, WHO WAS IN LINE TO BE THE NEXT SANTA CLAUS?
THEN WHEN WE KILLED HIM, HIS BODY RETURNED TO THE NORTH POLE?
WHICH BROUGHT SANTA AND HIS MINIONS SEARCHING HERE FOR YOU AND MRS. K?
THEN WE RAN INTO ALL OF SANTA'S ELVES AS THEY WERE TRYING TO FIND YOU, WHILE SIMULTANEOUSLY BUILDING SANTA'S EMPIRE, TURNING ALL KIDS INTO LAZY, TOY BUYING DRONES?
NOW YOU'RE HERE BECAUSE YOU WANT US TO HELP YOU KILL SANTA?

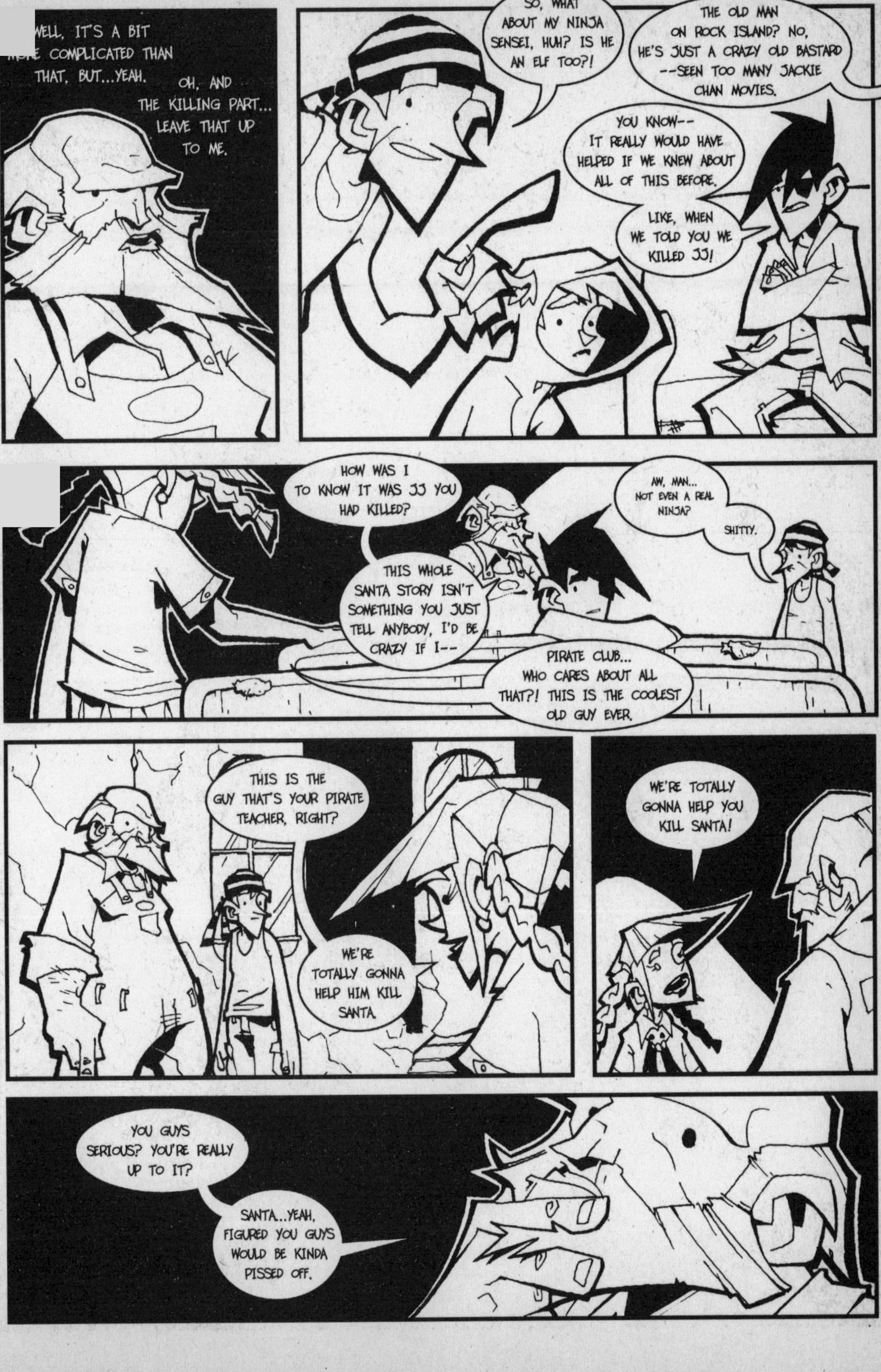
WELL, IT'S A BIT MORE COMPLICATED THAN THAT, BUT...YEAH.
OH, AND THE KILLING PART... LEAVE THAT UP TO ME.
SO, WHAT ABOUT MY NINJA SENSEI, HUH? IS HE AN ELF TOO?!
THE OLD MAN ON ROCK ISLAND? NO, HE'S JUST A CRAZY OLD BASTARD --SEEN TOO MANY JACKIE CHAN MOVIES.
YOU KNOW-- IT REALLY WOULD HAVE HELPED IF WE KNEW ABOUT ALL OF THIS BEFORE.
LIKE, WHEN WE TOLD YOU WE KILLED JJ!
HOW WAS I TO KNOW IT WAS JJ YOU HAD KILLED?
THIS WHOLE SANTA STORY ISN'T SOMETHING YOU JUST TELL ANYBODY, I'D BE CRAZY IF I--
AW, MAN... NOT EVEN A REAL NINJA?
SHITTY.
PIRATE CLUB... WHO CARES ABOUT ALL THAT?! THIS IS THE COOLEST OLD GUY EVER.
THIS IS THE GUY THAT'S YOUR PIRATE TEACHER, RIGHT?
WE'RE TOTALLY GONNA HELP HIM KILL SANTA.
WE'RE TOTALLY GONNA HELP YOU KILL SANTA!
YOU GUYS SERIOUS? YOU'RE REALLY UP TO IT?
SANTA...YEAH, FIGURED YOU GUYS WOULD BE KINDA PISSED OFF.

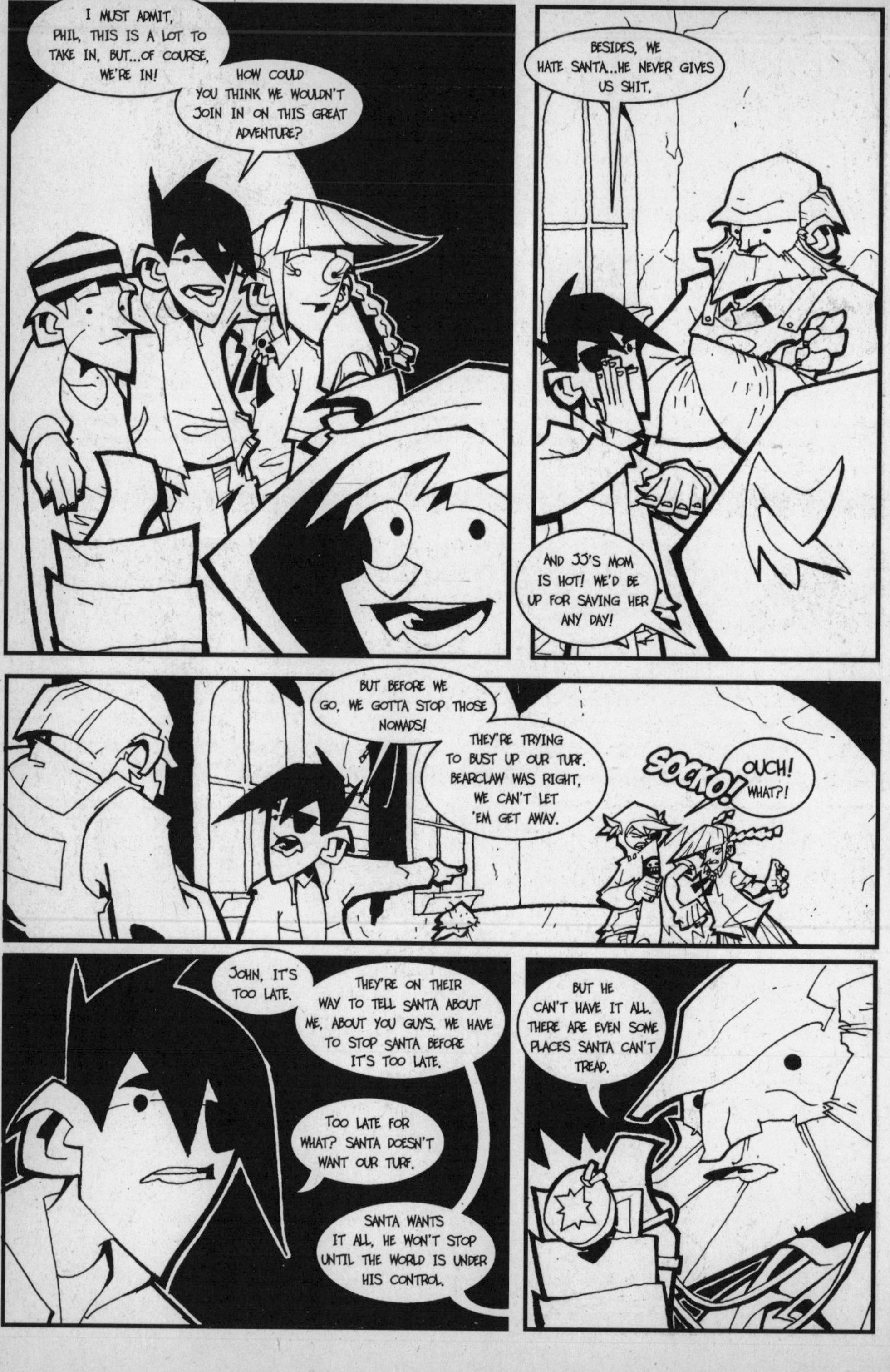
I MUST ADMIT, PHIL, THIS IS A LOT TO TAKE IN, BUT...OF COURSE, WE'RE IN!
HOW COULD YOU THINK WE WOULDN'T JOIN IN ON THIS GREAT ADVENTURE?
BESIDES, WE HATE SANTA...HE NEVER GIVES US SHIT.
AND JJ'S MOM IS HOT! WE'D BE UP FOR SAVING HER ANY DAY!
BUT BEFORE WE GO, WE GOTTA STOP THOSE NOMADS!
THEY'RE TRYING TO BUST UP OUR TURF. BEARCLAW WAS RIGHT, WE CAN'T LET 'EM GET AWAY.
SOCKO!
OUCH! WHAT?!
JOHN, IT'S TOO LATE.
THEY'RE ON THEIR WAY TO TELL SANTA ABOUT ME, ABOUT YOU GUYS. WE HAVE TO STOP SANTA BEFORE IT'S TOO LATE.
TOO LATE FOR WHAT? SANTA DOESN'T WANT OUR TURF.
SANTA WANTS IT ALL, HE WON'T STOP UNTIL THE WORLD IS UNDER HIS CONTROL.
BUT HE CAN'T HAVE IT ALL. THERE ARE EVEN SOME PLACES SANTA CAN'T TREAD.

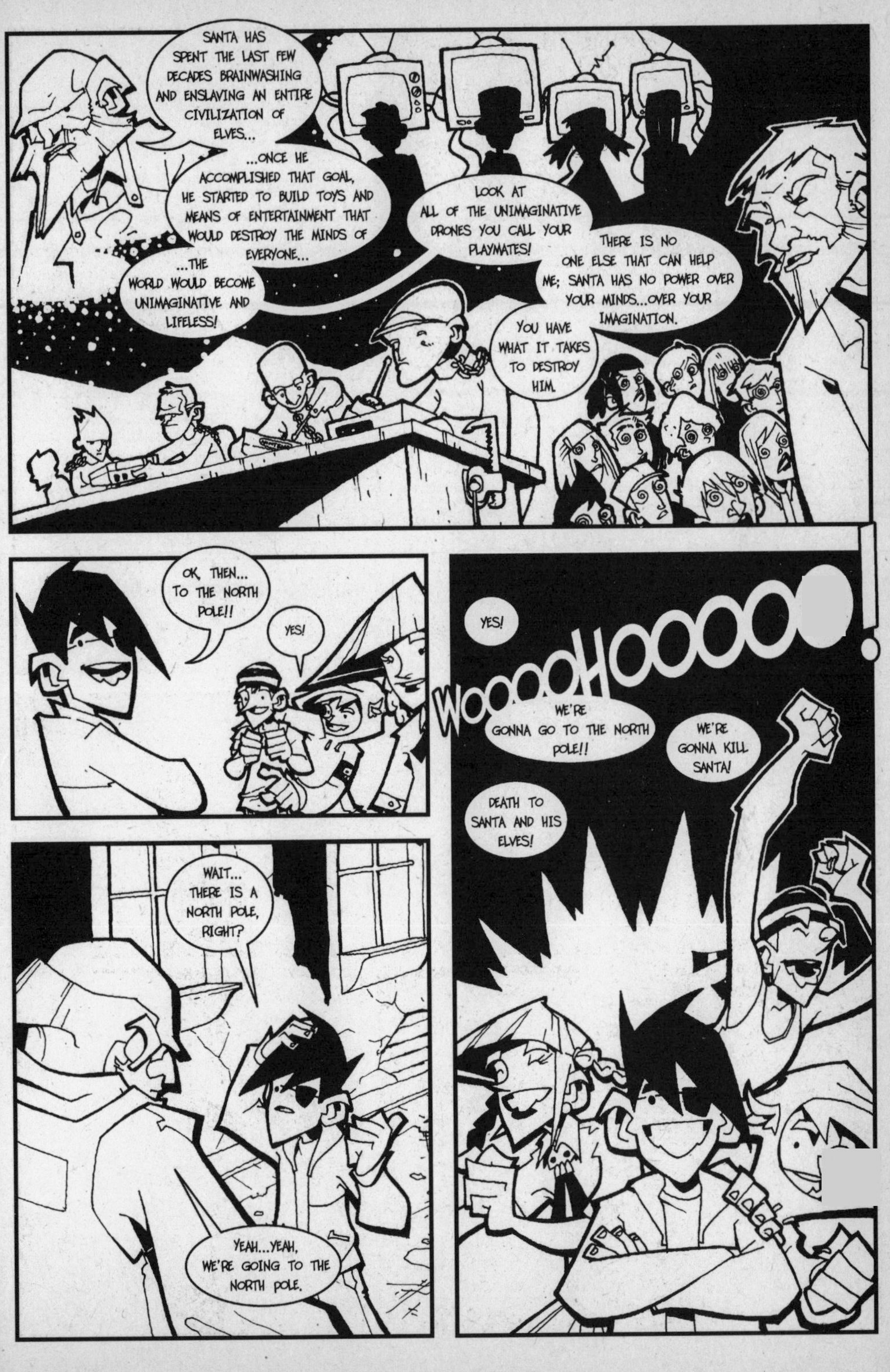
SANTA HAS SPENT THE LAST FEW DECADES BRAINWASHING AND ENSLAVING AN ENTIRE CIVILIZATION OF ELVES...
...ONCE HE ACCOMPLISHED THAT GOAL, HE STARTED TO BUILD TOYS AND MEANS OF ENTERTAINMENT THAT WOULD DESTROY THE MINDS OF EVERYONE...
...THE WORLD WOULD BECOME UNIMAGINATIVE AND LIFELESS!
LOOK AT ALL OF THE UNIMAGINATIVE DRONES YOU CALL YOUR PLAYMATES!
THERE IS NO ONE ELSE THAT CAN HELP ME; SANTA HAS NO POWER OVER YOUR MINDS...OVER YOUR IMAGINATION.
YOU HAVE WHAT IT TAKES TO DESTROY HIM.
OK, THEN... TO THE NORTH POLE!!
YES!
WAIT... THERE IS A NORTH POLE, RIGHT?
YEAH...YEAH, WE'RE GOING TO THE NORTH POLE.
YES!
WOOOOHOOOOO!
WE'RE GONNA GO TO THE NORTH POLE!!
WE'RE GONNA KILL SANTA!
DEATH TO SANTA AND HIS ELVES!

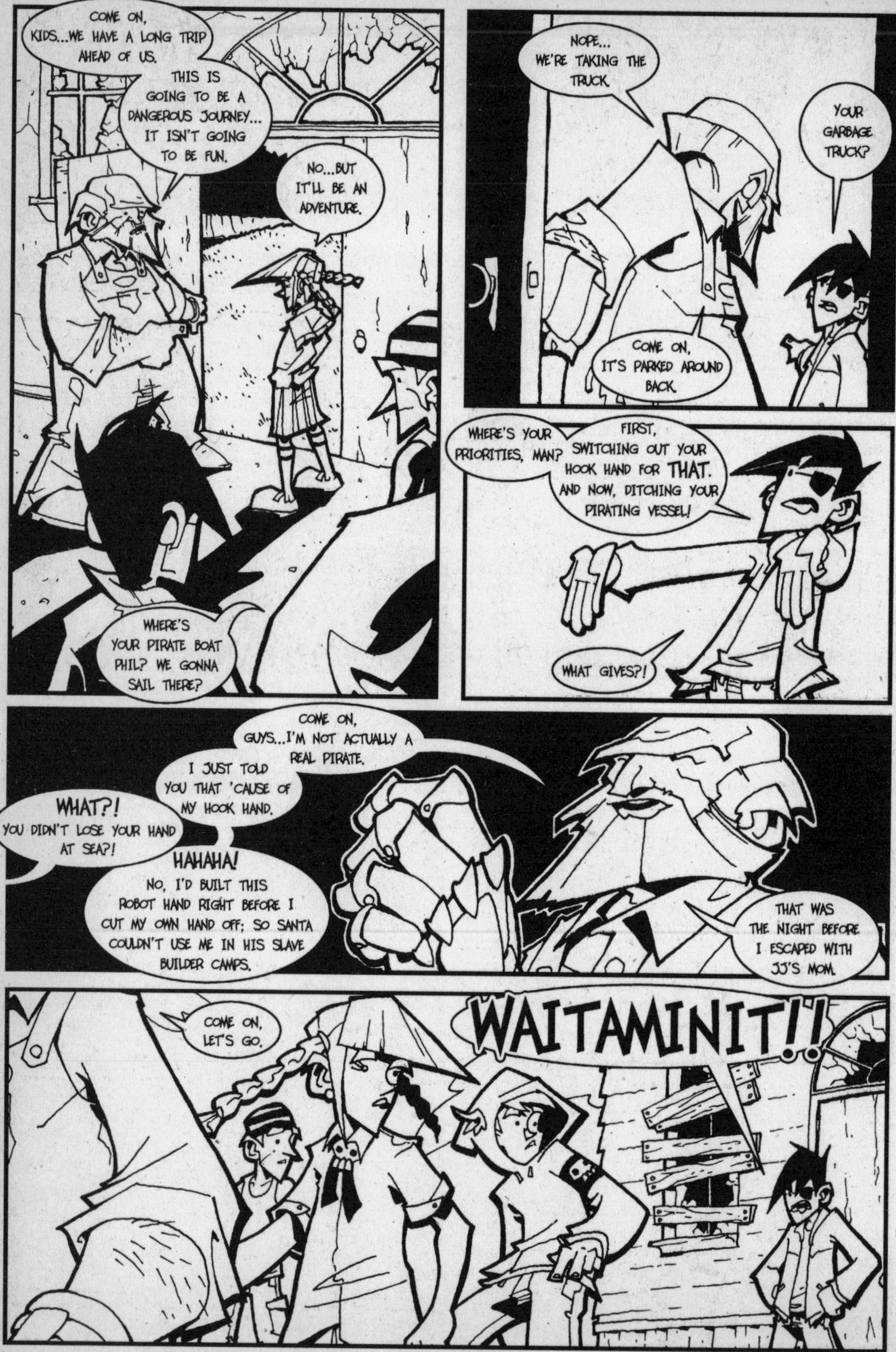
COME ON, KIDS...WE HAVE A LONG TRIP AHEAD OF US.
THIS IS GOING TO BE A DANGEROUS JOURNEY... IT ISN'T GOING TO BE FUN.
NO...BUT IT'LL BE AN ADVENTURE.
WHERE'S YOUR PIRATE BOAT PHIL? WE GONNA SAIL THERE?
NOPE... WE'RE TAKING THE TRUCK.
YOUR GARBAGE TRUCK?
COME ON, IT'S PARKED AROUND BACK.
WHERE'S YOUR PRIORITIES, MAN?
FIRST, SWITCHING OUT YOUR HOOK HAND FOR THAT. AND NOW, DITCHING YOUR PIRATING VESSEL!
WHAT GIVES?!
COME ON, GUYS...I'M NOT ACTUALLY A REAL PIRATE.
I JUST TOLD YOU THAT 'CAUSE OF MY HOOK HAND.
WHAT?! YOU DIDN'T LOSE YOUR HAND AT SEA?!
HAHAHA! NO, I'D BUILT THIS ROBOT HAND RIGHT BEFORE I CUT MY OWN HAND OFF; SO SANTA COULDN'T USE ME IN HIS SLAVE BUILDER CAMPS.
THAT WAS THE NIGHT BEFORE I ESCAPED WITH JJ'S MOM.
COME ON, LET'S GO.
WAITAMINIT!!

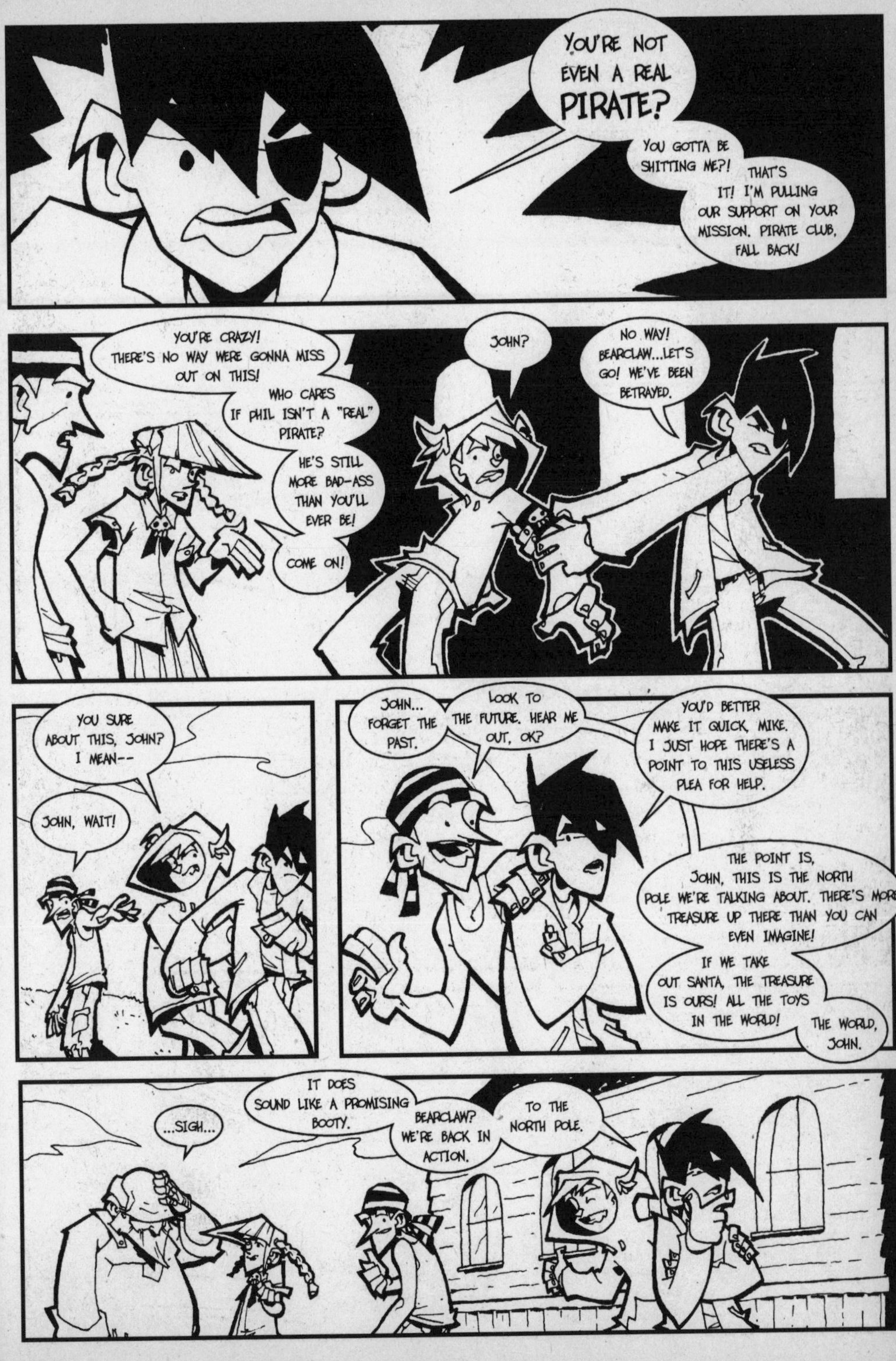
YOU'RE NOT EVEN A REAL PIRATE?
YOU GOTTA BE SHITTING ME?!
THAT'S IT! I'M PULLING OUR SUPPORT ON YOUR MISSION. PIRATE CLUB, FALL BACK!
YOU'RE CRAZY! THERE'S NO WAY WERE GONNA MISS OUT ON THIS!
WHO CARES IF PHIL ISN'T A "REAL" PIRATE?
HE'S STILL MORE BAD-ASS THAN YOU'LL EVER BE!
COME ON!
JOHN?
NO WAY! BEARCLAW...LET'S GO! WE'VE BEEN BETRAYED.
YOU SURE ABOUT THIS, JOHN? I MEAN--
JOHN, WAIT!
JOHN... FORGET THE PAST.
LOOK TO THE FUTURE. HEAR ME OUT, OK?
YOU'D BETTER MAKE IT QUICK, MIKE. I JUST HOPE THERE'S A POINT TO THIS USELESS PLEA FOR HELP.
THE POINT IS, JOHN, THIS IS THE NORTH POLE WE'RE TALKING ABOUT. THERE'S MORE TREASURE UP THERE THAN YOU CAN EVEN IMAGINE!
IF WE TAKE OUT SANTA, THE TREASURE IS OURS! ALL THE TOYS IN THE WORLD!
THE WORLD, JOHN.
...SIGH...
IT DOES SOUND LIKE A PROMISING BOOTY.
BEARCLAW? WE'RE BACK IN ACTION.
TO THE NORTH POLE.

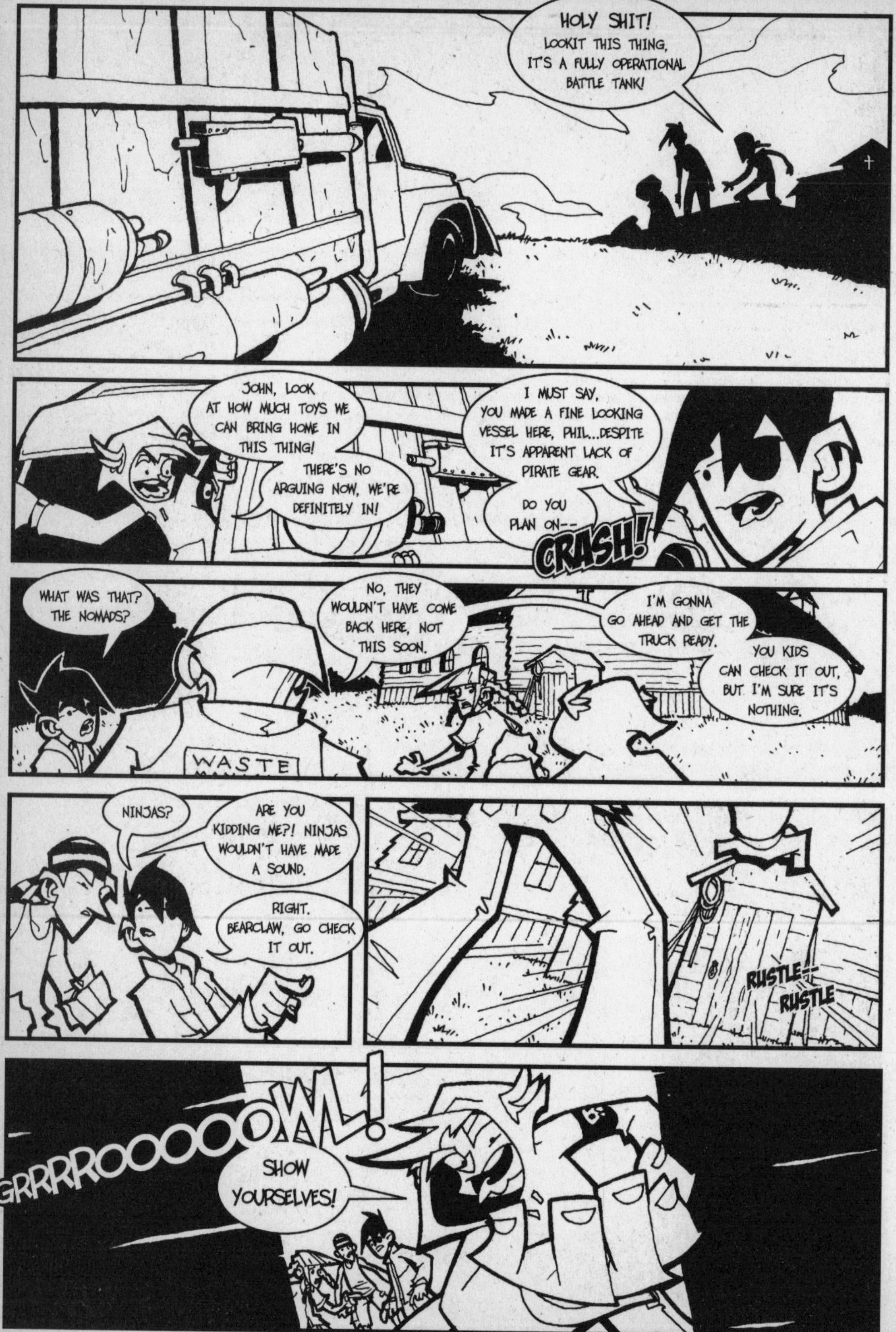
HOLY SHIT! LOOKIT THIS THING, IT'S A FULLY OPERATIONAL BATTLE TANK!
JOHN, LOOK AT HOW MUCH TOYS WE CAN BRING HOME IN THIS THING!
THERE'S NO ARGUING NOW, WE'RE DEFINITELY IN!
I MUST SAY, YOU MADE A FINE LOOKING VESSEL HERE, PHIL...DESPITE IT'S APPARENT LACK OF PIRATE GEAR.
DO YOU PLAN ON--
CRASH!
WHAT WAS THAT? THE NOMADS?
NO, THEY WOULDN'T HAVE COME BACK HERE, NOT THIS SOON.
I'M GONNA GO AHEAD AND GET THE TRUCK READY.
YOU KIDS CAN CHECK IT OUT, BUT I'M SURE IT'S NOTHING.
WASTE
NINJAS?
ARE YOU KIDDING ME?! NINJAS WOULDN'T HAVE MADE A SOUND.
RIGHT. BEARCLAW, GO CHECK IT OUT.
RUSTLE RUSTLE
GRRRROOOOOOWL!
SHOW YOURSELVES!

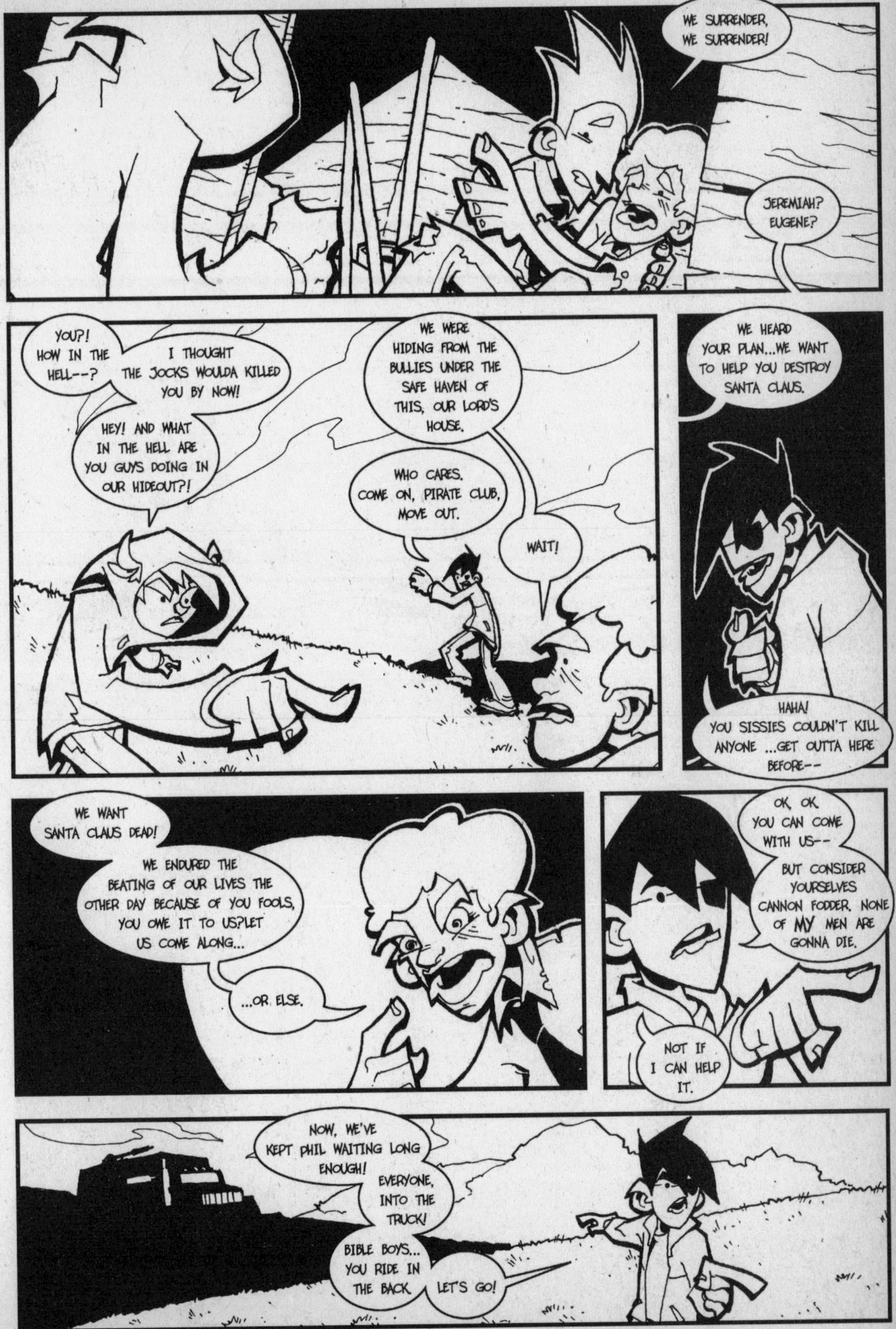
WE SURRENDER, WE SURRENDER!
JEREMIAH? EUGENE?
YOU?! HOW IN THE HELL--?
I THOUGHT THE JOCKS WOULDA KILLED YOU BY NOW!
HEY! AND WHAT IN THE HELL ARE YOU GUYS DOING IN OUR HIDEOUT?!
WE WERE HIDING FROM THE BULLIES UNDER THE SAFE HAVEN OF THIS, OUR LORD'S HOUSE.
WHO CARES. COME ON, PIRATE CLUB, MOVE OUT.
WAIT!
WE HEARD YOUR PLAN...WE WANT TO HELP YOU DESTROY SANTA CLAUS.
HAHA! YOU SISSIES COULDN'T KILL ANYONE ...GET OUTTA HERE BEFORE--
WE WANT SANTA CLAUS DEAD!
WE ENDURED THE BEATING OF OUR LIVES THE OTHER DAY BECAUSE OF YOU FOOLS, YOU OWE IT TO US?LET US COME ALONG...
...OR ELSE.
OK, OK, YOU CAN COME WITH US--
BUT CONSIDER YOURSELVES CANNON FODDER. NONE OF MY MEN ARE GONNA DIE.
NOT IF I CAN HELP IT.
NOW, WE'VE KEPT PHIL WAITING LONG ENOUGH!
EVERYONE, INTO THE TRUCK!
BIBLE BOYS... YOU RIDE IN THE BACK.
LET'S GO!

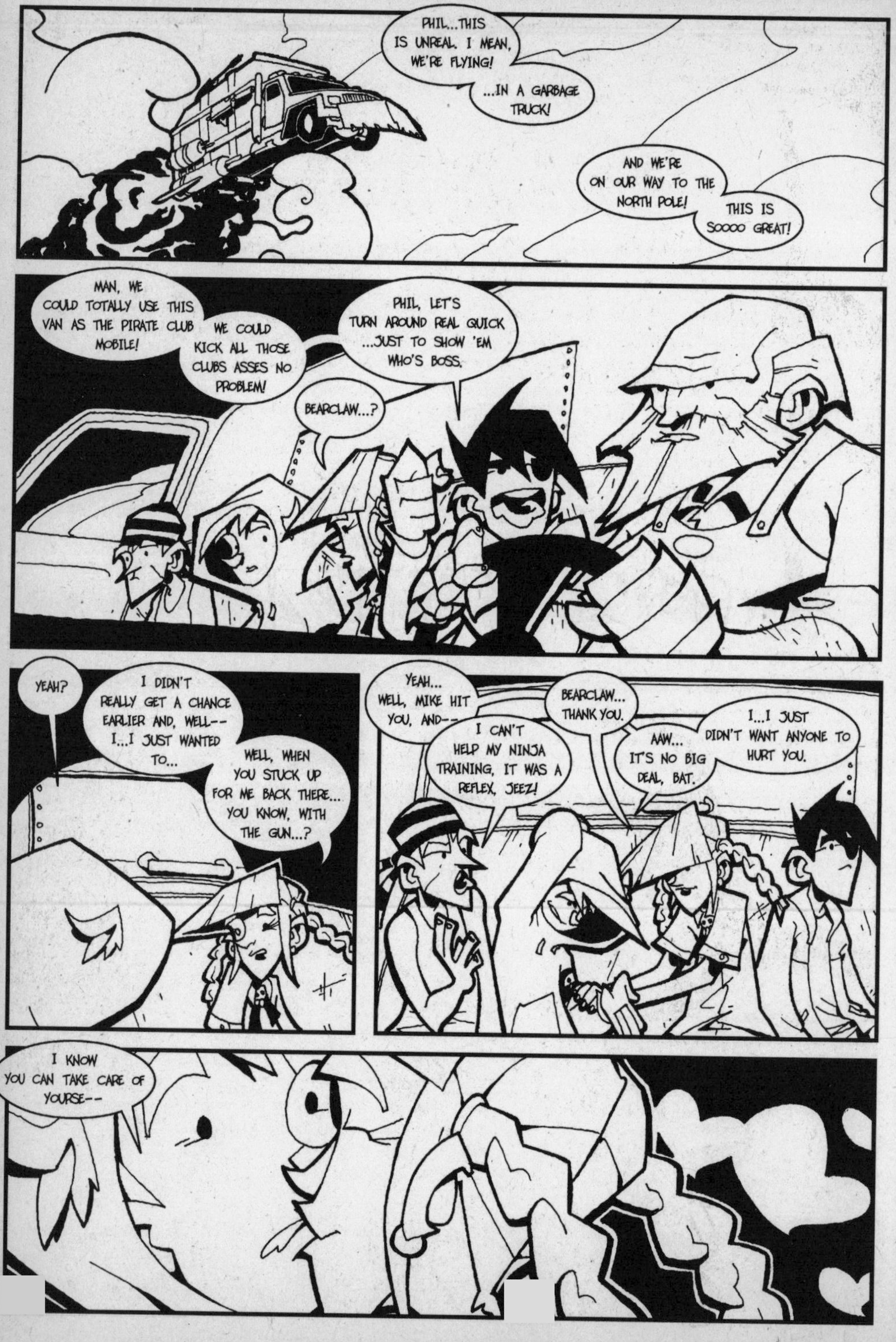
PHIL...THIS IS UNREAL. I MEAN, WE'RE FLYING!
...IN A GARBAGE TRUCK!
AND WE'RE ON OUR WAY TO THE NORTH POLE!
THIS IS SOOOO GREAT!
MAN, WE COULD TOTALLY USE THIS VAN AS THE PIRATE CLUB MOBILE!
WE COULD KICK ALL THOSE CLUBS ASSES NO PROBLEM!
PHIL, LET'S TURN AROUND REAL QUICK ...JUST TO SHOW 'EM WHO'S BOSS.
BEARCLAW...?
YEAH?
I DIDN'T REALLY GET A CHANCE EARLIER AND, WELL-- I...I JUST WANTED TO...
WELL, WHEN YOU STUCK UP FOR ME BACK THERE... YOU KNOW, WITH THE GUN...?
YEAH... WELL, MIKE HIT YOU, AND--
I CAN'T HELP MY NINJA TRAINING, IT WAS A REFLEX, JEEZ!
BEARCLAW... THANK YOU.
AAW... IT'S NO BIG DEAL, BAT.
I...I JUST DIDN'T WANT ANYONE TO HURT YOU.
I KNOW YOU CAN TAKE CARE OF YOURSE--

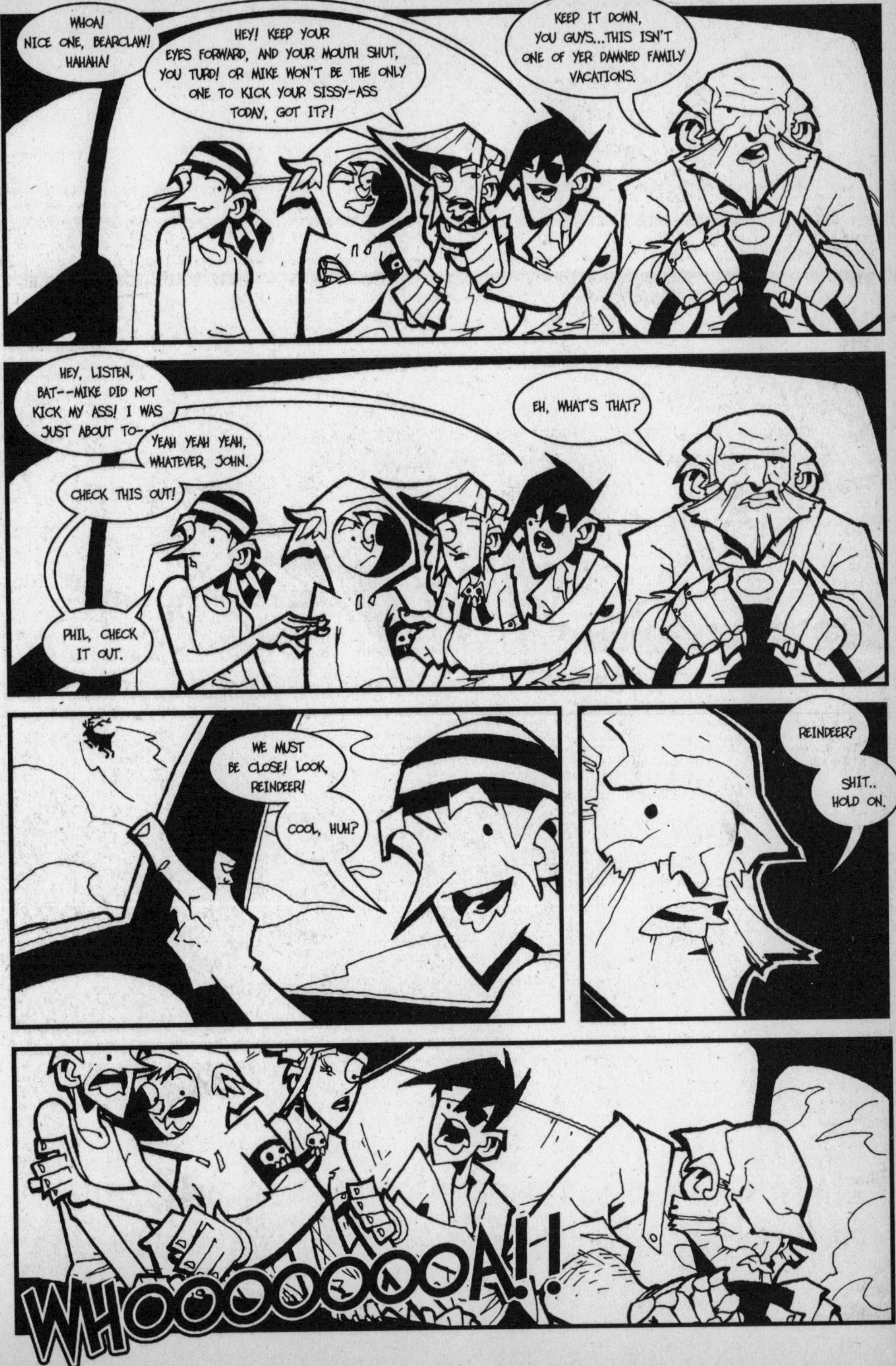
WHOA! NICE ONE, BEARCLAW! HAHAHA!
HEY! KEEP YOUR EYES FORWARD, AND YOUR MOUTH SHUT, YOU TURD! OR MIKE WON'T BE THE ONLY ONE TO KICK YOUR SISSY-ASS TODAY, GOT IT?!
KEEP IT DOWN, YOU GUYS...THIS ISN'T ONE OF YER DAMNED FAMILY VACATIONS.
HEY, LISTEN, BAT--MIKE DID NOT KICK MY ASS! I WAS JUST ABOUT TO--
YEAH YEAH YEAH, WHATEVER, JOHN.
EH, WHAT'S THAT?
CHECK THIS OUT!
PHIL, CHECK IT OUT.
WE MUST BE CLOSE! LOOK, REINDEER!
COOL, HUH?
REINDEER?
SHIT.. HOLD ON.
WHOOOOOOOOA!!

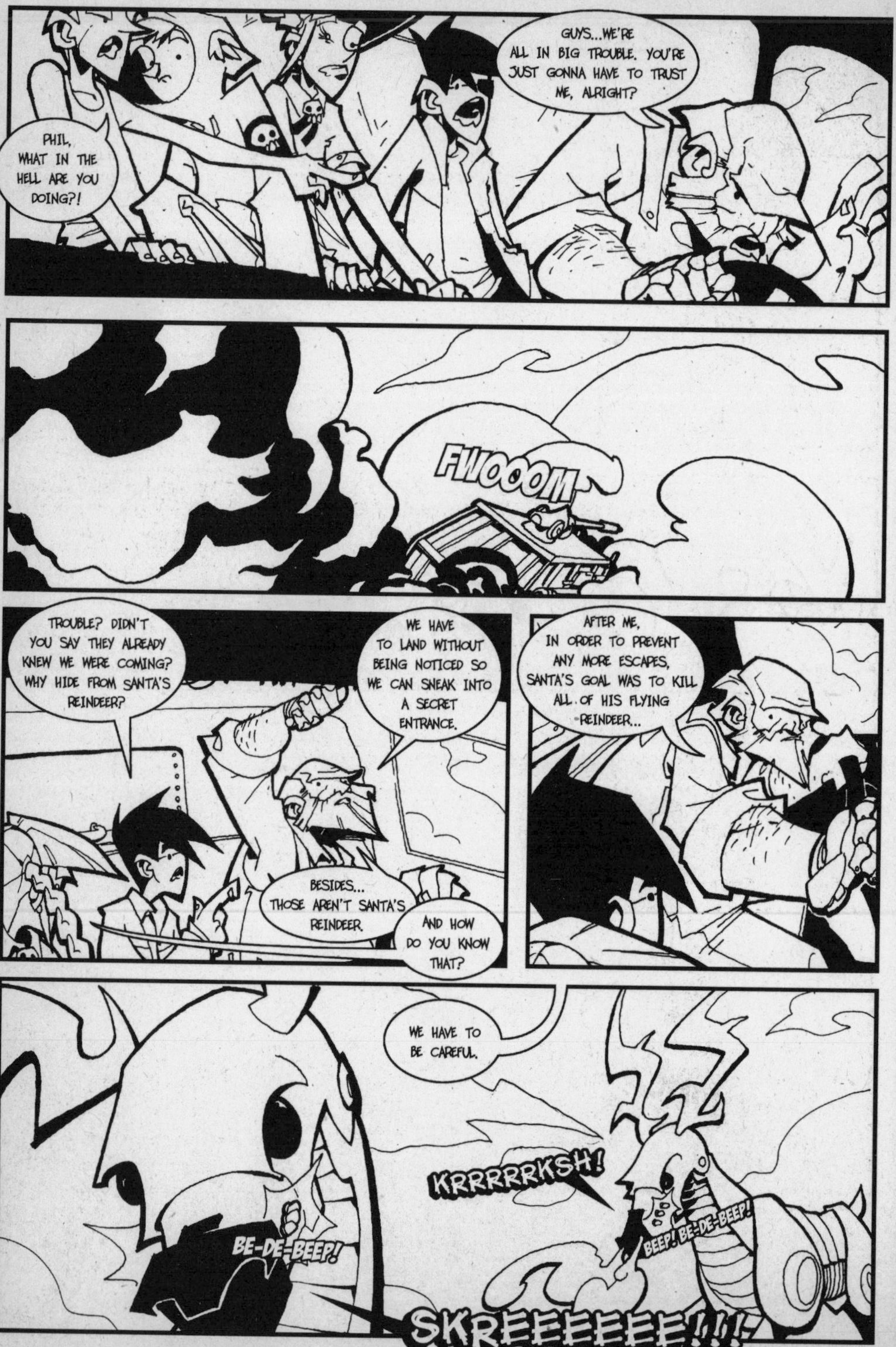
GUYS...WE'RE ALL IN BIG TROUBLE. YOU'RE JUST GONNA HAVE TO TRUST ME, ALRIGHT?
PHIL, WHAT IN THE HELL ARE YOU DOING?!
FWOOOM
TROUBLE? DIDN'T YOU SAY THEY ALREADY KNEW WE WERE COMING? WHY HIDE FROM SANTA'S REINDEER?
WE HAVE TO LAND WITHOUT BEING NOTICED SO WE CAN SNEAK INTO A SECRET ENTRANCE.
BESIDES... THOSE AREN'T SANTA'S REINDEER.
AND HOW DO YOU KNOW THAT?
AFTER ME, IN ORDER TO PREVENT ANY MORE ESCAPES, SANTA'S GOAL WAS TO KILL ALL OF HIS FLYING REINDEER...
WE HAVE TO BE CAREFUL.
KRRRRRKSH!
BE-DE-BEEP!
BEEP! BE-DE-BEEP!
SKREEEEEEE!!!

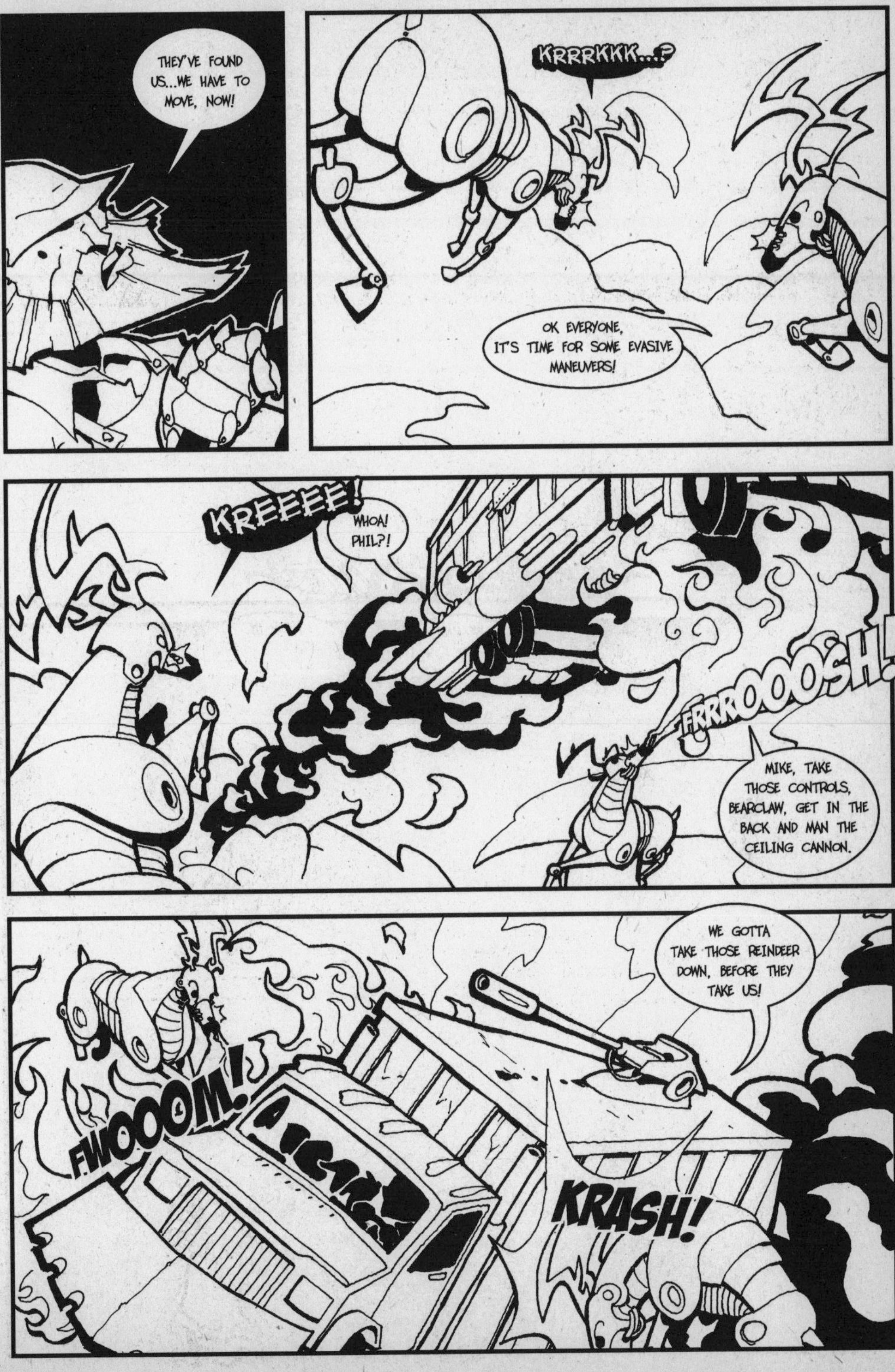
THEY'VE FOUND US...WE HAVE TO MOVE, NOW!
KRRRKKK...?
OK EVERYONE, IT'S TIME FOR SOME EVASIVE MANEUVERS!
KREEEEE!
WHOA! PHIL?!
FRRROOOOSH!
MIKE, TAKE THOSE CONTROLS, BEARCLAW, GET IN THE BACK AND MAN THE CEILING CANNON.
WE GOTTA TAKE THOSE REINDEER DOWN, BEFORE THEY TAKE US!
FWOOOM!
KRASH!

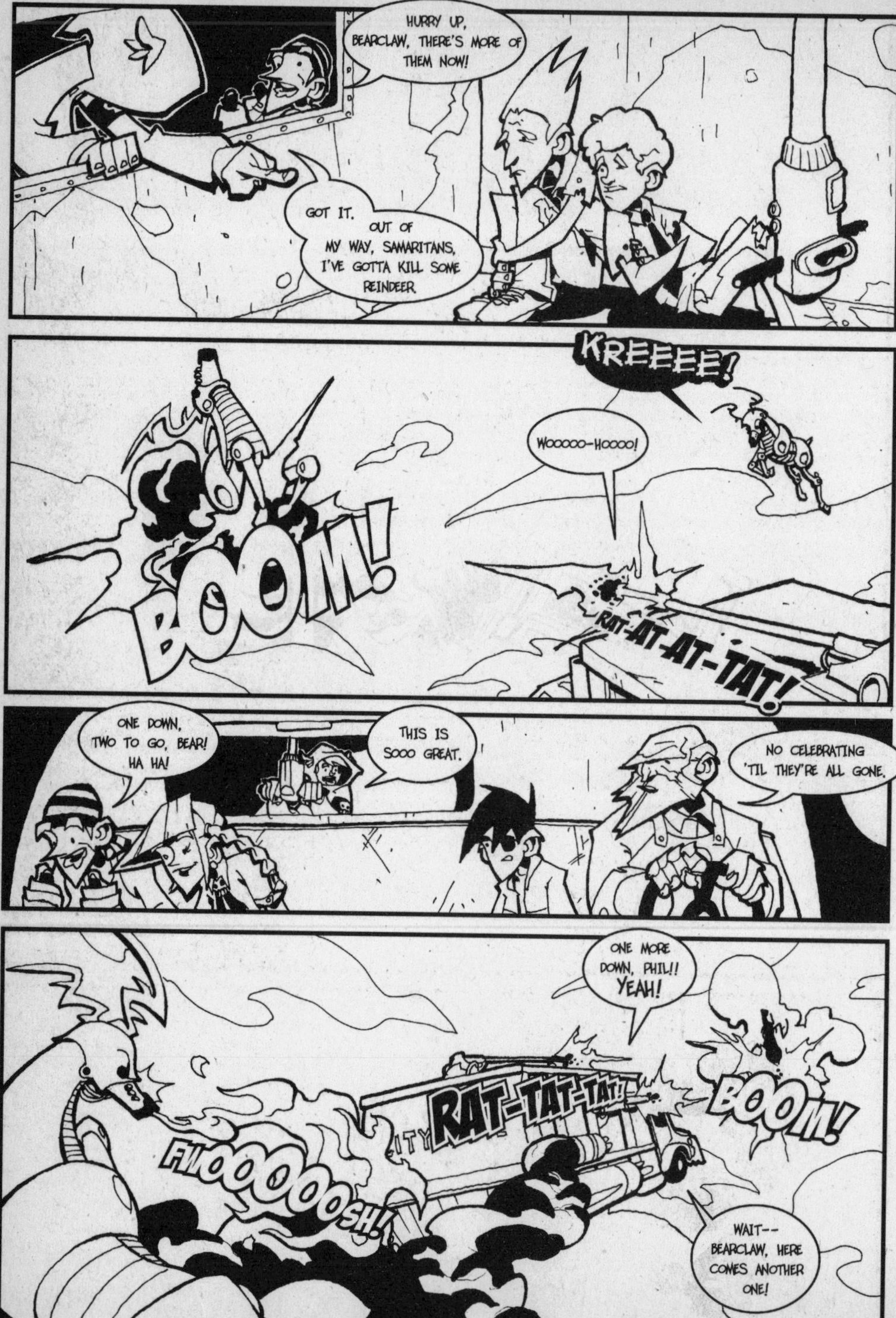
HURRY UP, BEARCLAW, THERE'S MORE OF THEM NOW!
GOT IT.
OUT OF MY WAY, SAMARITANS, I'VE GOTTA KILL SOME REINDEER
KREEEEE!
WOOOOO-HOOOO!
BOOM!
RAT-AT-AT-TAT!
ONE DOWN, TWO TO GO, BEAR! HA HA!
THIS IS SOOO GREAT.
NO CELEBRATING 'TIL THEY'RE ALL GONE.
ONE MORE DOWN, PHIL!! YEAH!
RAT-TAT-TAT!
BOOM!
FWOOOOOOSH!
WAIT-- BEARCLAW, HERE COMES ANOTHER ONE!

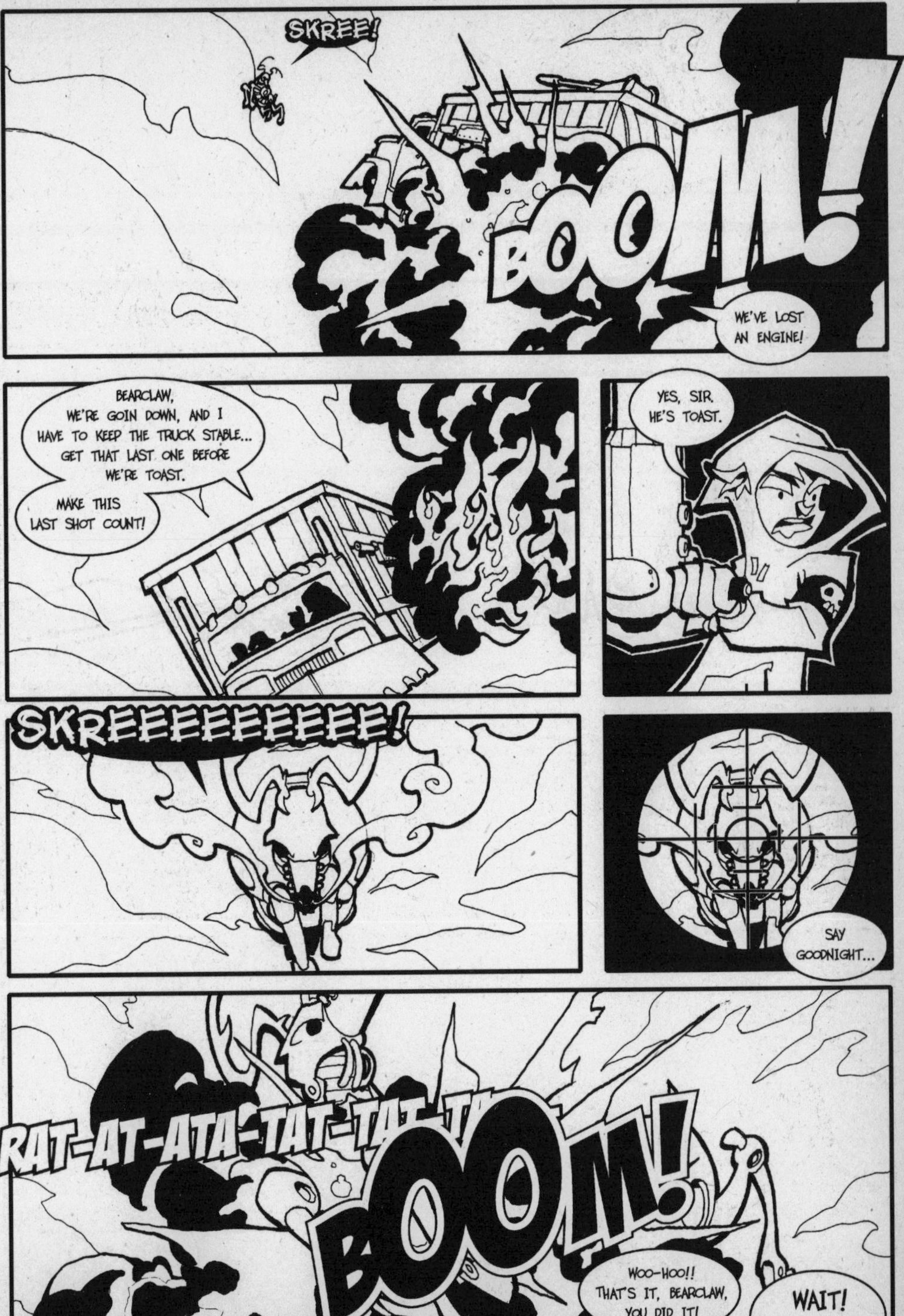

SKREE!
BOOM!
WE'VE LOST AN ENGINE!
BEARCLAW, WE'RE GOIN DOWN, AND I HAVE TO KEEP THE TRUCK STABLE... GET THAT LAST ONE BEFORE WE'RE TOAST.
MAKE THIS LAST SHOT COUNT!
YES, SIR. HE'S TOAST.
SKREEEEEEEEEEE!
SAY GOODNIGHT...
RAT-AT-ATA-TAT-TAT-TA
BOOM!
WOO-HOO!! THAT'S IT, BEARCLAW, YOU DID IT!
WAIT! OH NO!

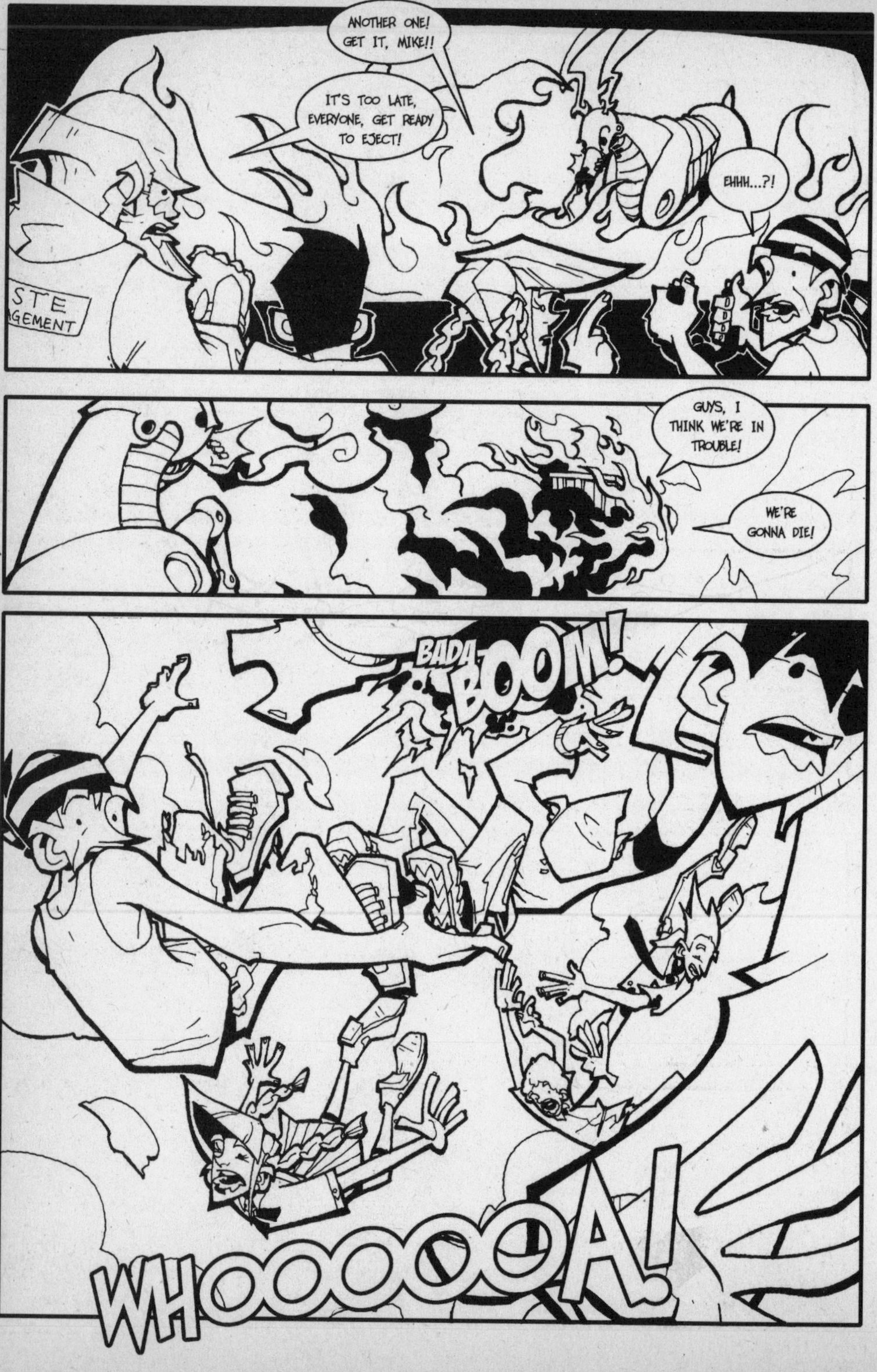
ANOTHER ONE! GET IT, MIKE!!
IT'S TOO LATE, EVERYONE, GET READY TO EJECT!
EHHH...?!
STE
AGEMENT
GUYS, I THINK WE'RE IN TROUBLE!
WE'RE GONNA DIE!
BADA BOOM!
WHOOOOOOA!

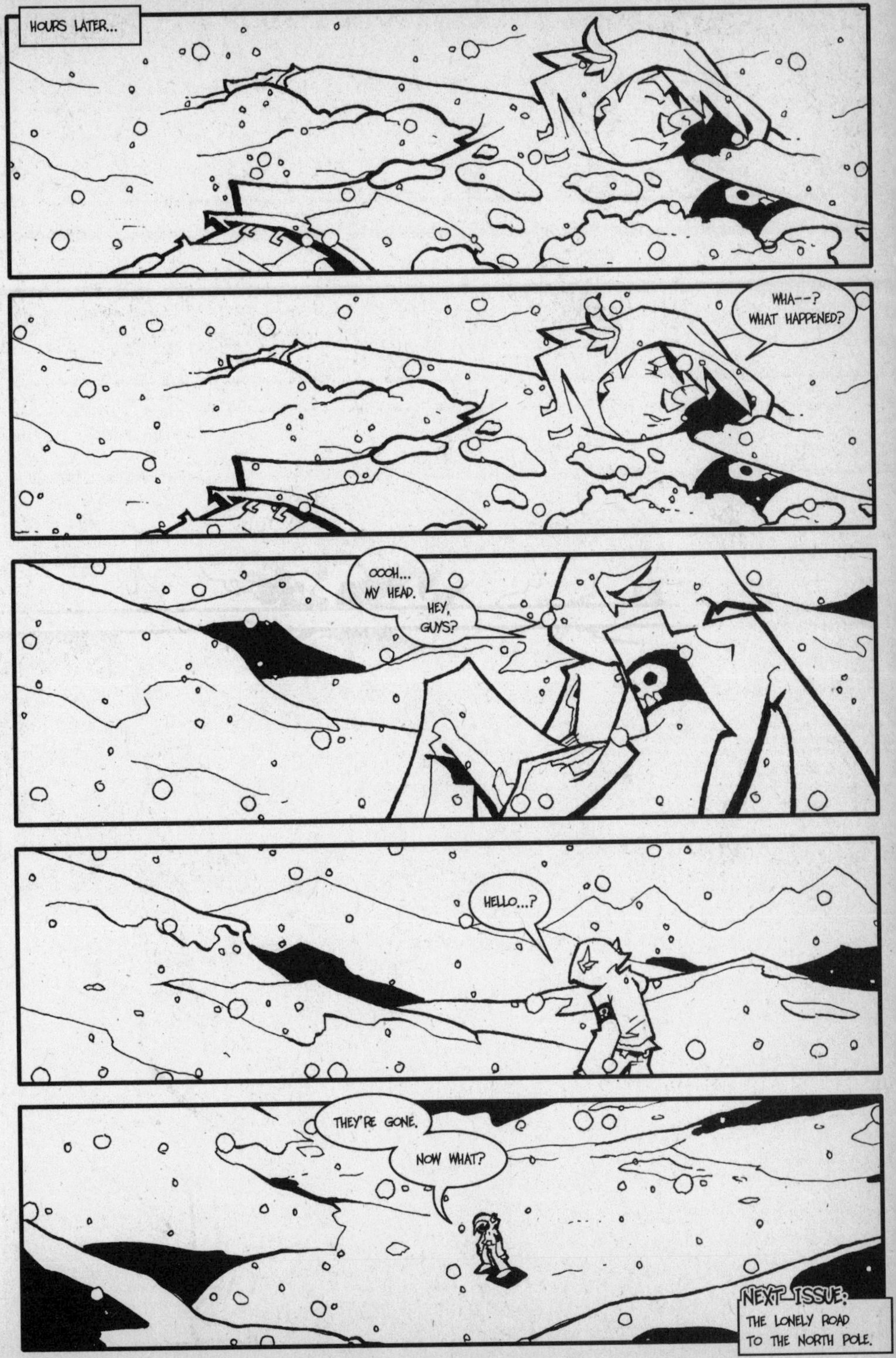
HOURS LATER...
WHA--? WHAT HAPPENED?
OOOH... MY HEAD.
HEY, GUYS?
HELLO...?
THEY'RE GONE.
NOW WHAT?
NEXT ISSUE:
THE LONELY ROAD TO THE NORTH POLE.

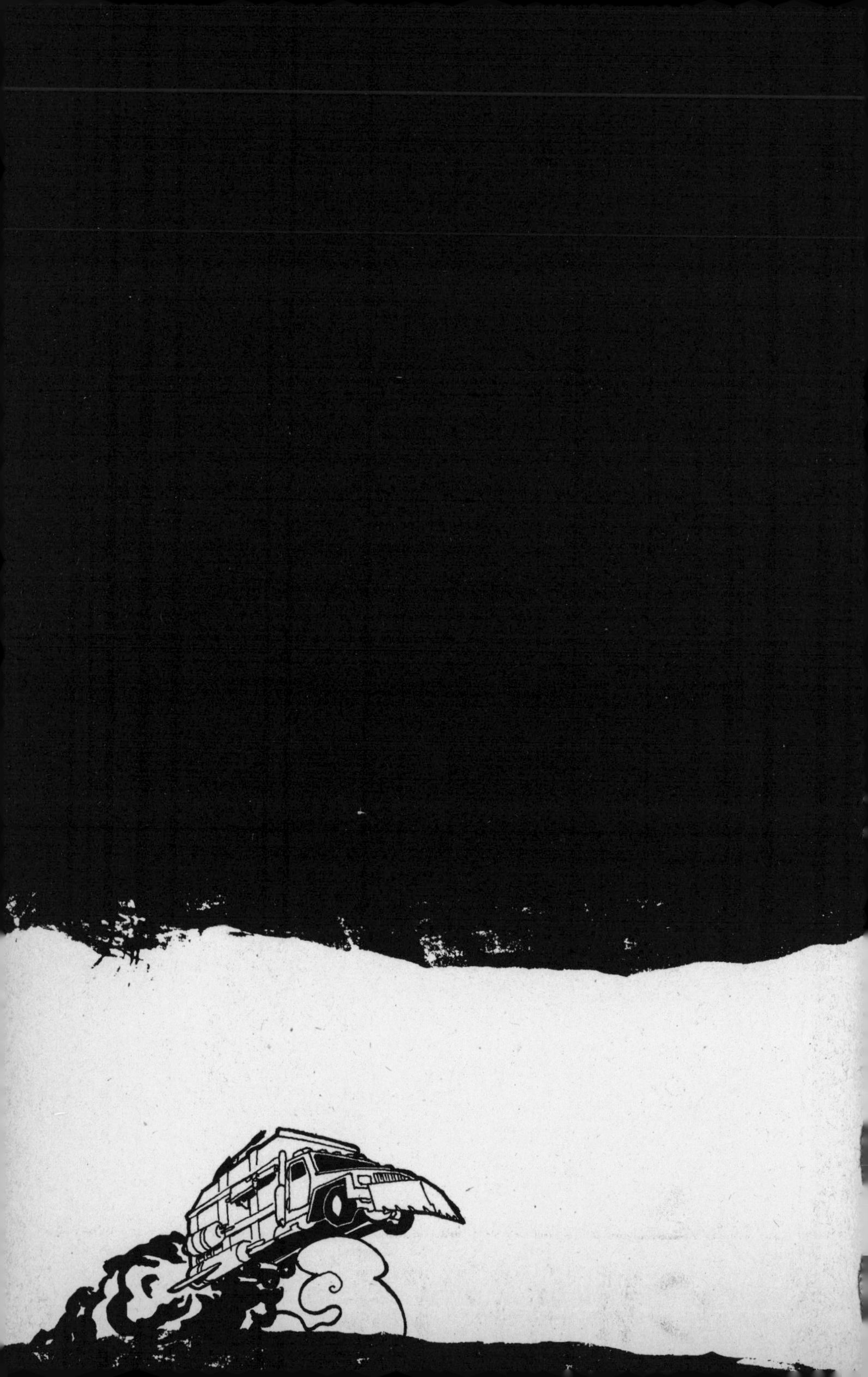

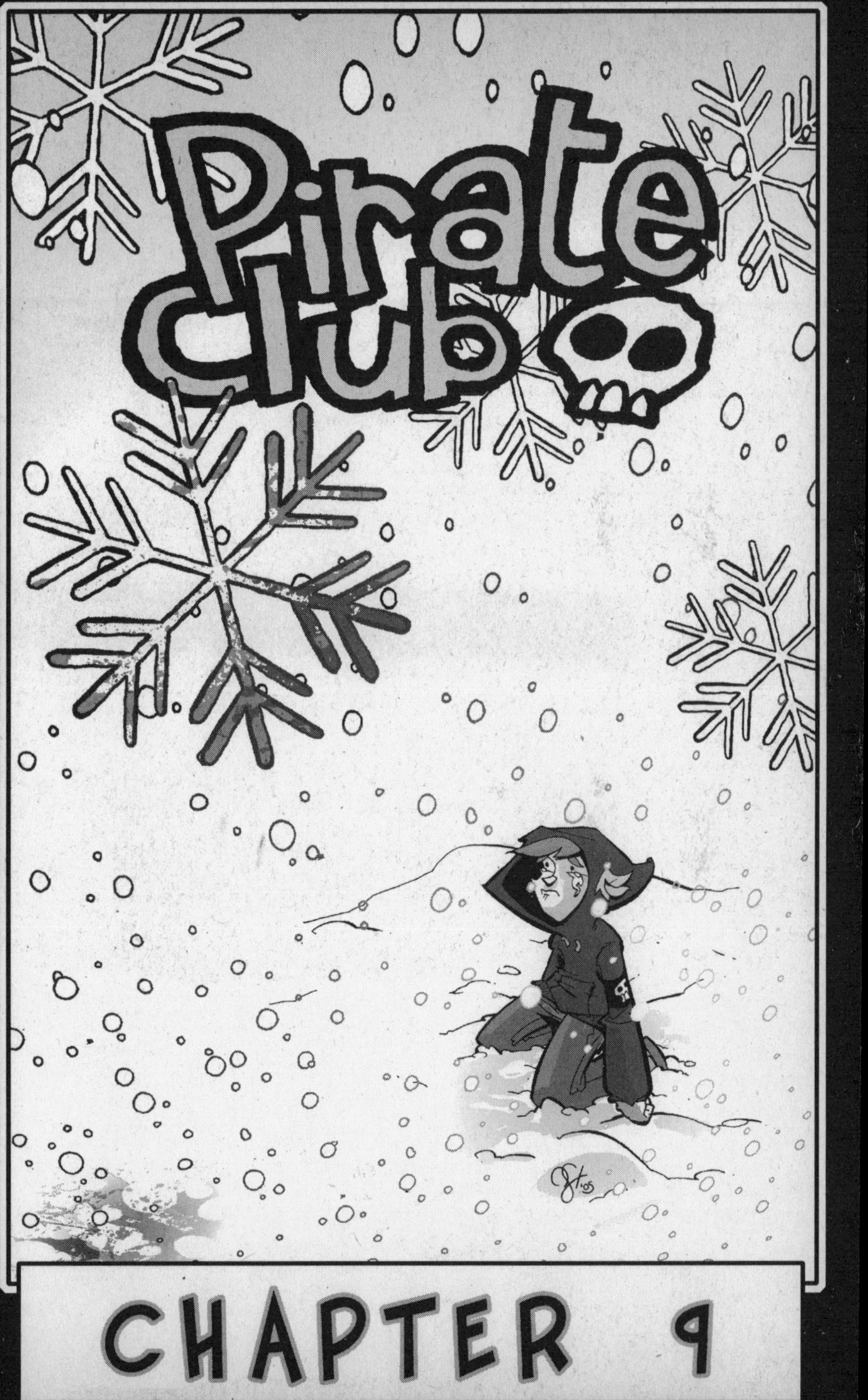
Pirate Club

# CHAPTER 9

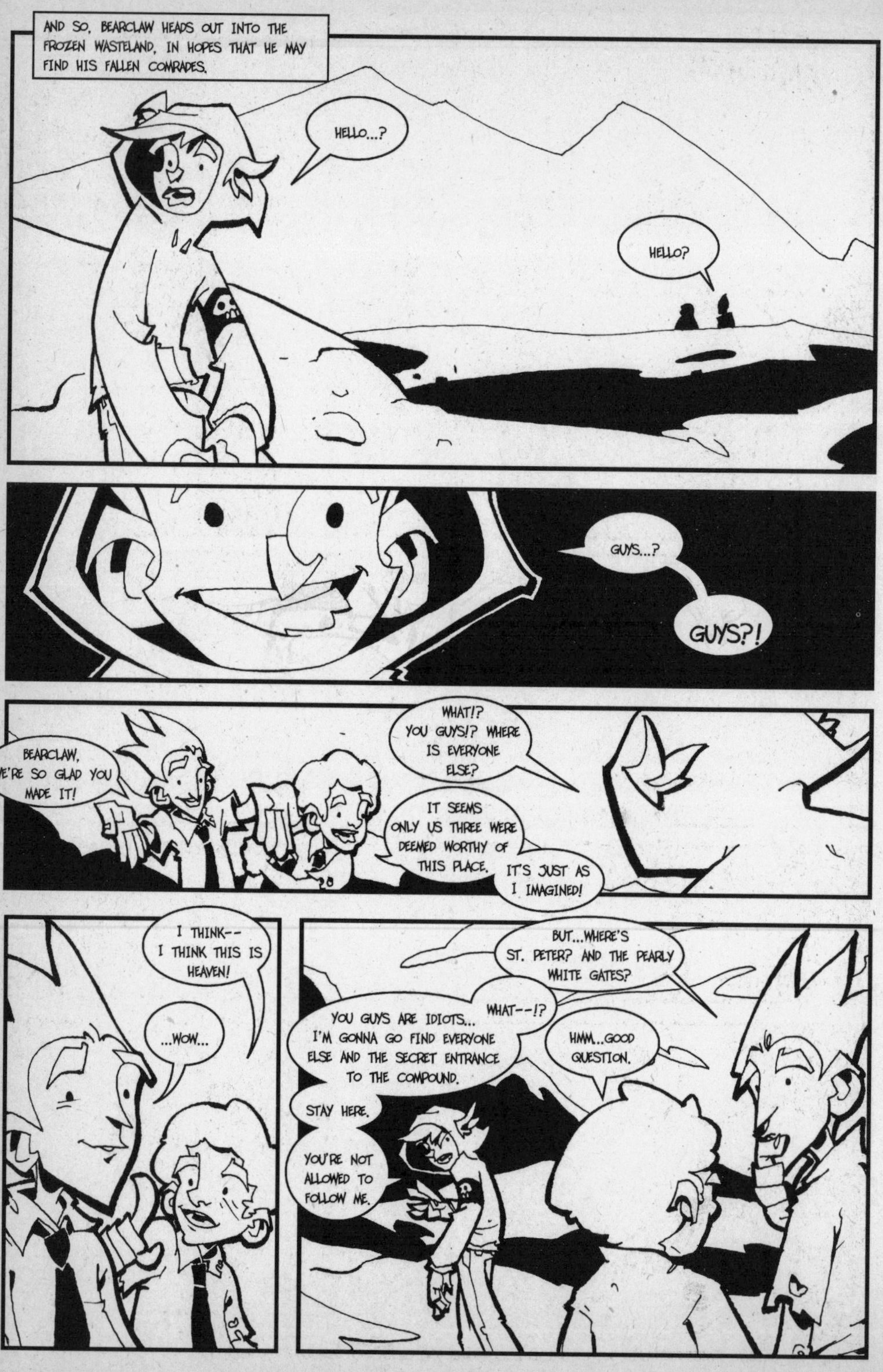
AND SO, BEARCLAW HEADS OUT INTO THE FROZEN WASTELAND, IN HOPES THAT HE MAY FIND HIS FALLEN COMRADES.
HELLO...?
HELLO?
GUYS...?
GUYS?!
BEARCLAW, WE'RE SO GLAD YOU MADE IT!
WHAT!? YOU GUYS!? WHERE IS EVERYONE ELSE?
IT SEEMS ONLY US THREE WERE DEEMED WORTHY OF THIS PLACE.
IT'S JUST AS I IMAGINED!
I THINK-- I THINK THIS IS HEAVEN!
...WOW...
BUT...WHERE'S ST. PETER? AND THE PEARLY WHITE GATES?
WHAT--!?
YOU GUYS ARE IDIOTS... I'M GONNA GO FIND EVERYONE ELSE AND THE SECRET ENTRANCE TO THE COMPOUND.
HMM..GOOD QUESTION.
STAY HERE.
YOU'RE NOT ALLOWED TO FOLLOW ME.

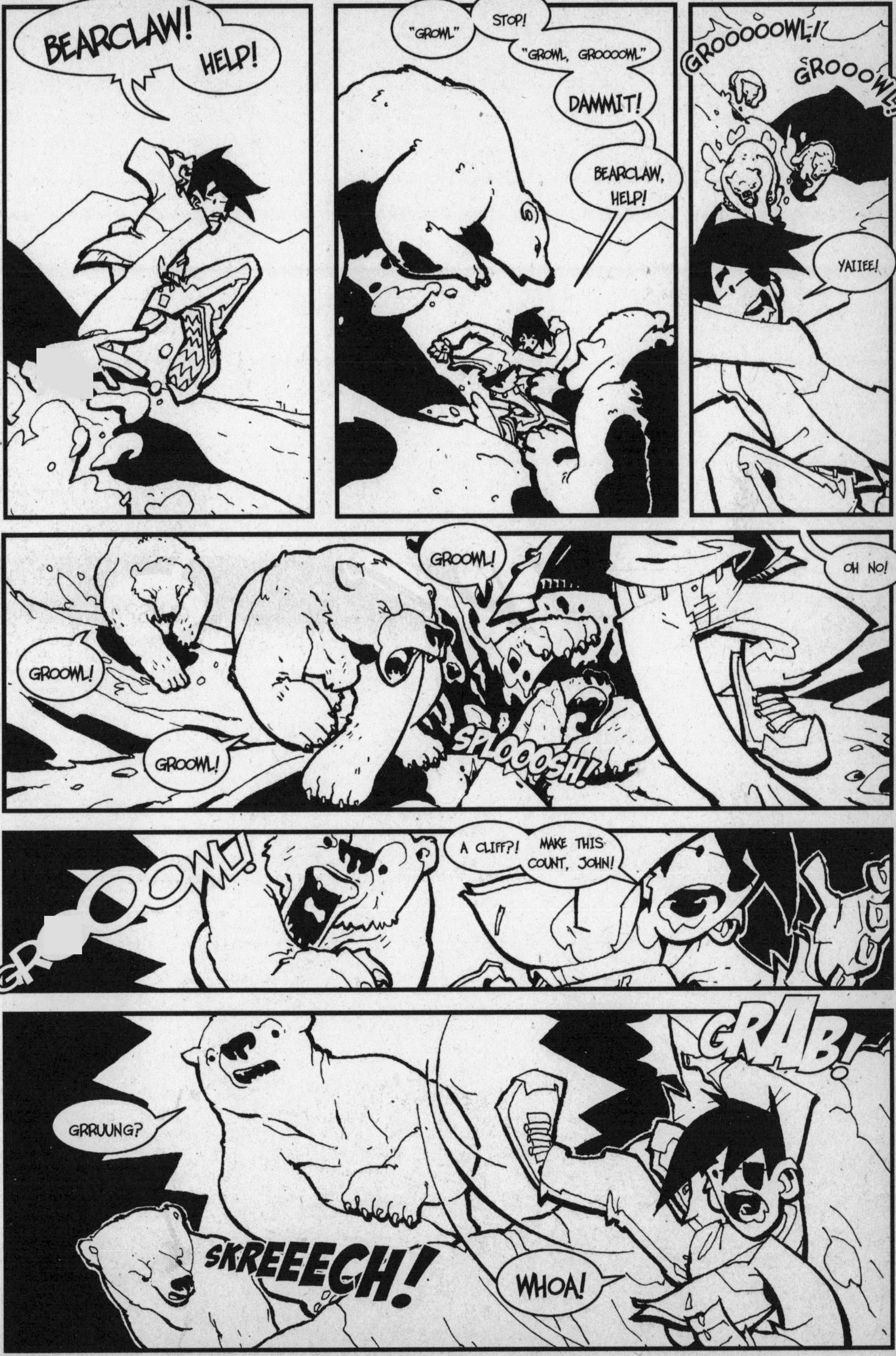
BEARCLAW!
HELP!
"GROWL"
STOP!
"GROWL, GROOOOWL"
DAMMIT!
BEARCLAW, HELP!
GROOOOOWL!
GROOOWL!
YAIIEE!
GROOWL!
GROOWL!
GROOWL!
SPLOOOSH!
OH NO!
A CLIFF?!
MAKE THIS COUNT, JOHN!
GRAB!
GRRUUNG?
SKREEECH!
WHOA!

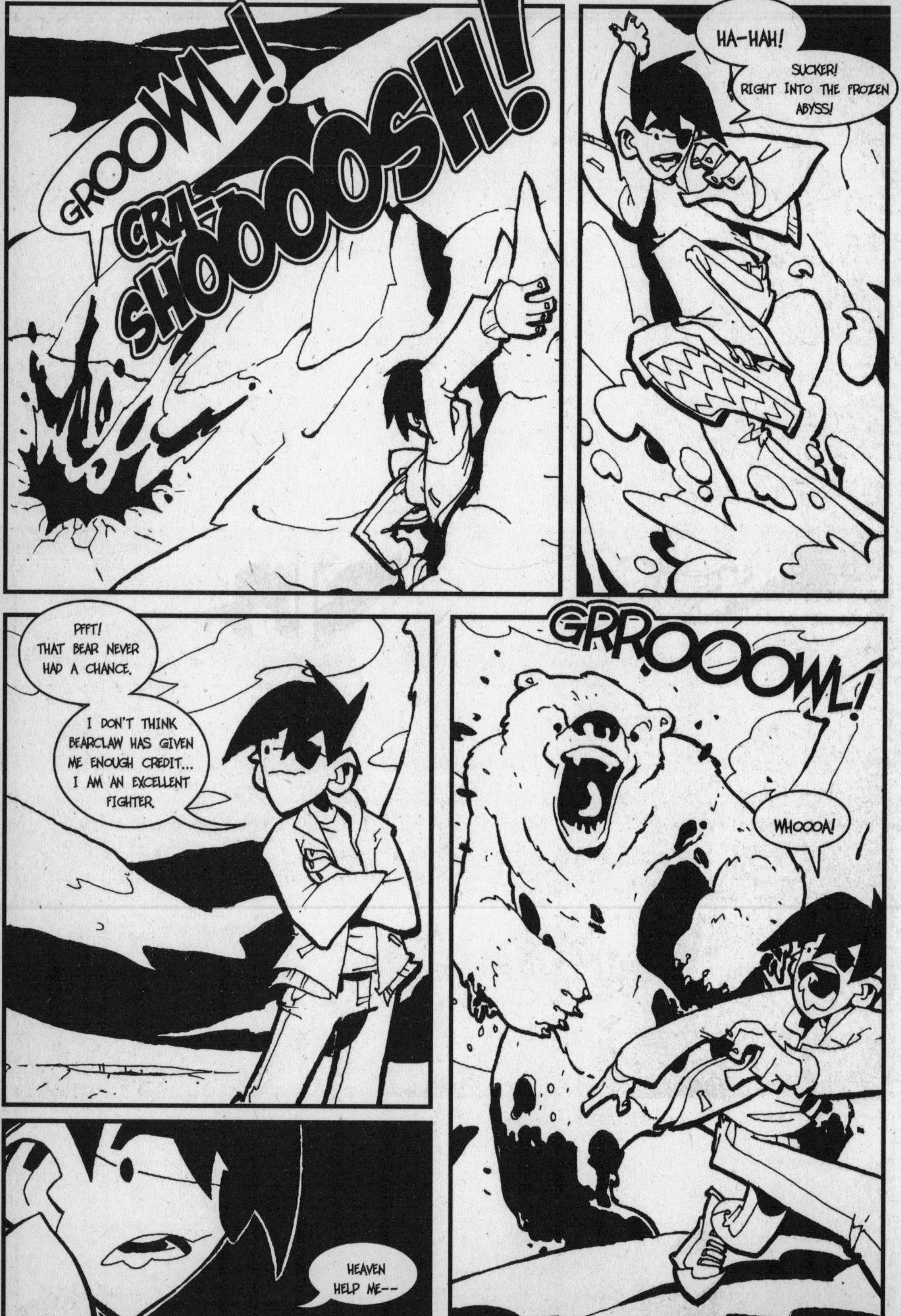
GROOWL!
CRA-SHOOOOOSH!
HA-HAH!
SUCKER! RIGHT INTO THE FROZEN ABYSS!
PFFT! THAT BEAR NEVER HAD A CHANCE.
I DON'T THINK BEARCLAW HAS GIVEN ME ENOUGH CREDIT... I AM AN EXCELLENT FIGHTER.
HEAVEN HELP ME--
GRROOOOWL!
WHOOOA!

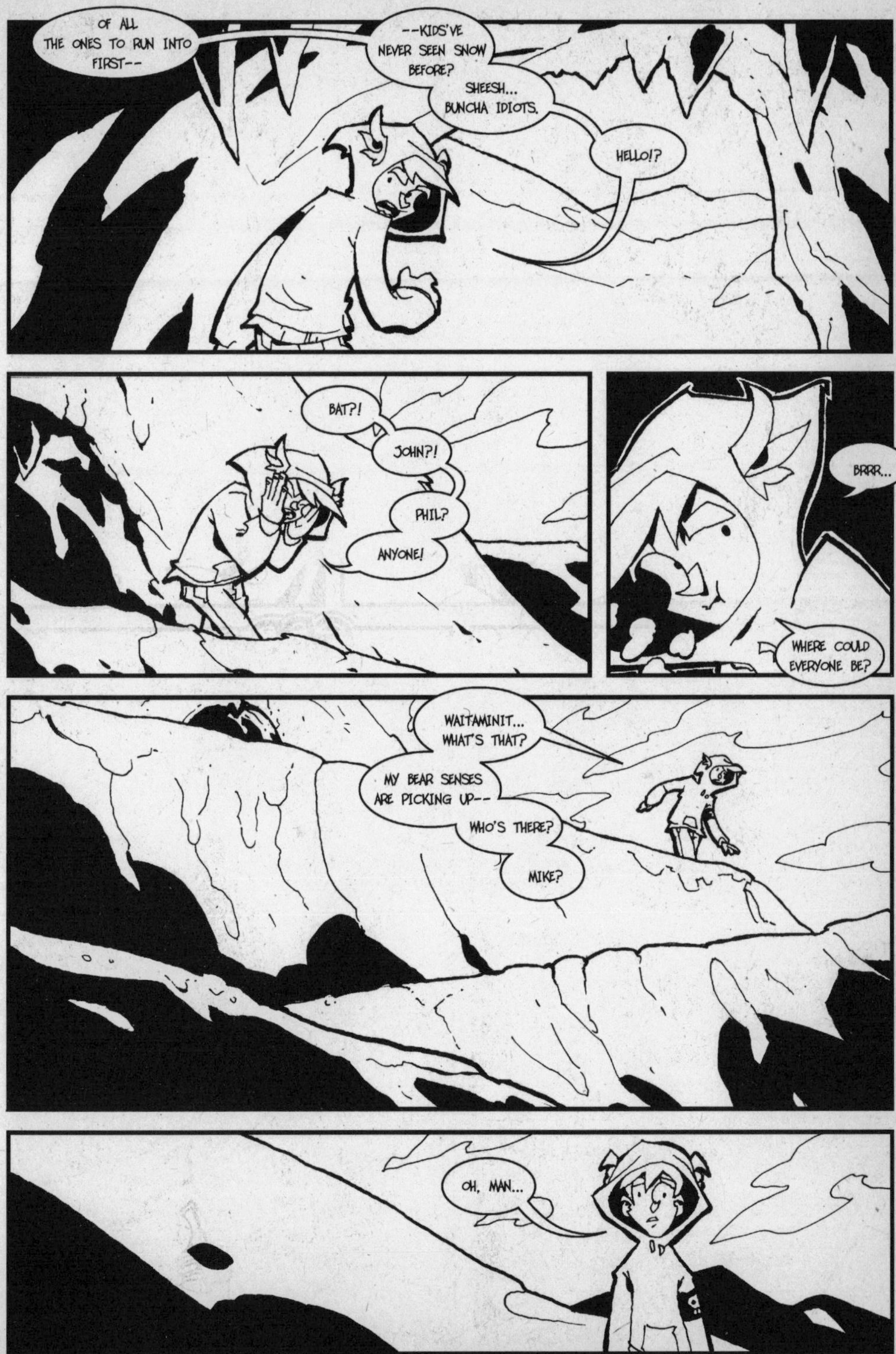

OF ALL THE ONES TO RUN INTO FIRST--
--KIDS'VE NEVER SEEN SNOW BEFORE?
SHEESH... BUNCHA IDIOTS.
HELLO!?
BAT?!
JOHN?!
PHIL?
ANYONE!
BRRR...
WHERE COULD EVERYONE BE?
WAITAMINIT... WHAT'S THAT?
MY BEAR SENSES ARE PICKING UP--
WHO'S THERE?
MIKE?
OH, MAN...

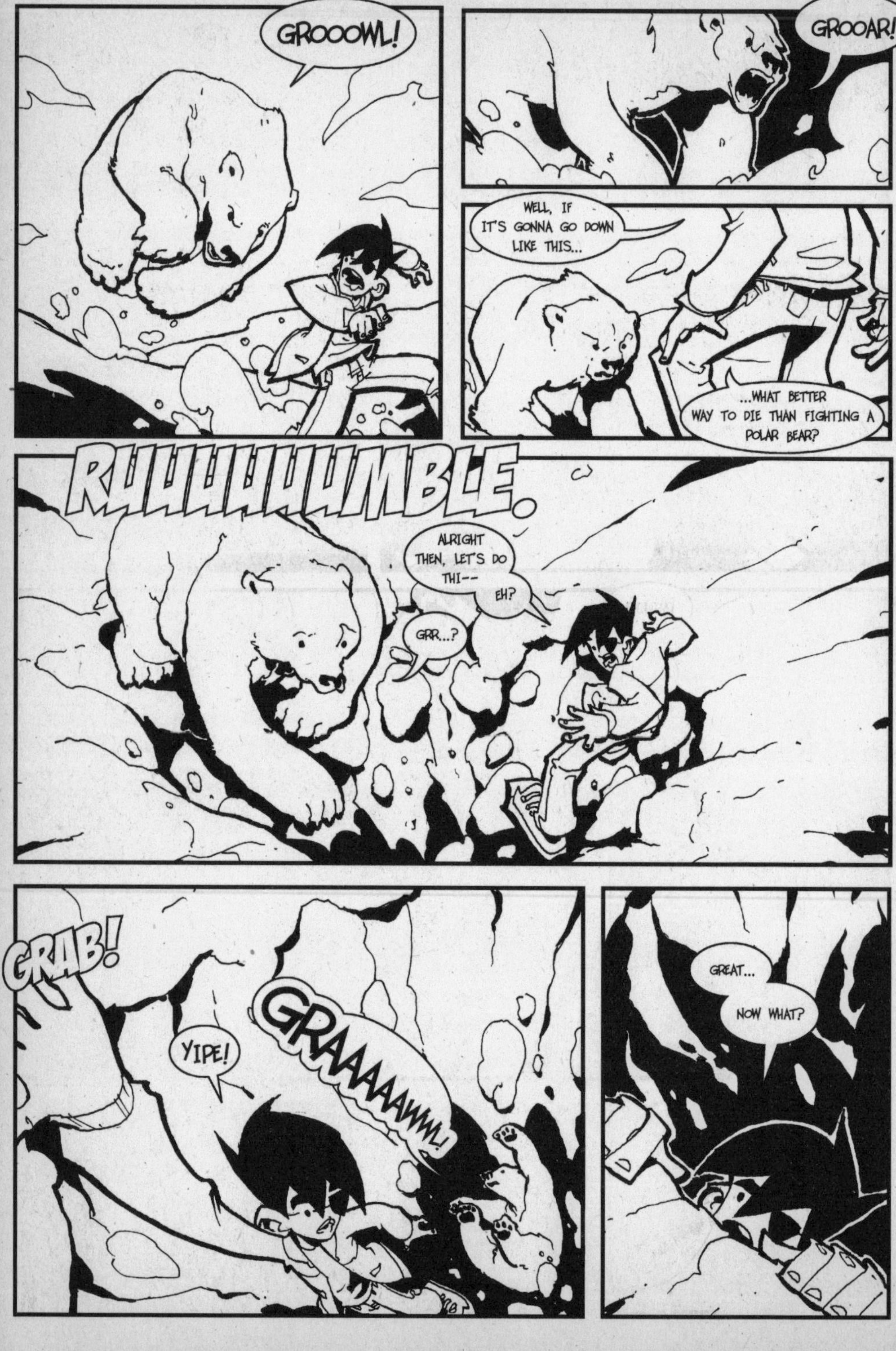
GROOOWL!
GROOAR!
WELL, IF IT'S GONNA GO DOWN LIKE THIS...
...WHAT BETTER WAY TO DIE THAN FIGHTING A POLAR BEAR?
RUUUUUUUMBLE.
ALRIGHT THEN, LET'S DO THI--
EH?
GRR...?
GRAB!
YIPE!
GRAAAAAWWL!
GREAT...
NOW WHAT?

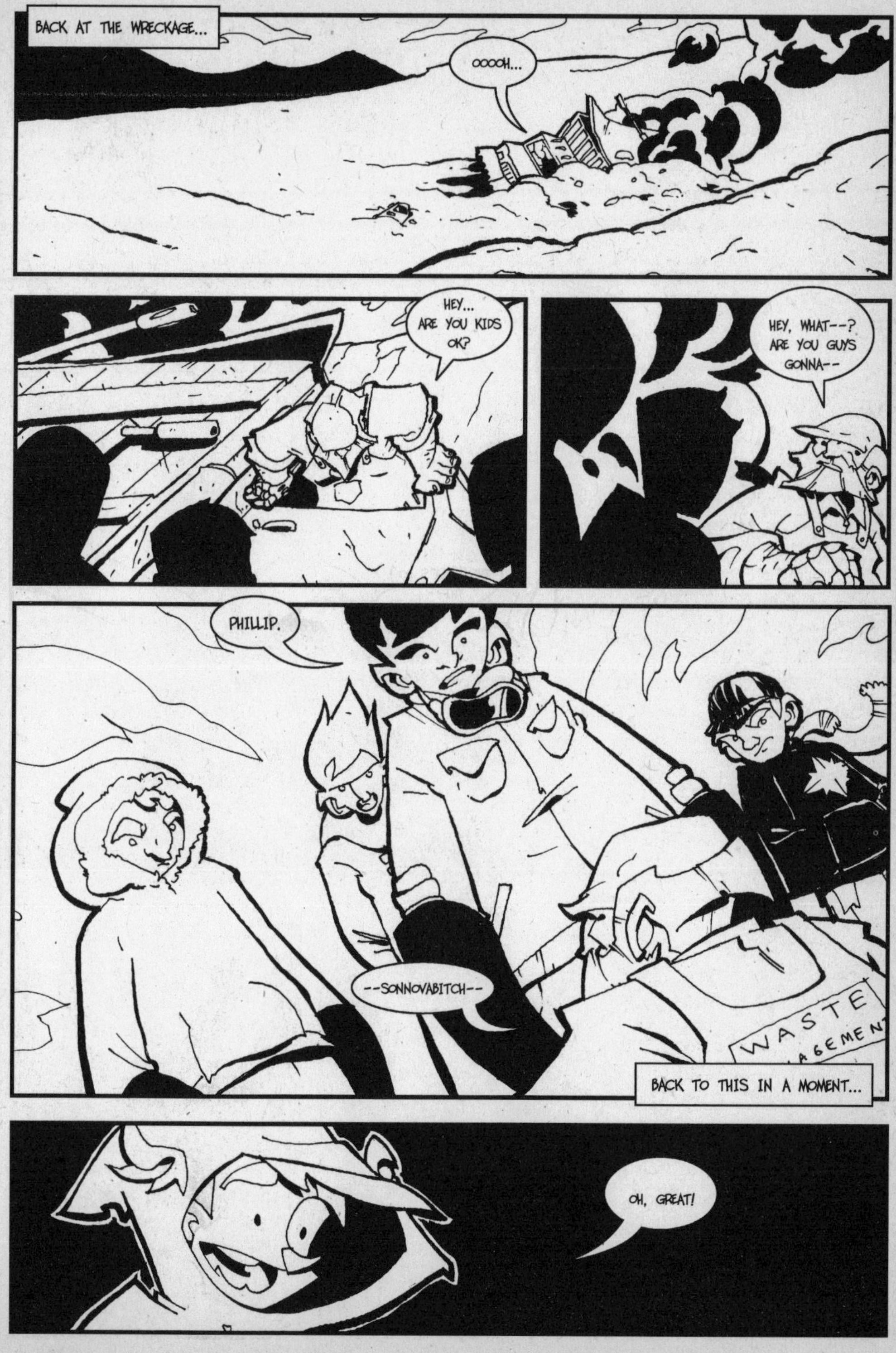
BACK AT THE WRECKAGE...
OOOOH...
HEY... ARE YOU KIDS OK?
HEY, WHAT--? ARE YOU GUYS GONNA--
PHILLIP.
--SONNOVABITCH--
WASTE
AGEMENT
BACK TO THIS IN A MOMENT...
OH, GREAT!

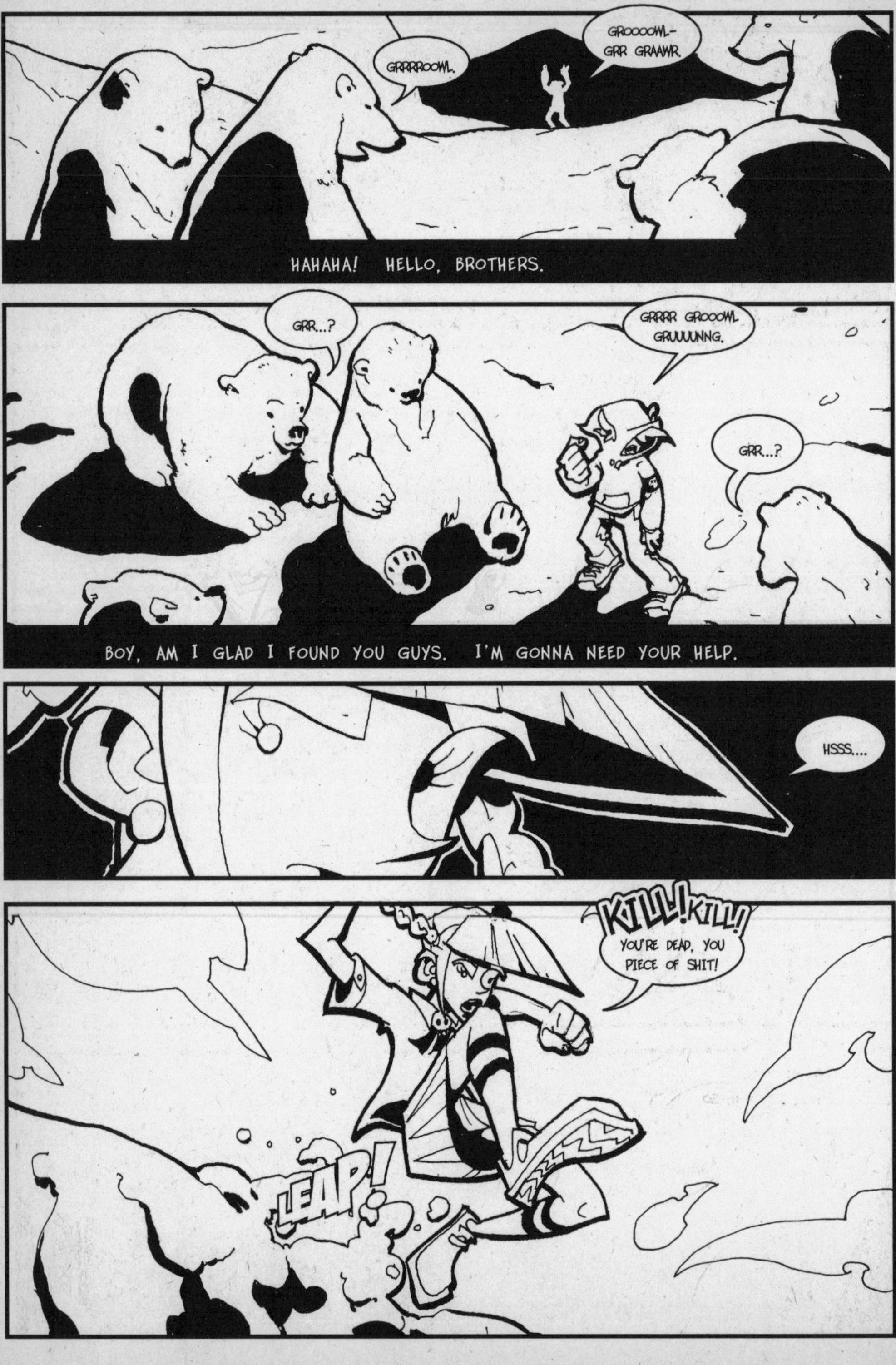
GRRRROOWL.
GROOOOWL-GRR GRAAWR.
HAHAHA! HELLO, BROTHERS.
GRR...?
GRRRR GROOOWL GRUUUUNG.
GRR...?
BOY, AM I GLAD I FOUND YOU GUYS. I'M GONNA NEED YOUR HELP.
HSSS....
KILL! KILL!
YOU'RE DEAD, YOU PIECE OF SHIT!
LEAP!

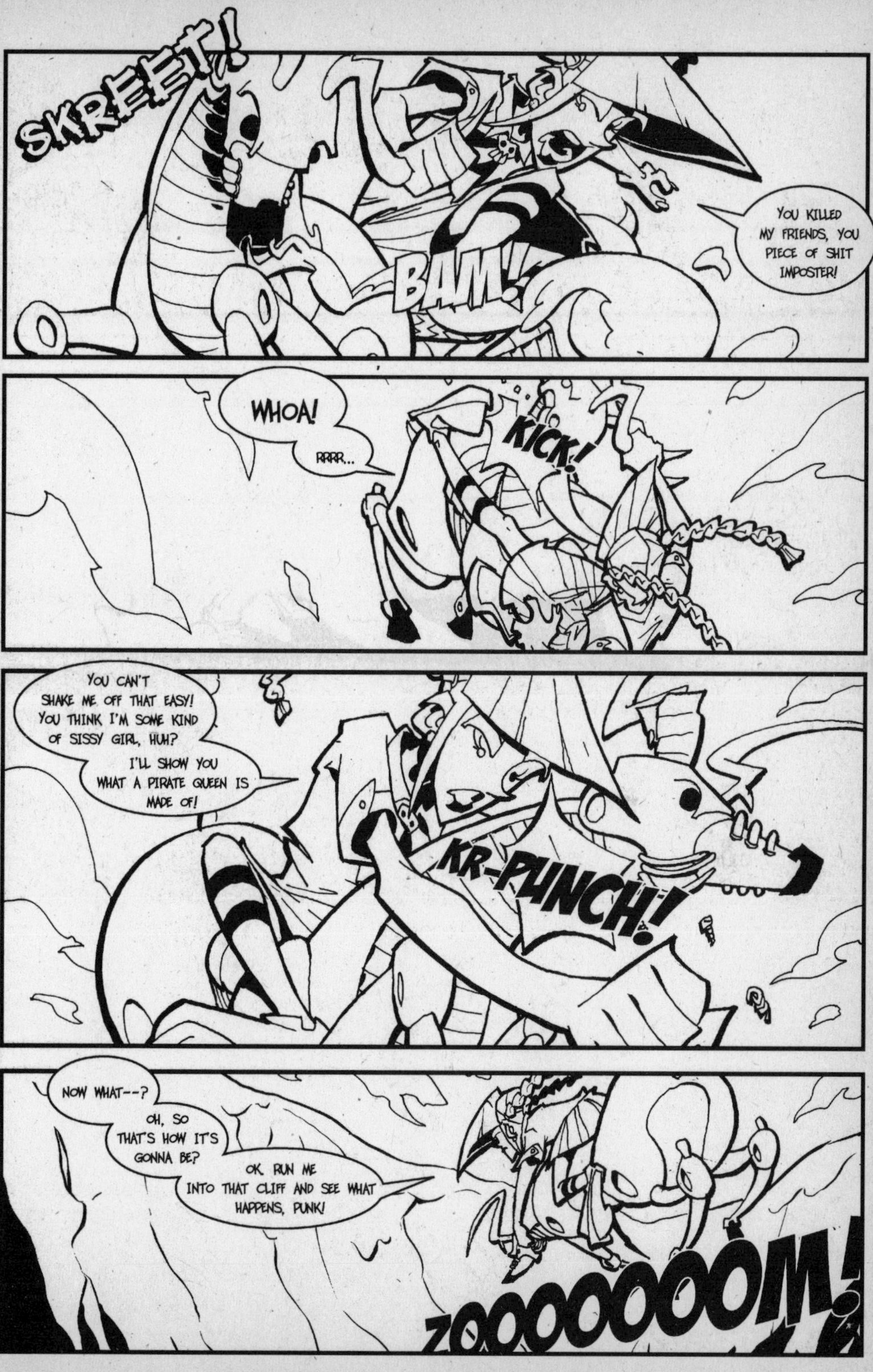
SKREEET!
YOU KILLED MY FRIENDS, YOU PIECE OF SHIT IMPOSTER!
BAM!
WHOA!
RRRR...
KICK!
YOU CAN'T SHAKE ME OFF THAT EASY! YOU THINK I'M SOME KIND OF SISSY GIRL, HUH?
I'LL SHOW YOU WHAT A PIRATE QUEEN IS MADE OF!
KR-PUNCH!
NOW WHAT--?
OH, SO THAT'S HOW IT'S GONNA BE?
OK. RUN ME INTO THAT CLIFF AND SEE WHAT HAPPENS, PUNK!
ZOOOOOOOOM!

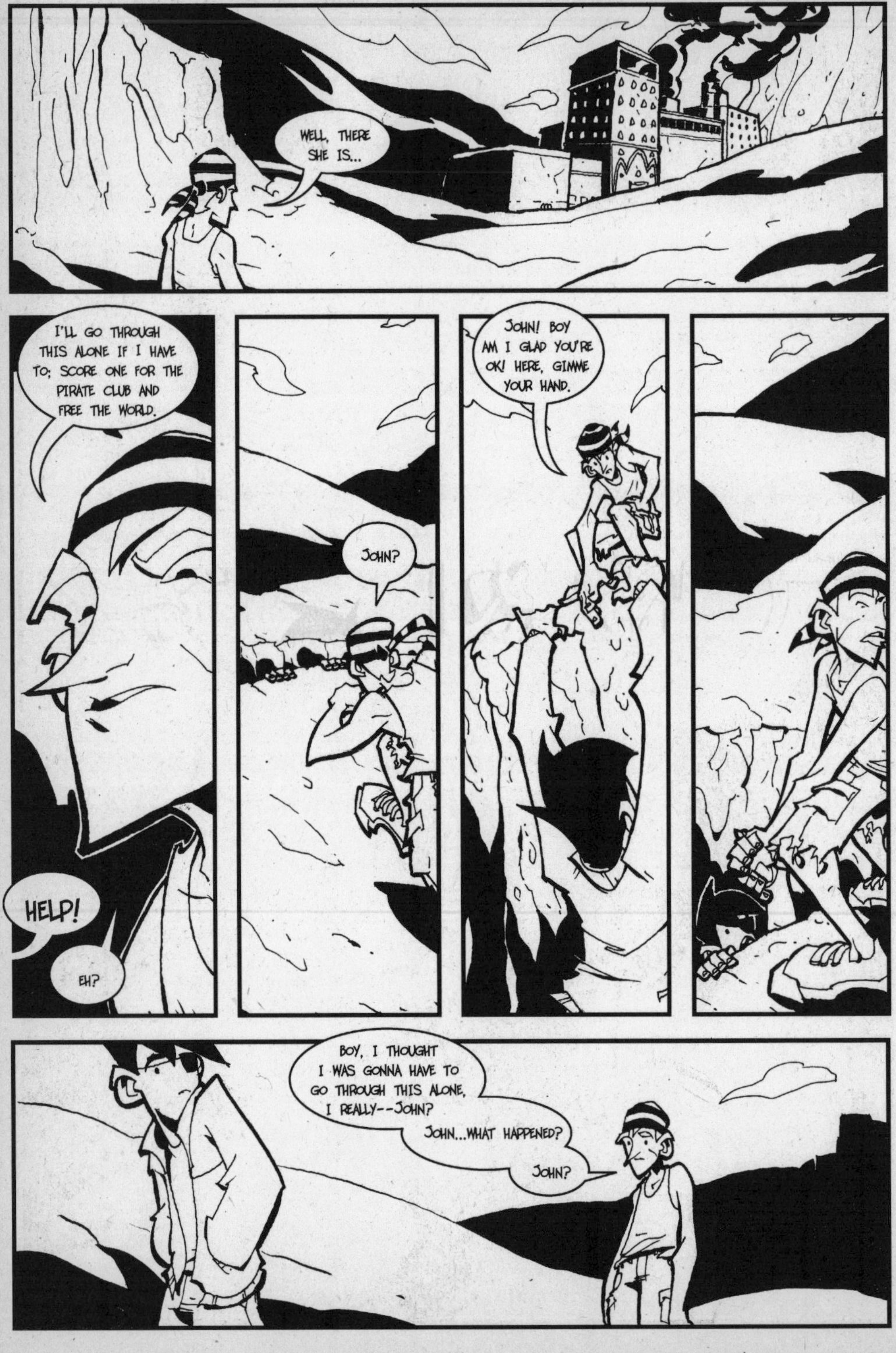
WELL, THERE SHE IS...
I'LL GO THROUGH THIS ALONE IF I HAVE TO; SCORE ONE FOR THE PIRATE CLUB AND FREE THE WORLD.
HELP!
EH?
JOHN?
JOHN! BOY AM I GLAD YOU'RE OK! HERE, GIMME YOUR HAND.
BOY, I THOUGHT I WAS GONNA HAVE TO GO THROUGH THIS ALONE, I REALLY--JOHN?
JOHN...WHAT HAPPENED?
JOHN?

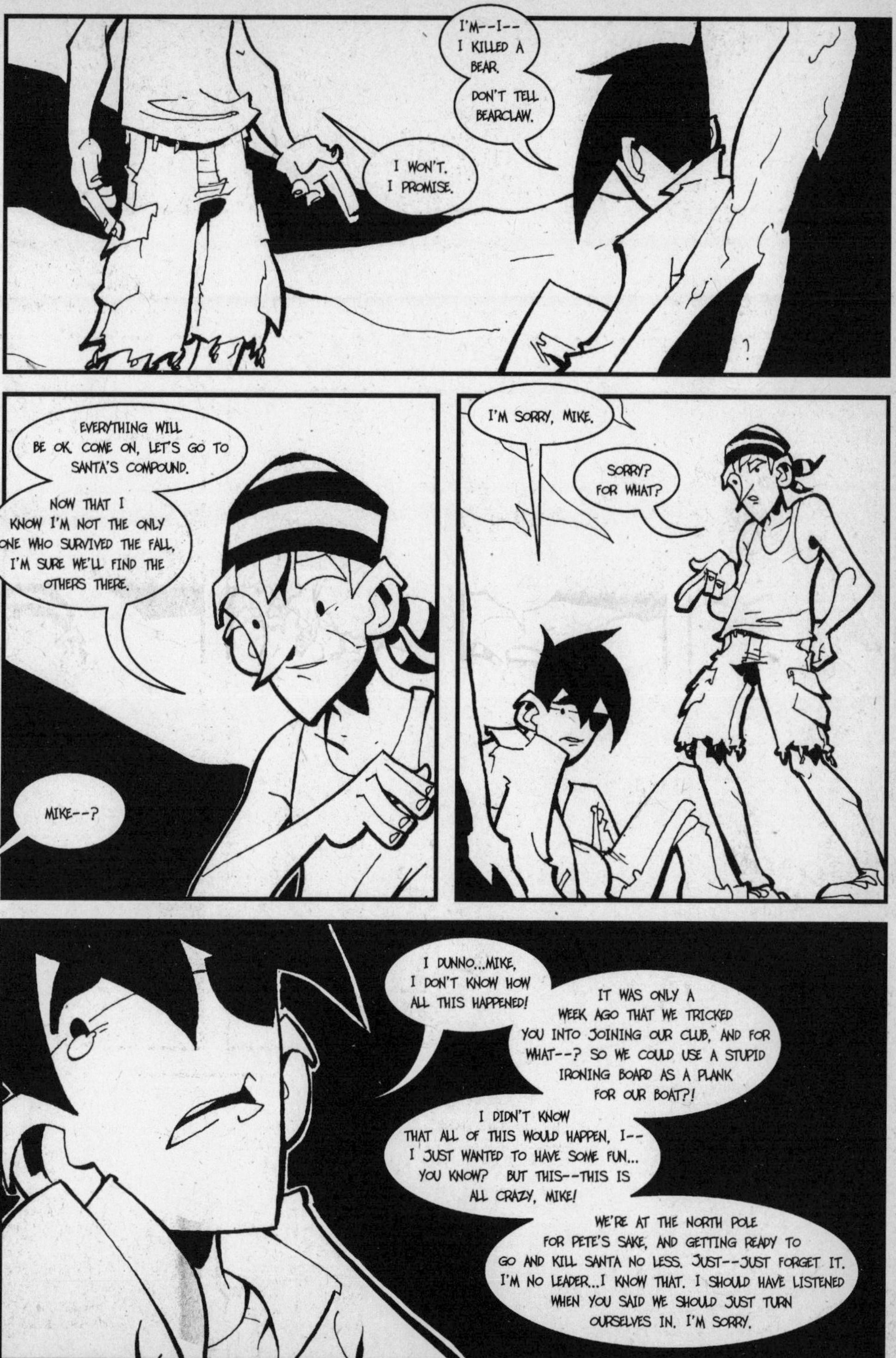

I'M--I--
I KILLED A BEAR.
DON'T TELL BEARCLAW.
I WON'T. I PROMISE.
EVERYTHING WILL BE OK. COME ON, LET'S GO TO SANTA'S COMPOUND.
NOW THAT I KNOW I'M NOT THE ONLY ONE WHO SURVIVED THE FALL, I'M SURE WE'LL FIND THE OTHERS THERE.
MIKE--?
I'M SORRY, MIKE.
SORRY? FOR WHAT?
I DUNNO...MIKE, I DON'T KNOW HOW ALL THIS HAPPENED!
IT WAS ONLY A WEEK AGO THAT WE TRICKED YOU INTO JOINING OUR CLUB, AND FOR WHAT--? SO WE COULD USE A STUPID IRONING BOARD AS A PLANK FOR OUR BOAT?!
I DIDN'T KNOW THAT ALL OF THIS WOULD HAPPEN, I-- I JUST WANTED TO HAVE SOME FUN... YOU KNOW? BUT THIS--THIS IS ALL CRAZY, MIKE!
WE'RE AT THE NORTH POLE FOR PETE'S SAKE, AND GETTING READY TO GO AND KILL SANTA NO LESS. JUST--JUST FORGET IT. I'M NO LEADER...I KNOW THAT. I SHOULD HAVE LISTENED WHEN YOU SAID WE SHOULD JUST TURN OURSELVES IN. I'M SORRY.

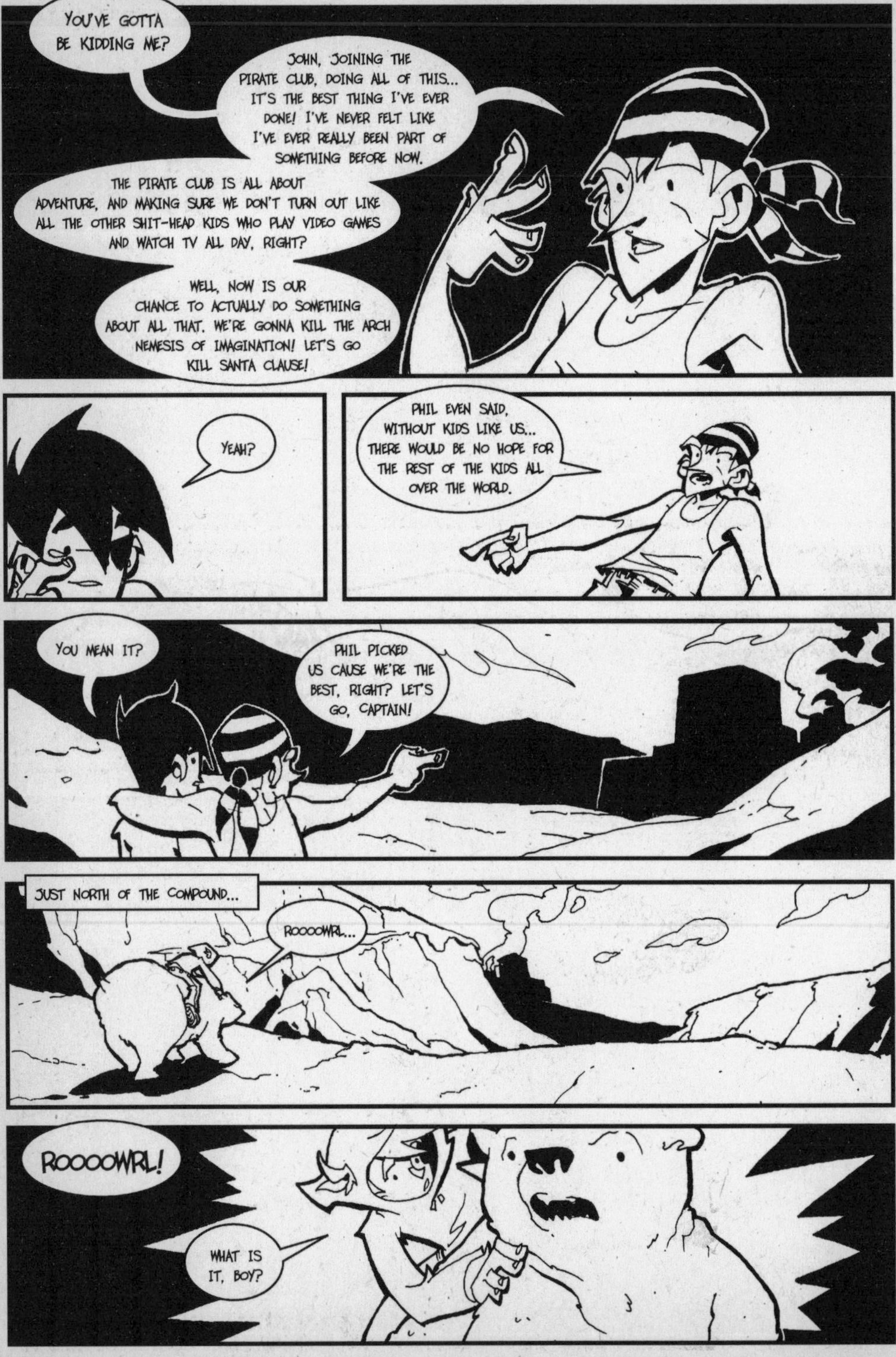
YOU'VE GOTTA BE KIDDING ME?
JOHN, JOINING THE PIRATE CLUB, DOING ALL OF THIS... IT'S THE BEST THING I'VE EVER DONE! I'VE NEVER FELT LIKE I'VE EVER REALLY BEEN PART OF SOMETHING BEFORE NOW.
THE PIRATE CLUB IS ALL ABOUT ADVENTURE, AND MAKING SURE WE DON'T TURN OUT LIKE ALL THE OTHER SHIT-HEAD KIDS WHO PLAY VIDEO GAMES AND WATCH TV ALL DAY, RIGHT?
WELL, NOW IS OUR CHANCE TO ACTUALLY DO SOMETHING ABOUT ALL THAT. WE'RE GONNA KILL THE ARCH NEMESIS OF IMAGINATION! LET'S GO KILL SANTA CLAUSE!
YEAH?
PHIL EVEN SAID, WITHOUT KIDS LIKE US... THERE WOULD BE NO HOPE FOR THE REST OF THE KIDS ALL OVER THE WORLD.
YOU MEAN IT?
PHIL PICKED US CAUSE WE'RE THE BEST, RIGHT? LET'S GO, CAPTAIN!
JUST NORTH OF THE COMPOUND...
ROOOOWRL...
ROOOOWRL!
WHAT IS IT, BOY?

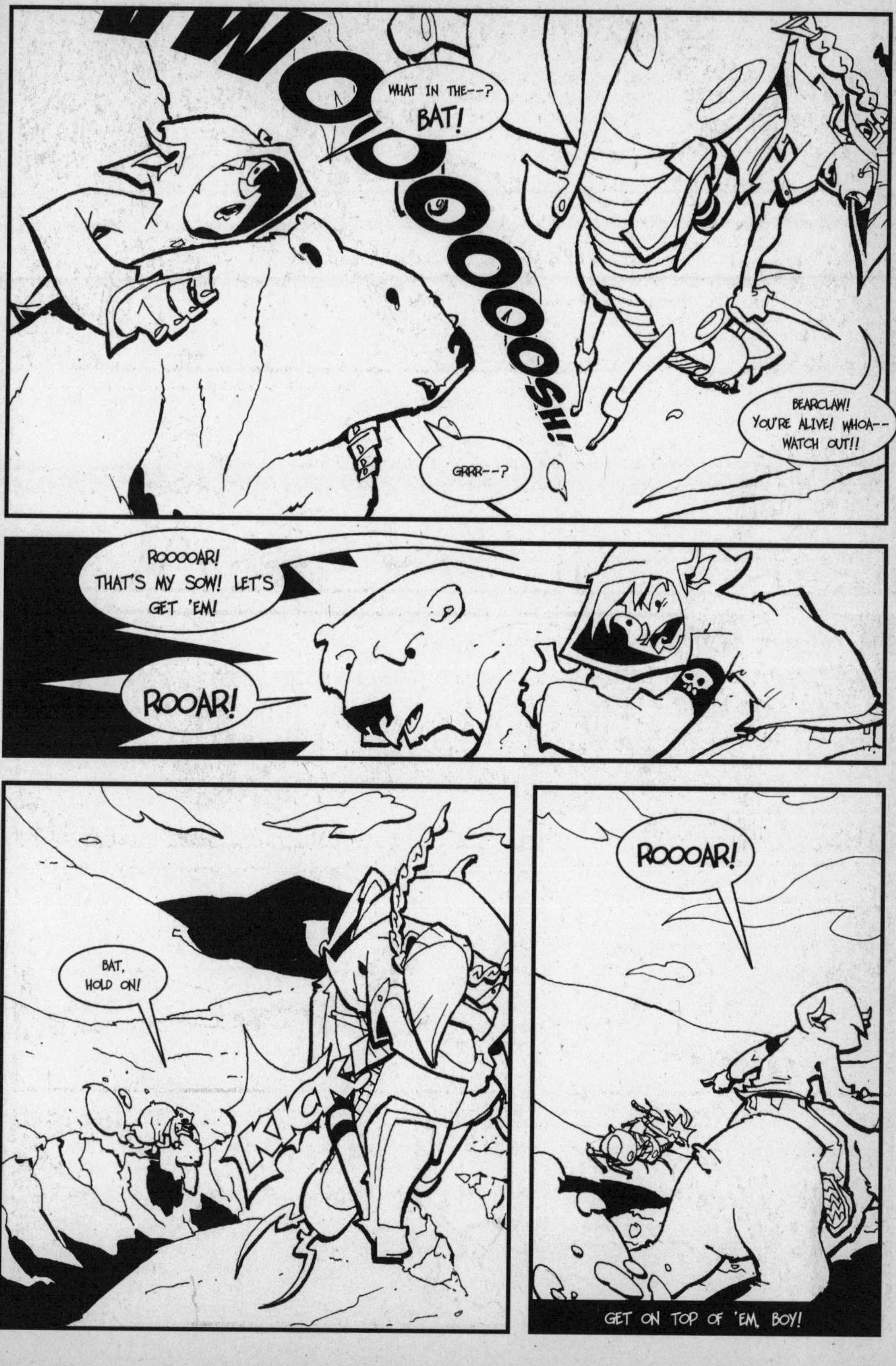
WOOOOOOOOOSH!!
WHAT IN THE--? BAT!
BEARCLAW! YOU'RE ALIVE! WHOA-- WATCH OUT!!
GRRR--?
ROOOOAR! THAT'S MY SOW! LET'S GET 'EM!
ROOAR!
BAT, HOLD ON!
KICK
ROOOAR!
GET ON TOP OF 'EM, BOY!

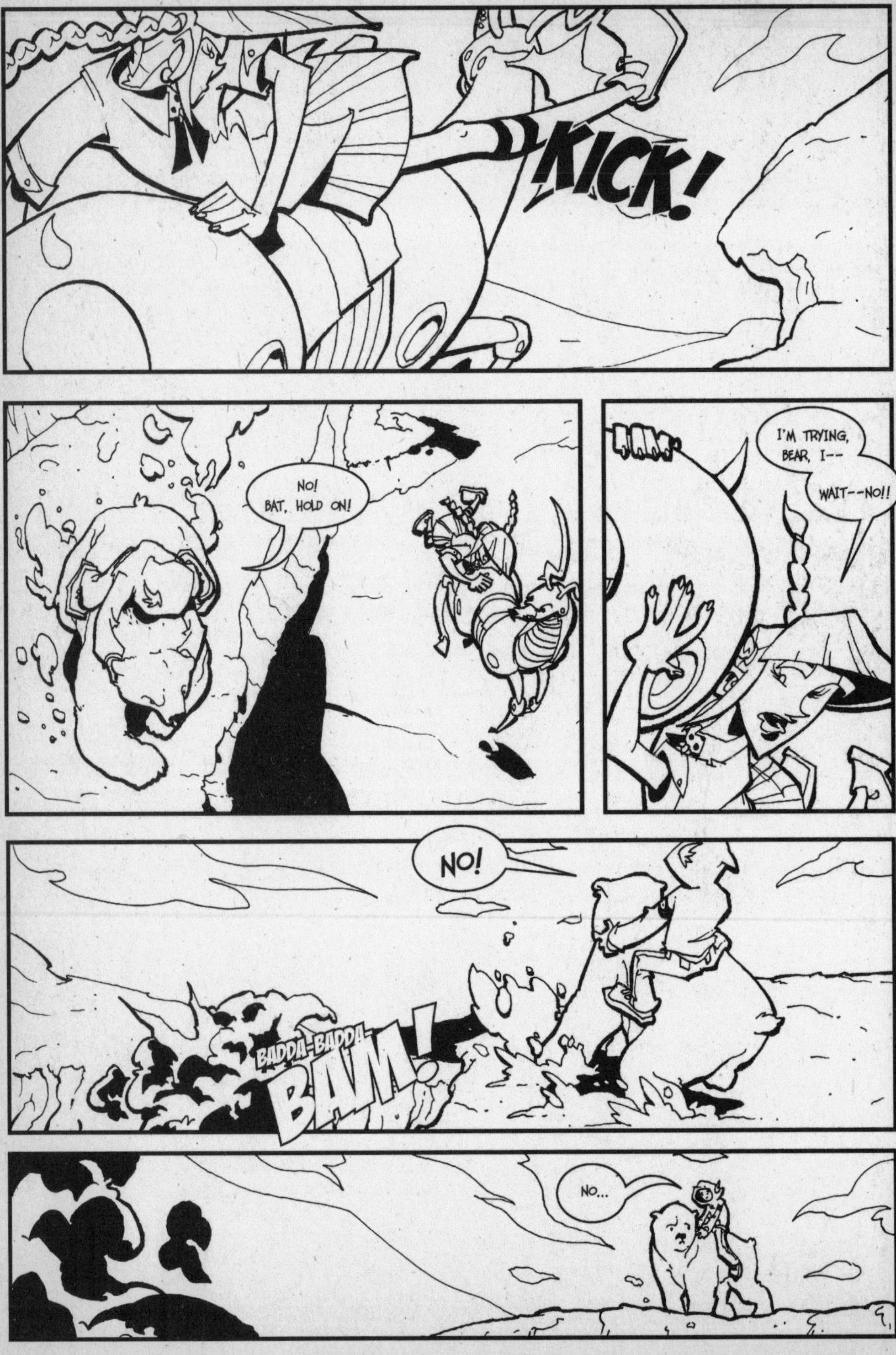
KICK!
NO! BAT, HOLD ON!
I'M TRYING, BEAR, I--
WAIT--NO!!
NO!
BADDA-BADDA-BAM!
NO...

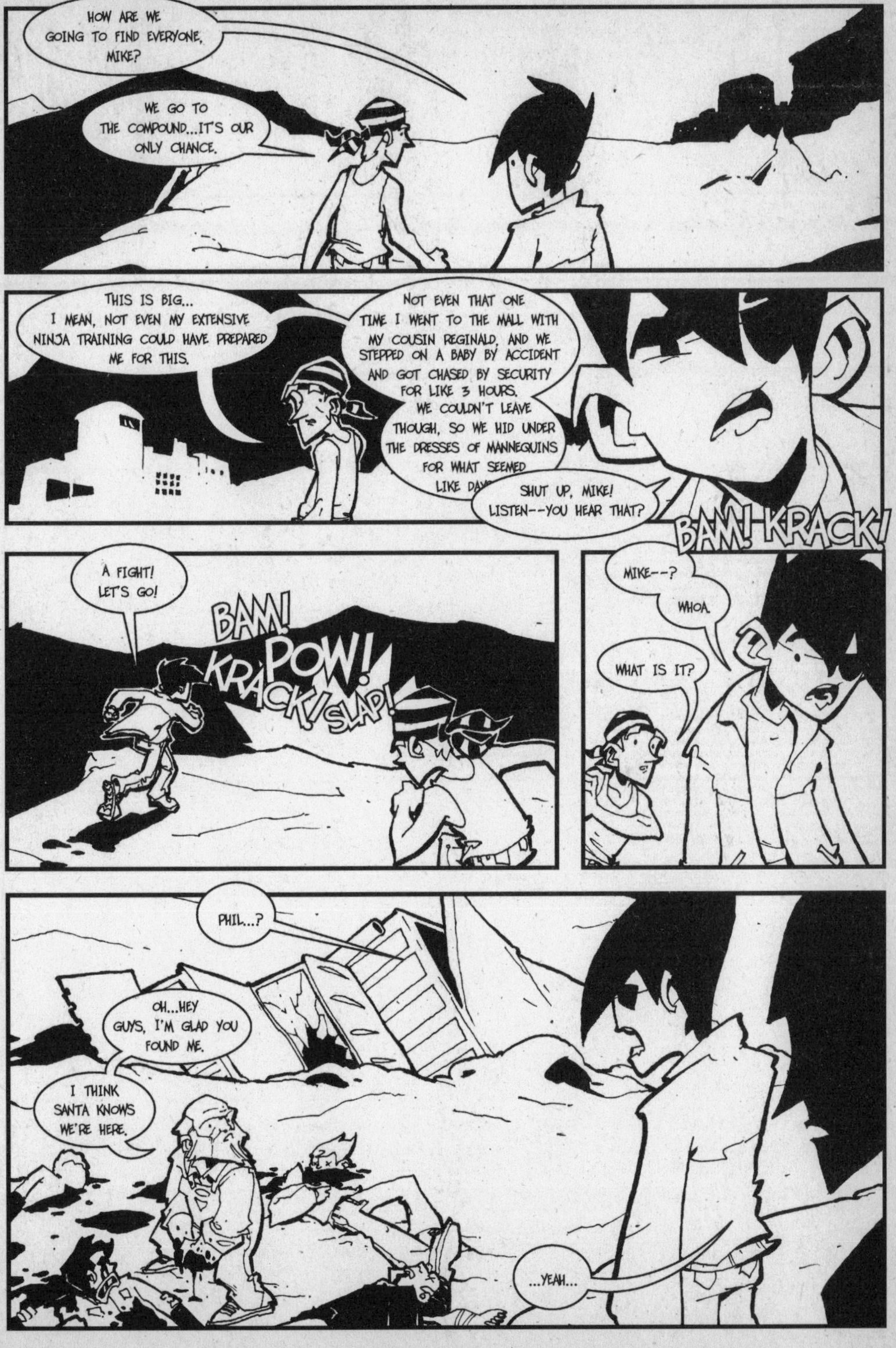

HOW ARE WE GOING TO FIND EVERYONE, MIKE?
WE GO TO THE COMPOUND...IT'S OUR ONLY CHANCE.
THIS IS BIG... I MEAN, NOT EVEN MY EXTENSIVE NINJA TRAINING COULD HAVE PREPARED ME FOR THIS.
NOT EVEN THAT ONE TIME I WENT TO THE MALL WITH MY COUSIN REGINALD, AND WE STEPPED ON A BABY BY ACCIDENT AND GOT CHASED BY SECURITY FOR LIKE 3 HOURS.
WE COULDN'T LEAVE THOUGH, SO WE HID UNDER THE DRESSES OF MANNEQUINS FOR WHAT SEEMED
SHUT UP, MIKE! LISTEN--YOU HEAR THAT?
BAM! KRACK!
A FIGHT! LET'S GO!
BAM! POW! KRACK! SLAP!
MIKE--?
WHOA.
WHAT IS IT?
PHIL...?
OH...HEY GUYS, I'M GLAD YOU FOUND ME.
I THINK SANTA KNOWS WE'RE HERE.
...YEAH...

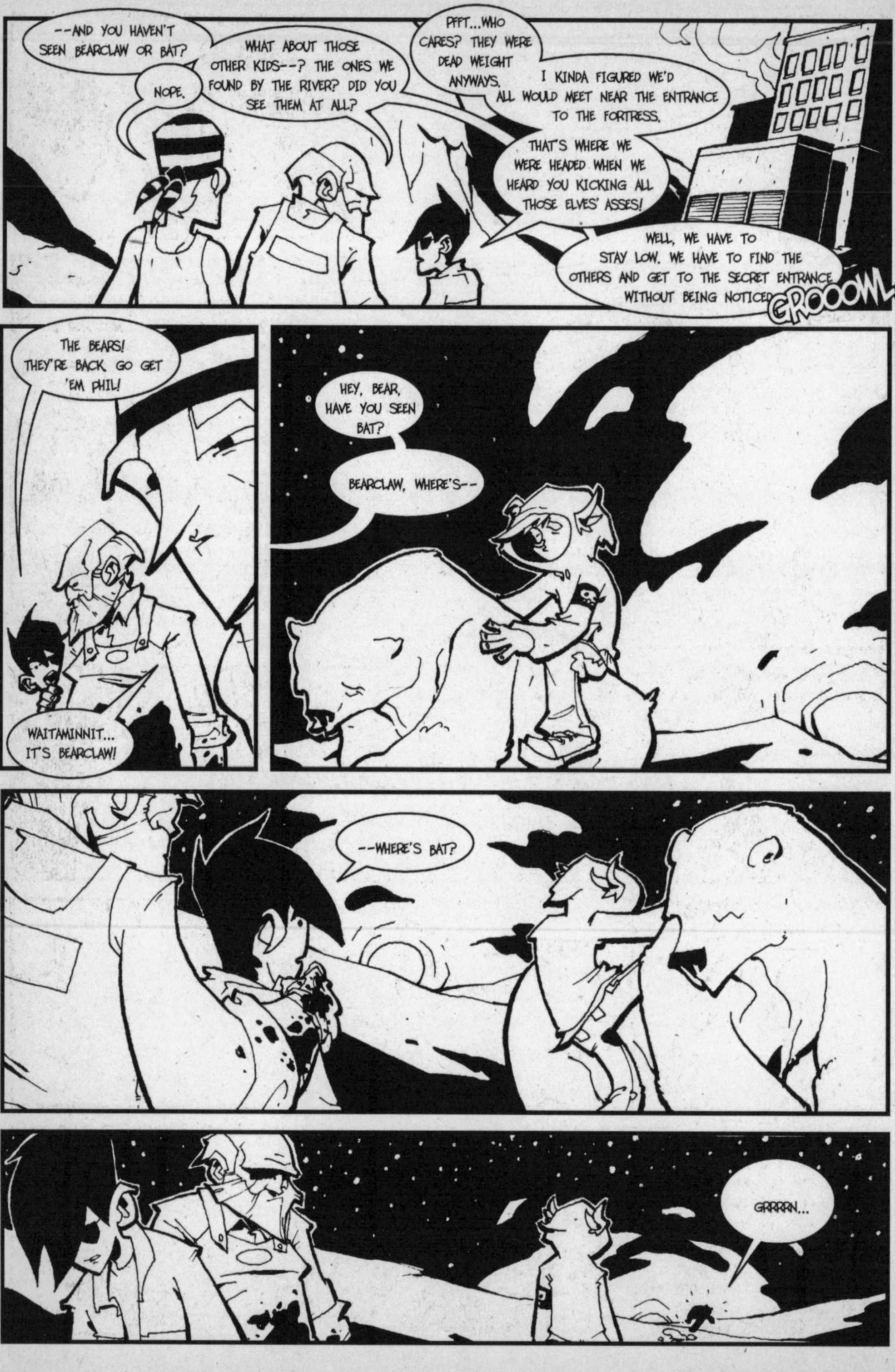
--AND YOU HAVEN'T SEEN BEARCLAW OR BAT?
NOPE.
WHAT ABOUT THOSE OTHER KIDS--? THE ONES WE FOUND BY THE RIVER? DID YOU SEE THEM AT ALL?
PFFT...WHO CARES? THEY WERE DEAD WEIGHT ANYWAYS.
I KINDA FIGURED WE'D ALL WOULD MEET NEAR THE ENTRANCE TO THE FORTRESS.
THAT'S WHERE WE WERE HEADED WHEN WE HEARD YOU KICKING ALL THOSE ELVES' ASSES!
WELL, WE HAVE TO STAY LOW. WE HAVE TO FIND THE OTHERS AND GET TO THE SECRET ENTRANCE WITHOUT BEING NOTICED
GROOOWL
THE BEARS! THEY'RE BACK. GO GET 'EM PHIL!
WAITAMINNIT... IT'S BEARCLAW!
HEY, BEAR, HAVE YOU SEEN BAT?
BEARCLAW, WHERE'S--
--WHERE'S BAT?
GRRRRN...

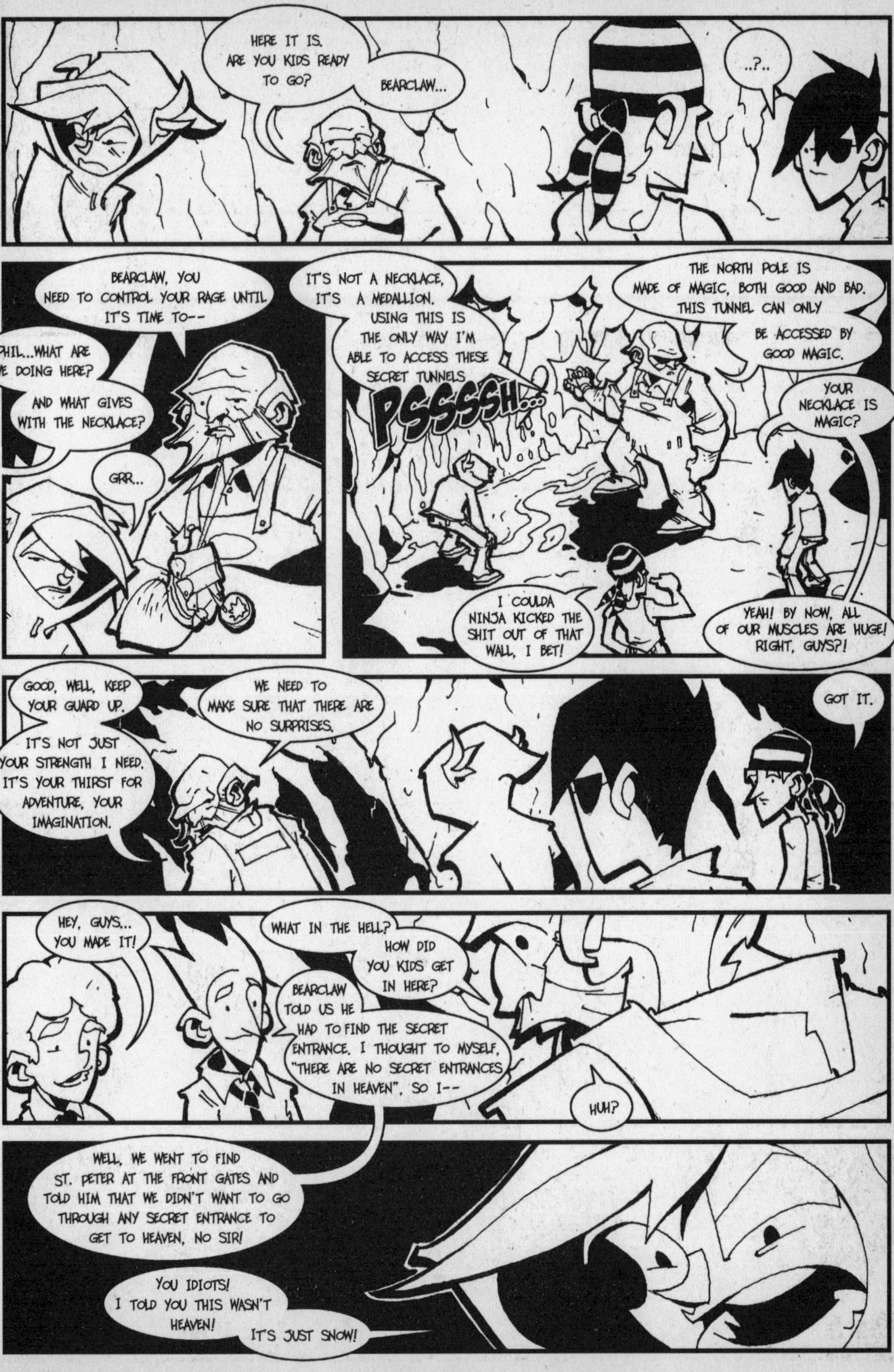
HERE IT IS. ARE YOU KIDS READY TO GO?
BEARCLAW...
..?..
BEARCLAW, YOU NEED TO CONTROL YOUR RAGE UNTIL IT'S TIME TO--
PHIL...WHAT ARE WE DOING HERE?
AND WHAT GIVES WITH THE NECKLACE?
GRR...
IT'S NOT A NECKLACE, IT'S A MEDALLION. USING THIS IS THE ONLY WAY I'M ABLE TO ACCESS THESE SECRET TUNNELS
PSSSSH...
THE NORTH POLE IS MADE OF MAGIC, BOTH GOOD AND BAD. THIS TUNNEL CAN ONLY
BE ACCESSED BY GOOD MAGIC.
YOUR NECKLACE IS MAGIC?
I COULDA NINJA KICKED THE SHIT OUT OF THAT WALL, I BET!
YEAH! BY NOW, ALL OF OUR MUSCLES ARE HUGE! RIGHT, GUYS?!
GOOD, WELL, KEEP YOUR GUARD UP.
WE NEED TO MAKE SURE THAT THERE ARE NO SURPRISES.
IT'S NOT JUST YOUR STRENGTH I NEED, IT'S YOUR THIRST FOR ADVENTURE, YOUR IMAGINATION.
GOT IT.
HEY, GUYS... YOU MADE IT!
WHAT IN THE HELL?
HOW DID YOU KIDS GET IN HERE?
BEARCLAW TOLD US HE HAD TO FIND THE SECRET ENTRANCE. I THOUGHT TO MYSELF, "THERE ARE NO SECRET ENTRANCES IN HEAVEN", SO I--
HUH?
WELL, WE WENT TO FIND ST. PETER AT THE FRONT GATES AND TOLD HIM THAT WE DIDN'T WANT TO GO THROUGH ANY SECRET ENTRANCE TO GET TO HEAVEN, NO SIR!
YOU IDIOTS! I TOLD YOU THIS WASN'T HEAVEN!
IT'S JUST SNOW!

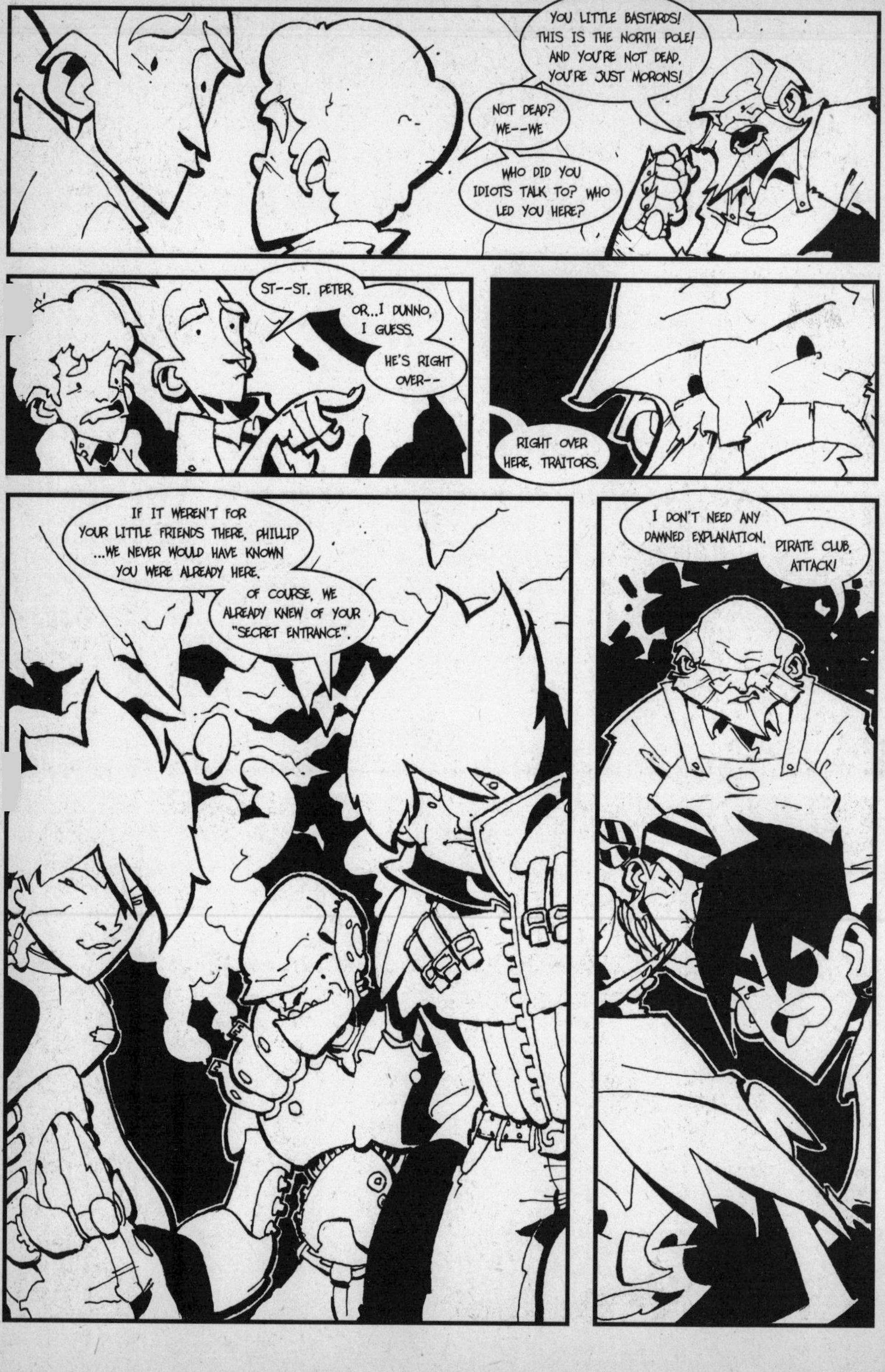
YOU LITTLE BASTARDS! THIS IS THE NORTH POLE! AND YOU'RE NOT DEAD, YOU'RE JUST MORONS!
NOT DEAD? WE--WE
WHO DID YOU IDIOTS TALK TO? WHO LED YOU HERE?
ST--ST. PETER.
OR...I DUNNO, I GUESS.
HE'S RIGHT OVER--
RIGHT OVER HERE, TRAITORS.
IF IT WEREN'T FOR YOUR LITTLE FRIENDS THERE, PHILLIP ...WE NEVER WOULD HAVE KNOWN YOU WERE ALREADY HERE.
OF COURSE, WE ALREADY KNEW OF YOUR "SECRET ENTRANCE".
I DON'T NEED ANY DAMNED EXPLANATION.
PIRATE CLUB, ATTACK!

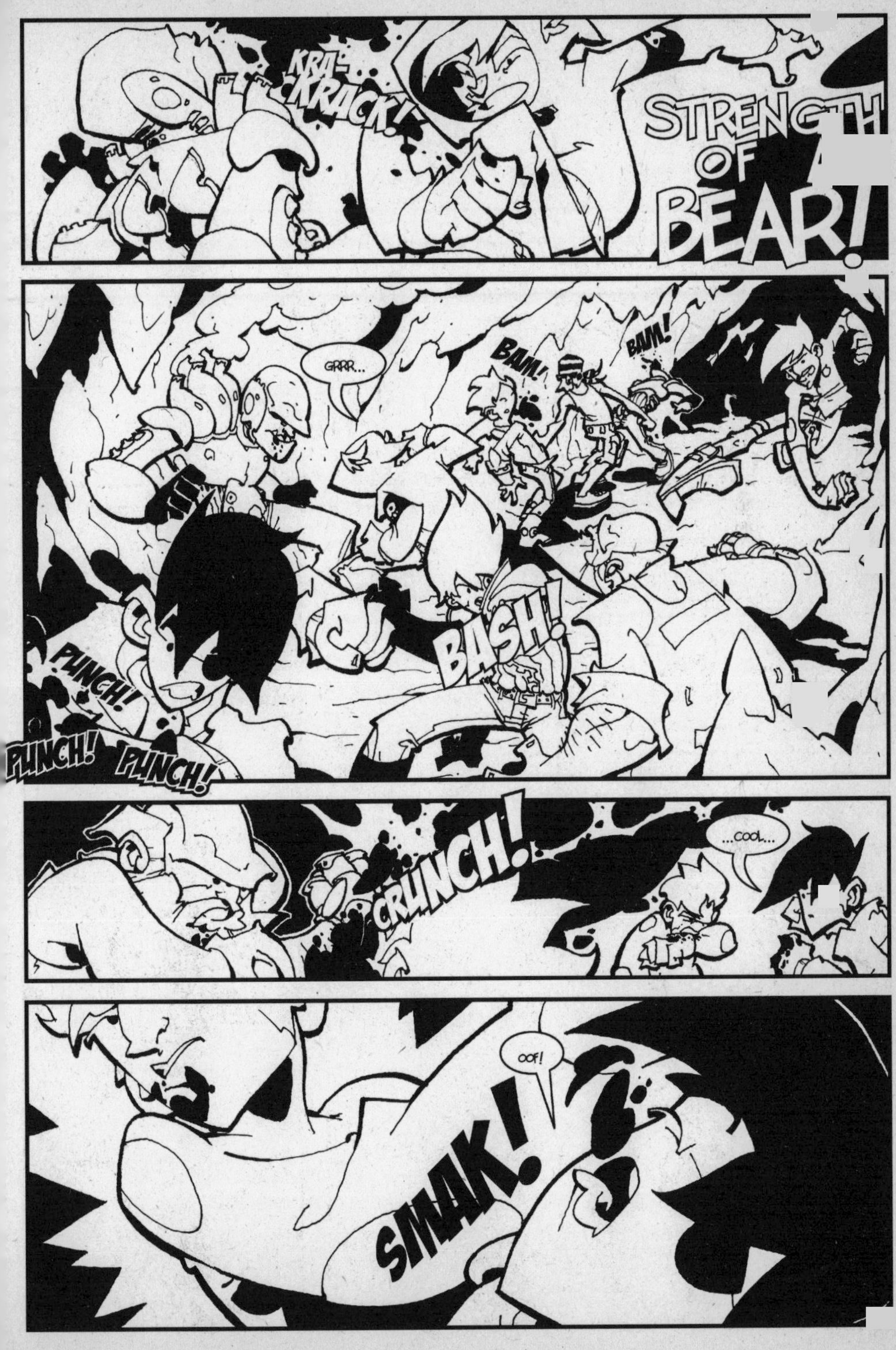

KRA-KRACK!
STRENGTH OF A BEAR!
GRRR...
BAM!
BAM!
BASH!
PUNCH!
PUNCH!
PUNCH!
CRUNCH!
...COOL...
OOF!
SMAK!

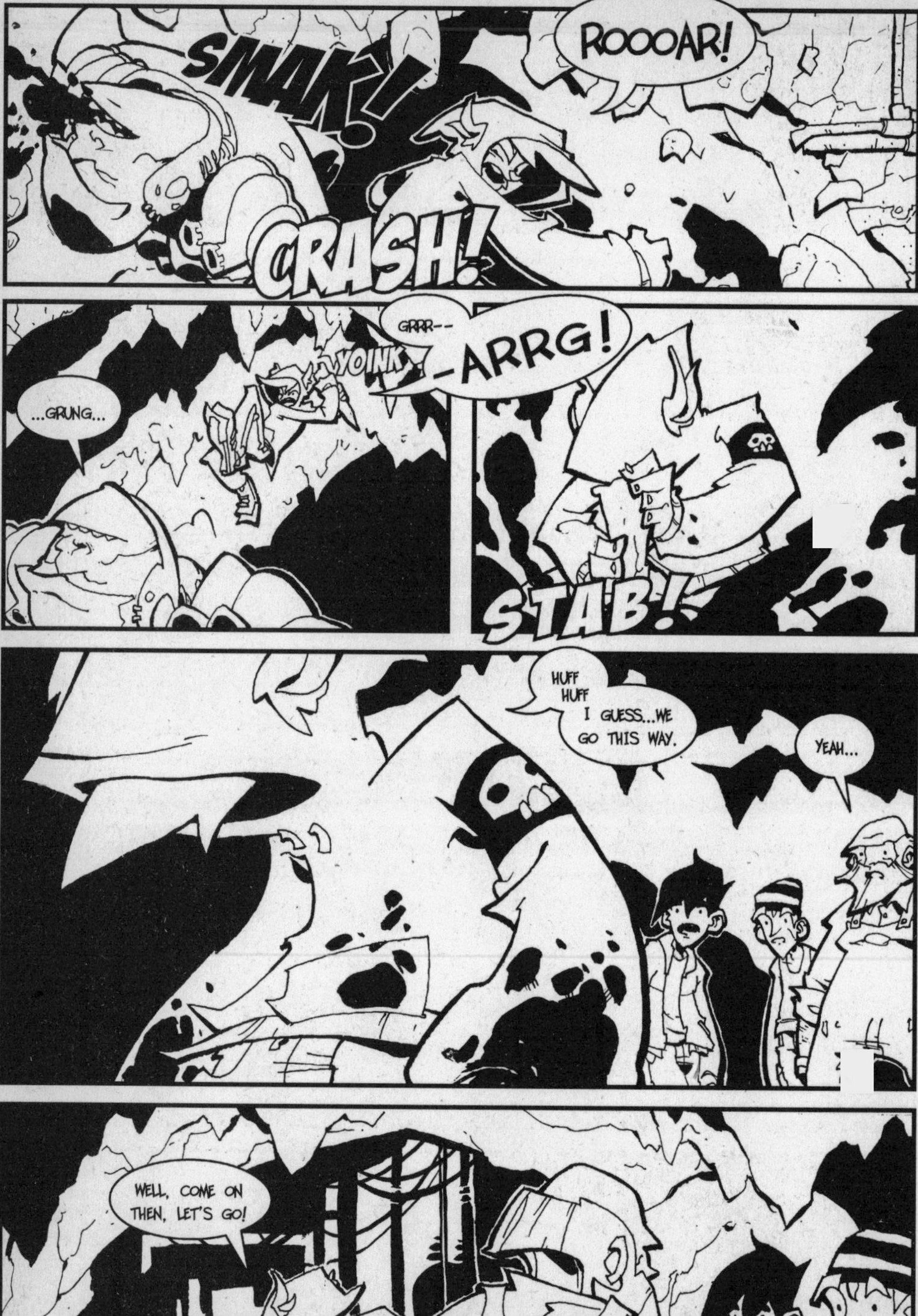

SMAK!
ROOOAR!
CRASH!
...GRUNG...
YOINK
GRRR--
-ARRG!
STAB!
HUFF HUFF
I GUESS...WE GO THIS WAY.
YEAH...
WELL, COME ON THEN, LET'S GO!

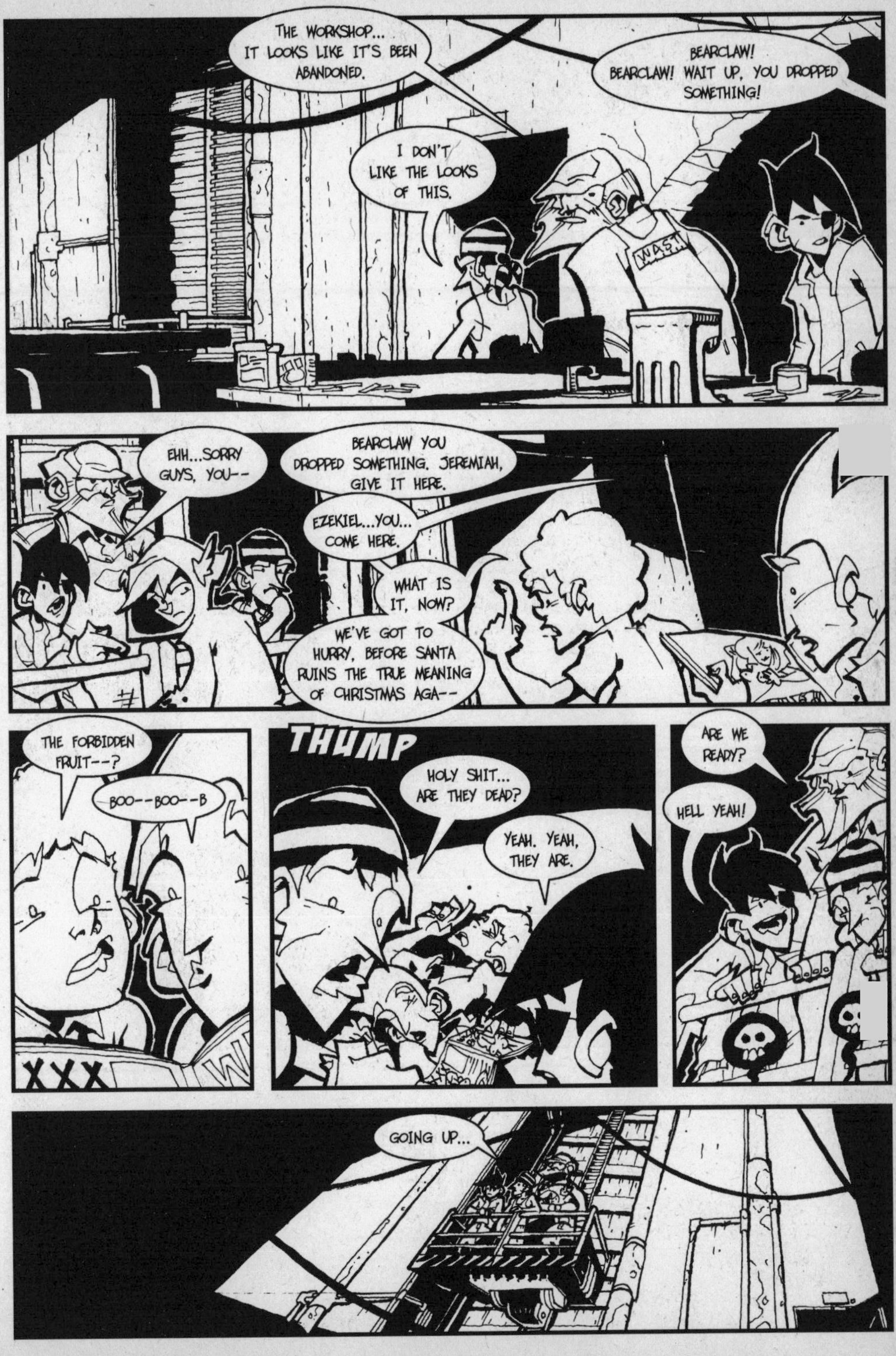
THE WORKSHOP... IT LOOKS LIKE IT'S BEEN ABANDONED.
BEARCLAW! BEARCLAW! WAIT UP, YOU DROPPED SOMETHING!
I DON'T LIKE THE LOOKS OF THIS.
WAST
EHH...SORRY GUYS, YOU--
BEARCLAW YOU DROPPED SOMETHING. JEREMIAH, GIVE IT HERE.
EZEKIEL...YOU... COME HERE.
WHAT IS IT, NOW?
WE'VE GOT TO HURRY, BEFORE SANTA RUINS THE TRUE MEANING OF CHRISTMAS AGA--
THE FORBIDDEN FRUIT--?
--BOO--BOO--B
XXX
THUMP
HOLY SHIT... ARE THEY DEAD?
YEAH. YEAH, THEY ARE.
ARE WE READY?
HELL YEAH!
GOING UP...

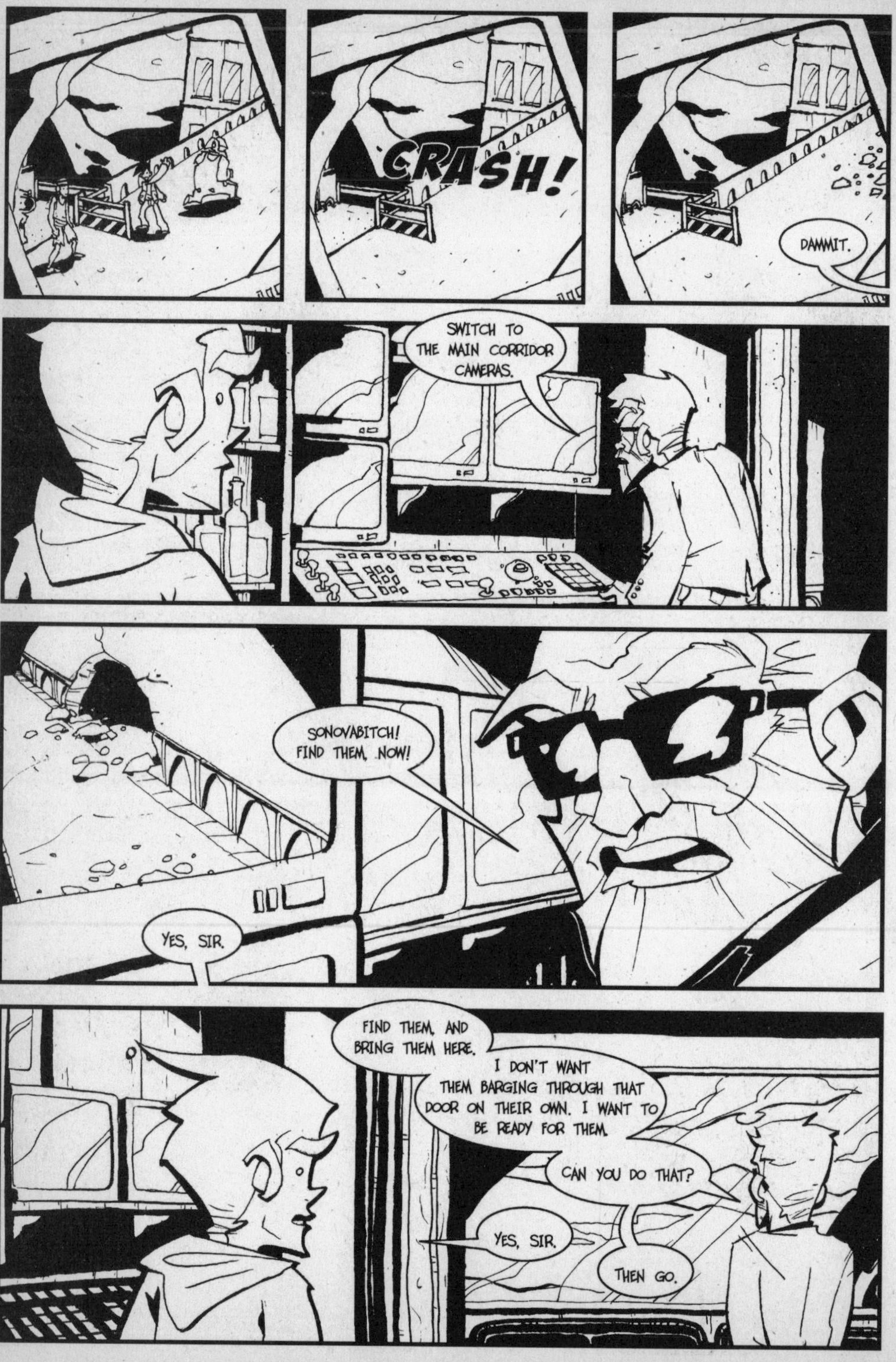
CRASH!
DAMMIT.
SWITCH TO THE MAIN CORRIDOR CAMERAS.
SONOVABITCH! FIND THEM, NOW!
YES, SIR.
FIND THEM, AND BRING THEM HERE.
I DON'T WANT THEM BARGING THROUGH THAT DOOR ON THEIR OWN. I WANT TO BE READY FOR THEM.
CAN YOU DO THAT?
YES, SIR.
THEN GO.

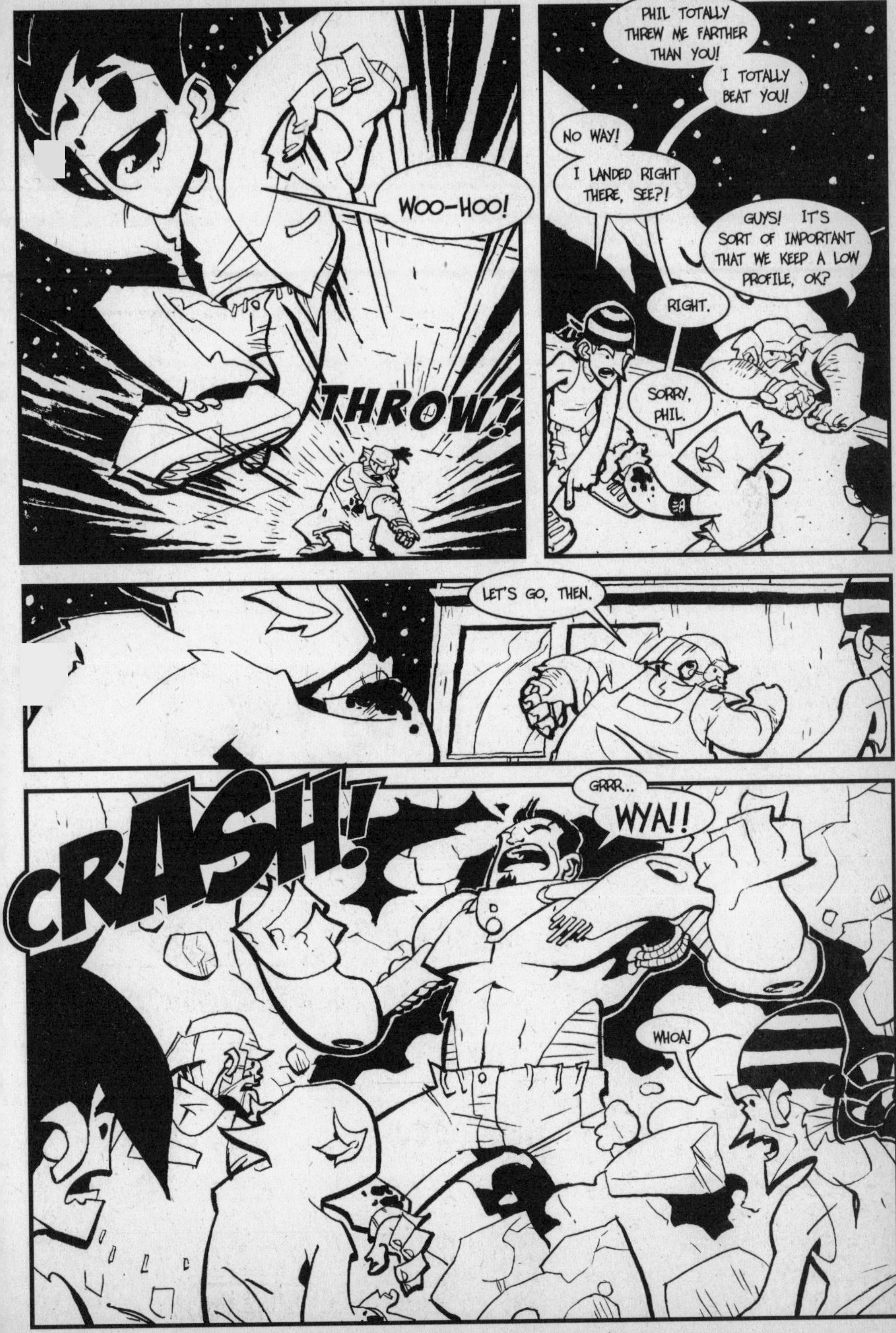
WOO-HOO!
THROW!
PHIL TOTALLY THREW ME FARTHER THAN YOU!
I TOTALLY BEAT YOU!
NO WAY!
I LANDED RIGHT THERE, SEE?!
GUYS! IT'S SORT OF IMPORTANT THAT WE KEEP A LOW PROFILE, OK?
RIGHT.
SORRY, PHIL.
LET'S GO, THEN.
CRASH!
GRRR...
WYA!!
WHOA!

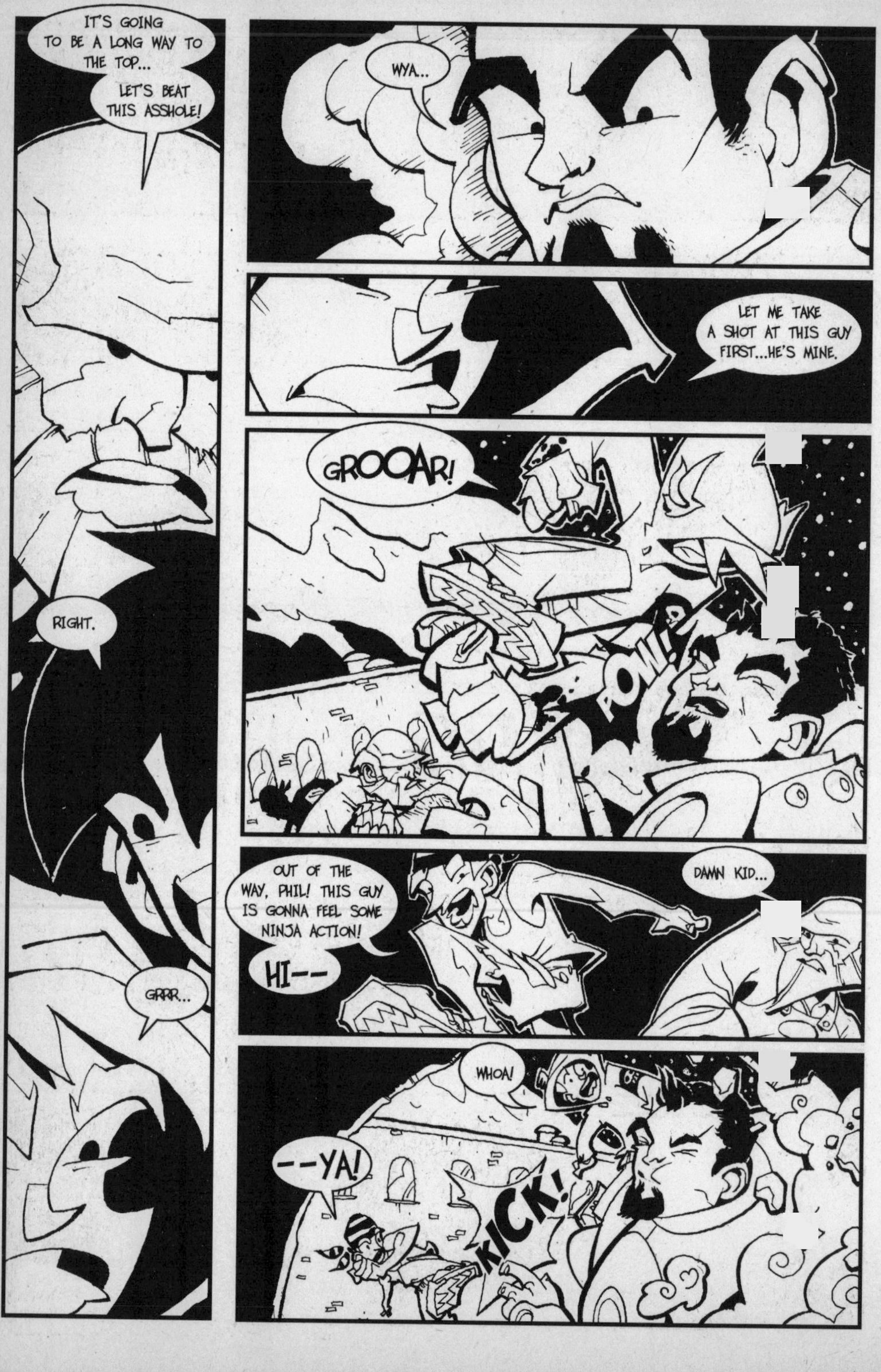
IT'S GOING TO BE A LONG WAY TO THE TOP...
LET'S BEAT THIS ASSHOLE!
RIGHT.
GRRR...
WYA...
LET ME TAKE A SHOT AT THIS GUY FIRST...HE'S MINE.
GROOAR!
POW!
OUT OF THE WAY, PHIL! THIS GUY IS GONNA FEEL SOME NINJA ACTION!
HI--
DAMN KID...
WHOA!
--YA!
KICK!

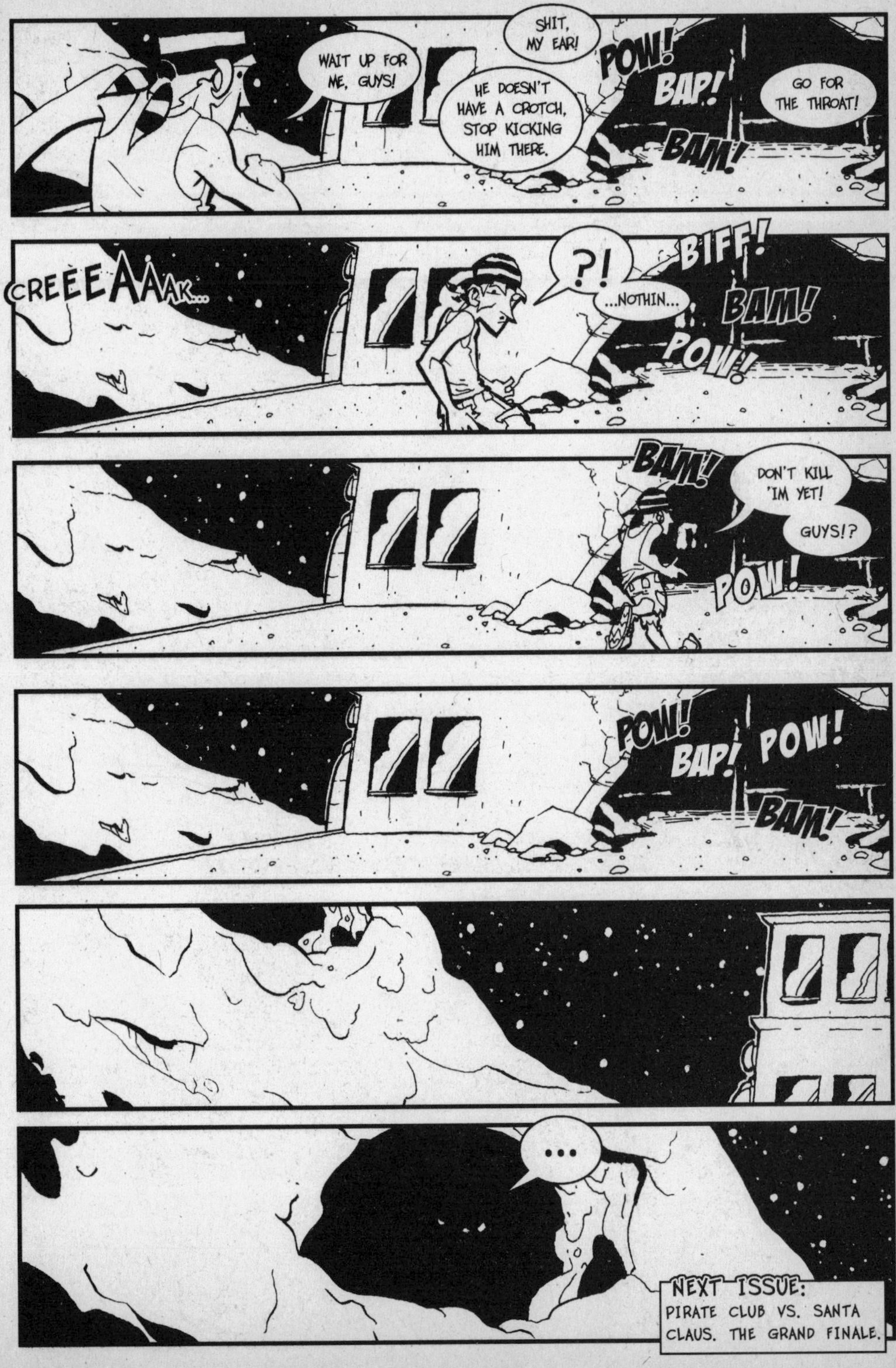
WAIT UP FOR ME, GUYS!
SHIT, MY EAR!
HE DOESN'T HAVE A CROTCH, STOP KICKING HIM THERE.
POW!
BAP!
BAM!
GO FOR THE THROAT!
CREEEAAAAK...
?!
...NOTHIN...
BIFF!
BAM!
POW!
BAM!
DON'T KILL 'IM YET!
GUYS!?
POW!
POW!
BAP!
POW!
BAM!
...
NEXT ISSUE:
PIRATE CLUB VS. SANTA CLAUS. THE GRAND FINALE.

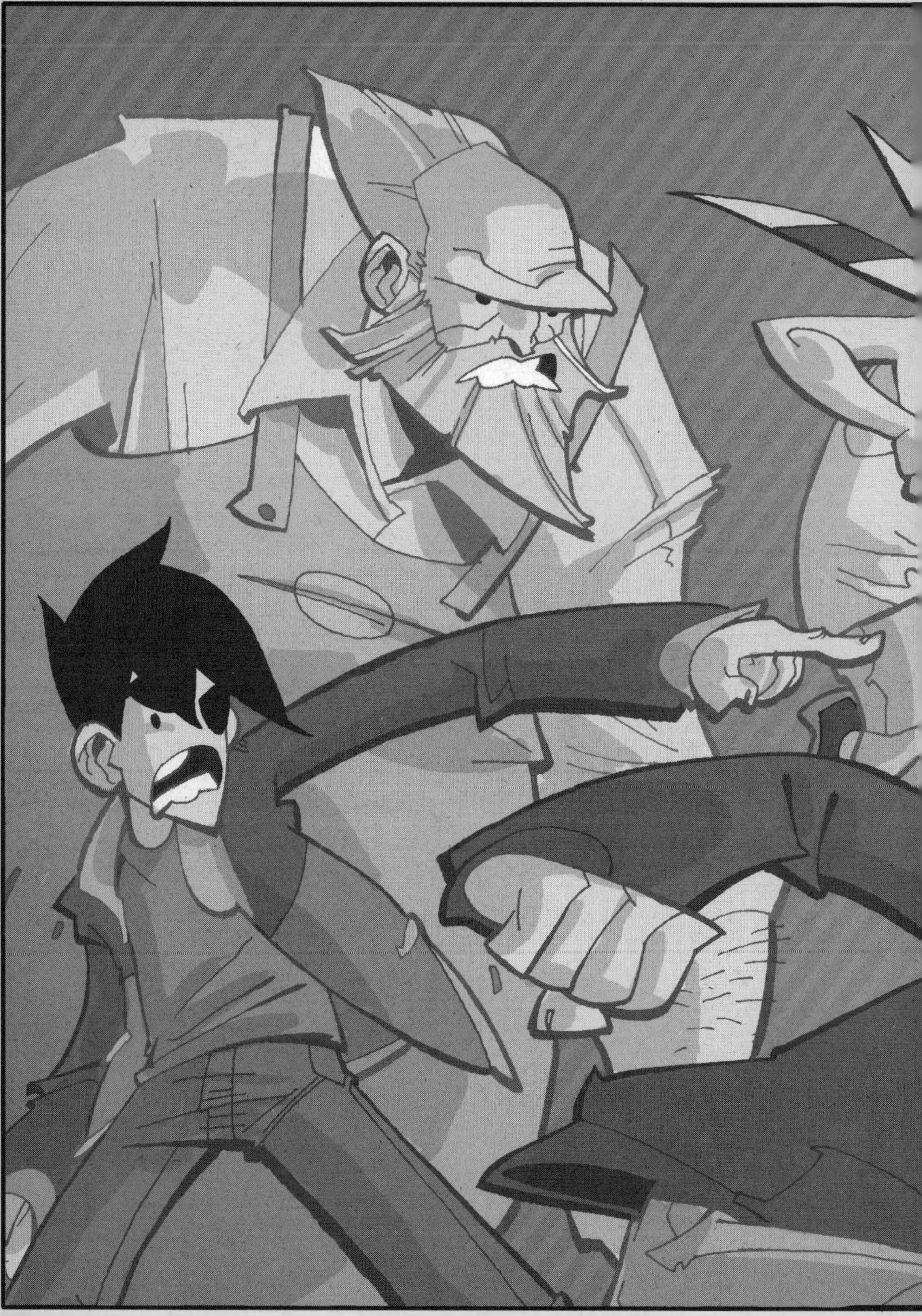

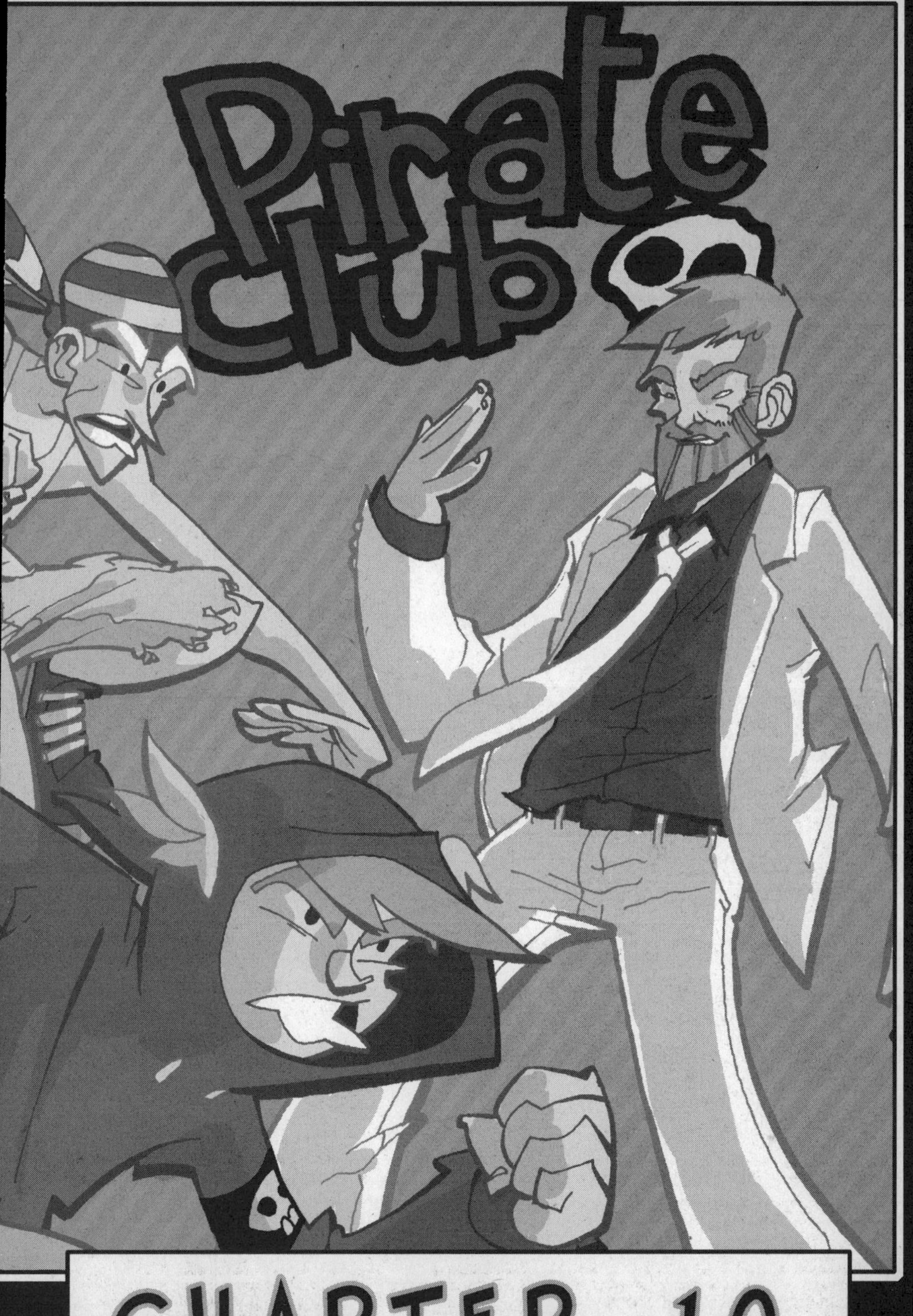
Pirate Club

# CHAPTER 10

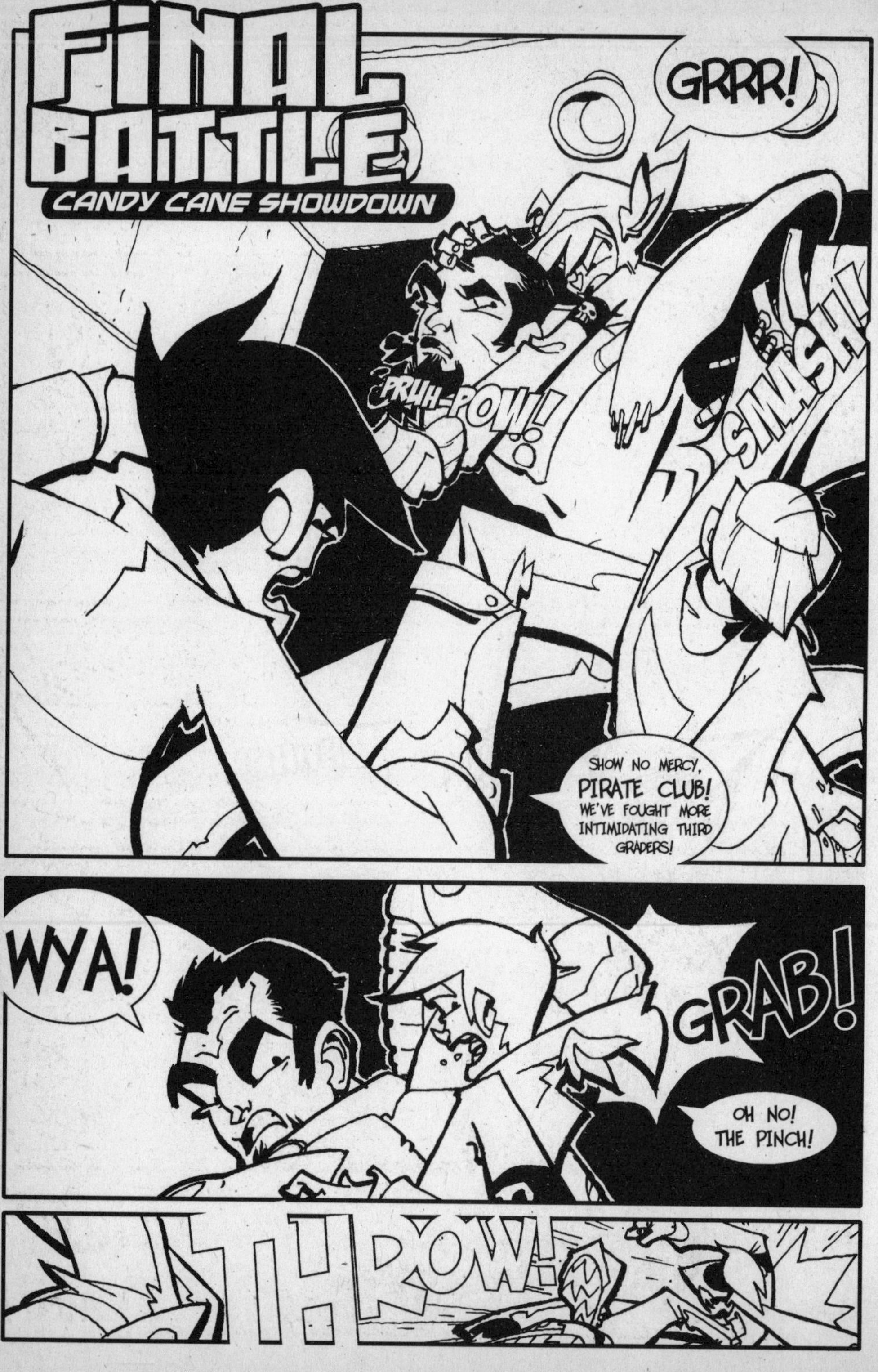
FINAL BATTLE
CANDY CANE SHOWDOWN
GRRR!
PRUH-POW!
SMASH!
SHOW NO MERCY, PIRATE CLUB! WE'VE FOUGHT MORE INTIMIDATING THIRD GRADERS!
WYA!
GRAB!
OH NO! THE PINCH!
THROW!

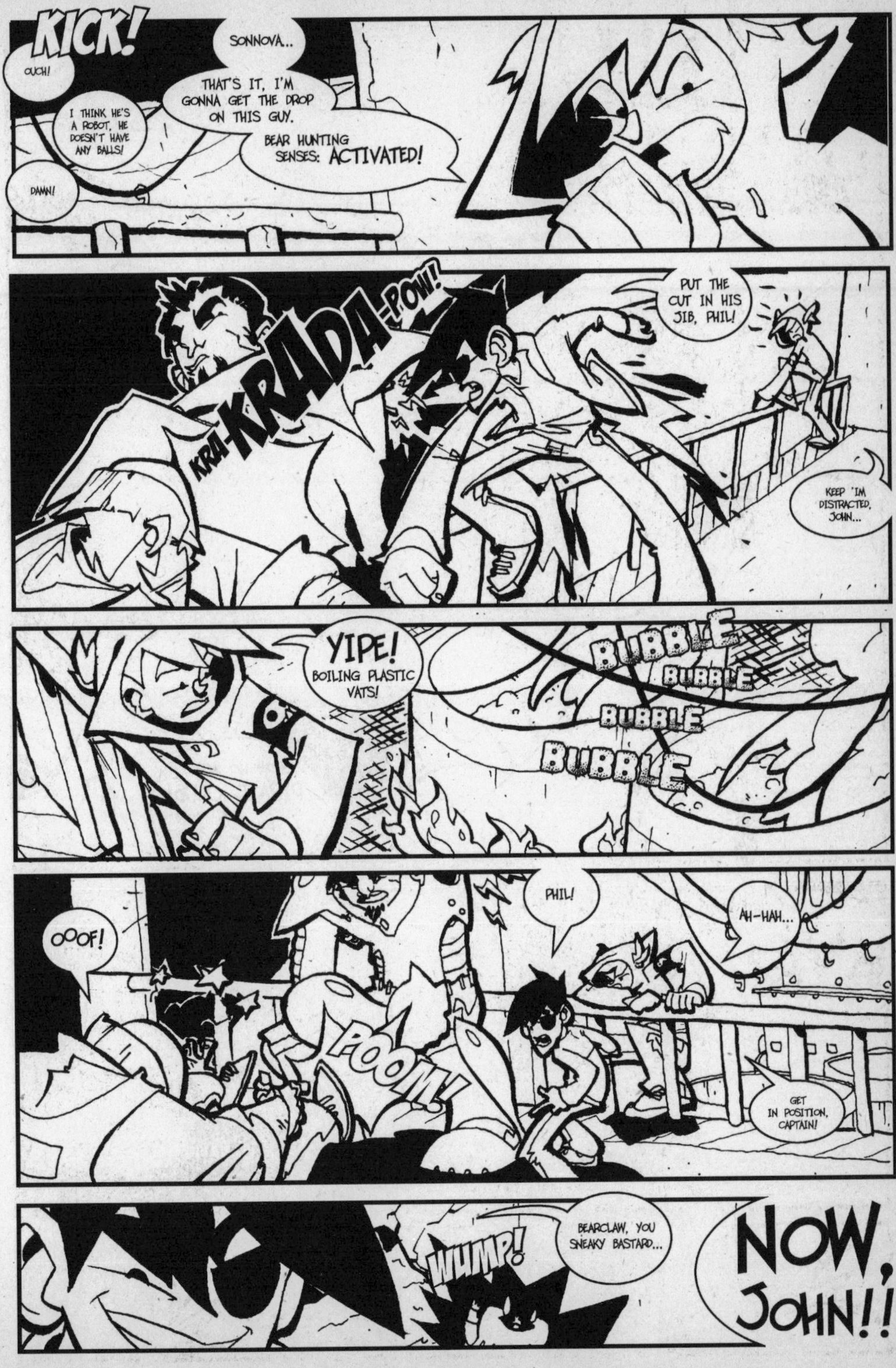

KICK!
OUCH!
I THINK HE'S A ROBOT, HE DOESN'T HAVE ANY BALLS!
DAMN!
SONNOVA...
THAT'S IT, I'M GONNA GET THE DROP ON THIS GUY.
BEAR HUNTING SENSES: ACTIVATED!
KRA-KRADA-POW!
PUT THE CUT IN HIS JIB, PHIL!
KEEP 'IM DISTRACTED, JOHN...
YIPE! BOILING PLASTIC VATS!
BUBBLE
BUBBLE
BUBBLE
BUBBLE
OOOF!
POOOM!
PHIL!
AH-HAH...
GET IN POSITION, CAPTAIN!
WUMP!
BEARCLAW, YOU SNEAKY BASTARD...
NOW, JOHN!!

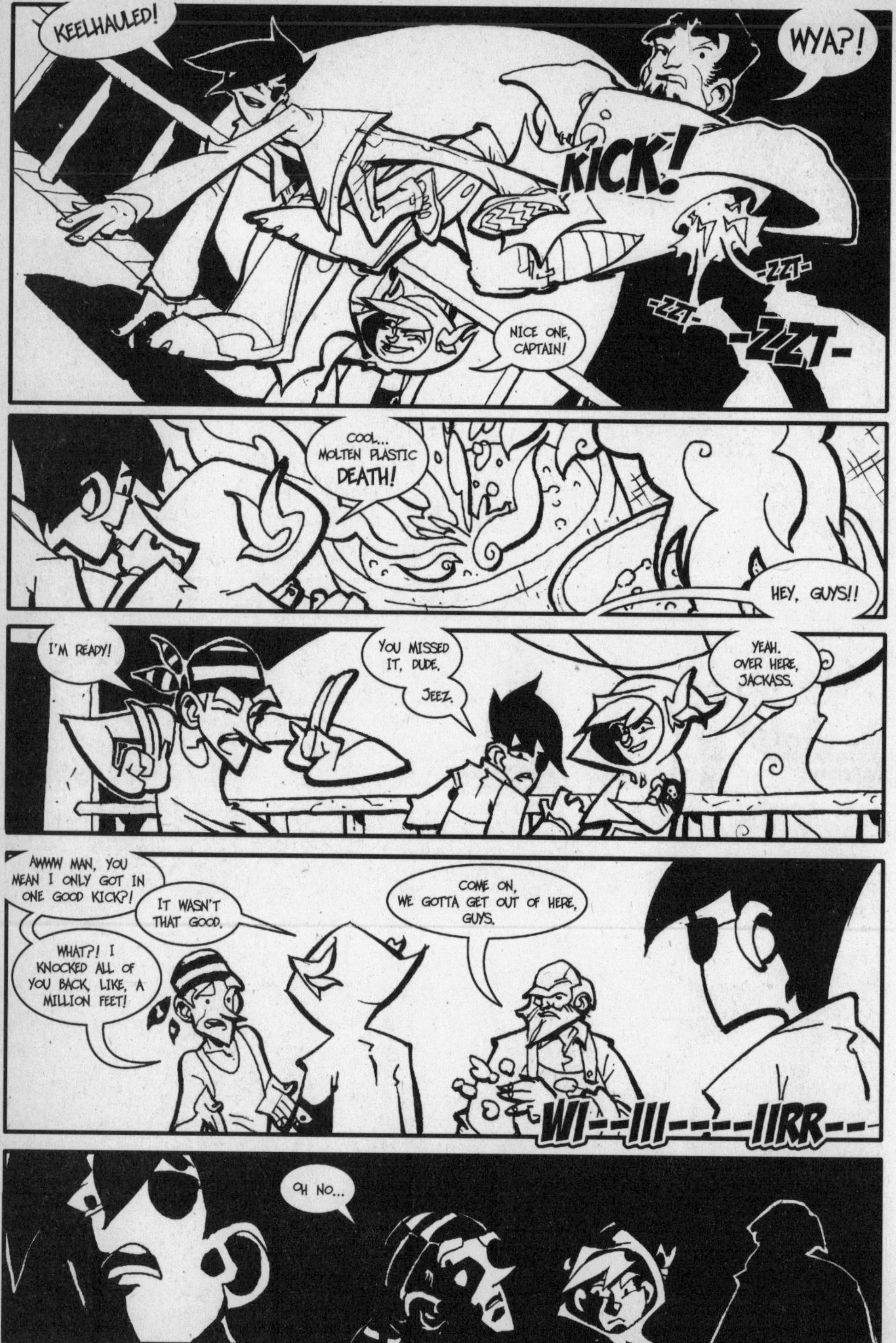
KEELHAULED!
WYA?!
KICK!
NICE ONE, CAPTAIN!
-ZZT-
-ZZT-
-ZZT-
COOL... MOLTEN PLASTIC DEATH!
HEY, GUYS!!
I'M READY!
YOU MISSED IT, DUDE.
JEEZ.
YEAH. OVER HERE, JACKASS.
AWWW MAN, YOU MEAN I ONLY GOT IN ONE GOOD KICK?!
IT WASN'T THAT GOOD.
WHAT?! I KNOCKED ALL OF YOU BACK, LIKE, A MILLION FEET!
COME ON, WE GOTTA GET OUT OF HERE, GUYS.
WI--III----IIRR--
OH NO...

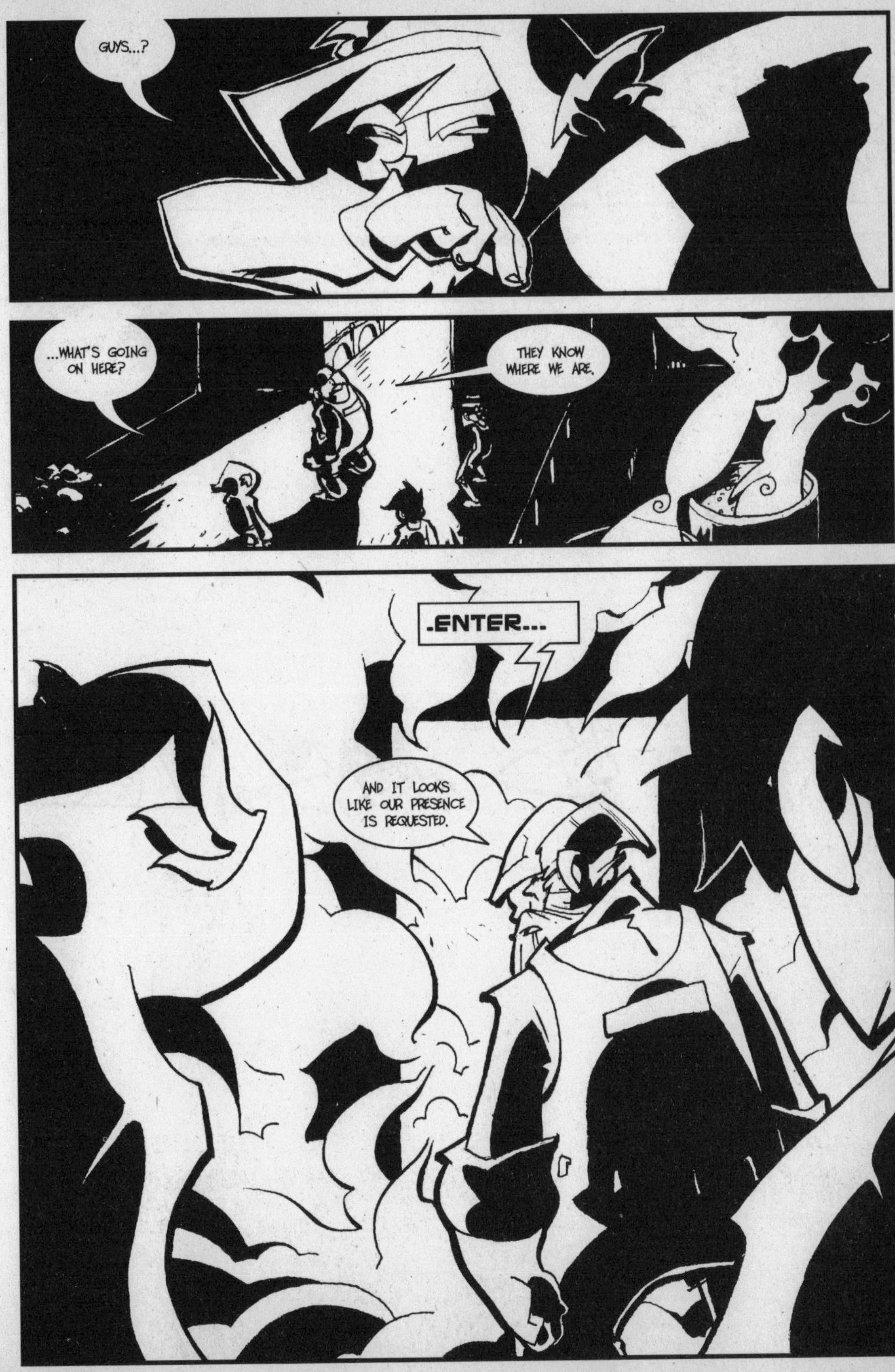
GUYS...?
...WHAT'S GOING ON HERE?
THEY KNOW WHERE WE ARE.
.ENTER...
AND IT LOOKS LIKE OUR PRESENCE IS REQUESTED.

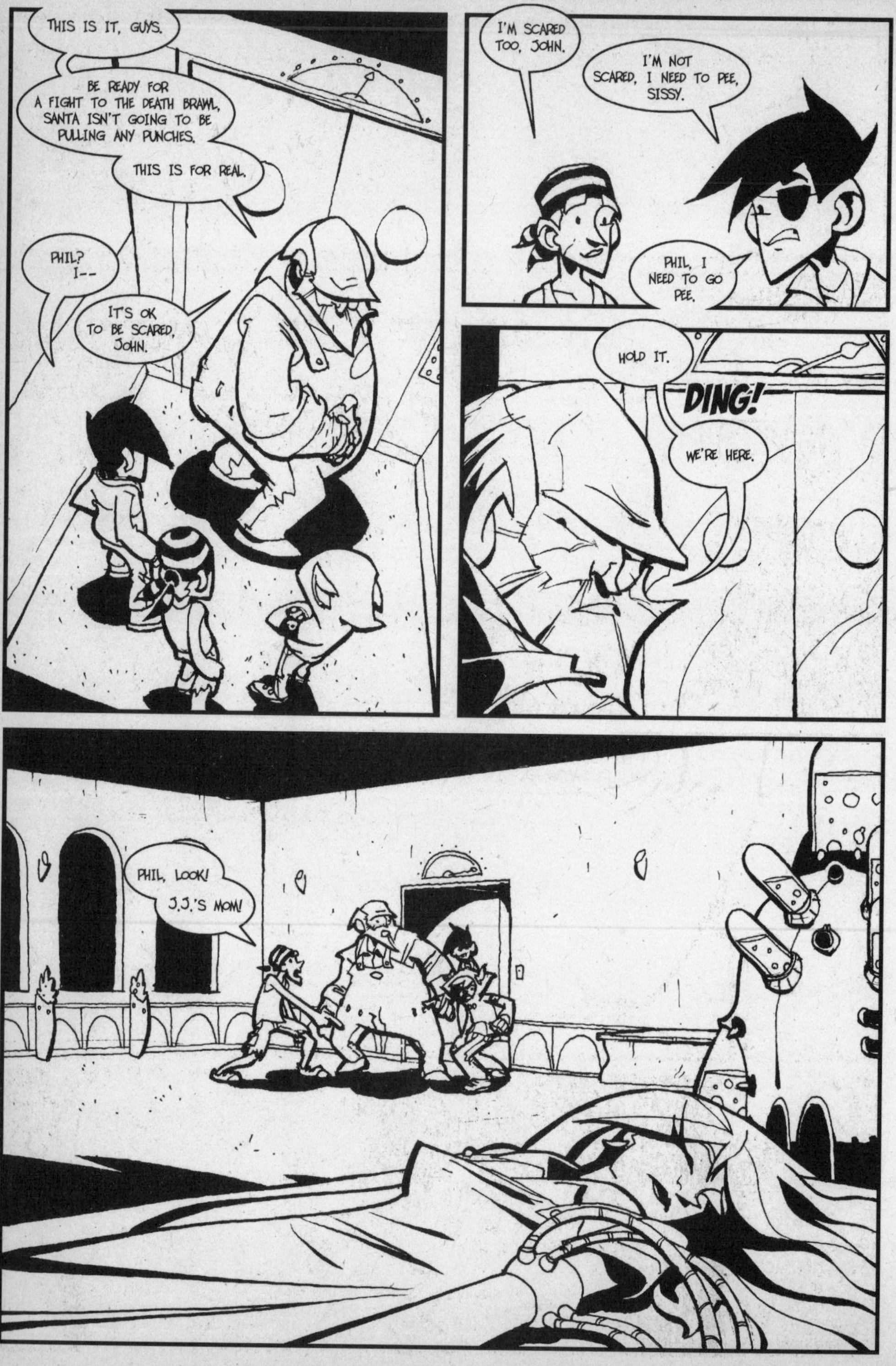
THIS IS IT, GUYS.
BE READY FOR A FIGHT TO THE DEATH BRAWL, SANTA ISN'T GOING TO BE PULLING ANY PUNCHES.
THIS IS FOR REAL.
PHIL? I--
IT'S OK TO BE SCARED, JOHN.
I'M SCARED TOO, JOHN.
I'M NOT SCARED, I NEED TO PEE, SISSY.
PHIL, I NEED TO GO PEE.
HOLD IT.
DING!
WE'RE HERE.
PHIL, LOOK!
J.J.'S MOM!

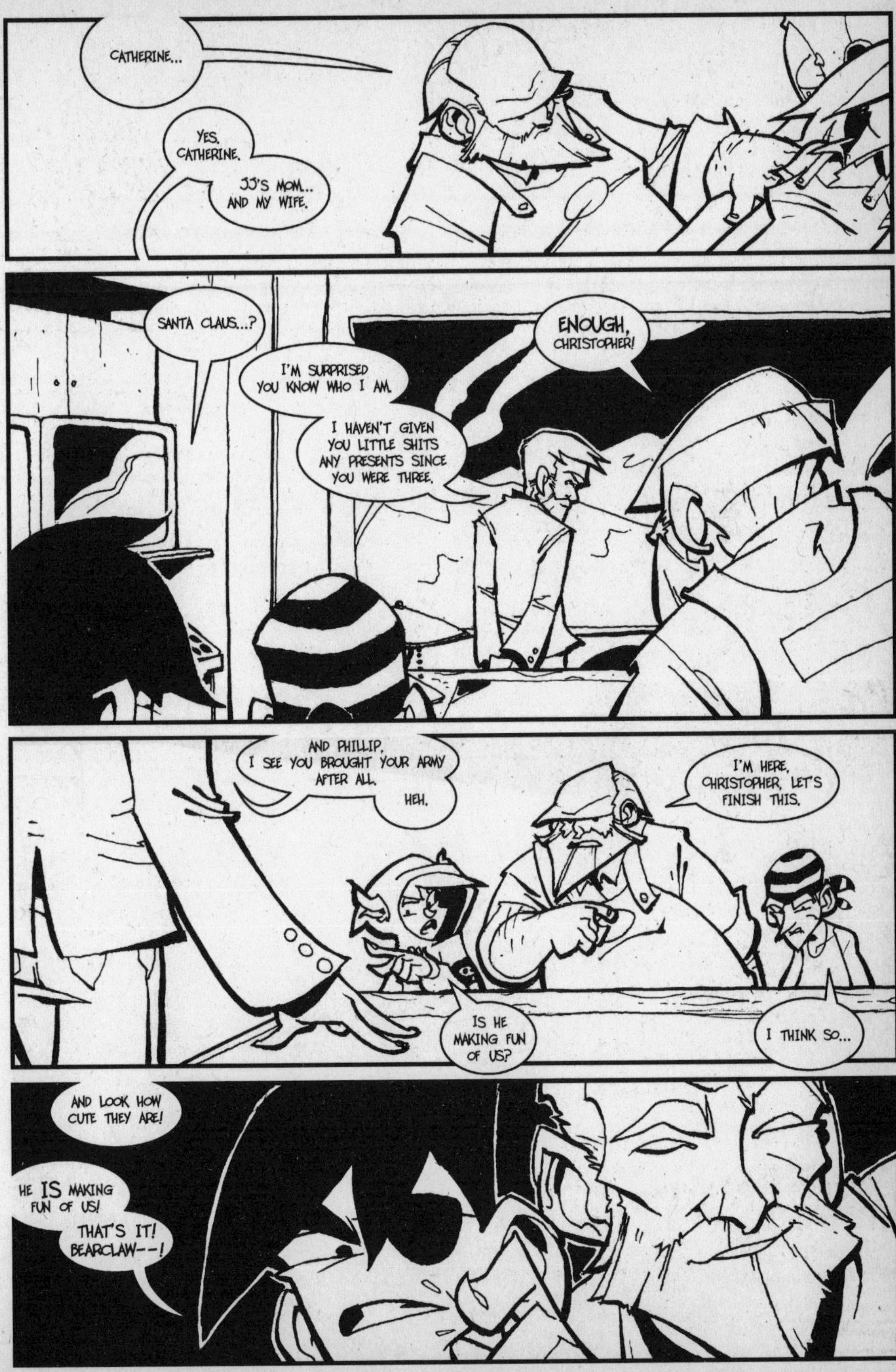

CATHERINE...
YES. CATHERINE.
JJ'S MOM... AND MY WIFE.
SANTA CLAUS...?
I'M SURPRISED YOU KNOW WHO I AM.
I HAVEN'T GIVEN YOU LITTLE SHITS ANY PRESENTS SINCE YOU WERE THREE.
ENOUGH, CHRISTOPHER!
AND PHILLIP, I SEE YOU BROUGHT YOUR ARMY AFTER ALL.
HEH.
I'M HERE, CHRISTOPHER. LET'S FINISH THIS.
IS HE MAKING FUN OF US?
I THINK SO...
AND LOOK HOW CUTE THEY ARE!
HE IS MAKING FUN OF US!
THAT'S IT! BEARCLAW--!

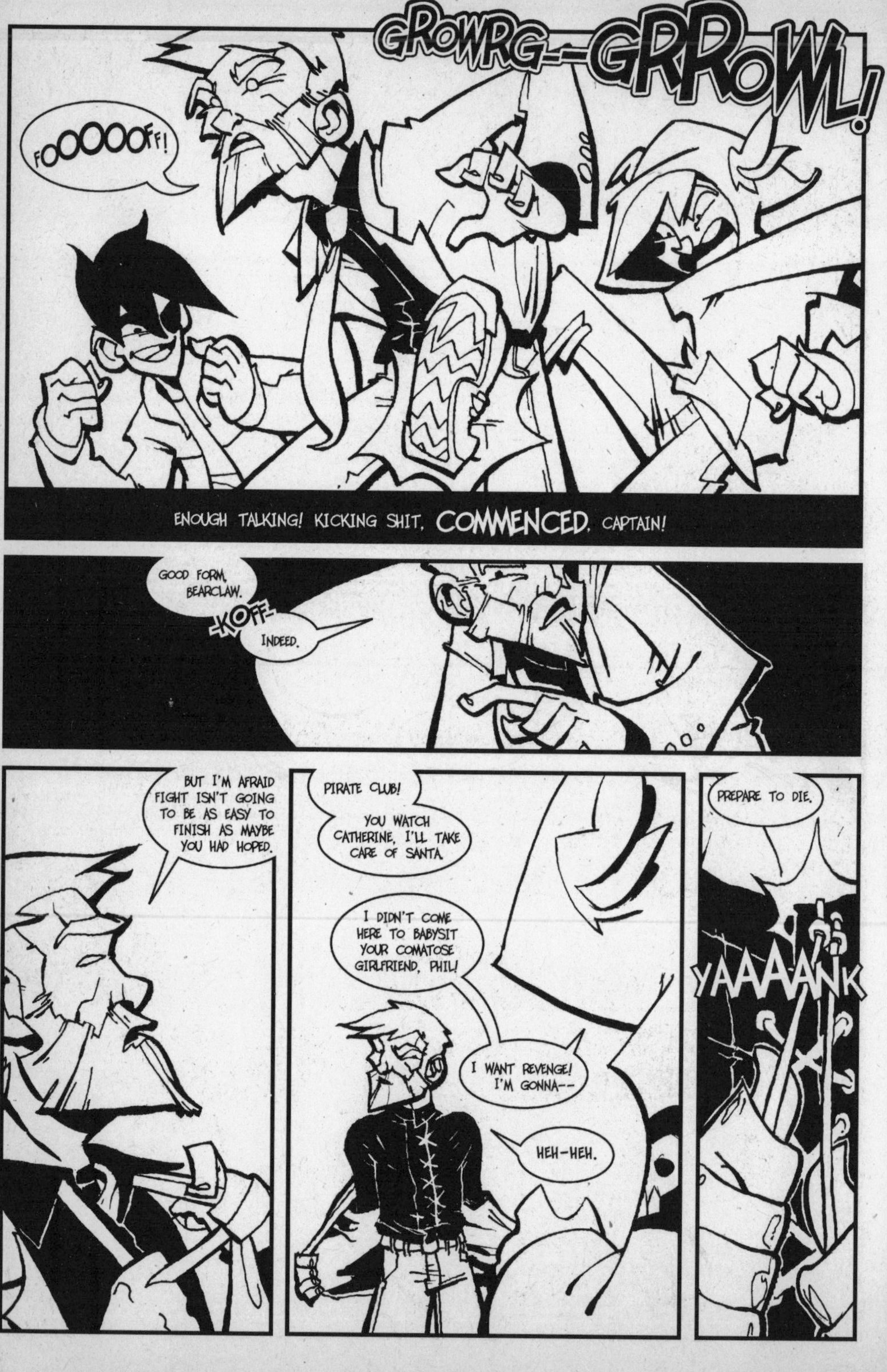
GROWRG--GRROWL!
FOOOOOFF!
ENOUGH TALKING! KICKING SHIT, COMMENCED, CAPTAIN!
GOOD FORM, BEARCLAW.
-KOFF-
INDEED.
BUT I'M AFRAID FIGHT ISN'T GOING TO BE AS EASY TO FINISH AS MAYBE YOU HAD HOPED.
PIRATE CLUB!
YOU WATCH CATHERINE, I'LL TAKE CARE OF SANTA.
I DIDN'T COME HERE TO BABYSIT YOUR COMATOSE GIRLFRIEND, PHIL!
I WANT REVENGE! I'M GONNA--
HEH-HEH.
PREPARE TO DIE.
YAAAANK

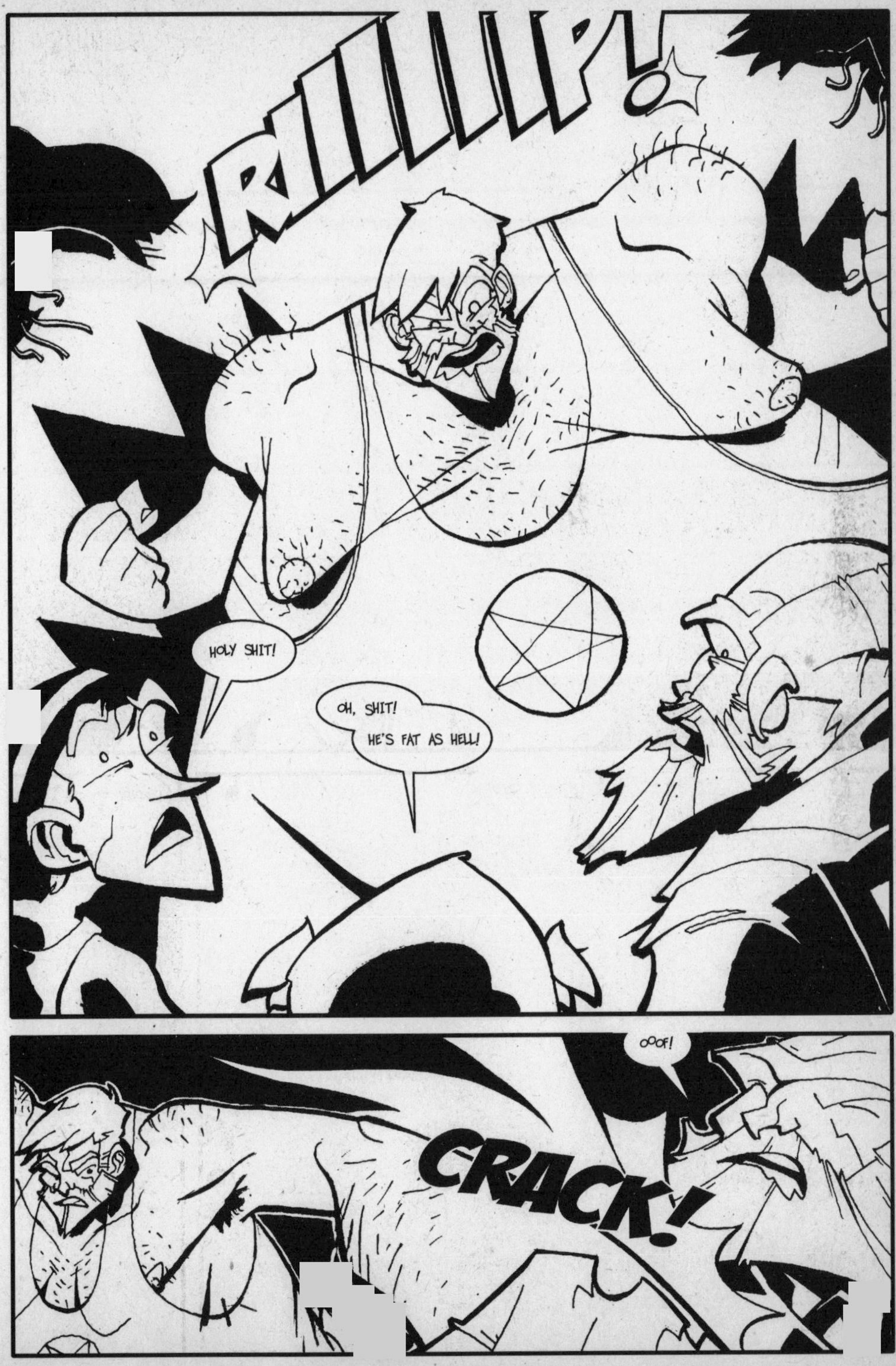
RIIIIIIP!
HOLY SHIT!
OH, SHIT!
HE'S FAT AS HELL!
OOOF!
CRACK!

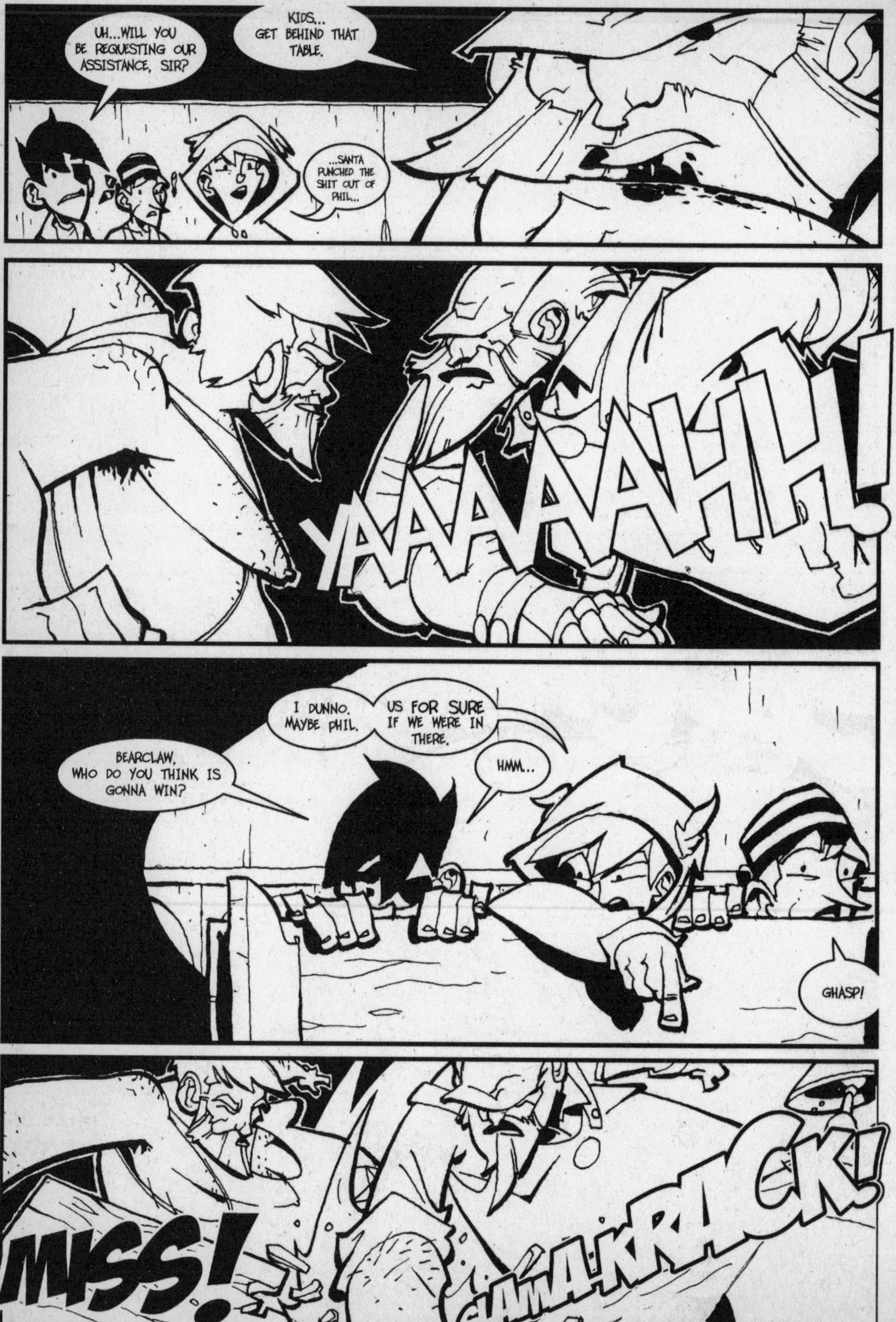
UH...WILL YOU BE REQUESTING OUR ASSISTANCE, SIR?
KIDS... GET BEHIND THAT TABLE.
...SANTA PUNCHED THE SHIT OUT OF PHIL...
YAAAAAHH!
BEARCLAW, WHO DO YOU THINK IS GONNA WIN?
I DUNNO. MAYBE PHIL.
US FOR SURE IF WE WERE IN THERE.
HMM...
GHASP!
MISS!
SLAMA-KRACK!

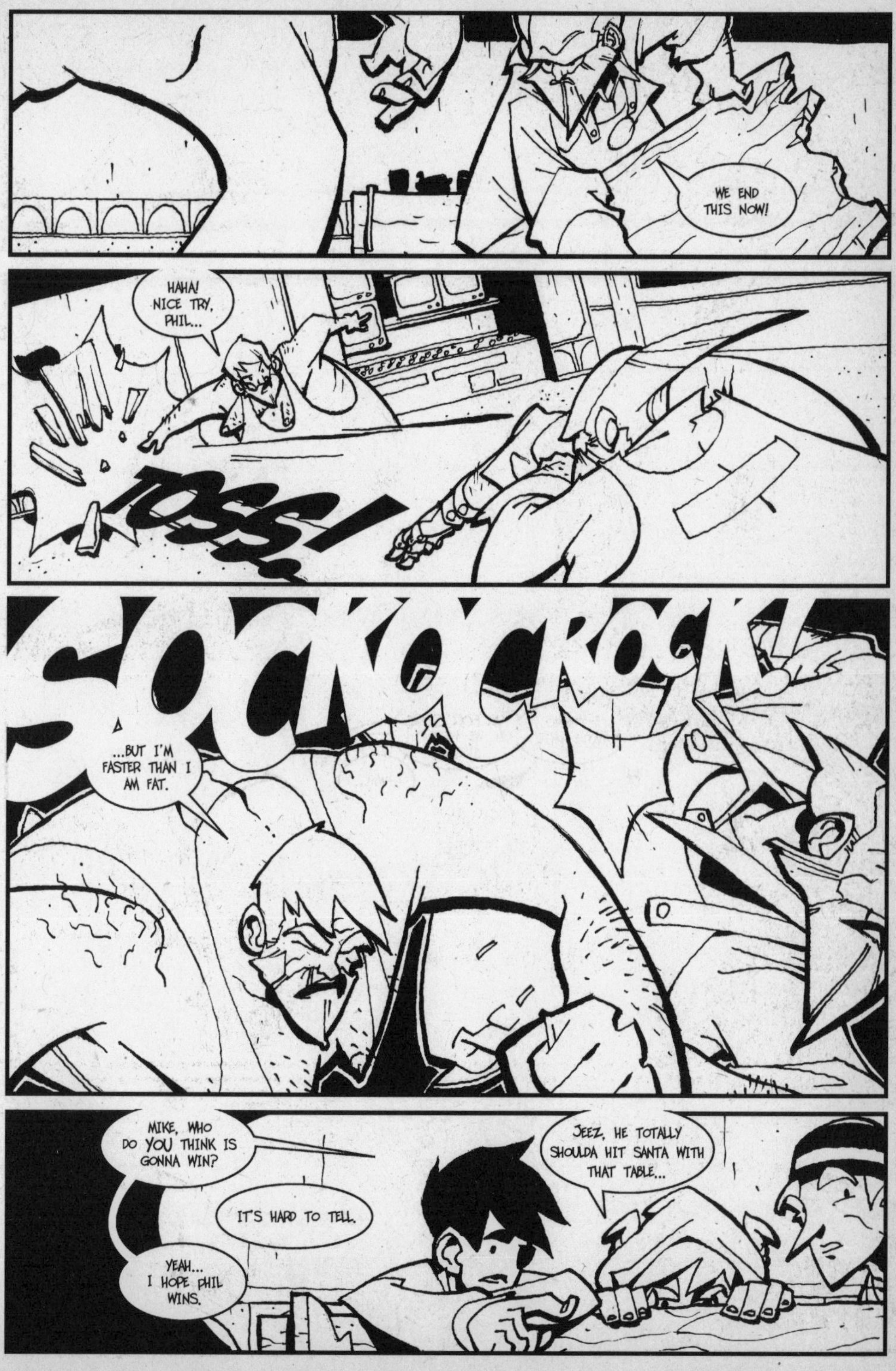
WE END THIS NOW!
HAHA! NICE TRY, PHIL...
TOSS!
SOCKO CROCK!
...BUT I'M FASTER THAN I AM FAT.
MIKE, WHO DO YOU THINK IS GONNA WIN?
IT'S HARD TO TELL.
YEAH... I HOPE PHIL WINS.
JEEZ, HE TOTALLY SHOULDA HIT SANTA WITH THAT TABLE...

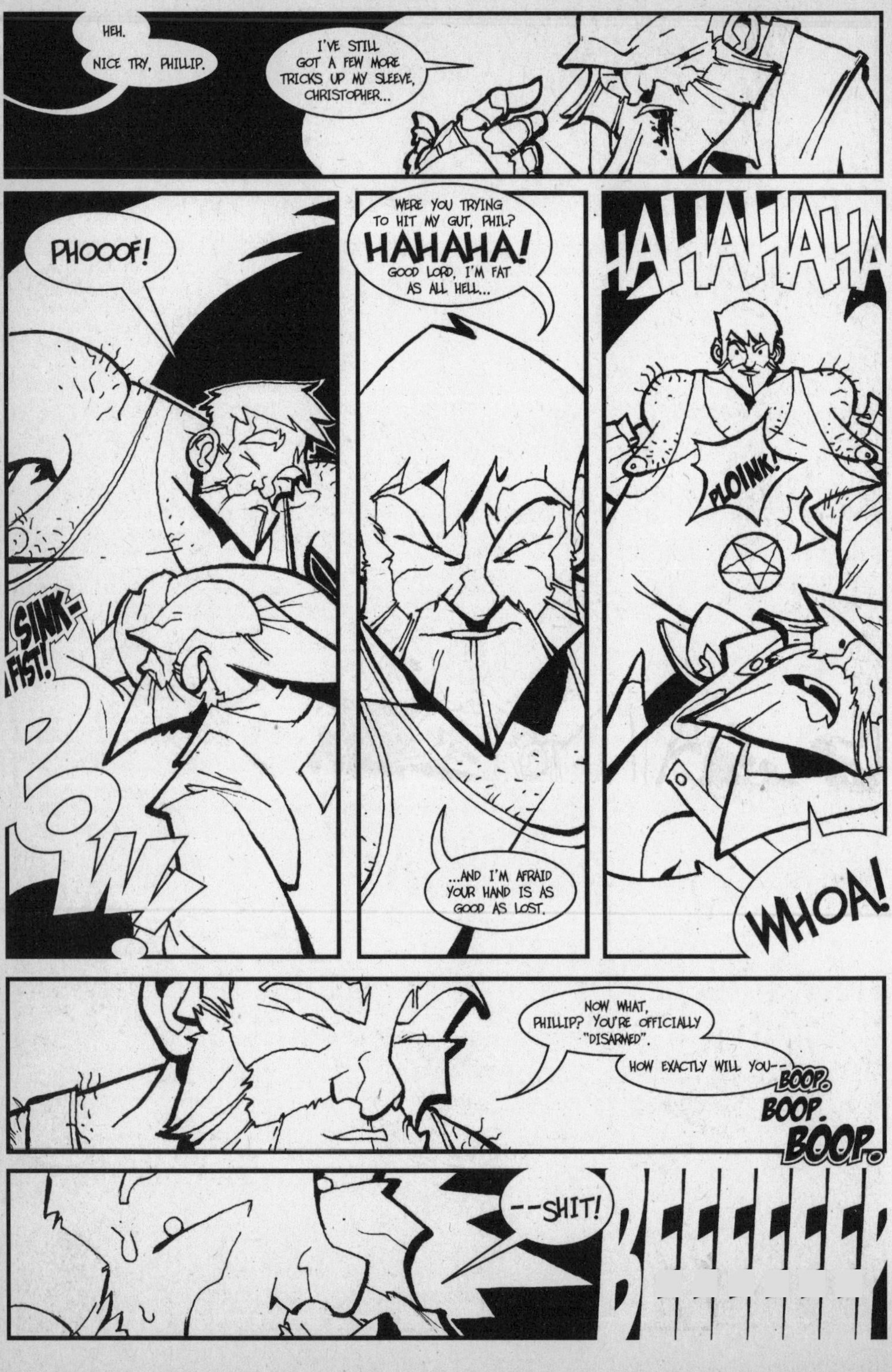
HEH.
NICE TRY, PHILLIP.
I'VE STILL GOT A FEW MORE TRICKS UP MY SLEEVE, CHRISTOPHER...
PHOOOF!
SINK-FIST!
POW!
WERE YOU TRYING TO HIT MY GUT, PHIL?
HAHAHA!
GOOD LORD, I'M FAT AS ALL HELL...
...AND I'M AFRAID YOUR HAND IS AS GOOD AS LOST.
HAHAHAHAHA
PLOINK!
WHOA!
NOW WHAT, PHILLIP? YOU'RE OFFICIALLY "DISARMED".
HOW EXACTLY WILL YOU--
BOOP.
BOOP.
BOOP.
--SHIT!
BEEEEEEP

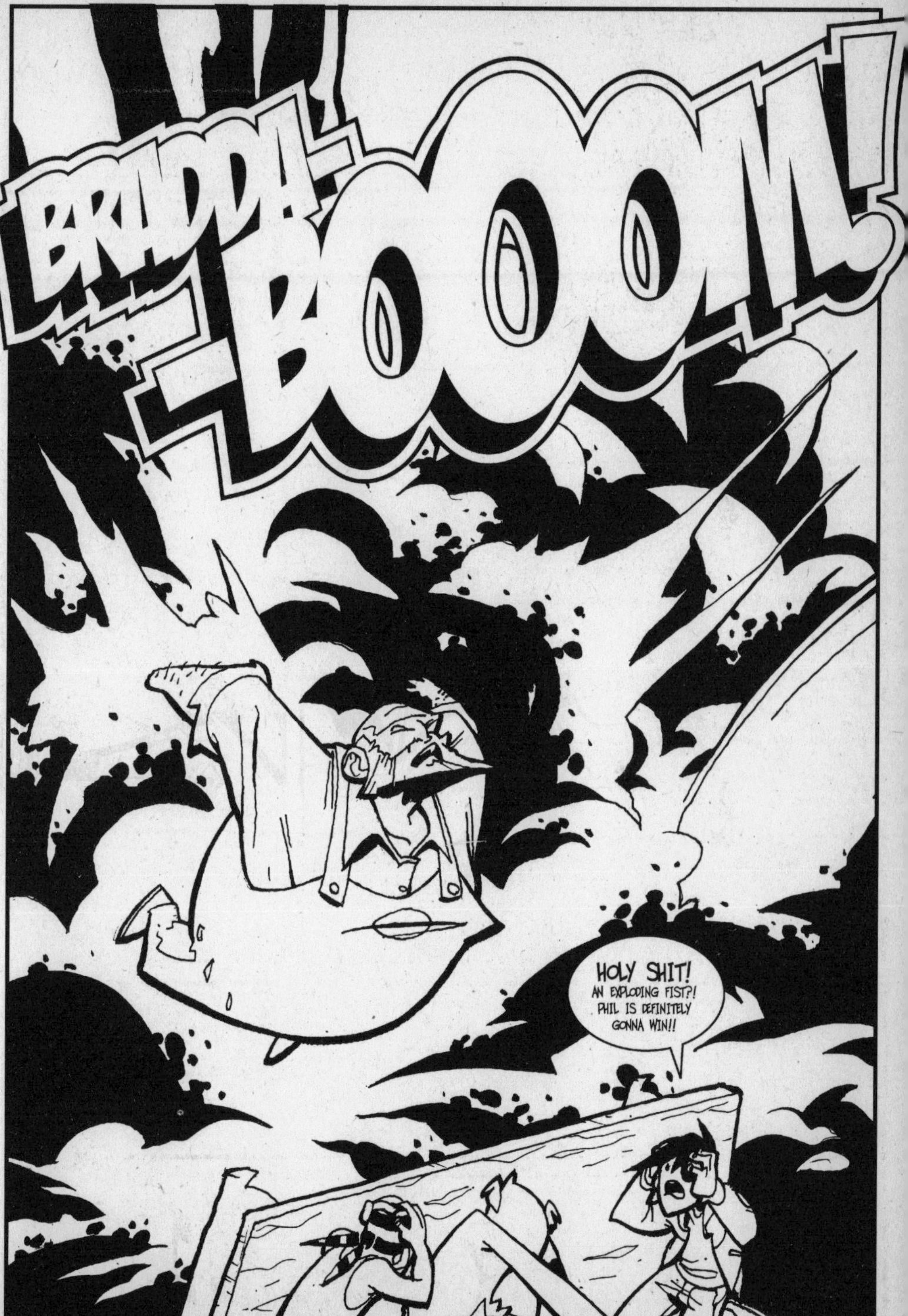
BRADDA-BOOOM!
HOLY SHIT!
AN EXPLODING FIST?!
PHIL IS DEFINITELY
GONNA WIN!!

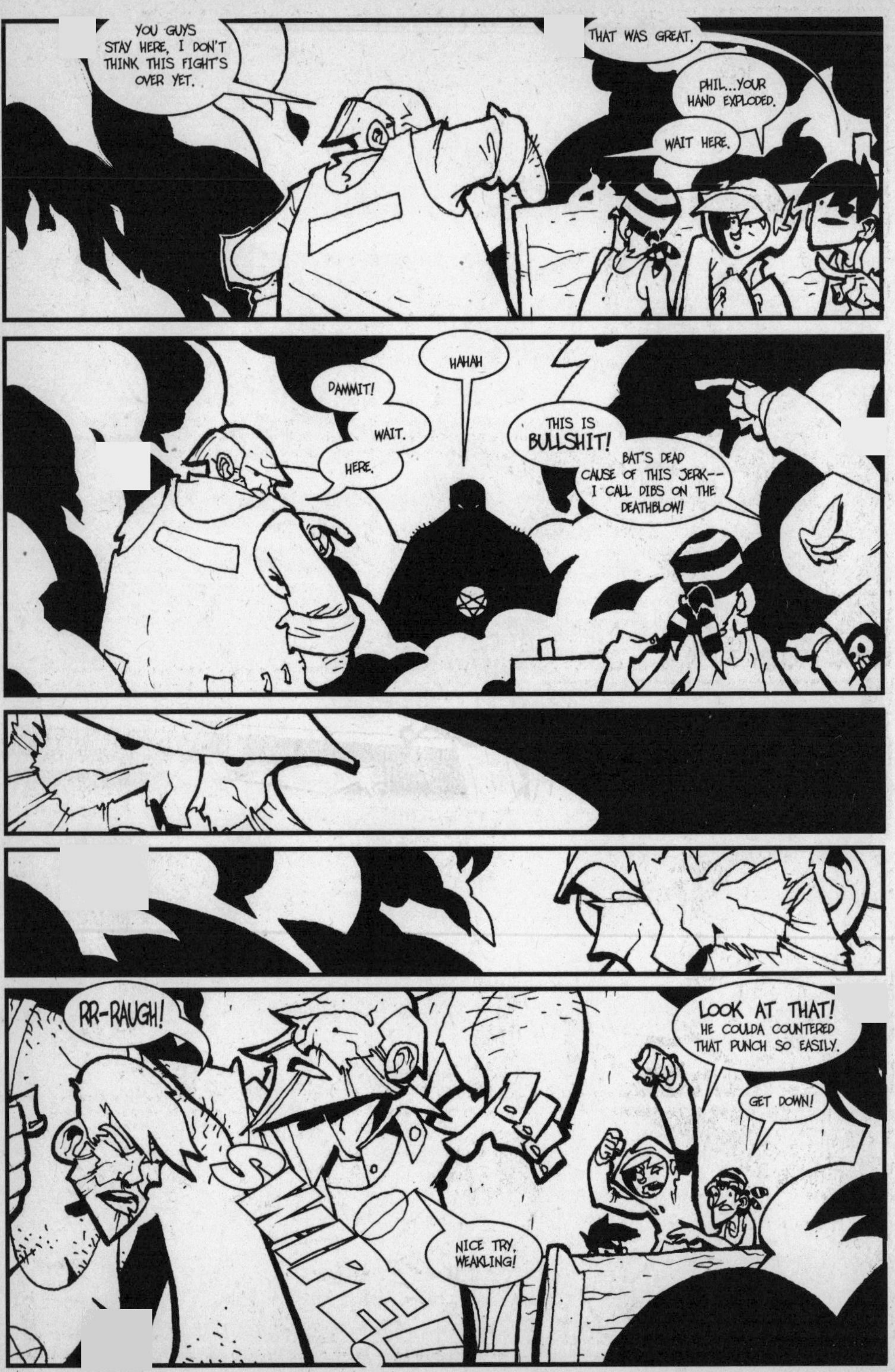
YOU GUYS STAY HERE, I DON'T THINK THIS FIGHT'S OVER YET.
THAT WAS GREAT.
PHIL...YOUR HAND EXPLODED.
WAIT HERE.
DAMMIT!
WAIT.
HERE.
HAHAH
THIS IS BULLSHIT!
BAT'S DEAD CAUSE OF THIS JERK-- I CALL DIBS ON THE DEATHBLOW!
RR-RAUGH!
SWIPE!
NICE TRY, WEAKLING!
LOOK AT THAT! HE COULDA COUNTERED THAT PUNCH SO EASILY.
GET DOWN!

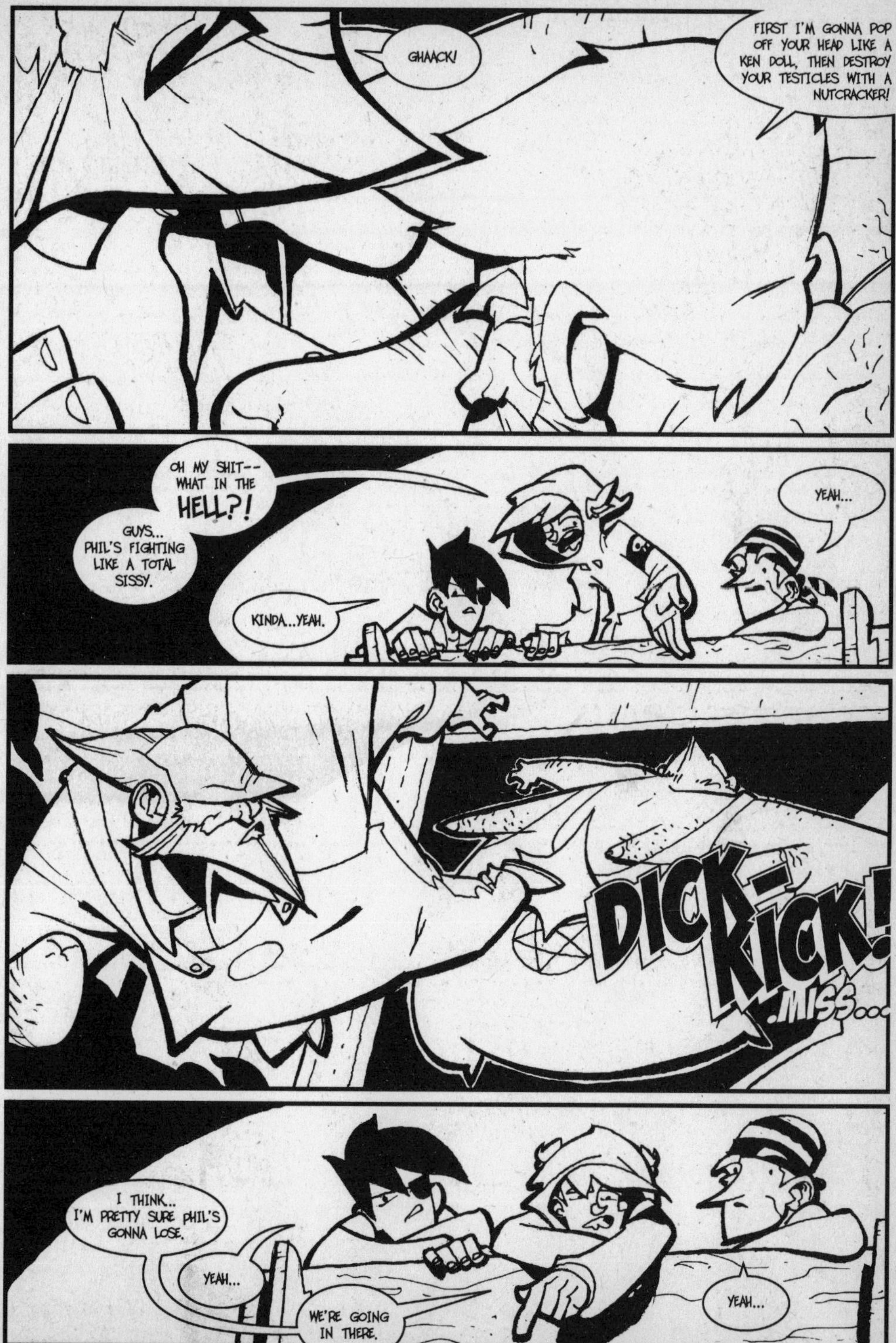
GHAACK!
FIRST I'M GONNA POP OFF YOUR HEAD LIKE A KEN DOLL, THEN DESTROY YOUR TESTICLES WITH A NUTCRACKER!
OH MY SHIT-- WHAT IN THE HELL?!
GUYS... PHIL'S FIGHTING LIKE A TOTAL SISSY.
YEAH...
KINDA...YEAH.
DICK-KICK!
.MISS...
I THINK.. I'M PRETTY SURE PHIL'S GONNA LOSE.
YEAH...
WE'RE GOING IN THERE.
YEAH...

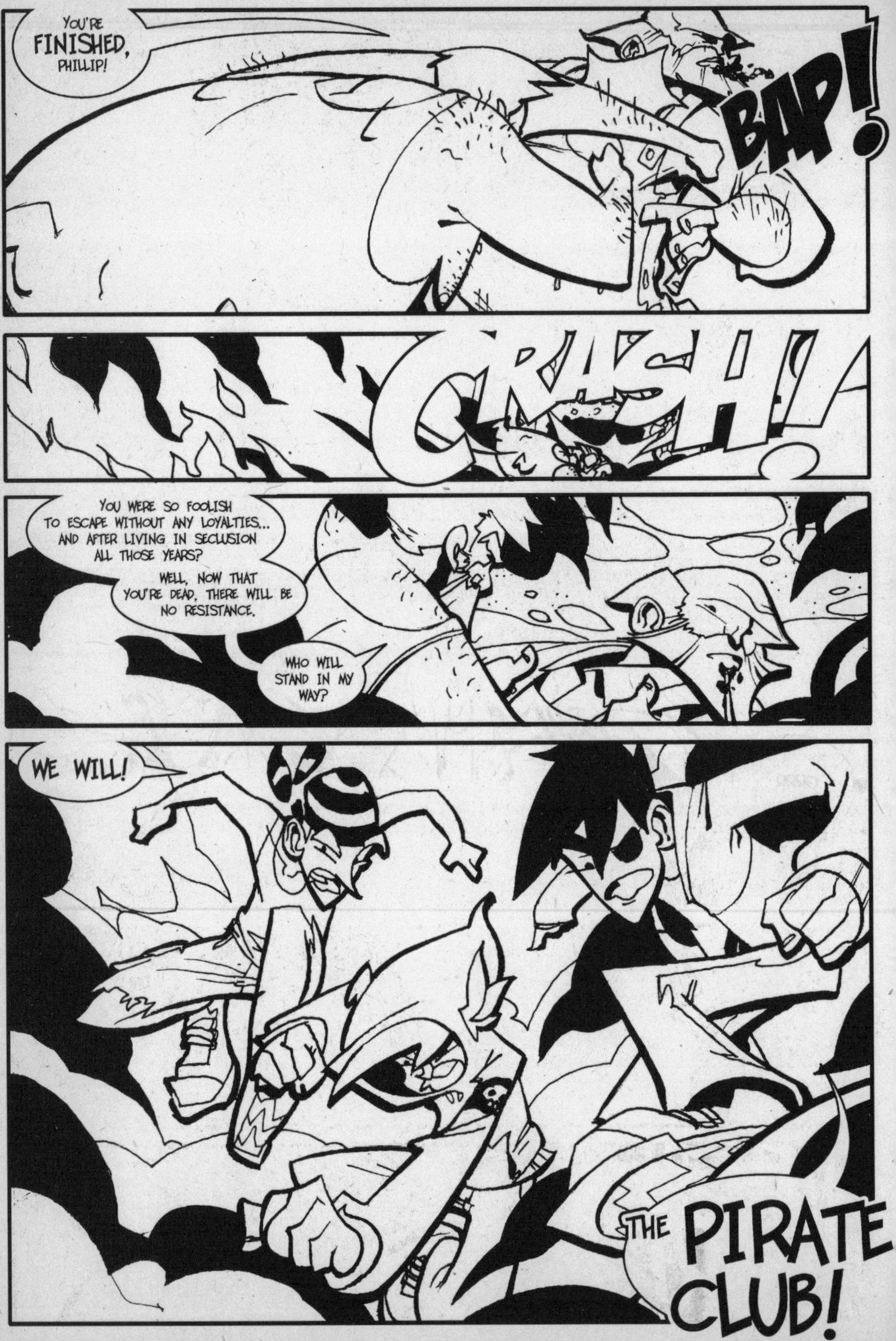
YOU'RE FINISHED, PHILLIP!
BAP!
CRASH!
YOU WERE SO FOOLISH TO ESCAPE WITHOUT ANY LOYALTIES... AND AFTER LIVING IN SECLUSION ALL THOSE YEARS?
WELL, NOW THAT YOU'RE DEAD, THERE WILL BE NO RESISTANCE.
WHO WILL STAND IN MY WAY?
WE WILL!
THE PIRATE CLUB!

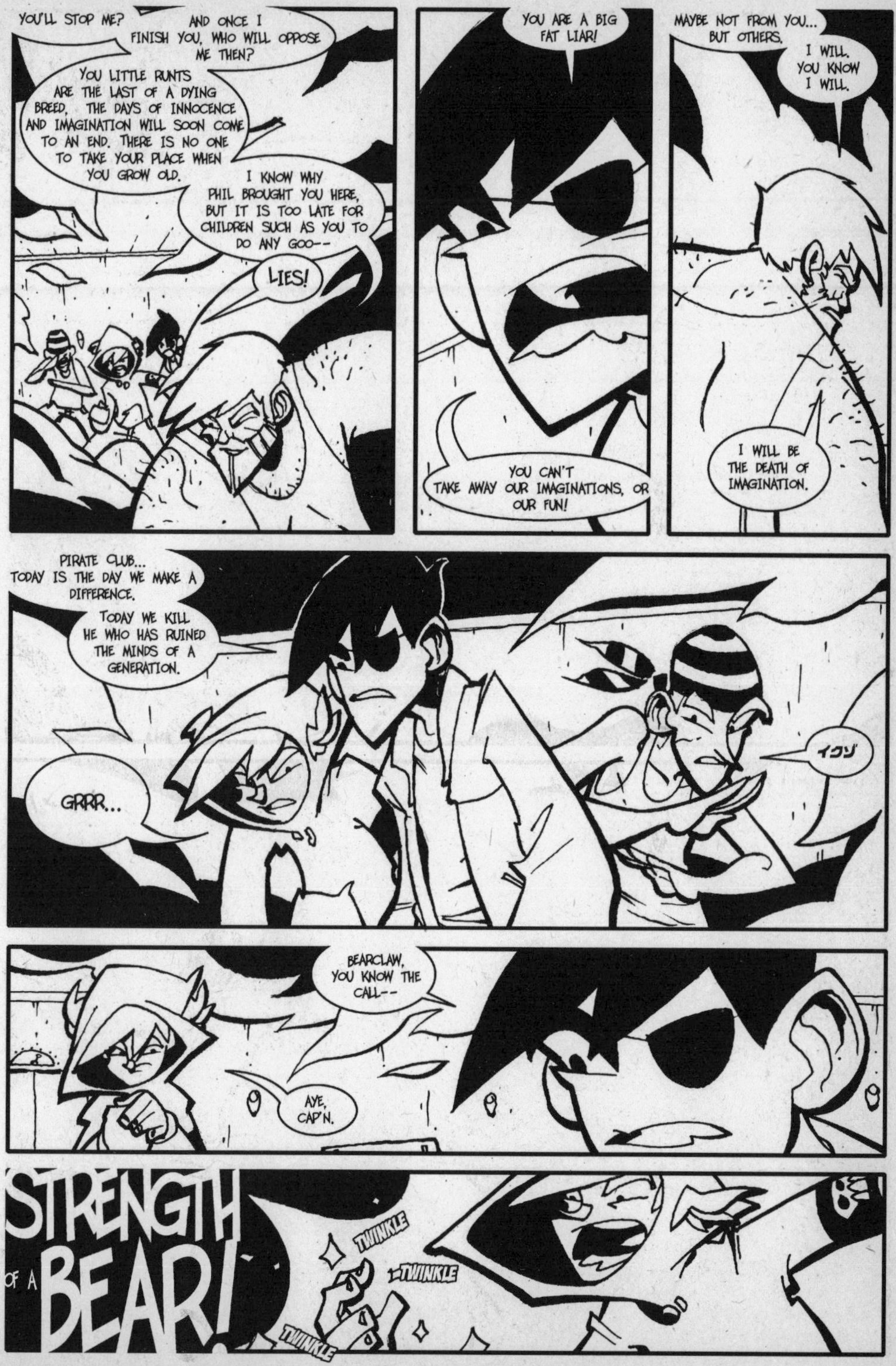
YOU'LL STOP ME?
AND ONCE I FINISH YOU, WHO WILL OPPOSE ME THEN?
YOU LITTLE RUNTS ARE THE LAST OF A DYING BREED. THE DAYS OF INNOCENCE AND IMAGINATION WILL SOON COME TO AN END. THERE IS NO ONE TO TAKE YOUR PLACE WHEN YOU GROW OLD.
I KNOW WHY PHIL BROUGHT YOU HERE, BUT IT IS TOO LATE FOR CHILDREN SUCH AS YOU TO DO ANY GOO--
LIES!
YOU ARE A BIG FAT LIAR!
YOU CAN'T TAKE AWAY OUR IMAGINATIONS, OR OUR FUN!
MAYBE NOT FROM YOU... BUT OTHERS.
I WILL. YOU KNOW I WILL.
I WILL BE THE DEATH OF IMAGINATION.
PIRATE CLUB... TODAY IS THE DAY WE MAKE A DIFFERENCE.
TODAY WE KILL HE WHO HAS RUINED THE MINDS OF A GENERATION.
GRRR...
イクゾ
BEARCLAW, YOU KNOW THE CALL--
AYE, CAP'N.
STRENGTH OF A BEAR!
TWINKLE
TWINKLE
TWINKLE

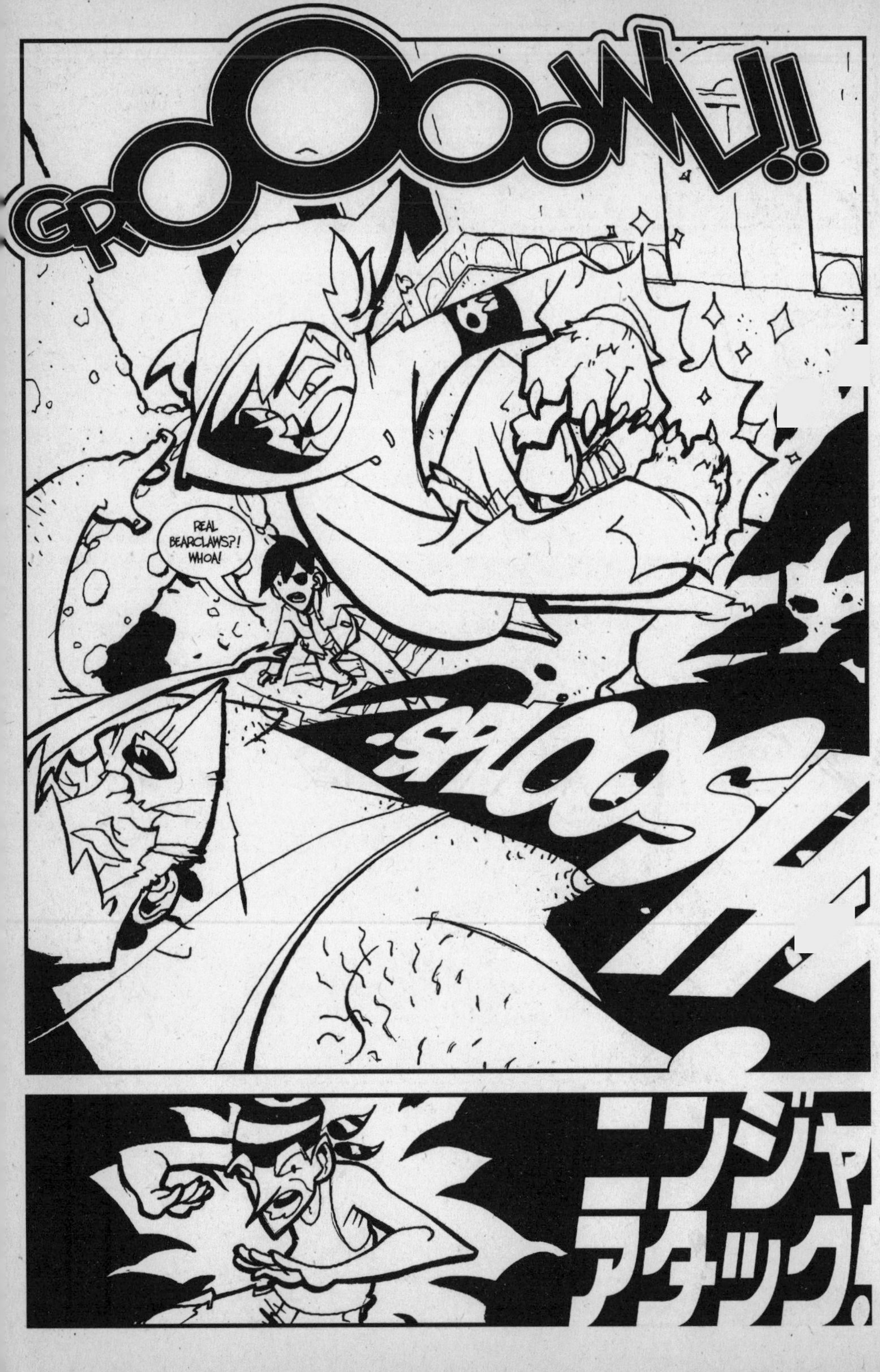
GROOOOOWL!!
REAL BEARCLAWS?! WHOA!
SPLOOSH
ニンジャアタック！

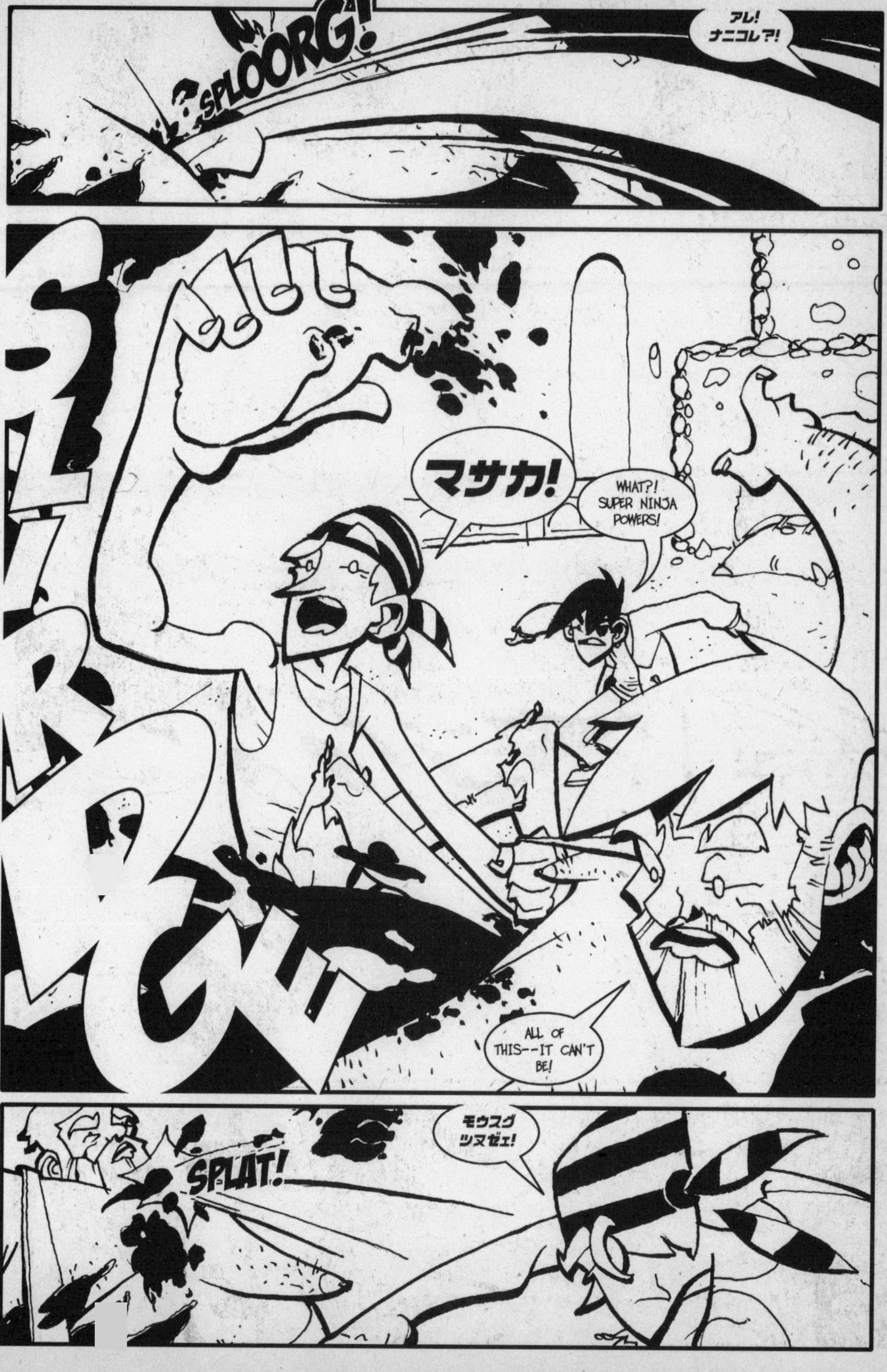
SPLOORG!
アレ!
ナニコレ?!
マサカ!
WHAT?! SUPER NINJA POWERS!
ALL OF THIS--IT CAN'T BE!
SPLAT!
モウスグ
ツヌゼェ!

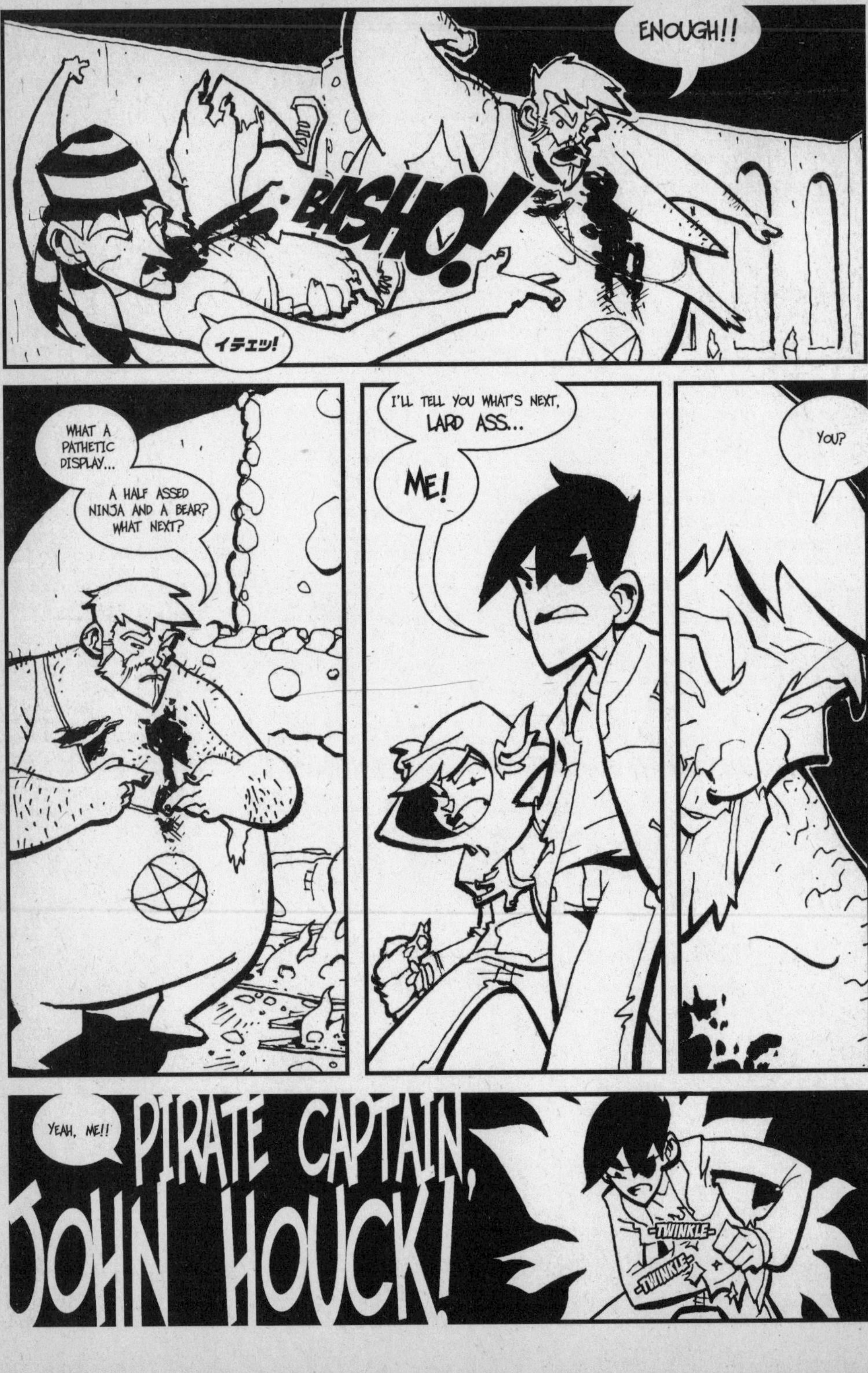

ENOUGH!!
BASHO!
イテェッ!
WHAT A PATHETIC DISPLAY...
A HALF ASSED NINJA AND A BEAR? WHAT NEXT?
I'LL TELL YOU WHAT'S NEXT, LARD ASS...
ME!
YOU?
YEAH, ME!!
PIRATE CAPTAIN, JOHN HOUCK!
TWINKLE
TWINKLE

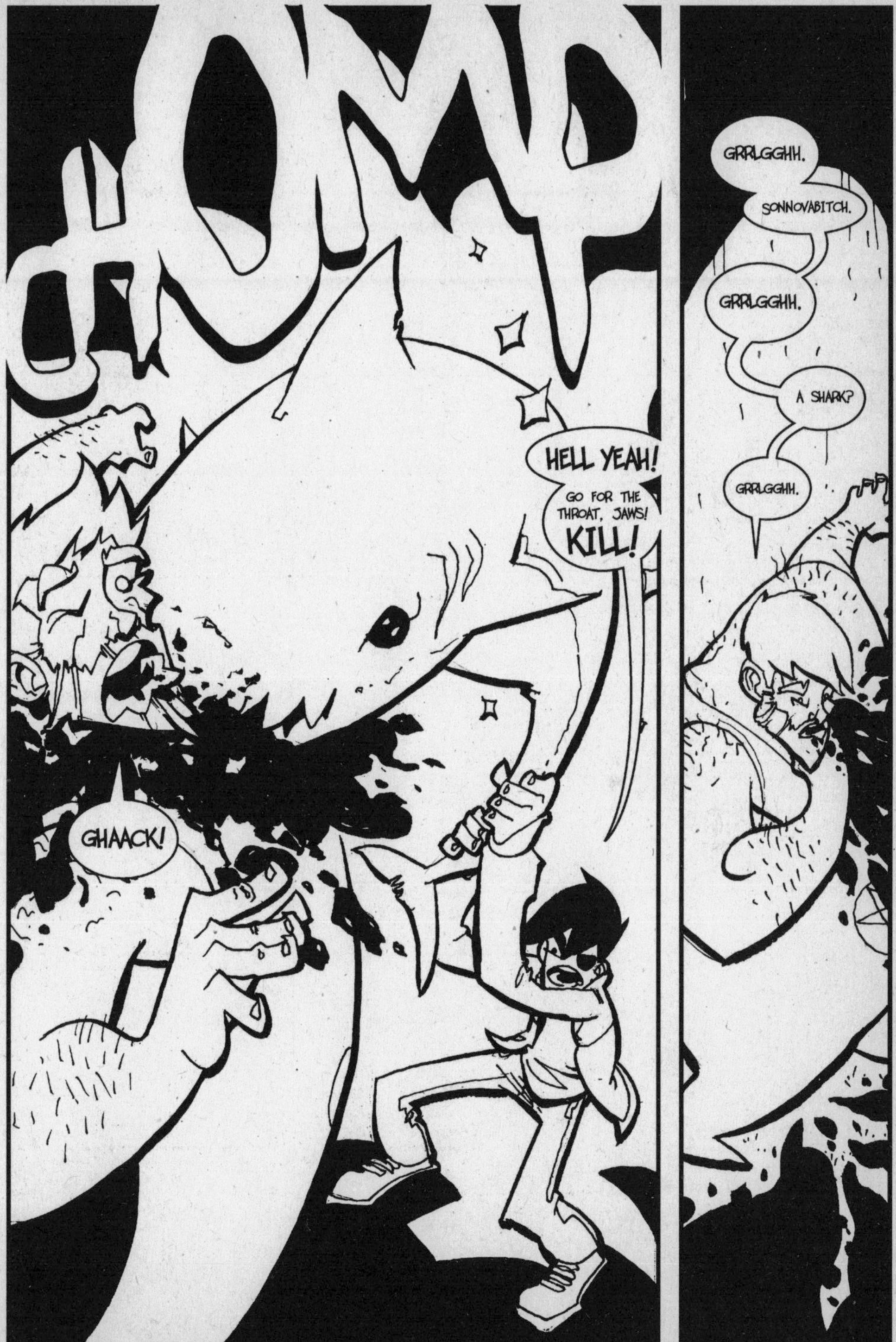
CHOMP
HELL YEAH!
GO FOR THE THROAT, JAWS!
KILL!
GHAACK!
GRRLGGHH.
SONNOVABITCH.
GRRLGGHH.
A SHARK?
GRRLGGHH.

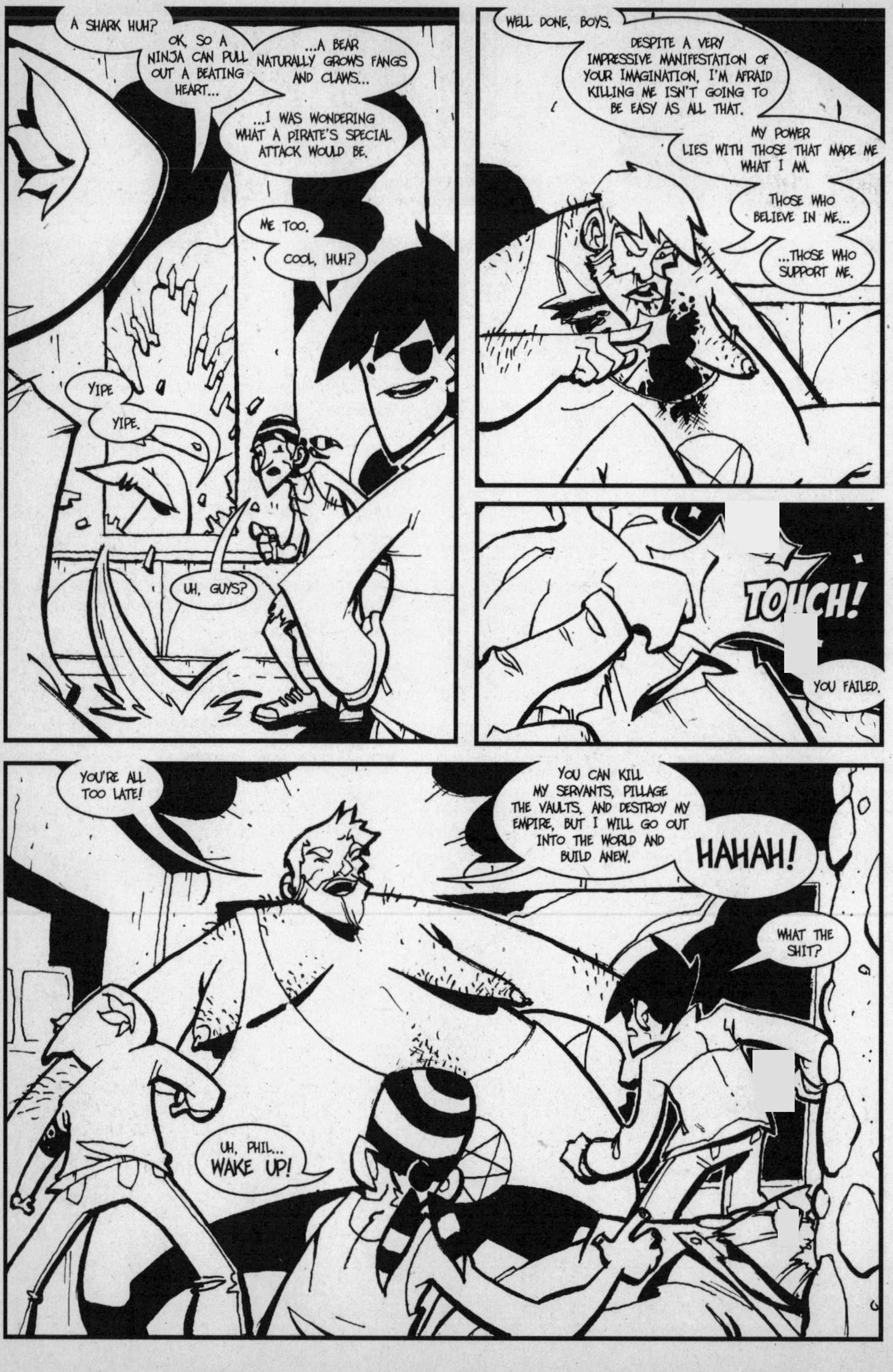
A SHARK HUH?
OK, SO A NINJA CAN PULL OUT A BEATING HEART...
...A BEAR NATURALLY GROWS FANGS AND CLAWS...
...I WAS WONDERING WHAT A PIRATE'S SPECIAL ATTACK WOULD BE.
ME TOO.
COOL, HUH?
YIPE
YIPE.
UH, GUYS?
WELL DONE, BOYS.
DESPITE A VERY IMPRESSIVE MANIFESTATION OF YOUR IMAGINATION, I'M AFRAID KILLING ME ISN'T GOING TO BE EASY AS ALL THAT.
MY POWER LIES WITH THOSE THAT MADE ME WHAT I AM.
THOSE WHO BELIEVE IN ME...
...THOSE WHO SUPPORT ME.
TOUCH!
YOU FAILED.
YOU'RE ALL TOO LATE!
YOU CAN KILL MY SERVANTS, PILLAGE THE VAULTS, AND DESTROY MY EMPIRE, BUT I WILL GO OUT INTO THE WORLD AND BUILD ANEW.
HAHAH!
WHAT THE SHIT?
UH, PHIL... WAKE UP!

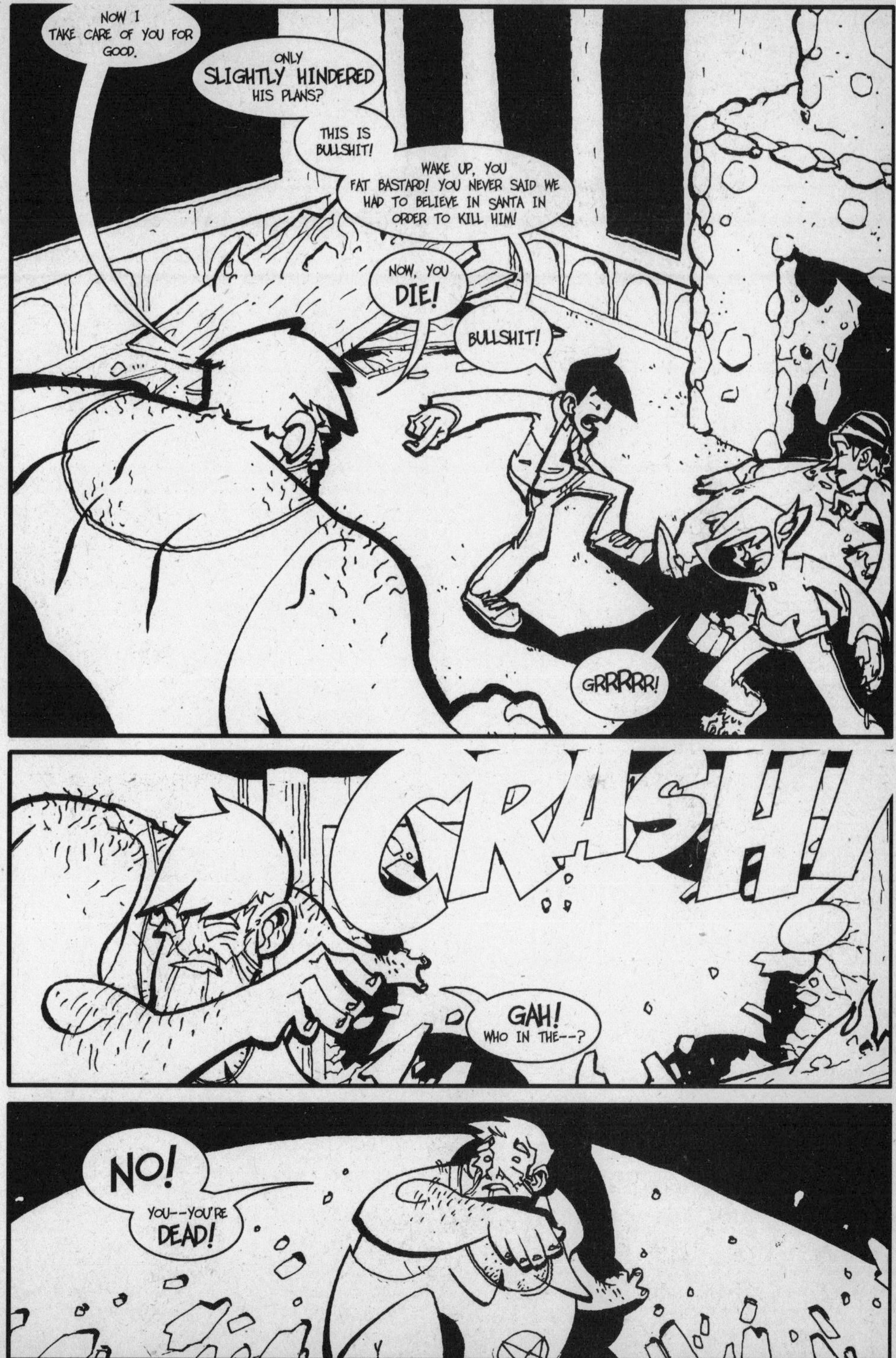
NOW I TAKE CARE OF YOU FOR GOOD.
ONLY SLIGHTLY HINDERED HIS PLANS?
THIS IS BULLSHIT!
WAKE UP, YOU FAT BASTARD! YOU NEVER SAID WE HAD TO BELIEVE IN SANTA IN ORDER TO KILL HIM!
NOW, YOU DIE!
BULLSHIT!
GRRRRR!
CRASH!
GAH! WHO IN THE--?
NO!
YOU--YOU'RE DEAD!

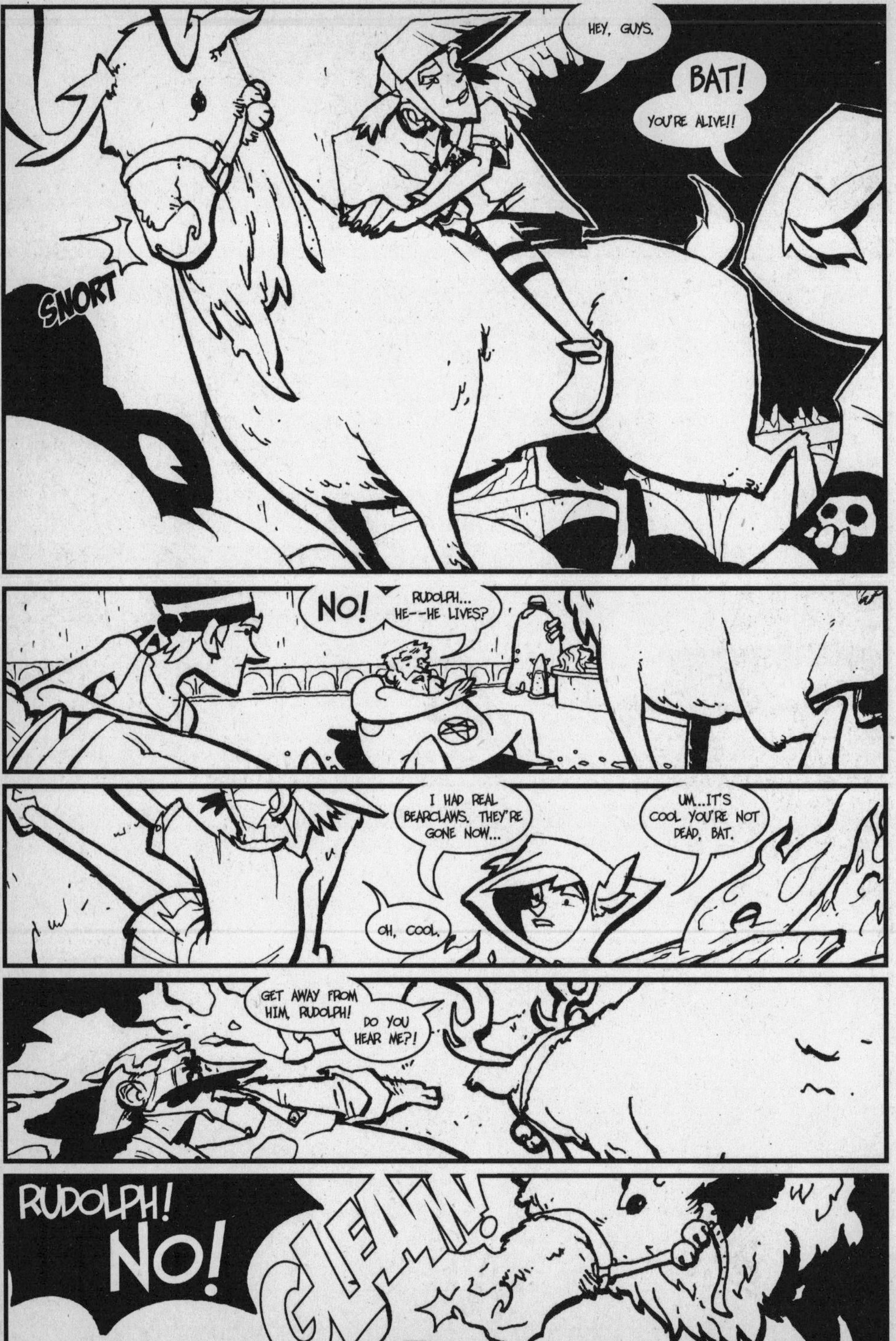
HEY, GUYS.
BAT!
YOU'RE ALIVE!!
SNORT
NO!
RUDOLPH... HE--HE LIVES?
I HAD REAL BEARCLAWS. THEY'RE GONE NOW...
OH, COOL.
UM...IT'S COOL YOU'RE NOT DEAD, BAT.
GET AWAY FROM HIM, RUDOLPH!
DO YOU HEAR ME?!
RUDOLPH!
NO!
CLFAM!

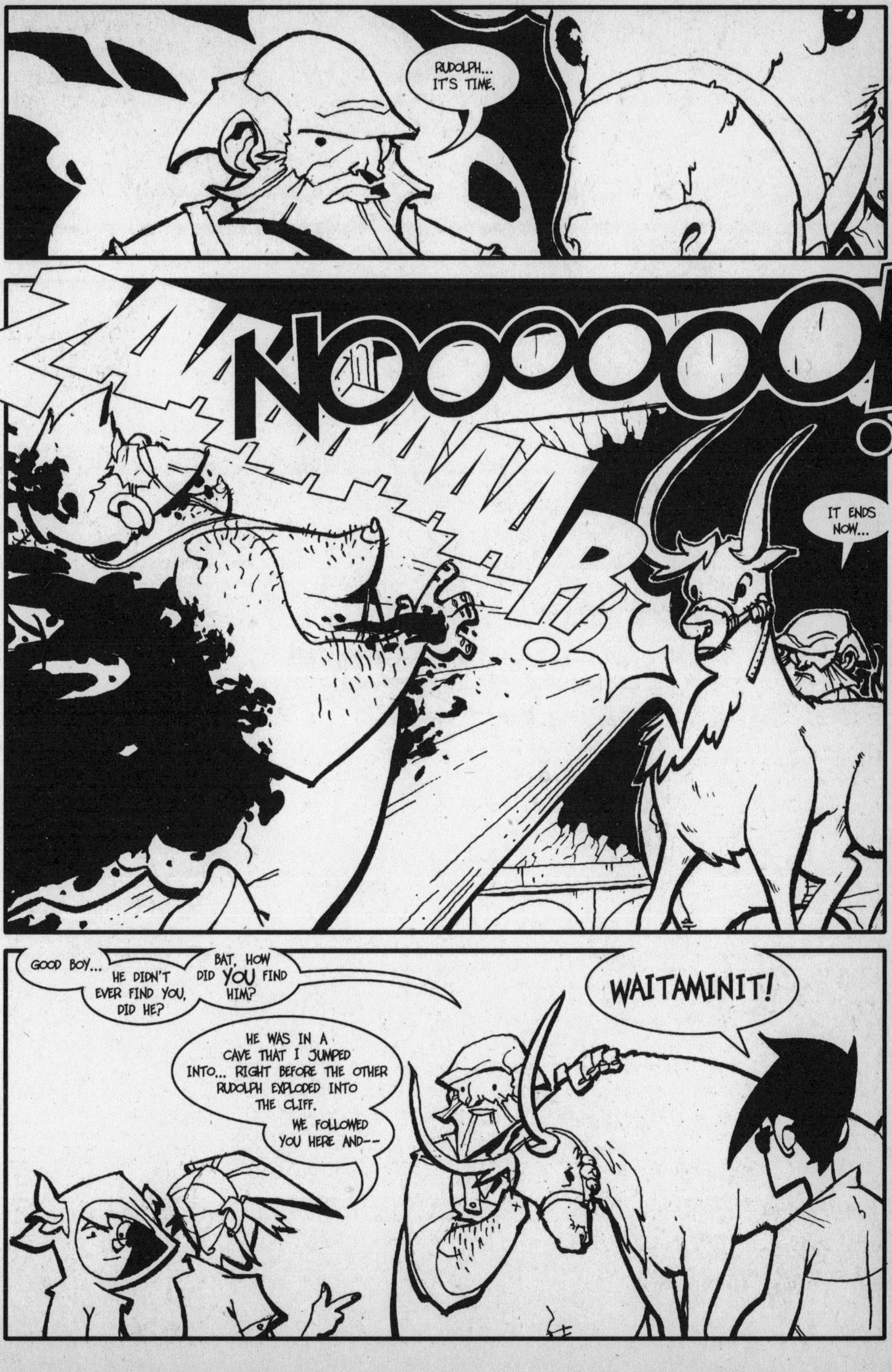
RUDOLPH... IT'S TIME.
ZAKNOOOOOO!
WAMR
IT ENDS NOW...
GOOD BOY...
HE DIDN'T EVER FIND YOU, DID HE?
BAT, HOW DID YOU FIND HIM?
WAITAMINIT!
HE WAS IN A CAVE THAT I JUMPED INTO... RIGHT BEFORE THE OTHER RUDOLPH EXPLODED INTO THE CLIFF.
WE FOLLOWED YOU HERE AND--

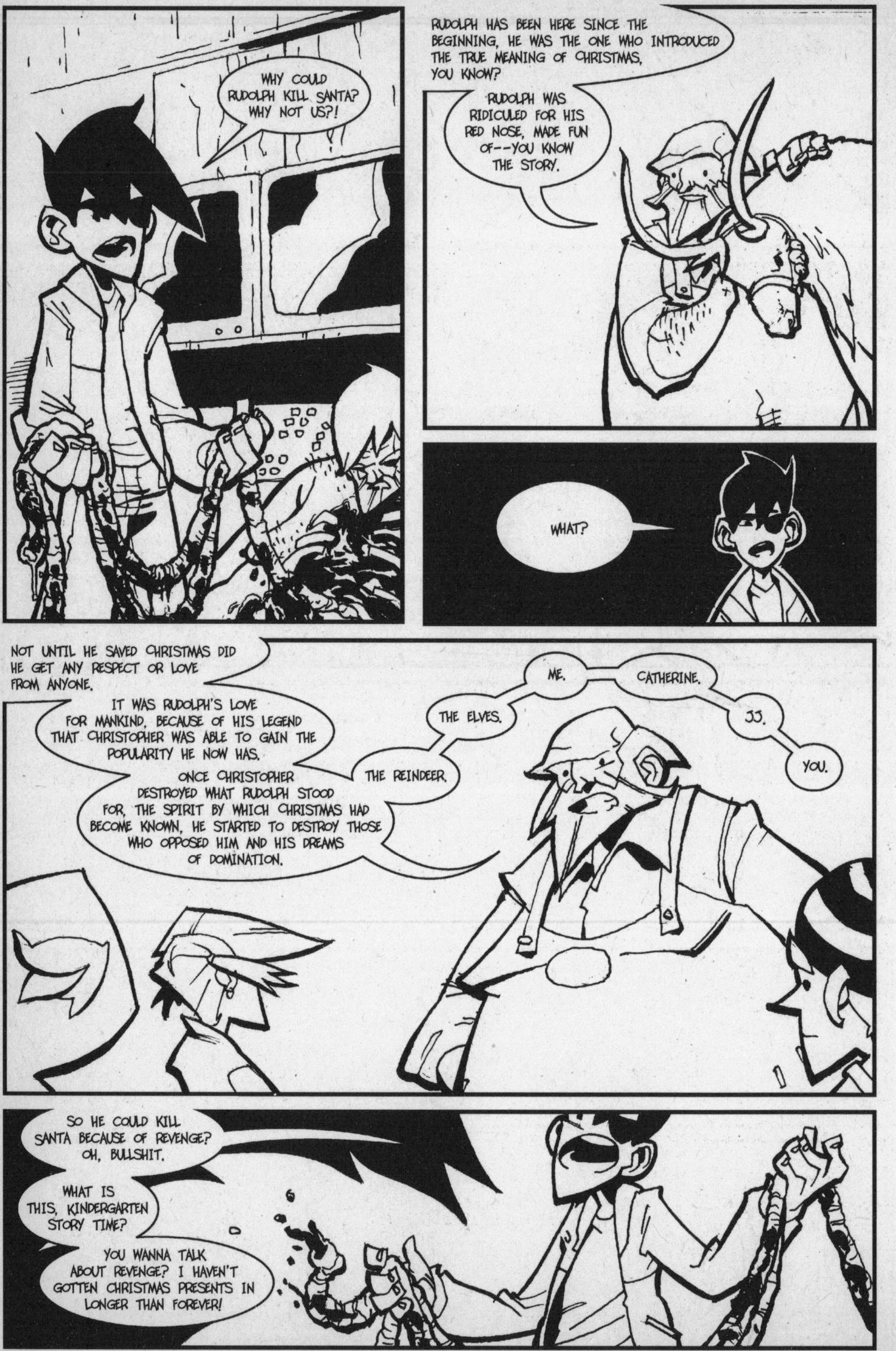
WHY COULD RUDOLPH KILL SANTA? WHY NOT US?!
RUDOLPH HAS BEEN HERE SINCE THE BEGINNING, HE WAS THE ONE WHO INTRODUCED THE TRUE MEANING OF CHRISTMAS, YOU KNOW?
RUDOLPH WAS RIDICULED FOR HIS RED NOSE, MADE FUN OF--YOU KNOW THE STORY.
WHAT?
NOT UNTIL HE SAVED CHRISTMAS DID HE GET ANY RESPECT OR LOVE FROM ANYONE.
IT WAS RUDOLPH'S LOVE FOR MANKIND, BECAUSE OF HIS LEGEND THAT CHRISTOPHER WAS ABLE TO GAIN THE POPULARITY HE NOW HAS.
ONCE CHRISTOPHER DESTROYED WHAT RUDOLPH STOOD FOR, THE SPIRIT BY WHICH CHRISTMAS HAD BECOME KNOWN, HE STARTED TO DESTROY THOSE WHO OPPOSED HIM AND HIS DREAMS OF DOMINATION.
THE REINDEER.
THE ELVES.
ME.
CATHERINE.
JJ.
YOU.
SO HE COULD KILL SANTA BECAUSE OF REVENGE? OH, BULLSHIT.
WHAT IS THIS, KINDERGARTEN STORY TIME?
YOU WANNA TALK ABOUT REVENGE? I HAVEN'T GOTTEN CHRISTMAS PRESENTS IN LONGER THAN FOREVER!

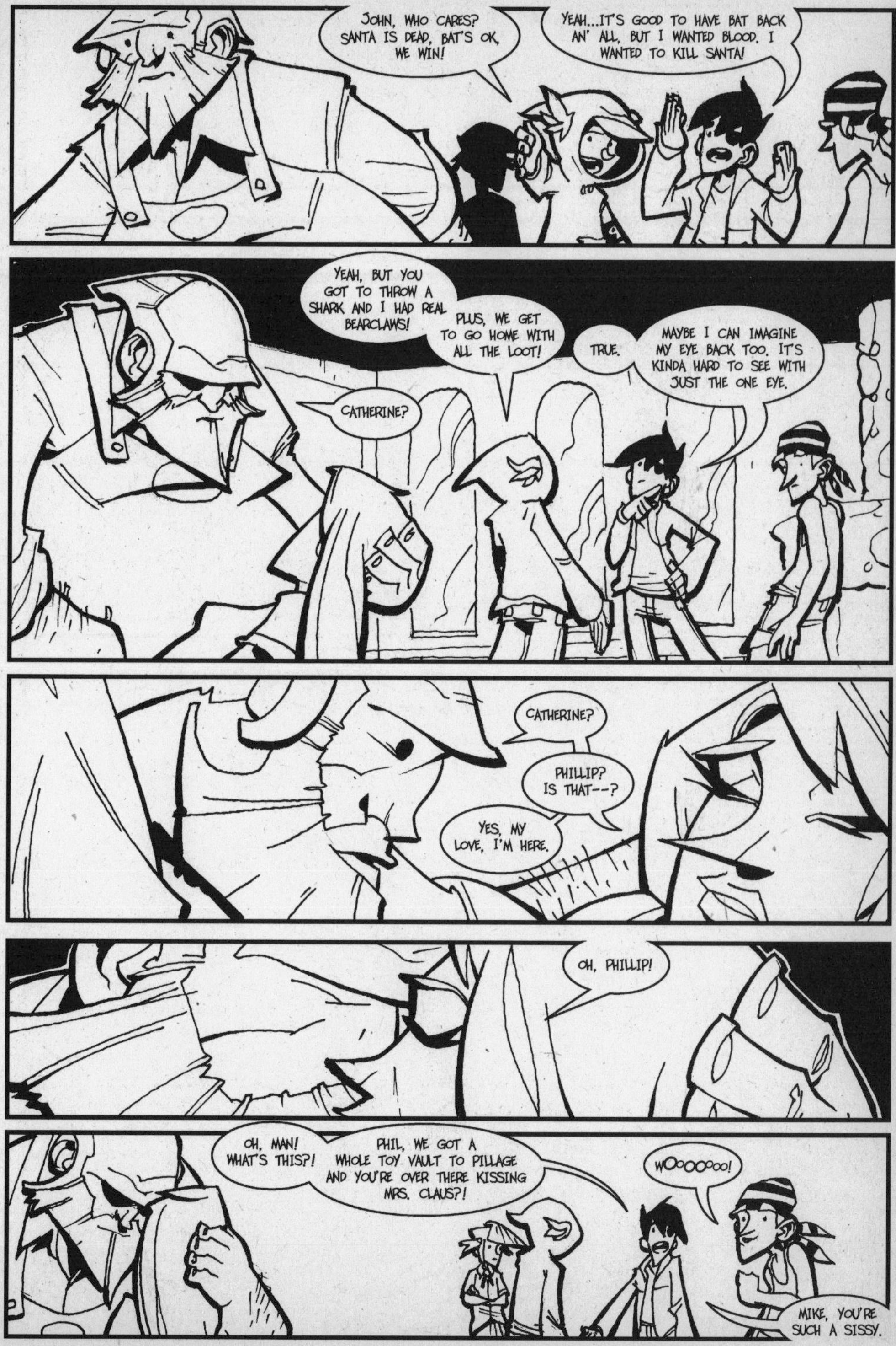
JOHN, WHO CARES? SANTA IS DEAD, BAT'S OK, WE WIN!
YEAH...IT'S GOOD TO HAVE BAT BACK AN' ALL, BUT I WANTED BLOOD. I WANTED TO KILL SANTA!
YEAH, BUT YOU GOT TO THROW A SHARK AND I HAD REAL BEARCLAWS!
PLUS, WE GET TO GO HOME WITH ALL THE LOOT!
TRUE.
MAYBE I CAN IMAGINE MY EYE BACK TOO. IT'S KINDA HARD TO SEE WITH JUST THE ONE EYE.
CATHERINE?
CATHERINE?
PHILLIP? IS THAT--?
YES, MY LOVE, I'M HERE.
OH, PHILLIP!
OH, MAN! WHAT'S THIS?!
PHIL, WE GOT A WHOLE TOY VAULT TO PILLAGE AND YOU'RE OVER THERE KISSING MRS. CLAUS?!
WOoooooo!
MIKE, YOU'RE SUCH A SISSY.

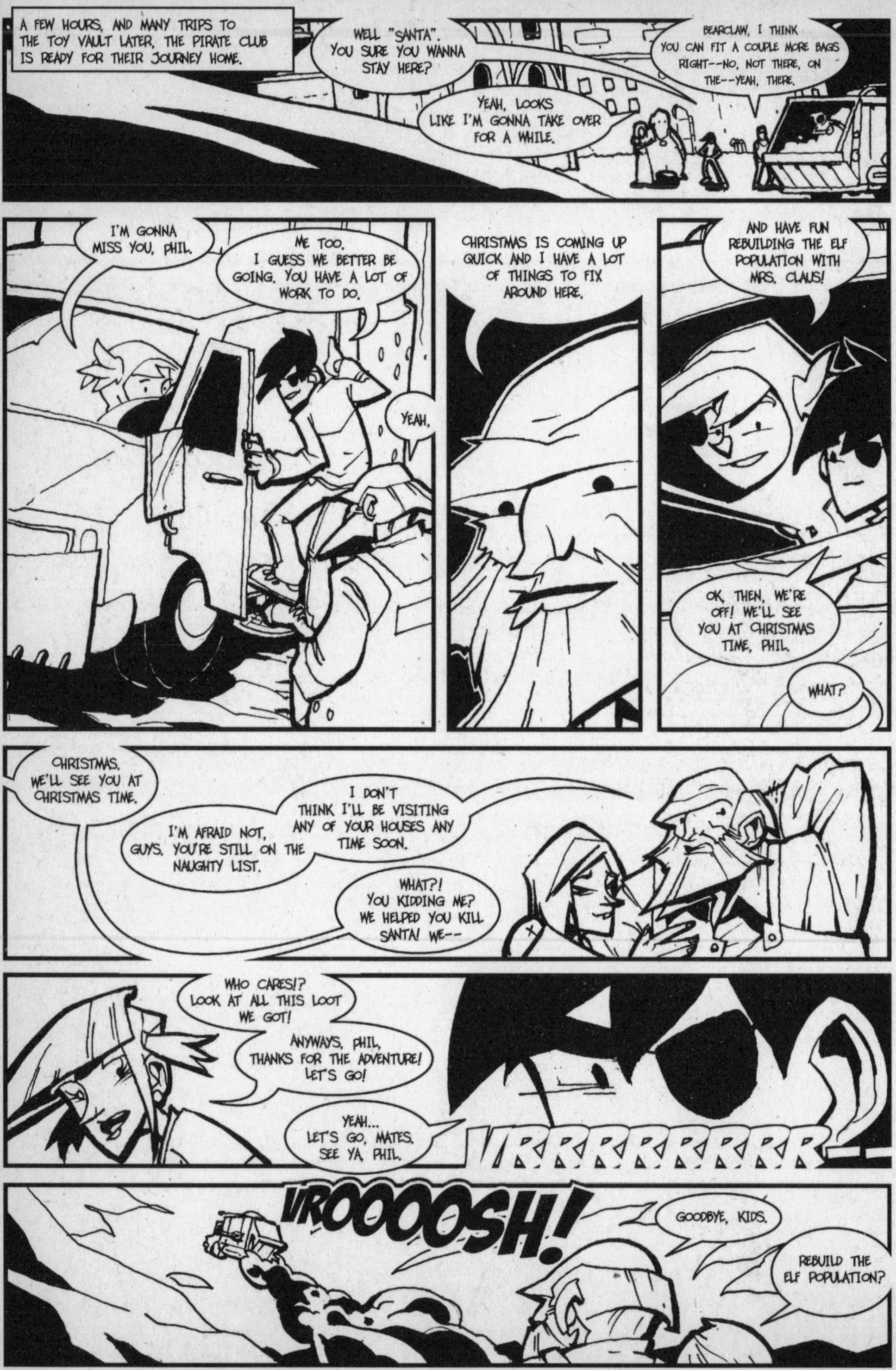
A FEW HOURS, AND MANY TRIPS TO THE TOY VAULT LATER, THE PIRATE CLUB IS READY FOR THEIR JOURNEY HOME.
WELL "SANTA". YOU SURE YOU WANNA STAY HERE?
YEAH, LOOKS LIKE I'M GONNA TAKE OVER FOR A WHILE.
BEARCLAW, I THINK YOU CAN FIT A COUPLE MORE BAGS RIGHT--NO, NOT THERE, ON THE--YEAH, THERE.
I'M GONNA MISS YOU, PHIL.
ME TOO. I GUESS WE BETTER BE GOING. YOU HAVE A LOT OF WORK TO DO.
YEAH.
CHRISTMAS IS COMING UP QUICK AND I HAVE A LOT OF THINGS TO FIX AROUND HERE.
AND HAVE FUN REBUILDING THE ELF POPULATION WITH MRS. CLAUS!
OK, THEN, WE'RE OFF! WE'LL SEE YOU AT CHRISTMAS TIME, PHIL.
WHAT?
CHRISTMAS. WE'LL SEE YOU AT CHRISTMAS TIME.
I'M AFRAID NOT, GUYS. YOU'RE STILL ON THE NAUGHTY LIST.
I DON'T THINK I'LL BE VISITING ANY OF YOUR HOUSES ANY TIME SOON.
WHAT?! YOU KIDDING ME? WE HELPED YOU KILL SANTA! WE--
WHO CARES!? LOOK AT ALL THIS LOOT WE GOT!
ANYWAYS, PHIL, THANKS FOR THE ADVENTURE! LET'S GO!
YEAH... LET'S GO, MATES. SEE YA, PHIL.
VRRRRRRRRR--
VROOOOOSH!
GOODBYE, KIDS.
REBUILD THE ELF POPULATION?

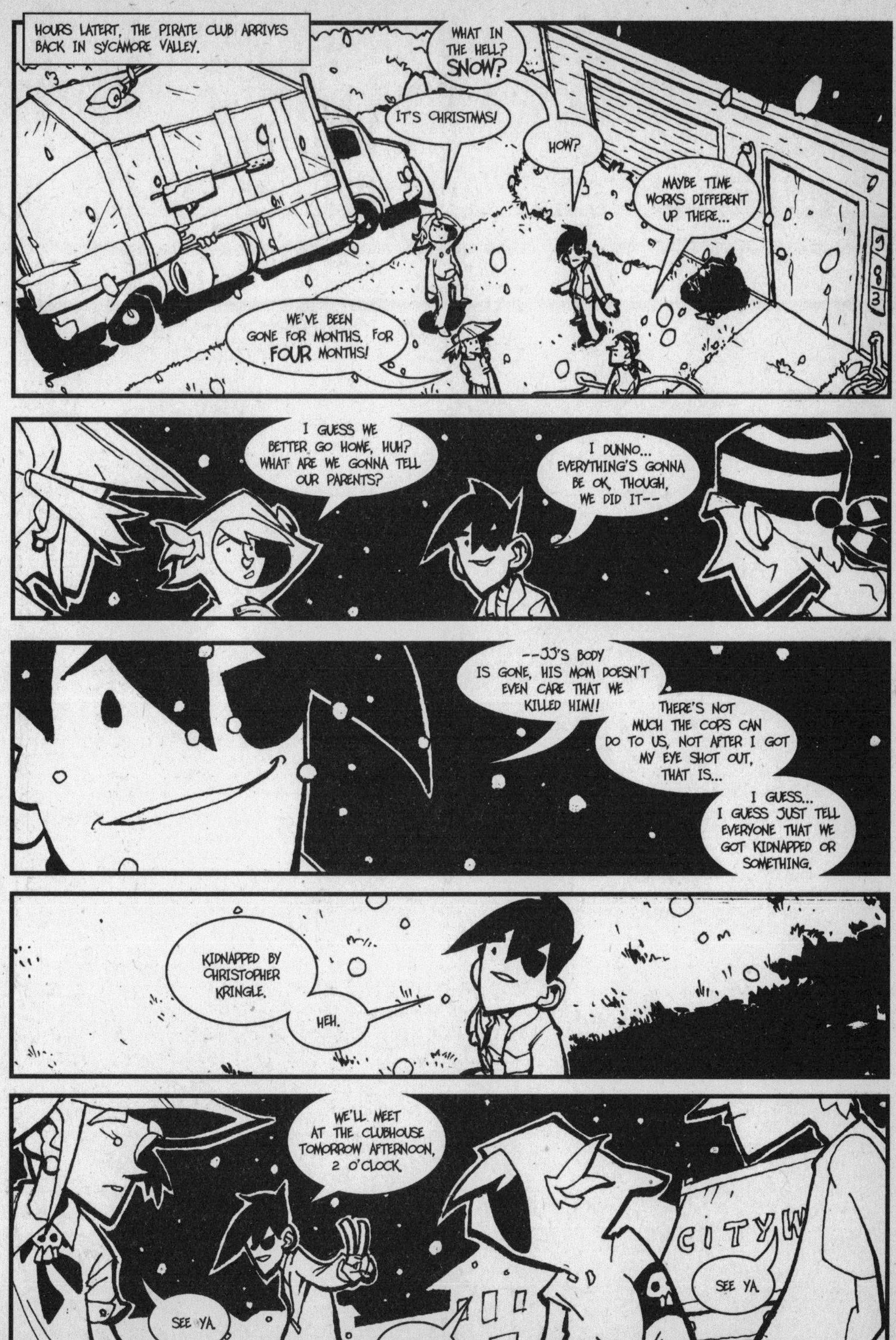
HOURS LATERT, THE PIRATE CLUB ARRIVES BACK IN SYCAMORE VALLEY.
WHAT IN THE HELL? SNOW?
IT'S CHRISTMAS!
HOW?
MAYBE TIME WORKS DIFFERENT UP THERE...
WE'VE BEEN GONE FOR MONTHS. FOR FOUR MONTHS!
9
8
3
I GUESS WE BETTER GO HOME, HUH? WHAT ARE WE GONNA TELL OUR PARENTS?
I DUNNO... EVERYTHING'S GONNA BE OK, THOUGH. WE DID IT--
--JJ'S BODY IS GONE, HIS MOM DOESN'T EVEN CARE THAT WE KILLED HIM!!
THERE'S NOT MUCH THE COPS CAN DO TO US, NOT AFTER I GOT MY EYE SHOT OUT, THAT IS...
I GUESS... I GUESS JUST TELL EVERYONE THAT WE GOT KIDNAPPED OR SOMETHING.
KIDNAPPED BY CHRISTOPHER KRINGLE.
HEH.
WE'LL MEET AT THE CLUBHOUSE TOMORROW AFTERNOON, 2 O'CLOCK.
CITYW
SEE YA.
SEE YA.
SEE YA.

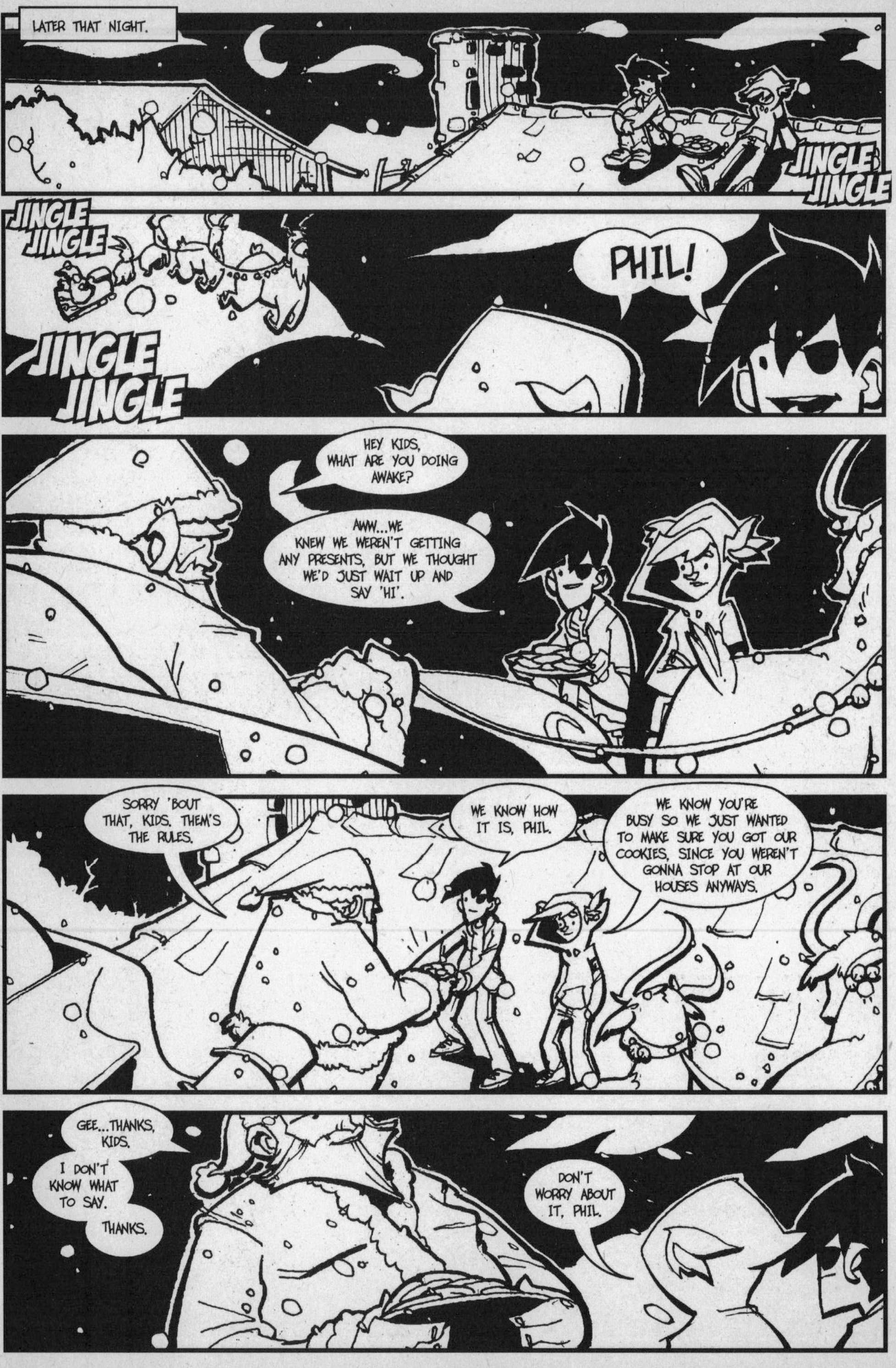
LATER THAT NIGHT.
JINGLE JINGLE
JINGLE JINGLE
JINGLE JINGLE
PHIL!
HEY KIDS, WHAT ARE YOU DOING AWAKE?
AWW...WE KNEW WE WEREN'T GETTING ANY PRESENTS, BUT WE THOUGHT WE'D JUST WAIT UP AND SAY 'HI'.
SORRY 'BOUT THAT, KIDS. THEM'S THE RULES.
WE KNOW HOW IT IS, PHIL.
WE KNOW YOU'RE BUSY SO WE JUST WANTED TO MAKE SURE YOU GOT OUR COOKIES, SINCE YOU WEREN'T GONNA STOP AT OUR HOUSES ANYWAYS.
GEE...THANKS, KIDS.
I DON'T KNOW WHAT TO SAY.
THANKS.
DON'T WORRY ABOUT IT, PHIL.

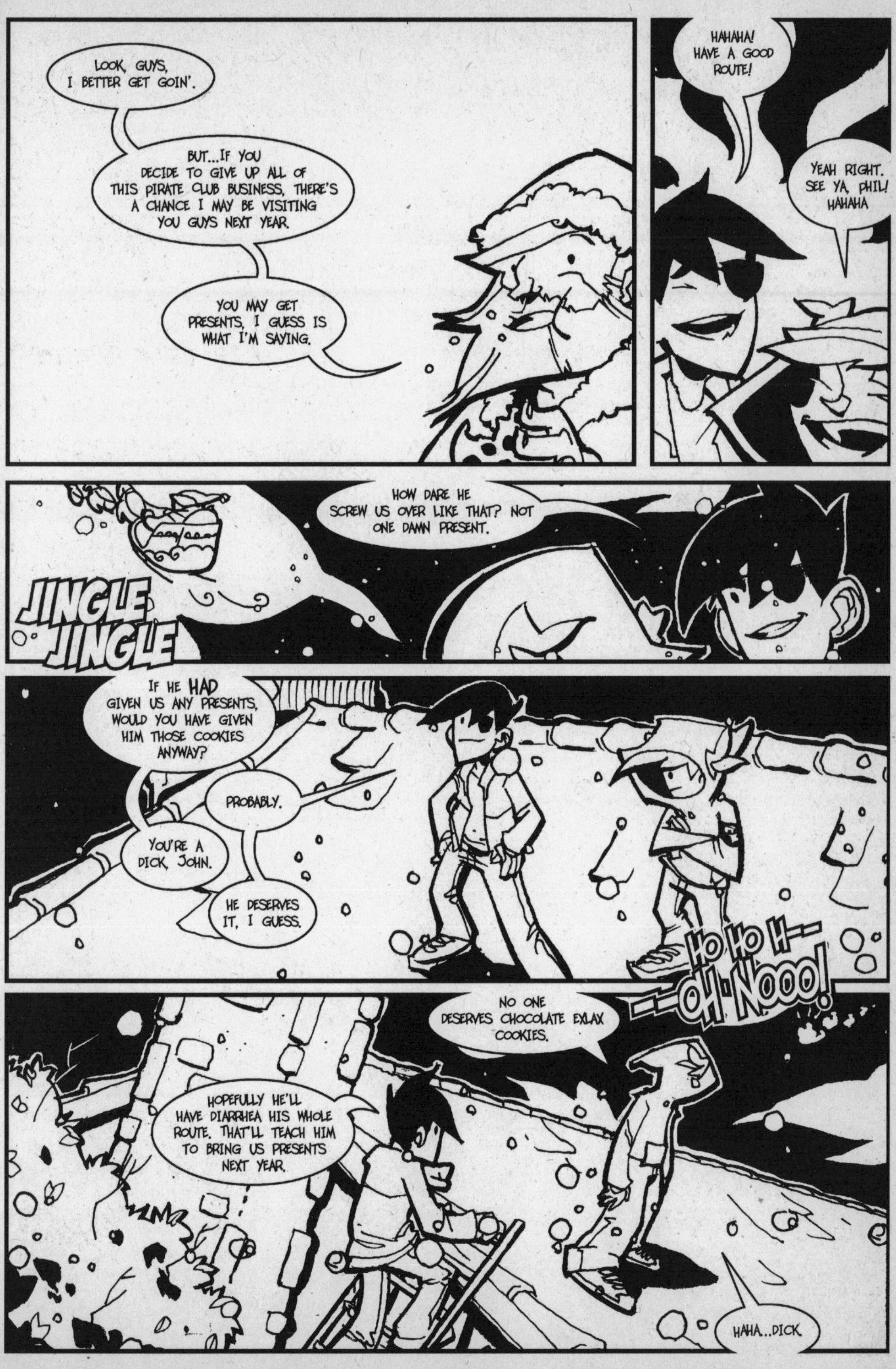
LOOK, GUYS, I BETTER GET GOIN'.
BUT...IF YOU DECIDE TO GIVE UP ALL OF THIS PIRATE CLUB BUSINESS, THERE'S A CHANCE I MAY BE VISITING YOU GUYS NEXT YEAR.
YOU MAY GET PRESENTS, I GUESS IS WHAT I'M SAYING.
HAHAHA! HAVE A GOOD ROUTE!
YEAH RIGHT. SEE YA, PHIL! HAHAHA
JINGLE JINGLE
HOW DARE HE SCREW US OVER LIKE THAT? NOT ONE DAMN PRESENT.
IF HE HAD GIVEN US ANY PRESENTS, WOULD YOU HAVE GIVEN HIM THOSE COOKIES ANYWAY?
PROBABLY.
YOU'RE A DICK, JOHN.
HE DESERVES IT, I GUESS.
HO HO H-- --OH NOOO!
NO ONE DESERVES CHOCOLATE EXLAX COOKIES.
HOPEFULLY HE'LL HAVE DIARRHEA HIS WHOLE ROUTE. THAT'LL TEACH HIM TO BRING US PRESENTS NEXT YEAR.
HAHA...DICK.

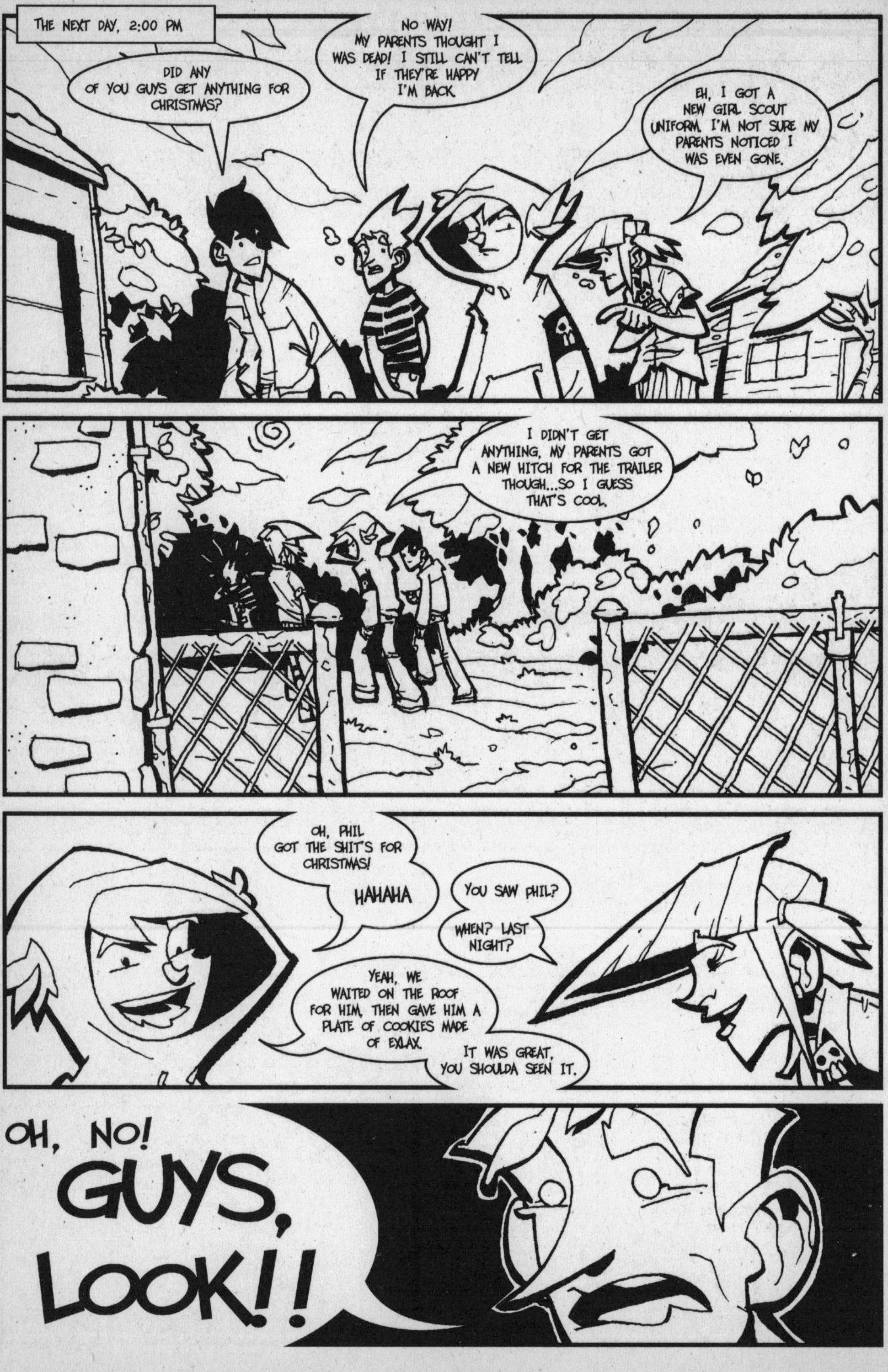
THE NEXT DAY, 2:00 PM
DID ANY OF YOU GUYS GET ANYTHING FOR CHRISTMAS?
NO WAY! MY PARENTS THOUGHT I WAS DEAD! I STILL CAN'T TELL IF THEY'RE HAPPY I'M BACK.
EH, I GOT A NEW GIRL SCOUT UNIFORM. I'M NOT SURE MY PARENTS NOTICED I WAS EVEN GONE.
I DIDN'T GET ANYTHING, MY PARENTS GOT A NEW HITCH FOR THE TRAILER THOUGH...SO I GUESS THAT'S COOL.
OH, PHIL GOT THE SHIT'S FOR CHRISTMAS!
HAHAHA
YOU SAW PHIL?
WHEN? LAST NIGHT?
YEAH, WE WAITED ON THE ROOF FOR HIM, THEN GAVE HIM A PLATE OF COOKIES MADE OF EXLAX.
IT WAS GREAT, YOU SHOULDA SEEN IT.
OH, NO!
GUYS, LOOK!!

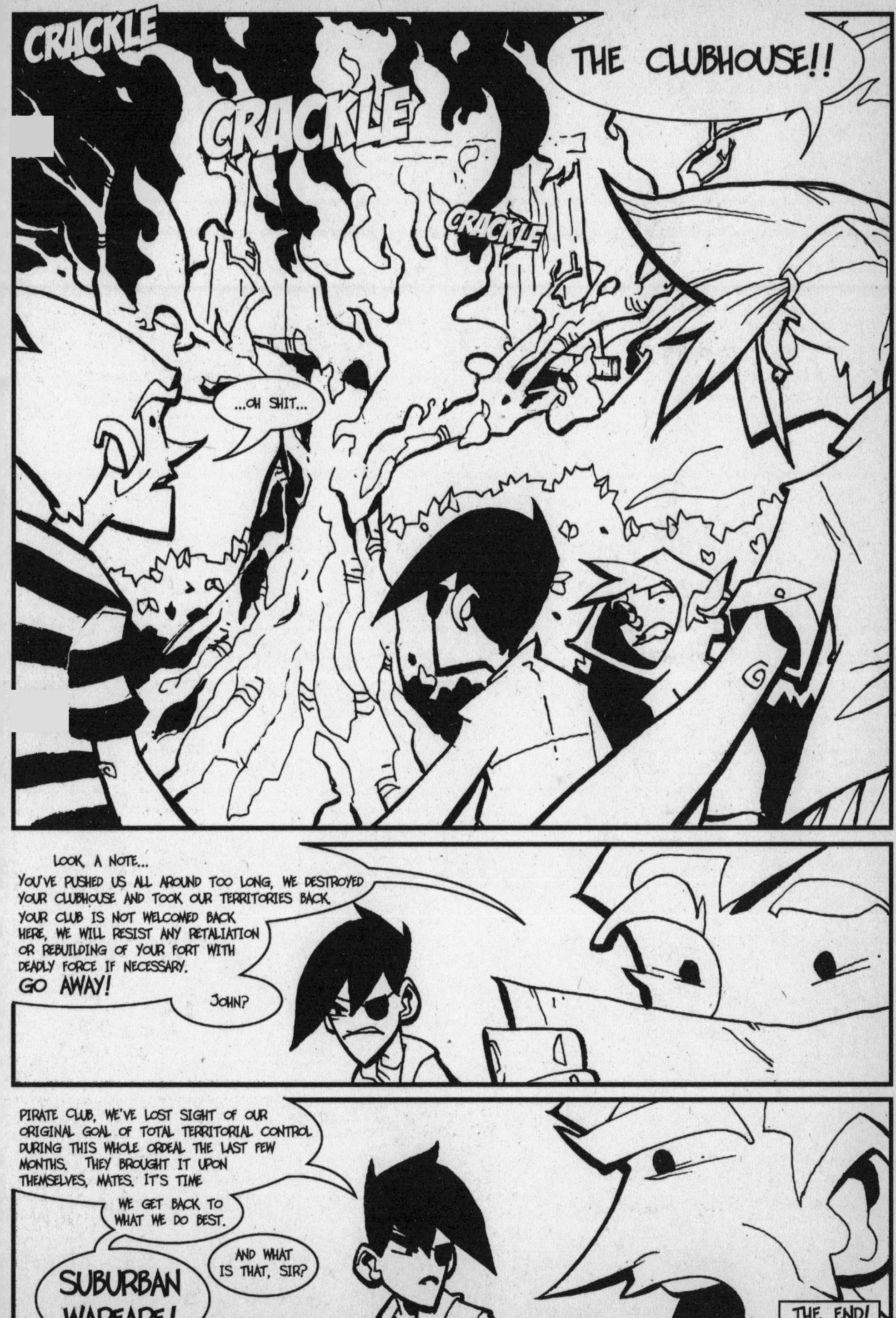
CRACKLE
CRACKLE
CRACKLE
THE CLUBHOUSE!!
...OH SHIT...
LOOK, A NOTE...
YOU'VE PUSHED US ALL AROUND TOO LONG, WE DESTROYED YOUR CLUBHOUSE AND TOOK OUR TERRITORIES BACK. YOUR CLUB IS NOT WELCOMED BACK HERE, WE WILL RESIST ANY RETALIATION OR REBUILDING OF YOUR FORT WITH DEADLY FORCE IF NECESSARY.
GO AWAY!
JOHN?
PIRATE CLUB, WE'VE LOST SIGHT OF OUR ORIGINAL GOAL OF TOTAL TERRITORIAL CONTROL DURING THIS WHOLE ORDEAL THE LAST FEW MONTHS. THEY BROUGHT IT UPON THEMSELVES, MATES. IT'S TIME
WE GET BACK TO WHAT WE DO BEST.
AND WHAT IS THAT, SIR?
SUBURBAN WARFARE!
THE END!
THANKS, FOLKS!

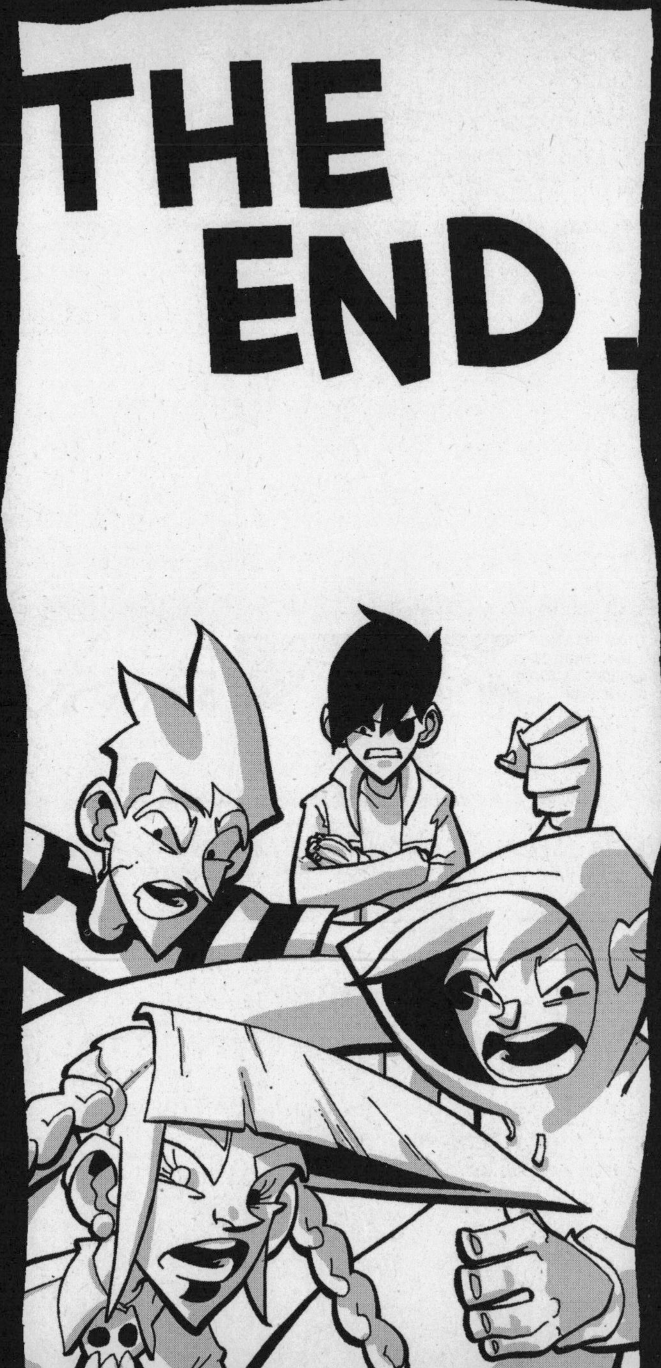
THE END.

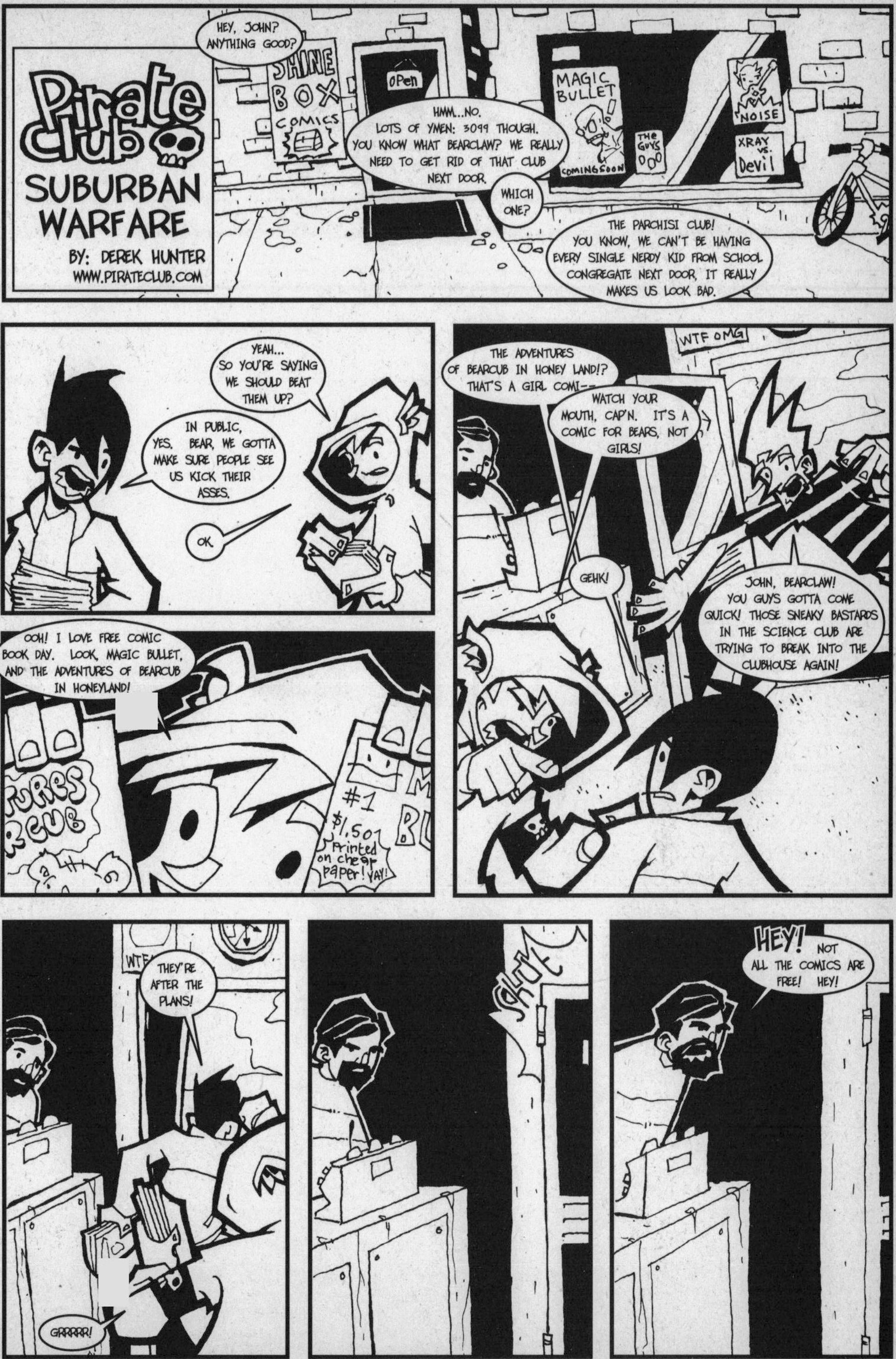
Pirate Club
SUBURBAN WARFARE
BY: DEREK HUNTER
WWW.PIRATECLUB.COM
HEY, JOHN? ANYTHING GOOD?
SHINE BOX COMICS
OPEN
MAGIC BULLET
COMING SOON
THE GUYS
NOISE
XRAY VS. DEVIL
HMM...NO. LOTS OF YMEN: 3099 THOUGH. YOU KNOW WHAT BEARCLAW? WE REALLY NEED TO GET RID OF THAT CLUB NEXT DOOR.
WHICH ONE?
THE PARCHISI CLUB! YOU KNOW, WE CAN'T BE HAVING EVERY SINGLE NERDY KID FROM SCHOOL CONGREGATE NEXT DOOR, IT REALLY MAKES US LOOK BAD.
YEAH... SO YOU'RE SAYING WE SHOULD BEAT THEM UP?
IN PUBLIC, YES. BEAR, WE GOTTA MAKE SURE PEOPLE SEE US KICK THEIR ASSES.
OK.
WTF OMG
THE ADVENTURES OF BEARCUB IN HONEY LAND!? THAT'S A GIRL COMI--
WATCH YOUR MOUTH, CAP'N. IT'S A COMIC FOR BEARS, NOT GIRLS!
GEHK!
JOHN, BEARCLAW! YOU GUYS GOTTA COME QUICK! THOSE SNEAKY BASTARDS IN THE SCIENCE CLUB ARE TRYING TO BREAK INTO THE CLUBHOUSE AGAIN!
OOH! I LOVE FREE COMIC BOOK DAY. LOOK, MAGIC BULLET, AND THE ADVENTURES OF BEARCUB IN HONEYLAND!
#1 $1.50 printed on cheap paper! yay!
THEY'RE AFTER THE PLANS!
GRRRRR!
SHUT
HEY! NOT ALL THE COMICS ARE FREE! HEY!

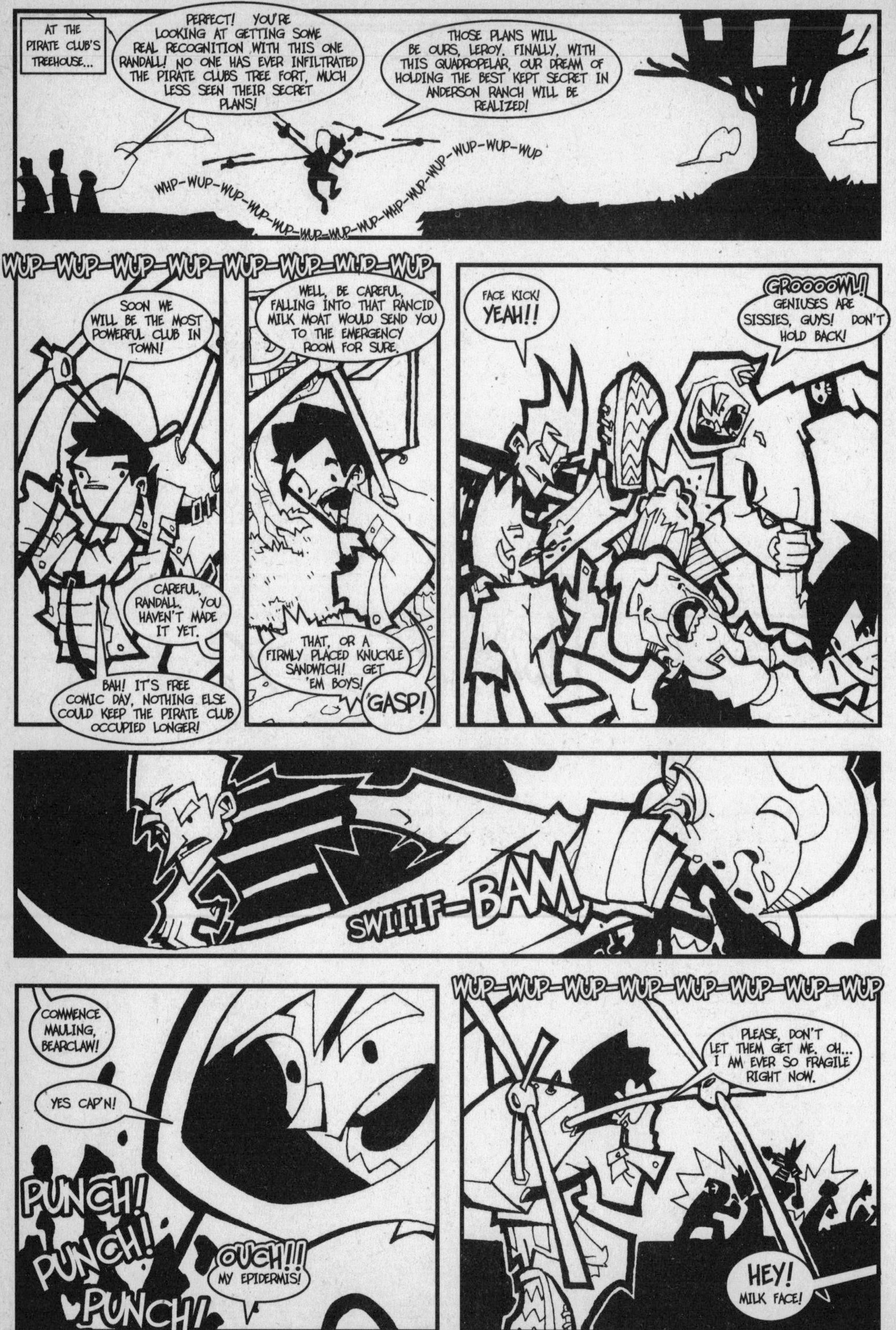
AT THE PIRATE CLUB'S TREEHOUSE...
PERFECT! YOU'RE LOOKING AT GETTING SOME REAL RECOGNITION WITH THIS ONE RANDALL! NO ONE HAS EVER INFILTRATED THE PIRATE CLUBS TREE FORT, MUCH LESS SEEN THEIR SECRET PLANS!
THOSE PLANS WILL BE OURS, LEROY. FINALLY, WITH THIS QUADROPELAR, OUR DREAM OF HOLDING THE BEST KEPT SECRET IN ANDERSON RANCH WILL BE REALIZED!
WHP-WUP-WUP-WUP-WUP-WUP-WUP-WUP-WHP-WUP-WUP-WUP-WUP-WUP
WUP-WUP-WUP-WUP-WUP-WUP-WUP-WUP
SOON WE WILL BE THE MOST POWERFUL CLUB IN TOWN!
CAREFUL, RANDALL. YOU HAVEN'T MADE IT YET.
BAH! IT'S FREE COMIC DAY, NOTHING ELSE COULD KEEP THE PIRATE CLUB OCCUPIED LONGER!
WELL, BE CAREFUL, FALLING INTO THAT RANCID MILK MOAT WOULD SEND YOU TO THE EMERGENCY ROOM FOR SURE.
THAT, OR A FIRMLY PLACED KNUCKLE SANDWICH! GET 'EM BOYS!
GASP!
FACE KICK! YEAH!!
GROOOOWL! GENIUSES ARE SISSIES, GUYS! DON'T HOLD BACK!
SWIIIF-BAM
COMMENCE MAULING, BEARCLAW!
YES CAP'N!
PUNCH! PUNCH! PUNCH!
OUCH!! MY EPIDERMIS!
WUP-WUP-WUP-WUP-WUP-WUP-WUP-WUP
PLEASE, DON'T LET THEM GET ME, OH... I AM EVER SO FRAGILE RIGHT NOW.
HEY! MILK FACE!

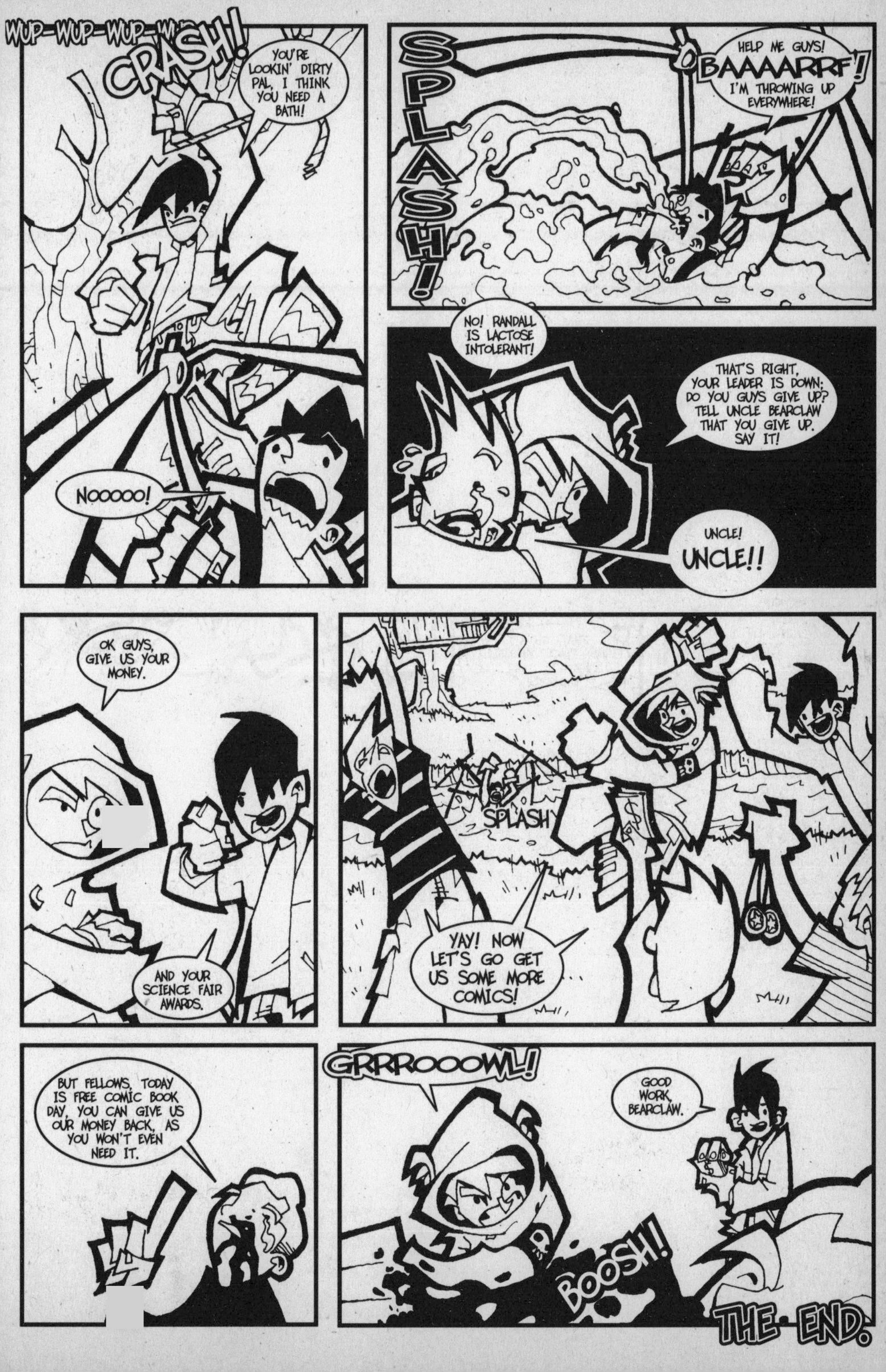
WUP-WUP-WUP-W
CRASH!
YOU'RE LOOKIN' DIRTY PAL, I THINK YOU NEED A BATH!
NOOOOO!
SPLASH!
HELP ME GUYS! BAAAARRF! I'M THROWING UP EVERYWHERE!
NO! RANDALL IS LACTOSE INTOLERANT!
THAT'S RIGHT, YOUR LEADER IS DOWN; DO YOU GUYS GIVE UP? TELL UNCLE BEARCLAW THAT YOU GIVE UP. SAY IT!
UNCLE! UNCLE!!
OK GUYS, GIVE US YOUR MONEY.
AND YOUR SCIENCE FAIR AWARDS.
SPLASH
YAY! NOW LET'S GO GET US SOME MORE COMICS!
BUT FELLOWS, TODAY IS FREE COMIC BOOK DAY, YOU CAN GIVE US OUR MONEY BACK, AS YOU WON'T EVEN NEED IT.
GRRROOOWL!
GOOD WORK, BEARCLAW.
BOOSH!
THE END.

PIRATE CLUB: ICE CREAM TAKE-OVER

CO-WRITTEN BY: BRYAN YOUNG

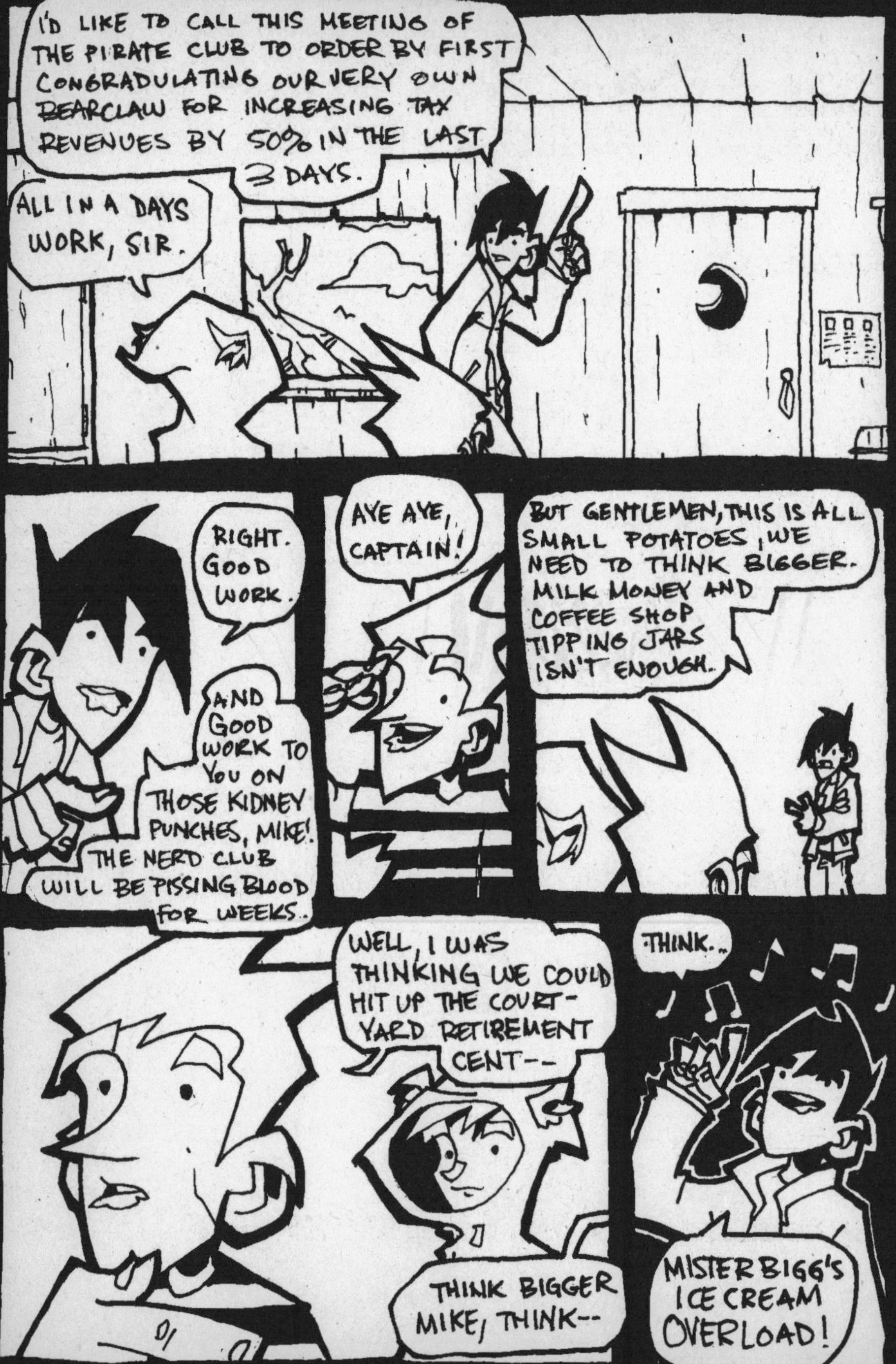
I'D LIKE TO CALL THIS MEETING OF THE PIRATE CLUB TO ORDER BY FIRST CONGRADULATING OUR VERY OWN ~~BEARCLAW~~ FOR INCREASING TAX REVENUES BY 50% IN THE LAST 3 DAYS.
ALL IN A DAYS WORK, SIR.
RIGHT. GOOD WORK.
AND GOOD WORK TO YOU ON THOSE KIDNEY PUNCHES, MIKE! THE NERD CLUB WILL BE PISSING BLOOD FOR WEEKS..
AYE AYE, CAPTAIN!
BUT GENTLEMEN, THIS IS ALL SMALL POTATOES, WE NEED TO THINK BIGGER. MILK MONEY AND COFFEE SHOP TIPPING JARS ISN'T ENOUGH.
WELL, I WAS THINKING WE COULD HIT UP THE COURT-YARD RETIREMENT CENT--
THINK BIGGER MIKE, THINK--
THINK..
MISTER BIGG'S ICE CREAM OVERLOAD!

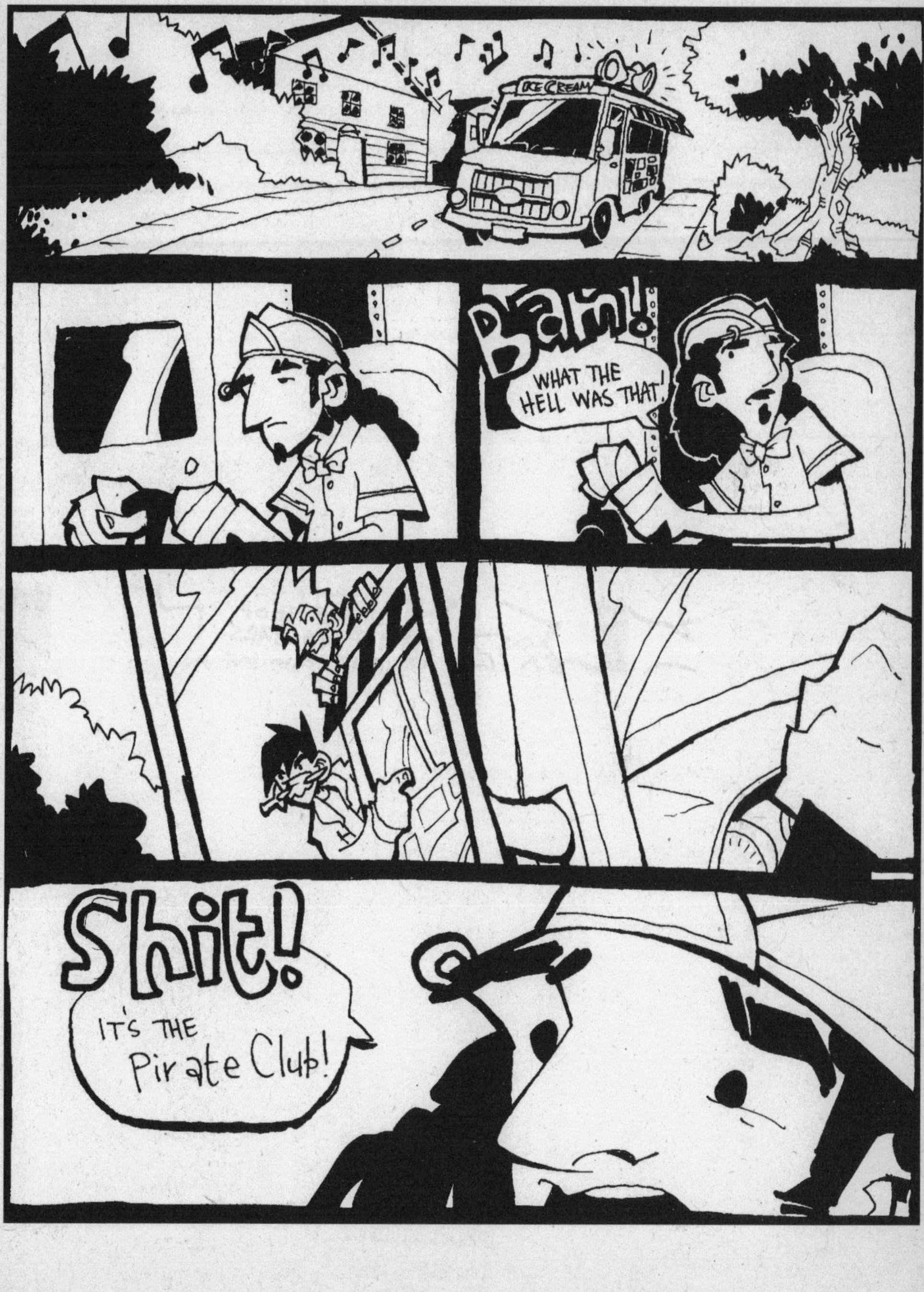
ICE CREAM
BAM!
WHAT THE HELL WAS THAT!
Shit!
IT'S THE Pirate Club!

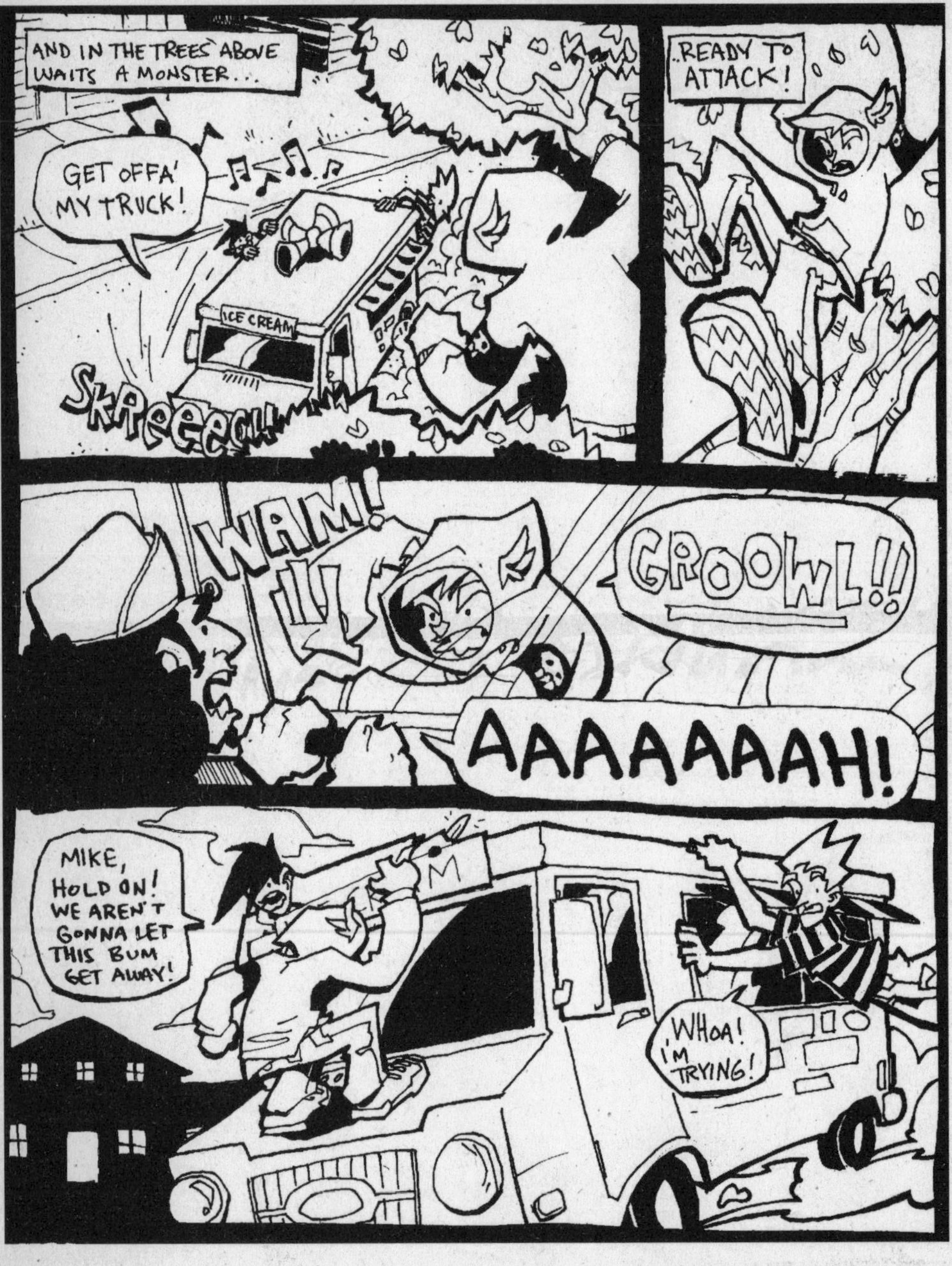

AND IN THE TREES ABOVE WAITS A MONSTER...
GET OFFA' MY TRUCK!
ICE CREAM
SKREEEEC!!!
..READY TO ATTACK!
WAM!
GROOWL!!
AAAAAAAH!
MIKE, HOLD ON! WE AREN'T GONNA LET THIS BUM GET AWAY!
M
WHOA! I'M TRYING!

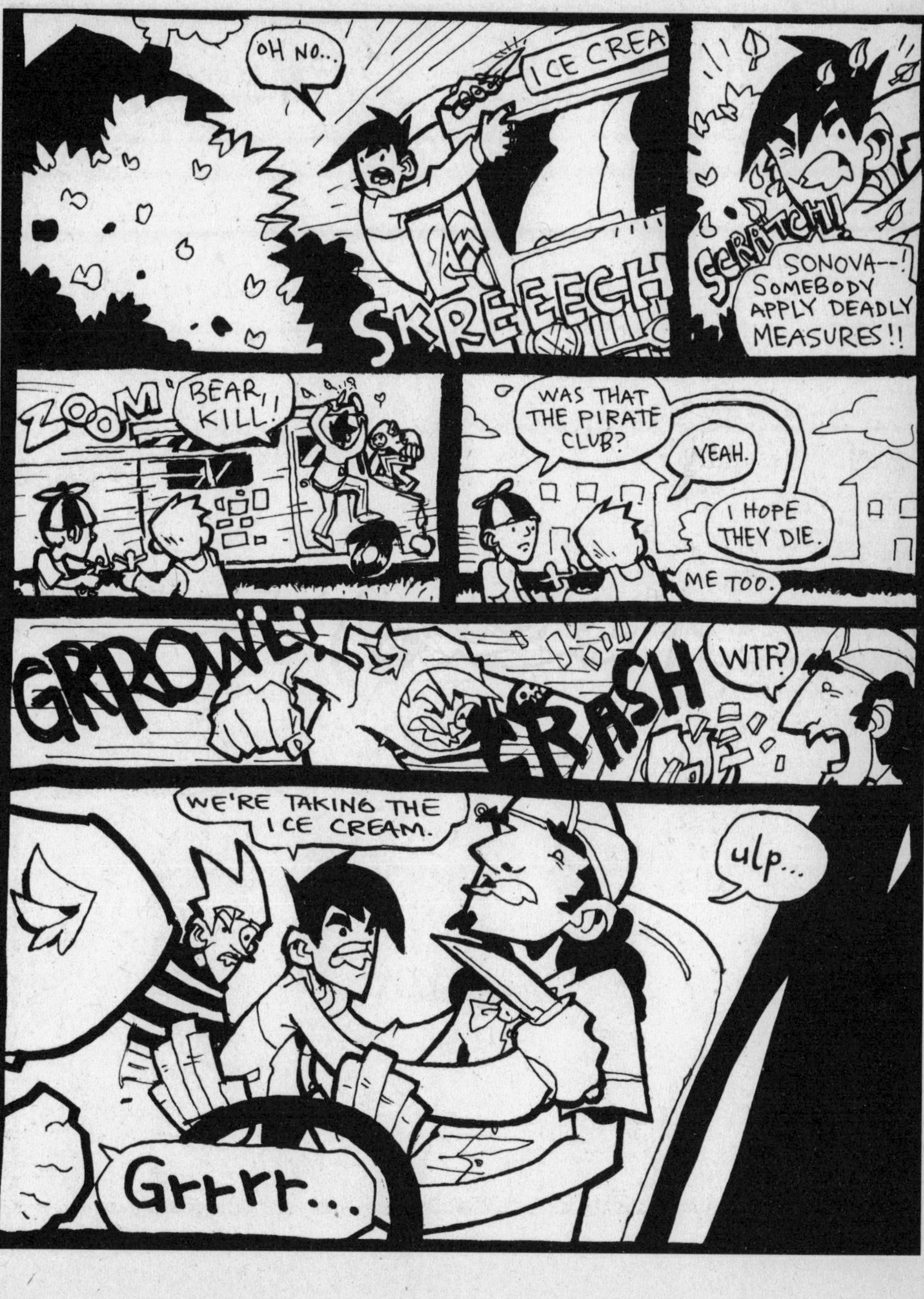
OH NO...
ICE CREA
SKREEECH
SCRITCH!
SONOVA--! SOMEBODY APPLY DEADLY MEASURES!!
ZOOM
BEAR KILL!!
WAS THAT THE PIRATE CLUB?
YEAH.
I HOPE THEY DIE.
ME TOO.
GRROWL!
CRASH
WTF?
WE'RE TAKING THE ICE CREAM.
ulp...
Grrrr...

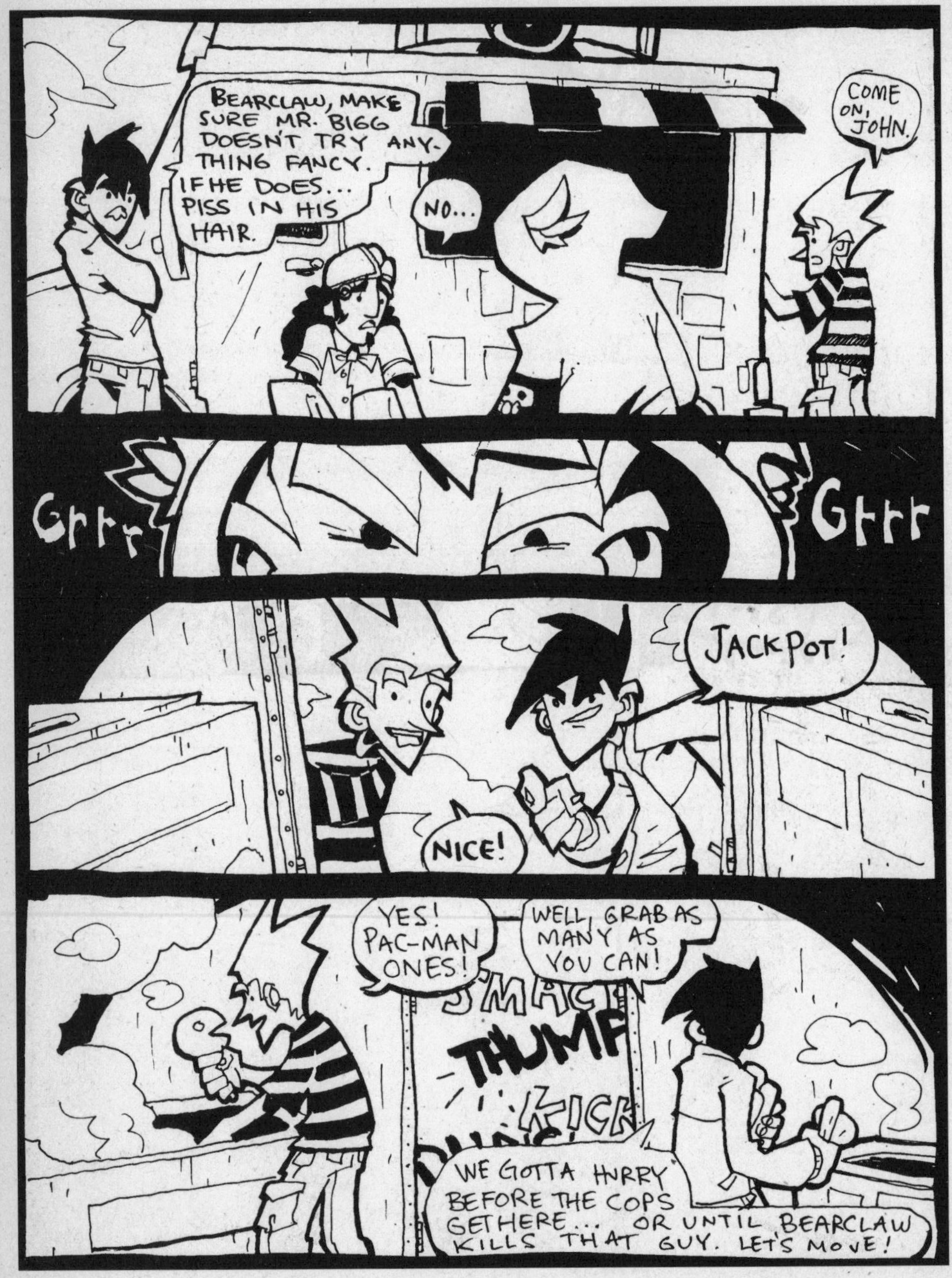
BEARCLAW, MAKE SURE MR. BIGG DOESN'T TRY ANYTHING FANCY. IF HE DOES... PISS IN HIS HAIR.
NO...
COME ON, JOHN.
Grrr
Grrr
JACKPOT!
NICE!
YES! PAC-MAN ONES!
WELL, GRAB AS MANY AS YOU CAN!
THUMP
KICK
WE GOTTA HURRY BEFORE THE COPS GET HERE... OR UNTIL BEARCLAW KILLS THAT GUY. LET'S MOVE!

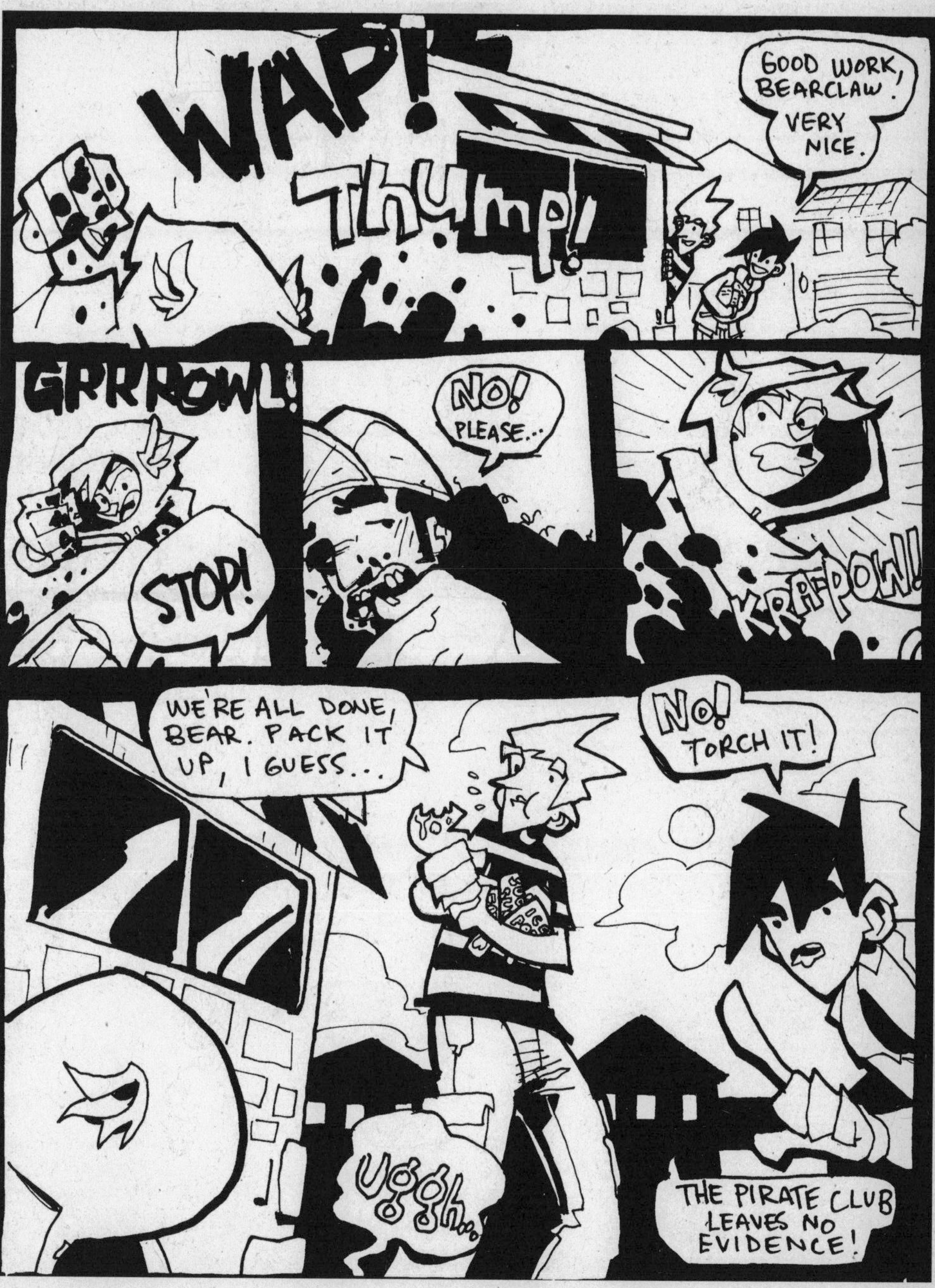
WAP!
Thump!
GOOD WORK, BEARCLAW. VERY NICE.
GRRROWL!
STOP!
NO! PLEASE...
KRAPOW!
WE'RE ALL DONE, BEAR. PACK IT UP, I GUESS...
NO! TORCH IT!
Uggh...
THE PIRATE CLUB LEAVES NO EVIDENCE!

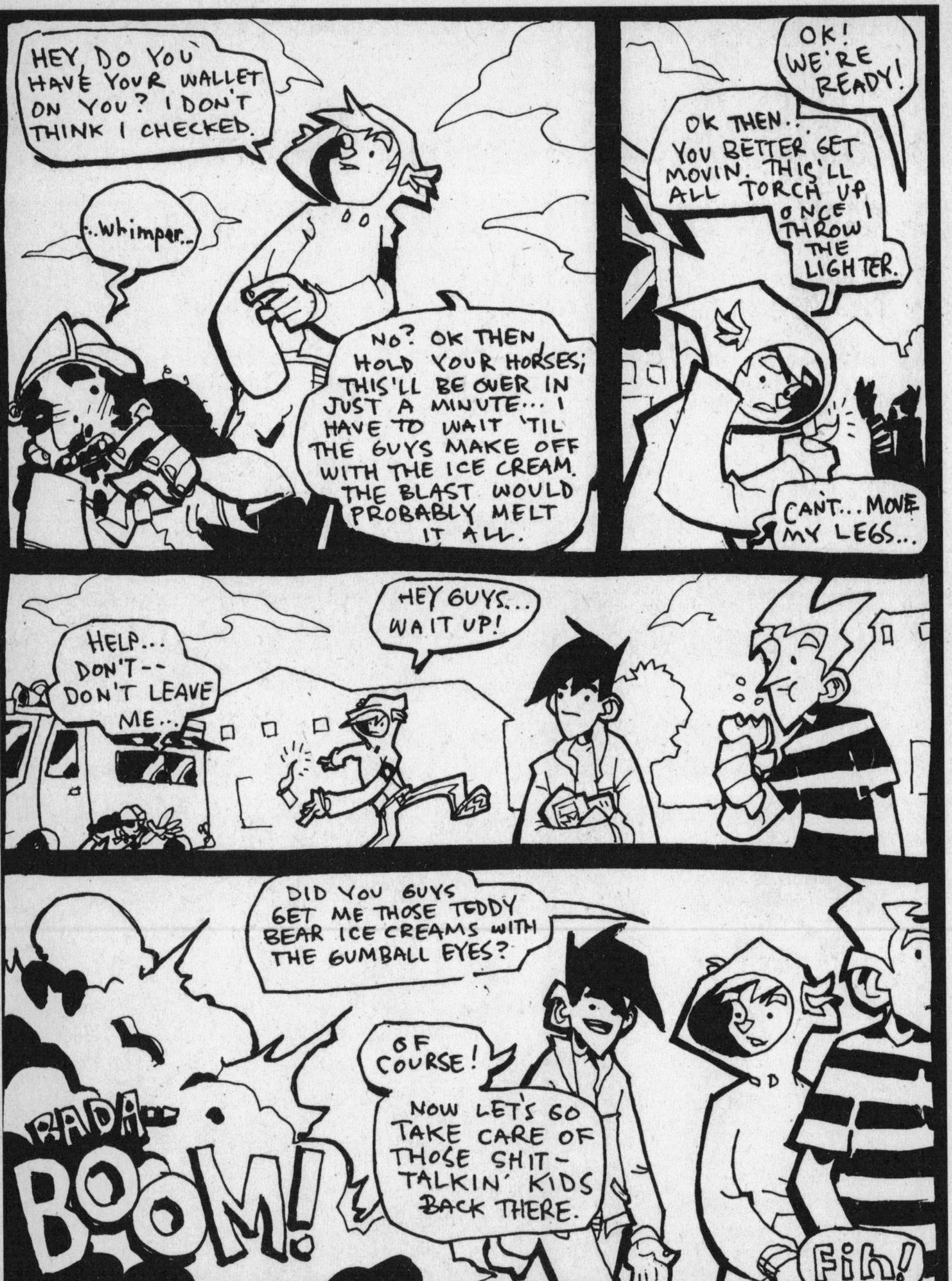
HEY, DO YOU HAVE YOUR WALLET ON YOU? I DON'T THINK I CHECKED.
..whimper..
NO? OK THEN, HOLD YOUR HORSES; THIS'LL BE OVER IN JUST A MINUTE... I HAVE TO WAIT 'TIL THE GUYS MAKE OFF WITH THE ICE CREAM. THE BLAST WOULD PROBABLY MELT IT ALL.
OK! WE'RE READY!
OK THEN... YOU BETTER GET MOVIN. THIS'LL ALL TORCH UP ONCE I THROW THE LIGHTER.
CAN'T... MOVE MY LEGS...
HELP... DON'T-- DON'T LEAVE ME...
HEY GUYS... WAIT UP!
DID YOU GUYS GET ME THOSE TEDDY BEAR ICE CREAMS WITH THE GUMBALL EYES?
OF COURSE!
NOW LET'S GO TAKE CARE OF THOSE SHIT-TALKIN' KIDS BACK THERE.
BADA-BOOM!
Fih!